ADVANCED GRAMMAR

HELEN HOYT SCHMIDT

W9-BTS-484

ADVANCED GRAMMAR

Copyright © 2015 by Pearson Education, Inc.
All rights reserved. No part of this publication may be reproduced, stored in a retrieval system or transmitted in any form or by any means, electronic, mechanical, photocopying, recording or otherwise, without prior permission of the publisher.

Pearson Education, 10 Bank Street, White Plains, NY 10606

Staff credits: The people who made up the *Advanced Grammar* team, representing editorial, production, and design, are Stephanie Bullard, Tracey Cataldo, Rosa Chapinal, Aerin Csigay, Nancy Flaggman, Gosia Jaros-White, Barry Katzen, Amy McCormick, Joan Poole, Lindsay Richman, Robert Ruvo, and Marian Wassner.

Editorial services: Barbara Lyons, Lyons Publishing Services, LLC and Leigh Stolle, Goathaus Studio

Cover design: Yin Ling Wong

Cover photos: (left) Photos 12/Alamy, (middle left) Henry Westheim Photography/Alamy, (middle) agsandrew/Shutterstock, (middle right) siloto/Fotolia, (right) fotoliaxrender/Fotolia.

Text design: Yin Ling Wong
Text composition: Yin Ling Wong and Clea Chmela

Library of Congress Cataloging-in-Publication Data
Schmidt, Helen Hoyt.
   Advanced grammar / Helen Hoyt Schmidt.
      pages cm
Includes bibliographical references.
ISBN 978-0-13-304180-4 -- ISBN 0-13-304180-8
   1. English language--Grammar--Study and teaching (Higher)--Foreign speakers.
   2. English language--Study and teaching (Higher)--Foreign speakers. 3. Universities and colleges--Entrance examinations--Foreign speakers. I. Title.
PE1128.A2S3197 2015
428.2'4--dc23

         2015013675

Printed in the United States of America

ISBN 10: 0-13-304180-8
ISBN 13: 978-0-13-304180-4

1 2 3 4 5 6 7 8 9 10—V057—20 19 18 17 16 15

CONTENTS

PART 1

The Verb Tense System:
Using Academic Verb Tense Patterns

INTRODUCTION TO ADVANCED GRAMMAR

Advanced Grammar is the result of years of teaching intensive grammar and writing to international students preparing to enter a U.S. college or university. Once enrolled, these students face enormous challenges in their basic coursework. One course in the social sciences, for example, may require more than 100 pages of reading a week plus writing assignments quite different from the personal writing most international students have been taught. There have been a few ESL reading textbooks based on unabridged academic textbook material, but no grammar textbooks. The grammar that students are exposed to tends to be simplified. The result is that often students cannot identify and grasp previously studied grammar structures in their academic textbook reading. At the same time, the demands of academia to write in academic prose are frequently beyond the scope of most ESL textbooks.

The *Advanced Grammar* Approach

To better prepare students for college-level course work, *Advanced Grammar* focuses on the academic forms and uses of grammatical structures without oversimplifying either the content or the grammar structures. Students review the grammar, identify and practice the targeted structures in context, and finally produce them in academic speaking and writing tasks. This approach is made possible by the authentic textbook content—from a variety of disciplines—upon which each chapter is based. By working with genuine academic material as they focus on the grammatical structures used in academic writing, students will be better prepared to read and understand textbook content, write academic papers, and discuss academic topics with their professors and classmates.

Key Features of *Advanced Grammar*

- **Discipline-specific and universal academic vocabulary:** Students learn meanings and develop knowledge of vocabulary inductively and deductively.

- **In-depth exposure to authentic academic language via textbook excerpts:** Students become accustomed to and use authentic academic language as it is spoken and written.

- **Contextualized grammar presented in authentic academic texts:** Students broaden their knowledge of grammar in real academic contexts from a variety of disciplines.

- **Comprehensive range of advanced grammar structures:** Grammar is presented in clear, accessible charts that incorporate both explanations and examples. Students are exposed to complex meanings and learn to use grammar in a more natural manner.

- **Varied range of inductive and deductive exercises:** Students with different learning styles are helped to practice and understand the target grammar using authentic textbook content.

- **Application of the grammar to speaking:** Students learn to use the target grammar to discuss and present academic topics.

- **Application of the grammar to writing:** Students learn to use the target grammar to discuss academic topics in written summaries and paragraphs.

- **Focused analytical review of the grammar structures taught in each Part:** At the end of each of the five Parts, in the "Putting It All Together" review, students do reading-based analysis of the grammar from that Part, complete an additional error analysis exercise, take a review-oriented self-study quiz / Part achievement test, and have further opportunities for speaking and writing practice.

Organization of *Advanced Grammar*

Advanced Grammar contains five Parts, each of which includes a review entitled "Putting It All Together." Each Part focuses on a particular discipline, such as computer science, anthropology, or history, and teaches grammar structures within the context of that discipline, using texts and examples from a well-regarded introductory textbook in the field. Each chapter follows a three-part progression from a text-based "Preview" section, to grammar introduction and practice, to a final "Application" section.

1. **Preview** begins with a list of relevant thematic vocabulary complemented in Appendix A by opportunities for self-assessment and practice. Grammar structures are then introduced inductively in a high-interest authentic reading. Students are encouraged to discuss and analyze the passage in order to access their background knowledge of the grammar.

2. **Grammar** presents and illustrates new structures in easy-to-understand charts. The grammar structures are practiced in varied, accessible exercises that conclude with a student essay for error analysis.

3. **Application** provides opportunities for speaking and writing practice incorporating the chapter grammar.

At the end of each of the five three-chapter Parts, a "Putting It All Together" section provides immediate review within an expanded context introduced by an authentic reading with related grammar analysis. The chapter provides additional grammar practice, a self-study quiz / Part achievement test entitled "What Did You Learn?" and further opportunities for speaking and writing.

SCOPE AND SEQUENCE

Part 1: The Verb Tense System: Using Academic Verb Tense Patterns
ACADEMIC DISCIPLINE: COMPUTER SCIENCE

Outcomes:
• Understand why the passive voice is used in academic speech and writing.
• Give a formal presentation using a variety of verb tenses and forms.
• State an opinion in a paragraph, supported by the appropriate verb tenses.

	PREVIEW	GRAMMAR	APPLICATION
Chapter 1: **Review of the Verb Tenses**	**Reading:** The First Programmer: Augusta Ada Byron **Inductive exercise:** Identify verbs and verb tenses in context.	Chart 1-1 Verbs Chart 1-2 Present Tenses (Active) Chart 1-3 Future Tenses (Active) Chart 1-4 Present Perfect Chart 1-5 Past Tenses Chart 1-6 Time Frames	**"Apply It to Speaking":** Discuss Augusta Ada Byron in small groups. Prepare a presentation about a historical person. **"Apply It to Writing":** Write a summary. Write a paragraph about the changing roles of men and women.
Chapter 2: **Passive Verbs**	**Reading:** Computer Miniaturization **Inductive exercise:** Identify passive verbs in context.	Chart 2-1 Active Voice v. Passive Voice Chart 2-2 Passive Forms of Verbs Chart 2-3 When to Choose Passive	**"Apply It to Speaking":** Read a paragraph and discuss it in small groups. Prepare a brief presentation explaining the meaning of a quotation. **"Apply It to Writing":** Write a paragraph about a procedure.
Chapter 3: **Modal Auxiliary Verbs**	**Reading:** Considering the Consequences **Inductive exercise:** Identify modal auxiliary verbs in context. Identify verb tenses and forms.	Chart 3-1 Modal Auxiliary Verbs (Active) Chart 3-2 Modal Auxiliary Verbs (Passive) Chart 3-3 Degrees of Certainty Chart 3-4 Degrees of Necessity Chart 3-5 Modal Auxiliary Verbs Used to Express Doubt (Hedging)	**"Apply It to Speaking":** Discuss a paragraph in small groups and report on its meaning. In small groups agree or disagree with the author of a paragraph. **"Apply It to Writing":** Write a paragraph based on the discussion in the preceding exercise.

PUTTING IT ALL TOGETHER

Reading:
"The Science of Algorithms"

In-depth Practice:
Analysis of the Reading Passage
Identifying Time Frames
Error Analysis

Highlights
"What Did You Learn?"
"Apply It to Speaking":
  Prepare a Presentation
"Apply It to Writing"

COMPUTER SCIENCE

Part 2: Nouns and Noun Phrases: Adding Variety and Detail
ACADEMIC DISCIPLINE: SOCIOLOGY

Outcomes:
- Understand how noun phrases are used in academic speech and writing.
- Participate in an extended discussion using a variety of nouns and noun phrases.
- Use noun phrases to strengthen a written argument or point-of-view.

SOCIOLOGY

	PREVIEW	GRAMMAR	APPLICATION
Chapter 4: **Noun Functions**	**Reading:** What Do Clothing and Adornment Communicate about Culture? **Inductive exercise:** Identify noun and noun functions in context.	Chart 4-1 Types of Nouns Chart 4-2 Nouns, Gerunds, and Infinitives as Subjects and Objects Chart 4-3 Complements Chart 4-4 Appositives	**"Apply It to Speaking":** Have a group discussion about changing hairstyles. **"Apply It to Writing":** Write two paragraphs about the connection between appearance and social position.
Chapter 5: **Elements of Noun Phrases: Premodifiers**	**Reading:** Gender and Garments **Inductive exercise:** Identify descriptive nouns.	Chart 5-1 Elements of Noun Phrases Chart 5-2 Determiners as Premodifiers Chart 5-3 Adjective, Adverb, and Noun Premodifiers Chart 5-4 Order of Premodifiers in Noun Phrases	**"Apply It to Speaking":** Discuss in small groups personal clothing styles and celebrities' influence on fashion. Using noun phrases, discuss clothing that is specific to certain cultures. **"Apply It to Writing":** Using noun phrases, write a paragraph about an interesting fashion.
Chapter 6: **Elements of Noun Phrases: Postmodifiers**	**Reading:** Sumptuary Laws and Clothing **Inductive exercise:** Identify postmodifiers.	Chart 6-1 Postmodifiers: Nouns and Adjectives Chart 6-2 Prepositional Phrases and Participles Chart 6-3 Forming Sentences with Participles	**"Apply It to Speaking":** Hold a group discussion about dress codes. Using postmodifiers, give a brief presentation about professional attire. **"Apply It to Writing":** Write one or two paragraphs about a specific dress code.

PUTTING IT ALL TOGETHER

Reading:
Business Dress

In-depth Practice:
Analysis of the Reading Passage
Identifying Noun Functions
Analyzing Grammatical Structure in a Text
Error Analysis

Highlights
"What Did You Learn?"
"Apply It to Speaking":
 Prepare a Presentation
"Apply It to Writing"

Part 3: Adjectives Clauses and Phrases: Adding Prediction, Description, Historical Explanation, and Emphasis
ACADEMIC DISCIPLINE: HISTORY

Outcomes:
- Understand how adjective clauses are used in academic speech and writing.
- Create and discuss a narrative, using a variety of adjective clauses and phrases.
- Use adjective clauses, phrases, and cleft sentences to add rich detail to writing.

	PREVIEW	GRAMMAR	APPLICATION
Chapter 7: **Review of Adjective Clauses**	**Reading:** Ötzi, the 5,000-year-old man **Inductive exercise:** Identify adjective clauses.	Chart 7-1 Overview of Adjective Clauses Chart 7-2 Relative Pronouns That Introduce Adjective Clauses Chart 7-3 Adjective Clauses after Prepositions, Quantity Expressions, and Nouns Chart 7-4 Restrictive and Nonrestrictive Adjective Clauses	**"Apply It to Speaking":** Give a presentation about the technical accomplishments of Neanderthals. Discuss in small groups a statement about a Neanderthal man. **"Apply It to Writing":** Describe the final moments of Ötzi's life.
Chapter 8: **Reduced Adjective Clauses and Adjective Phrases**	**Reading:** The Agony of Athletics **Inductive exercise:** Identify adjective phrases.	Chart 8-1 Adjective Phrases	**"Apply It to Speaking":** Using adjectives phrases, describe the Olympic games. **"Apply It to Writing":** Write a paragraph about ancient and contemporary attitudes towards sports. Write a paragraph describing contemporary athletes and their motivation.
Chapter 9: **Academic Uses of Adjective Clauses, Phrases, and Cleft Sentences**	**Reading:** The Roman Domus, the Family House **Inductive exercise:** Identify adjective phrases and clauses.	Chart 9-1 Purposes of Adjective Clauses and Adjective Phrases in Academic Writing Chart 9-2 Summary: Punctuation of Adjective Clauses and Adjective Phrases Chart 9-3 Cleft Sentences	**"Apply It to Speaking":** Discuss the Roman Domus using adjective clauses and phrases. **"Apply It to Writing":** Write a description of the image of a Roman atrium using adjective clauses and phrases.

PUTTING IT ALL TOGETHER

Reading:
Reading: A Closer Look: A Working Woman

In-depth Practice:
Analysis of the Reading Passage
Error Analysis

Highlights
"What Did You Learn?"

"Apply It to Speaking and Writing":
Research and Prepare a Presentation

Part 4: Adverb Clauses, Adverb Phrases, and Other Structures That Express Complex Relationships
ACADEMIC DISCIPLINE: ANTHROPOLOGY

Outcomes:
- Understand how adverb clauses and phrases are used in academic speech and writing.
- Read and interpret data on a chart.
- Write paragraphs that clearly express cause / effect, purpose, manner, concession, and contrast.

ANTHROPOLOGY

	PREVIEW	GRAMMAR	APPLICATION
Chapter 10: **Adverb Clauses and Other Structures That Express Time, Cause / Effect, Purpose, and Manner**	**Reading:** Australian Aborigines **Inductive exercise:** Distinguish adverb phrases from clauses.	Chart 10-1 An Overview of Connectors Chart 10-2 Adverb Clauses of Time Chart 10-3 Adverb Clauses with Special Meanings Chart 10-4 Other Structures That Express Time Relationships Chart 10-5 Adverb Clauses of Cause / Effect (Reason / Result), Purpose, and Manner Chart 10-6 Other Structures That Express Cause / Effect, Purpose, and Manner	**"Apply It to Speaking":** Describe the marriage customs in your country. **"Apply It to Writing":** Write a paragraph about marriage customs in your country, using time, cause / effect, purpose, and manner.
Chapter 11: **Adverb Clauses and Other Structures That Express Concession, Opposition, and Condition**	**Reading:** Courtship and Marriage **Inductive exercise:** Distinguish adverb phrases from clauses.	Chart 11-1 Adverb Clauses of Concession and Opposition Chart 11-2 Other Structures that Express Opposition Chart 11-3 A Few Rules about Conjunction Usage Chart 11-4 Adverb Clauses of Condition: Real (True) Conditions Chart 11-5 Adverb Clauses of Condition: Unreal (Contrary-to-Fact) Conditions Chart 11-6 Other Structures That Express Conditions	**"Apply It to Speaking":** Discuss and evaluate data in a chart, "Gender Profiles of News Audiences." Summarize the findings of "Gender Profiles of News Audiences."
Chapter 12: **Reduced Adverb Clauses and Absolute Constructions**	**Reading:** The Tiv People **Inductive exercise:** Identify adverb phrases and their functions.	Chart 12-1 Reducing Adverb Clauses to Phrases: Time and Cause Phrases Chart 12-2 Reducing Adverb Clauses to Phrases: Result, Concession, and Condition Phrases Chart 12-3 Reducing Purpose, Cause, Concession, and Conditional Clauses to Prepositional Phrases Chart 12-4 Absolute Constructions	**"Apply It to Speaking and Writing":** Read information in a chart, and compare and contrast the labor roles of men and women. Write statements that explain why labor roles exist. Incorporate the statements into a two-paragraph essay on labor division.

PUTTING IT ALL TOGETHER

Reading:
Natural Disasters as Social Problems

In-depth Practice:
Analysis of the Reading Passage
Analyzing Individual Sentences
Error Analysis

Highlights
"What Did You Learn?"

"Apply It to Speaking":
Read and Discuss a Passage

"Apply It to Writing"

Part 5: Noun Clauses
ACADEMIC DISCIPLINE: PHYSICS

Outcomes:
- Understand how noun clauses are used in academic speech and writing.
- Synthesize and discuss information from multiple sources.
- Write paragraphs that provide an interpretive or critical response to academic text.

PHYSICS

	PREVIEW	GRAMMAR	APPLICATION
Chapter 13: **Noun Clauses Used as Objects**	**Reading:** The Scientific Method **Inductive exercise:** Identify noun clauses as objects.	Chart 13-1 Noun Clauses as Objects Overview Chart 13-2 Noun Clauses as Objects Introduced by *That* Chart 13-3 Subjunctive Noun Clauses Chart 13-4 Noun Clauses as Objects Introduced by *Wh-* Words Chart 13-5 Noun Clauses as Objects Introduced by *If* or *Whether*	**"Apply It to Speaking":** Discuss a scientific text using noun clauses. **"Apply It to Writing":** Using noun clauses, write a paragraph about an observed phenomenon.
Chapter 14: **Noun Clauses as Subjects, Complements, and Appositives**	**Reading:** Global Warming **Inductive exercise:** Identify noun clauses and their functions.	Chart 14-1 Noun Clauses as Subjects Chart 14-2 Noun Clauses as Complements Chart 14-3 Noun Clauses as Appositives Chart 14-4 Noun Clauses Used for Hedging	**"Apply It to Speaking":** Discuss and evaluate data in multiple charts. **"Apply It to Writing":** Write an interpretive paragraph about the information in the charts.
Chapter 15: **Noun Clauses Used for Academic Purposes**	**Reading:** Atomic Materialism: Atoms and Empty Space **Inductive exercise:** Examine the punctuation used for direct speech.	Chart 15-1 Punctuation of Direct Speech Chart 15-2 Reported Speech for Authorities' Opinions and Support Chart 15-3 Reported Speech Verb Tense and Other Changes	**"Apply It to Speaking and Writing":** Discuss a topic related to technology and science. Summarize a classmate's ideas. **"Apply It to Writing":** Summarize a scientific text.

PUTTING IT ALL TOGETHER

Reading:

Special Relativity and Quantum Physics

In-depth Practice:

Analysis of the Reading Passage

Noun Clauses Used for Hedging and Reported Speech

Error Analysis

Highlights

"What Did You Learn?"

"Apply It to Speaking":
 Discuss and Summarize an Essay

"Apply It to Writing"

KEY FEATURES OF *ADVANCED GRAMMAR*

PART OPENER

Advanced Grammar is organized around five Parts, each Part consisting of three chapters and one review section. Each Part focuses on a particular academic discipline and teaches grammar structures within the context of that discipline.

> Each Part opens with a captivating **image** that draws students into the Part's academic discipline.

> A list of **objectives** outlines the grammar covered in the Part.

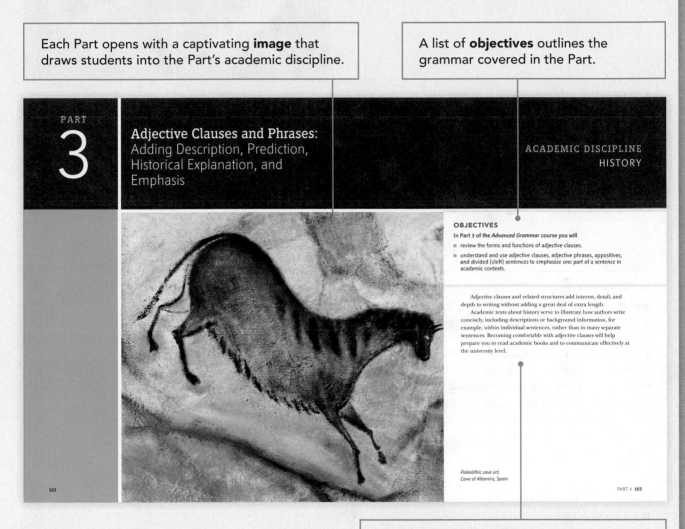

PART 3

Adjective Clauses and Phrases:
Adding Description, Prediction, Historical Explanation, and Emphasis

ACADEMIC DISCIPLINE
HISTORY

OBJECTIVES

In Part 3 of the *Advanced Grammar* course you will

- review the forms and functions of adjective clauses.
- understand and use adjective clauses, adjective phrases, appositives, and divided (cleft) sentences to emphasize one part of a sentence in academic contexts.

Adjective clauses and related structures add interest, detail, and depth to writing without adding a great deal of extra length.

Academic texts about history serve to illustrate how authors write concisely, including descriptions or background information, for example, within individual sentences, rather than in many separate sentences. Becoming comfortable with adjective clauses will help prepare you to read academic books and to communicate effectively at the university level.

Paleolithic cave art,
Cave of Altamira, Spain

102

PART 3 **103**

> A short **description of the grammar** focus explains how academic texts from a particular discipline illustrate the functions of the grammatical structures.

PREVIEW

This section presents the target grammar in a **high-interest authentic academic reading**. Students are encouraged to discuss and analyze the reading passage in order to access their background knowledge of the grammar.

CHAPTER

1

Review of the Verb Tenses

Charles Babbage *Augusta Ada Byron*

PREVIEW

VOCABULARY Here are some words that you will encounter in Chapter 1. How much do you know about each word? Turn to Appendix A to assess and expand your word knowledge.

algorithm	application	array	artificial intelligence	autonomous
contend	impact	miniaturization	program	task

Each unit opens with a list of **relevant thematic vocabulary**. Optional vocabulary exercises are available in Appendix A, which allows opportunities for self-assessment and practice.

Prepare to Read activities build schema and provide warm-up before students read the opening text. They create interest, elicit students' knowledge about the topic, and encourage them to make predictions about the reading. These activities are then followed by an **authentic unabridged reading** from a well-regarded introductory textbook in the field. Grammar structures are introduced inductively in a **real academic context**.

Prepare to Read
1. What was a well-educated woman's role in society in the nineteenth century?
2. How did computers in the nineteenth century look?
3. What could computers do in the nineteenth century?

Read the following paragraph from *Computer Science: An Overview*, 11th Edition, by J. Glenn Brookshear.[1]

THE FIRST PROGRAMMER

Augusta Ada Byron

[1]Augusta Ada Byron, Countess of Lovelace, **has been** the subject of much commentary in the computing community. [2]She **lived** a somewhat tragic life of less than thirty-seven years (1815–1852) that was complicated by poor health and the fact that she **was** a nonconformist in a society that limited the professional role of women. [3]Although she was interested in a wide range of science, she concentrated her studies in mathematics. [4]Her interest in "compute science" began when she became fascinated by the machines of Charles Babbage at a demonstration of a prototype of his Difference Engine in 1833. [5]Her contribution to computer science **stems** from her translation from French into English of a paper discussing Babbage's designs for the Analytical Engine. [6]To this translation, Babbage encouraged her to attach an addendum describing applications of the engine and containing examples of how the engine could be programmed to perform various tasks. [7]Babbage's enthusiasm for Ada Byron's work was apparently motivated by his hope that its publication would lead to financial backing for the construction of his Analytical Engine. [8](As the daughter of Lord Byron*, Ada Byron held celebrity status with potentially significant financial connections.) [9]This backing never materialized, but Ada Byron's addendum has survived and is considered to contain the first examples of computer programs. [10]The degree to which Babbage influenced Ada Byron's work is debated by historians. [11]Some argue that Babbage made major contributions whereas others contend that he was more of an obstacle than an aid. [12]Nonetheless, Augusta Ada Byron is recognized today as the world's first programmer, a status that was certified by the U.S. Department of Defense when it named the prominent programming language (Ada) in her honor.[2]

Lord Byron (1788–1824) was a notorious English nobleman and Romantic poet.

Review the Ideas questions allow students to check their comprehension of the text.

Review the Ideas
1. Who was Augusta Ada Byron and why is she known as the first programmer?
2. Who was Charles Babbage and what did he do?
3. What did you learn about computers in the nineteenth century?

In **Analyze the Grammar** exercises, students are encouraged to discuss and analyze the reading passage in order to access their background knowledge of the grammar.

Analyze the Grammar
Work in pairs to answer the following questions about the reading.
1 Look at the boldfaced words in the first, second, and fifth sentences. What do we call them? How do they differ from one another?
2 Underline other examples of these kinds of words in the passage.
3 Label the tenses you know.
4 Discuss your findings with your classmates.

Charles Babbage's Difference Engine

Review of the Verb Tenses 5

GRAMMAR

This section gives students a **comprehensive and explicit overview** of the grammar and ample opportunities for practice. The exercises in this section provide practice of the grammar structures in an **increasingly complex and challenging way**, starting with concept checks and/or structured, controlled exercises, moving to less-controlled practice. Many activities use **authentic texts**.

The **grammar charts** provide clear and logical presentations, concise explanations of terms and usage, clear references, and authentic examples to help reacquaint students with the grammar concepts and terminology.

GRAMMAR

SOCIOLOGY

| CHART 5-1 | Elements of Noun Phrases |

A **noun phrase** is a group of words that functions as a single noun. The most important word in a noun phrase is the **head noun**, which is usually the last noun in the phrase.

article adjective noun head noun (hn)
a beautiful cotton **skirt**

adjective noun hn
their cotton **skirts**

A noun phrase includes the head noun and other words that modify it, such as an article, quantifier, adverb, adjective, or other noun. All the words preceding the head noun are called **premodifiers**.

quantifier adjective hn
several wrapped skirts

PREMODIFIERS
article number adverb adjective noun hn
the ten **extraordinarily beautiful cotton skirts**

Exercise 1 Identifying Head Nouns in Noun Phrases
Write parentheses around each noun phrase and underline the head noun.

1. The East Indian woman is adorned with a red or saffron tika mark on her forehead.[5]
2. At the end of the nineteenth century, rich and powerful English businessmen wore a high, tight white collar with their heavy, stiff Edwardian suits. Physical exertion of any kind was inhibited and probably would have caused difficulty in breathing. Thus the term *white-collar worker* came into use. This term as well

---

The grammar charts are followed by a number of practice exercises. **Concept check exercises** practice material that is review in nature. They enable students to check their understanding of the basic concepts presented in the charts.

Exercise 6 Determining the Reason for Choosing Passive
Read the text and underline the passive verbs. Then, with a small group of classmates, decide why the passive is used in each instance. Choose the reason(s) from the list below. In many instances there may be more than one reason.

1 Agent not important or unknown
2 Sounds scientific
3 Describes a scientific procedure
4 Helps the paragraph flow smoothly

   The World Wide Web is an Internet service application that is based on hypertext. Hypertext documents contain hyperlinks that are connected to other documents containing audio, images, or video. A mouse is used to point and click on a hyperlink to move from document to document. Such a hypertext document is called a web page, and a group of related web pages is known as a website.
   Firefox®, Safari®, and Chrome® are called browsers. A browser is software that allows users to access hypertext documents on the Internet. A user employs a browser to request the documents from web servers. The documents are then transferred from the web servers to the browser. Each document has been given an Internet address or URL (universal resource locator), which is used to access the appropriate server and obtain the correct document. A typical URL looks like this: http://www.iastate.edu/~hschmidt/homepage.html.

Exercise 7 Completing the Description of a Process
On a separate sheet of paper, use passive voice to complete the following scrambled sentences. Write the sentences in the form of a paragraph. Be sure to write each verb in the correct tense.

1. A word processing program / use / research papers and business letters / to write
   In the past, word processing programs / to the purchaser of a computer / on CDs / give
   they / from the Internet / easily / download / Now
   The purchaser / a special code at the time / give / of the purchase
   When the code / at the word processing website, / enter / the program / download / onto the computer
   After the preferences / choose, / the other settings / adjust / and the program is ready to use
2. In the first processing systems, jobs / by instructions / accompany
   First, the instructions / encode / and store / in a job queue
   the jobs / select / for execution / Then
   by the operating system / print / the instructions / at a printer / After that,
   they / read / by the computer operator / there / Finally,

Focused exercises provide practice of the grammar structures in a structured, focused, and increasingly challenging way. They progress from simple to more complex. Early exercises include receptive practice; more challenging exercises combine grammar points, make more demand on productive tasks, and are based on longer, authentic texts.

Error analysis exercises allow students to build their awareness of incorrect usage of the target grammar structures. Students identify and correct errors in targeted grammar in written material, usually a student essay.

Exercise 9 Error Analysis
The following student essay contains ten errors in the use of verbs. The first error is corrected for you. Find and correct nine more.

The Global Positioning System (GPS)

                decided
   In 1973, it was decide to develop a satellite navigation system based on existing systems of the U.S. Air Force and Navy. This system of twenty-four satellites is knows as the GPS (Global Positioning System). GPS is using in aviation, marine, and onshore navigation to locate one's position on the earth within about 200 feet. Between 1973 and 1983, the system was limit to the government, but in 1983, ordinary people given access to it.
   Now GPS is use by millions of people all over the world to find out where they are and where they are going. Nowadays, the miniaturization of computers was allowed tiny GPS units to be placed into all sorts of devices. Airplane, ship, and automobile engines, radios, and phone communication systems contain GPS devices that is controlled by such tiny computers.
   It's amazing to think that even when a boat is a thousand miles out to sea and the captain needs to know his or her position, a satellite will pinpoint the position exactly. If a hiker who is carried a cell phone gets lost, others can find him or her by using GPS. Currently, similar systems are been developed by other nations. It's possible that someday GPS units will be implanted directly inside people so that they can always be found. This idea is sure to cause a lot of controversy.

APPLICATION

The **Application** section includes **open-ended productive activities** that allow students to apply the chapter grammar in extended contexts. The goal is to have students produce higher-level spoken and written discourse incorporating grammar they have learned.

Writing activities are open-ended productive written activities in which students use chapter vocabulary and information they read about on the topic. They include pair and /or group work in preparation for writing and take a variety of forms, including summary, description, opinion piece, and analysis.

Speaking activities are open-ended, productive oral activities in which students use chapter vocabulary and information they read about on the topic. These exercises take the form of individual or group presentations, pair or group discussions, or conversations.

Exercise 9 Apply It to Speaking and Writing

1 Select one of the following questions and prepare to present your thoughts about it for two minutes. Support your ideas with examples. See Appendix B for help.

- Americans use the "English" system of measurements, feet and pounds rather than meters and kilograms. Why should the United States change its system of measurement? Explain.
- Why should people learn about physics even if they do not use physics in their professions? Explain.
- Is it a good idea to accept the power of technology without also accepting the responsibility to use that power wisely? Explain.

2 With a partner, take turns presenting your ideas to each other. As your partner speaks, take notes.

3 Write a one-paragraph summary of your partner's ideas in your own words, including some direct quotations and reported speech. Conclude, in a second paragraph, by indicating whether you agree or disagree with his or her conclusions and why.

Exercise 10 Apply It to Writing

1 Read the following passage, underlining the main ideas and most important details.

2 Prepare a one-paragraph summary of these ideas in your own words, incorporating some direct quotes as appropriate. See Appendix B for help.

A Near Disaster

Without the courage of a handful of curious researchers in the mid-1970s, the world would have learned too late of the deadly hidden dangers associated with rapidly expanding use of CFCs. The now legendary hypothesis of Sherwood Rowland and Mario Molina . . . initially unleashed a firestorm of criticism and controversy. . . . They were vindicated* by the 1995 Nobel Peace Prize in Chemistry. . . .[16]

The story begins in 1928 when the General Motors Corporation first synthesized chlorofluorocarbons (CFCs), molecules made from atoms of chlorine, fluorine, and carbon for its Frigidaire refrigerators. . . . CFCs soon became a universal coolant. Production soared. In the 1940s CFCs were found to be useful as pressurized gases to propel* aerosol sprays. In the 1950s, they created the air-conditioning revolution. . . .

CFCs created a lot of business and little fuss until 1974 when scientists began to ask where all these inert gases might be drifting. . . .

In 1974, two university chemists suggested an alarming possibility. Mario Molina and Sherwood Rowland . . . discovered that because CFC molecules are inert and gaseous, they are not chemically broken down or rained out in the lower atmosphere. Instead, they drift slowly into the upper atmosphere or stratosphere, 10 to 50 kilometers overhead, where they may remain intact for decades or centuries. Molina and Rowland theorized that high-energy solar ultraviolet radiation should eventually split CFC molecules apart, releasing large quantities of chlorine (Cl). This was alarming because chlorine reacts strongly with O_3, known as ozone. . . . Scientists found that a single Cl atom destroyed about 100,000 ozone molecules. . . .

But stratospheric ozone is essential to most life on Earth. Because ozone molecules vibrate naturally at ultraviolet frequencies and so absorb much of the sun's ultraviolet radiation, they protect us from this biologically harmful radiation.[17]

*vindicate—to prove to be correct
*propel—to push forward

Exercise 18 Apply It to Speaking

1 In small groups, discuss the information in the chart entitled "Gender Profile of News Audiences."[35] Answer the following questions in your discussion.

a. Who published the chart?
b. What does *gender* mean?
c. What is a profile?
d. What are news audiences?
e. What does the chart compare?
f. What does it tell us about the differences between the genders in general?

2 Conclude by evaluating the information the chart presents. Address the questions below, using adverb clauses and other structures of concession and contrast to express your ideas. Use some of the words in the box. Be prepared to share your conclusions with the class.

a. What are some of the most interesting specific differences?
b. What is your reaction to the data in the chart?

although	but	conversely	even if	even though	however
if	in contrast	nevertheless	nonetheless	on the other hand	otherwise
though	unless	whereas	while	yet	

GENDER PROFILES OF NEWS AUDIENCES		
	Percent who are...	
	MEN	WOMEN
Of those who closely follow:	%	%
Sports news	74	26
Science / technology	69	31
Business / finance	65	35
International	63	37
Washington news	59	41
Local government	55	45
Consumer news	51	49
National Population:	48	52
The weather	47	53
Crime news	46	54
Culture and arts	42	56
Community news	42	58
Entertainment news	39	61
Health news	37	63
Religion	36	64

Source: "Online Papers Modestly Boost Newspaper Readership," Pew Research Center for the People & the Press, July 30, 2006.

PUTTING IT ALL TOGETHER

Each Part in the book culminates with the **Putting It All Together** (PIAT) review. It consists of **review and analysis** exercises that cover all the material in that Part. **No new material** has been added, so the PIAT can serve as a brief one-day **review** of the Part or as a Part achievement test.

PART
4
Putting It All Together

Following a volcanic eruption, rain evaporates on a lava field in Goma, Democratic Republic of Congo.

ADVANCED GRAMMAR **195**

A **longer authentic reading** passage in the PIAT contains multiple examples of grammar structures presented in the preceding chapters. It provides **substantive content** that includes examples of chapter grammar and academic discourse.

Read the following passage from *Anthropology*, 13th Edition, by Carol R. Ember, Melvin Ember, and Peter N. Peregrine.[1]

Natural Disasters as Social Problems

[1] Natural events such as floods, droughts, earthquakes, and insect infestations are usually but not always beyond human control, but their effects are not (Aptekar 1994). We call such events accidents or emergencies when only a few people are affected, but we call them disasters when large numbers of people or large areas are affected. . . . Climatic and other events in the physical environment become disasters because of events or conditions in the social environment.

[2] If people live in houses that are designed to withstand earthquakes—if governing bodies require such construction and the economy is developed enough so that people can afford such construction—the effects of an earthquake will be minimized. If poor people are forced to live in deforested floodplains to be able to find land to farm (as in coastal Bangladesh), if the poor are forced to live in shanties built on precarious hillsides (like those of Rio de Janeiro), the floods and landslides that follow severe hurricanes and rainstorms can kill thousands and even hundreds of thousands.

[3] Thus, natural disasters can have greater or lesser effects on human life, depending on social conditions. And therefore disasters are also social problems, problems that have social causes and possible social solutions. Legislating safe construction of a house is a social solution. The 1976 earthquake in Tangsham, China, killed 250,000 people, mostly because they lived in top-heavy adobe houses that could not withstand severe shaking, whereas the 1989 Loma Prieta earthquake in California, which was of comparable intensity, killed 65 people.

[4] One might think that floods, of all disasters, are the least influenced by social factors. After all, without a huge runoff from heavy rains or snowmelt, there cannot be a flood. But consider why so many people have died from Hwang River floods in China. (One such flood, in 1931, killed nearly 4 million people, making it the deadliest single disaster in history.) The floods in the Hwang River basin have occurred mostly because the clearing of nearby forests for fuel and farmland has allowed enormous quantities of silt to wash into the river, raising the riverbed and increasing the risk of floods that burst the dams that normally would contain them. The risk of disastrous flooding would be greatly reduced if different social conditions prevailed—if people were not so dependent on firewood for fuel, if they did not have to farm close to the river, or if the dams were higher and more numerous.[2]

Review the Ideas verifies students' understanding of the reading.

Review the Ideas

1. According to the passage, what is the difference between an accident and a disaster?
2. What causes disasters?
3. What are some examples of social conditions that can cause disasters?

196 PART 4

EXERCISES

Students demonstrate their understanding of the grammatical structures taught in preceding chapters by completing **exercises** that require **analysis and deep understanding**. These exercises can be used as self-study quizzes or a review.

Analytical exercises allow students to notice the grammatical structures in a fresh context. Students have the opportunity to demonstrate their understanding of the grammatical structures by identifying uses of these structures in an extended authentic text.

2. One adverb clause expressing cause
3. One adverb clause expressing contrast

Paragraph 4
1. One adverb phrase meaning "if not having"
2. Three adverb phrases expressing result
3. One adverb clause expressing cause
4. Four unreal conditional clauses

Exercise 2 Analyzing Individual Sentences

Answer the questions about sentences from the reading passage.

1. This sentence is a compound-complex sentence. Underline the independent clauses and put parentheses around the dependent clauses. Then explain why the sentence is called compound-complex.

   We call such events accidents or emergencies when only a few people are affected, but we call them disasters when large numbers of people or large areas are affected.

2. What is the function of the dashes in the following sentence?

   If people live in houses that are designed to withstand earthquakes—if governing bodies require such construction and the economy is developed enough so that people can afford such construction—the effects of an earthquake will be minimized.

3. Underline the independent clause and put parentheses around the dependent clauses of the following sentence. How is this sentence different from most sentences? (Hint: Note the number of dependent clauses and their positions relative to the independent clause.)

   The 1976 earthquake in Tangsham, China, killed 250,000 people, mostly because they lived in top-heavy adobe houses that could not withstand severe shaking, whereas the 1989 Loma Prieta earthquake in California, which was of comparable intensity, killed 65 people.

4. What is unusual about the following sentence?

   The risk of disastrous flooding would be greatly reduced if different social conditions prevailed—if people were not so dependent on firewood for fuel, if they did not have to farm close to the river, or if the dams were higher and more numerous.

Putting It All Together **197**

Focused exercises usually combine more than one grammar point. These exercises are challenging and require meta-analysis, such as labeling structures, explaining what structures in a sentence or paragraph express, completing or unscrambling sentences, or writing new sentences.

Exercise 2 Identifying Time Frames

Place each of the boldfaced verbs in this sentence from the reading passage into the correct time frame by completing the time line provided.

It was in this context that the theoretical work of mathematicians **began** to pay dividends. . . . Mathematicians **had already been investigating** those questions regarding algorithmic processes that advancing technology **was not raising**. With that, the stage **was set** for the emergence of a new discipline known as *computer science*.

Past Present Future

Error analysis exercises allow students to build their awareness of incorrect usage of the target grammar structures. Students identify and correct errors in targeted grammar in written material, usually a student essay.

Exercise 3 Error Analysis

The following student essay contains ten errors in verb tenses and forms. The first error is corrected for you. Find and correct nine more.

Social Media

                                                          registered
In November 2011, one of the social media companies registers more than 721 million active users, more than twice the population of the United States (314 million). This and other social media have easily outdistanced even e-mail in popularity. People who use social media say that they have been changed the way they communicate. They can actually see their families while they chat online and share information to keep up with family and friends on various social media such as Skype®. However, social media have definite disadvantages compared to traditional means of communication that may outweigh the advantages.

While it is true that social media have changed the way people communicate, the illusion of privacy is puts users at risk. First, young people may post photos that attract stalkers or worse. Or people share personal information such as dates of birth, Social Security numbers, and medical information that identity thieves steal. In addition, employees may talk negatively about employers on social media and then lose their jobs. For example, in 2010, several of the students at my school were suspended after a teacher discovered that they have been writing negative comments about their teachers and other students on Facebook®. They had been forwarding copies of e-mails that are sent to them about other students and that made nasty comments about them on the site. Someone told the director, and of course they are reprimanded.

Another problem with social media is that instead of bringing people together, it may be isolate them. Many people spend so much time developing long-distance friendships online that they don't develop personal relationships with the people around them and in some cases had lost their friends completely. It is sad that some students are as addicted to social media as other addicts are to drugs and alcohol.

A final disadvantage of social media is that it is unreliable. Anyone can post anything online, and there is no way to prove whether or not it is true. Bad or fake products may advertise by unscrupulous businesses; identity thieves and other criminals can pose as professionals or friends to rob or kidnap victims. Politicians and other activists have started rumors about their opponents that spread instantly all over the world.

In sum, social media is one of the great developments of technology, but it has some serious disadvantages. People should therefore be careful when using social media and always remember that everyone everywhere can see and hear everything that put on social media sites.

The **What Did You Learn?** exercises at the end of each PIAT are very comprehensive and can be used as either a self-study quiz or Part achievement test.

WHAT DID YOU LEARN?

A Review the forms and functions of verbs in Part 1. Decide if the grammar in the following sentences is correct. Write *C* for correct and *I* for incorrect. Correct the errors. Then check your answers in Appendix D.

_____ 1. History tells us that the abacus had its roots in ancient China and used in the early Greek and Roman civilizations.

_____ 2. For control of an algorithm's execution, the machine is relies on the human operator.

_____ 3. As desktop computers were being accepted and used in homes, the miniaturization of computing machines continued.[5]

_____ 4. The algorithm followed by the loom could changed to produce different woven designs.

_____ 5. John Atanasoff from Iowa State University and Clifford Berry, his assistant, has finally received credit for creating the first electronic digital computer.

_____ 6. Once an algorithm for performing a task has been found, the performance of the task no longer requires an understanding of the principles on which the algorithm is based.[4]

_____ 7. Pascal has already designed a computing machine by the time that Babbage created his Difference Engine.

_____ 8. In the field of artificial intelligence, autonomous machines were being built that can operate without human intervention.

_____ 9. Thomas Edison is credited with inventing the incandescent lamp, but other researchers were developing similar lamps and in a sense Edison was lucky to be the one to obtain the patent.[5]

_____ 10. Computer scientists want to develop their knowledge about artificial intelligence—knowledge that allowed them to create new intelligent machines.

B On a separate sheet of paper, describe the time frame of each paragraph.

1. The machines designed by Charles Babbage were truly the forerunners of modern computer design. If technology had been able to produce his machines in an economically feasible manner and if the data processing demands of commerce and government had been on the scale of today's requirements, Babbage's ideas could have led to a computer revolution in the 1880s.[6]

2. The old adage "an ounce of prevention is worth a pound of cure" is certainly true in the context of controlling vandalism over network connections. A primary prevention technique is to filter traffic passing through a point in the network, usually with a program called a firewall. For instance, a firewall might be installed at the gateway of an organization's intranet to filter messages passing in and out of the region.[6]

C On a separate sheet of paper, explain why the passive is used in the following paragraphs.

1. When a user sends e-mail from his or her local machine, it is first transferred to the user's mail server. There it is forwarded to the destination mail server where it is stored until the recipient contacts the mail server and asks to view the accumulated mail.[8]

2. As for the ability to follow an algorithm, we can see a progression of flexibility in these machines. Pascal's machine was built to perform only addition. Consequently, the appropriate sequence of steps was embedded into the structure of the machine itself. . . . Babbage's Difference Engine . . . could be modified to perform a variety of calculations, but his Analytical Engine . . . was designed to read instructions in the form of holes in paper cards.[9]

(continued on next page)

Putting It All Together **57**

Speaking activities are open-ended, productive oral activities in which students apply the Part grammar, vocabulary, and information in an extended context. These exercises take the form of individual or group presentations, pair or group discussions, or conversations. Their goal is to have students produce higher-level spoken discourse incorporating grammar they have learned.

Exercise 5 Apply It to Speaking

With a small group of classmates, prepare a brief presentation (two to three minutes) about clothing trends you've noticed among today's students. Follow these steps:

1 Brainstorm current clothing trends among students. For example, consider trends among: students from China, Japan, Russia, or Malaysia; students who belong to fraternities or sororities; students who admire sports teams; or students who don't care about fashion.

2 Make a list of noun phrases you can use to describe these trends, for example, *colorful high-top shoes; long, straight hair; status clothing; spectator sports apparel; body-conforming jeans;* and *dirty white T-shirts*.

3 Prepare and practice your presentation. See Appendix B for help preparing your presentation.

4 Give your presentation.

Writing activities are open-ended productive written activities in which students apply the Part grammar, vocabulary, and information in an extended context. They take a variety of forms, including summary, description, opinion piece, and analysis. Their goal is to have students produce higher-level written discourse incorporating grammar they have learned.

Exercise 6 Apply It to Writing

Write a paragraph about traditional clothing popular in your country. Follow these steps:

1 Choose the clothing you will write about.

2 Answer these questions about the clothing:
  • What does it look like?
  • Who wears it?
  • When (on what occasions) is it worn?
  • Why do people wear this clothing?

3 Use your answers to the questions to write your paragraph. See Appendix B for help.

4 Check your paragraph to make sure you have included varied noun phrases to make your descriptions interesting and informative.

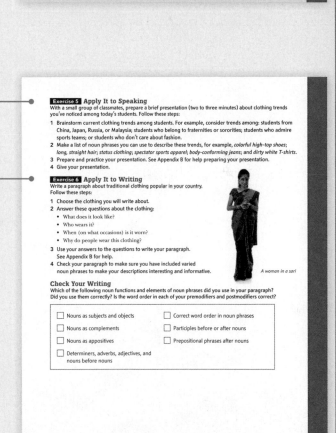

A woman in a sari

Check Your Writing

Which of the following noun functions and elements of noun phrases did you use in your paragraph? Did you use them correctly? Is the word order in each of your premodifiers and postmodifiers correct?

☐ Nouns as subjects and objects

☐ Nouns as complements

☐ Nouns as appositives

☐ Determiners, adverbs, adjectives, and nouns before nouns

☐ Correct word order in noun phrases

☐ Participles before or after nouns

☐ Prepositional phrases after nouns

Putting It All Together **101**

Key Features **xxi**

ABOUT THE AUTHOR

Helen Hoyt Schmidt was born in Cambridge, Massachusetts, graduated from the Cambridge School in Weston, Massachusetts, Rollins College in Winter Park, Florida, and was awarded her advanced degree from Teachers College, Columbia University, New York. She teaches in the Intensive English and Orientation Program at Iowa State University.

She has spent most of her teaching career developing materials based on authentic academic textbook and journal articles. She has frequently presented at TESOL and published articles on reading, vocabulary, and grammar. She is the author of *Advanced English Grammar*. She has been refining her ideas and working to make the most advanced grammatical structures in context more accessible to non-native speakers. *Advanced Grammar,* published in 2015 by Pearson, is the result of those efforts.

ACKNOWLEDGEMENTS

I would like to thank several people who have made this text possible.

My first interest in a then brand new field, teaching English as a second language, began at Teachers College, Columbia University, where I had outstanding professors, three of whom remain in my mind as the most inspirational; Robert L. Allen, who opened the door to the fascination of sector analysis, now known as Xword grammar, and inspired my love of grammar; Virginia French Allen, who excited my interest in teaching the new subject: English as a second language, and Christina Bratt Paulston, my supervising practice teaching professor, who taught me the value of the inductive approach.

As a new teacher, it was my great fortune to have the opportunity to work with Barbara Matthies in the Intensive English and Orientation Program at Iowa State University. Just before I arrived, Betty Schrampfer Azar had been an instructor there. Azar was writing her first textbook and Matthies wrote the teachers manual. These books have been an inspiration ever since. Over the years, my goal became to write a grammar text as well. Both Mattheis and Azar gave me valuable advice and support, which culminated in my book *Advanced English Grammar* with Prentice- Hall.

My new book, *Advanced Grammar*, published by Pearson, was made possible thanks to a team of amazing people. Barbara Sohombing, Pearson book representative, encouraged me and passed my sample manuscript to the publishers. This resulted in meetings with Massimo Rubini, and Lise Minowitz, who guided the project in its first stages.

I also want to thank the many ESL teachers who reviewed the manuscript and made many excellent suggestions that have made this book a truly advanced grammar text that is accessible and interesting.

Thank you, too, to the team of Amy McCormick, Joan Poole, and Gosia Jaros-White. My editors, Marian Wassner and then Barbara Lyons, have been enormously helpful. Their expert knowledge of grammar and true understanding of the purpose of *Advanced Grammar* have been of immeasurable help. They along with copy editor Leigh Stolle's insightful questions and careful examination of every word kept me on the track of logically and correctly explaining difficult grammatical concepts within authentic materials. Thanks, too, to Lindsay Richman, who provided help and advice with obtaining just the right photos to enhance the text.

To anyone I have missed inadvertently, thank you.

Finally, and most important of all, I thank my unbelievably supportive husband who has helped me in uncountable ways when the going got tough and has enjoyed the successes right along with me.

Helen Hoyt Schmidt

The publisher would like to thank the following reviewers for their detailed and insightful comments:

Sharon Cavusgil, Georgia State University; Sally Gearheart, Santa Rosa Junior College; Ann Hall, University of Texas at Austin; Kathi Hart, University of Denver; Patty Heiser, University of Washington; Joseph C. Hughes, University of Missouri; Barbara Inerfeld, Rutgers University; Ruth Luman, Modesto Junior College; Sherrie Malleis, Loyola University; Felicia Manor, University of Denver; Molly Ann McClennan, Marshall University in Huntington; Susanne McLaughlin, Roosevelt University; Y. Dana Miho, Mt. San Antonio College; Mary Lou Ninan, San Francisco State University; Susan Orias, Broward College; Grace Osborne, University of San Diego; Nancy Peritz, University of California at San Diego; Sandra Reno, Divine Word College; Tom Riedmiller, University of Northern Iowa; Mary Kay Wedum, Colorado State University.

PART

1

The Verb Tense System:
Using Academic Verb Tense Patterns

OBJECTIVES

In Part 1 of the *Advanced Grammar* course you will

- review verb forms and their uses.
- understand and use verb time frames to express ideas.
- review passive verb forms and their uses.
- understand and use active and passive verbs.
- review modal verb forms and their uses.
- understand and use modal auxiliary verbs to hedge.

Verbs* and verb phrases are used to express actions and states of being, show time relationships between actions, enhance cohesion within and between paragraphs, and provide a way to express facts, attitudes, and noncommittal statements.

Academic texts about computer science serve to illustrate the functions of verbs and verb phrases in academic English. Becoming proficient in using the verb system will help prepare you to read textbooks efficiently and to communicate effectively in speaking and writing at the university level.

All terms highlighted in yellow are defined and illustrated in the Glossary of Grammar and Writing Terms.

Review of the Verb Tenses

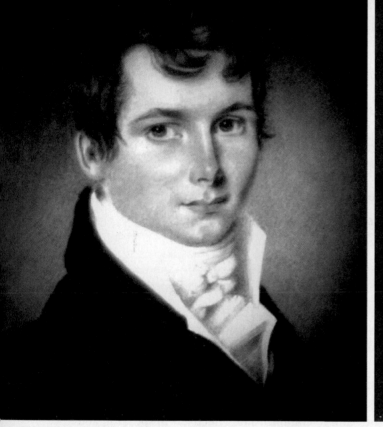

Charles Babbage

Augusta Ada Byron

VOCABULARY Here are some words that you will <u>encounter</u> in Chapter 1. How much do you know about each word? Turn to Appendix A to assess and expand your word knowledge.

		Tableau		
algorithm	application	array	artificial intelligence	autonomous
contend	impact	miniaturization	program	task

Prepare to Read

1. What was a well-educated woman's role in society in the nineteenth century?
2. How did computers in the nineteenth century look?
3. What could computers do in the nineteenth century?

Read the following paragraph from *Computer Science: An Overview*, **11th Edition, by J. Glenn Brookshear.**[1]

THE FIRST PROGRAMMER

Augusta Ada Byron

[1]Augusta Ada Byron, Countess of Lovelace, **has been** the subject of much commentary in the computing community. [2]She **lived** a somewhat tragic life of less than thirty-seven years (1815–1852) that was complicated by poor health and the fact that she **was** a nonconformist in a society that limited the professional role of women. [3]Although she was interested in a wide range of science, she concentrated her studies in mathematics. [4]Her interest in "compute science" began when she became fascinated by the machines of Charles Babbage at a demonstration of a prototype of his Difference Engine in 1833. [5]Her contribution to computer science **stems** from her translation from French into English of a paper discussing Babbage's designs for the Analytical Engine. [6]To this translation, Babbage encouraged her to attach an addendum describing applications of the engine and containing examples of how the engine could be programmed to perform various tasks. [7]Babbage's enthusiasm for Ada Byron's work was apparently motivated by his hope that its publication would lead to financial backing for the construction of his Analytical Engine. [8](As the daughter of Lord Byron*, Ada Byron held celebrity status with potentially significant financial connections.) [9]This backing never materialized, but Ada Byron's addendum has survived and is considered to contain the first examples of computer programs. [10]The degree to which Babbage influenced Ada Byron's work is debated by historians. [11]Some argue that Babbage made major contributions whereas others contend that he was more of an obstacle than an aid. [12]Nonetheless, Augusta Ada Byron is recognized today as the world's first programmer, a status that was certified by the U.S. Department of Defense when it named the prominent programming language (Ada) in her honor.[2]

Lord Byron (1788–1824) was a notorious English nobleman and Romantic poet.

Review the Ideas

1. Who was Augusta Ada Byron and why is she known as the first programmer?
2. Who was Charles Babbage and what did he do?
3. What did you learn about computers in the nineteenth century?

Analyze the Grammar

Work in pairs to answer the following questions about the reading.

1 Look at the boldfaced words in the first, second, and fifth sentences. What do we call them? How do they differ from one another?
2 Underline other examples of these kinds of words in the passage.
3 Label the tenses you know.
4 Discuss your findings with your classmates.

Charles Babbage's Difference Engine

CHART 1-1 | Verbs

Verbs are words that describe actions (*discuss, program, investigate*) or states (*be, seem, appear*).

1. Verbs can be divided into auxiliary verbs (*be, have, can, should*) and main verbs (*influence, program, consider*).	1. The engine **was** programmed. Charles Babbage **influenced** Augusta Ada Byron's work.
2. Auxiliary verbs are used together with main verbs to form verb tenses (*is working*) or passive voice (*was complicated*), or to add the speaker's attitude to the meaning of the main verb (*should consider*).	2. The computer **is working**. Byron's life **was complicated** by poor health. Engineers **should consider** the cost of production.
3. After the first auxiliary verb, repetition of the auxiliary can be omitted when there are two or more verbs in a list within a sentence.	3. The researchers **had created**, **tested**, and **refined** the program.
4. A verb phrase may be made up of a single verb (*store*), or one or more auxiliary verbs + (an adverb) + a main verb (*had already been studying*).	4. A computer **stores** data. Byron **had** already **been studying** mathematics by the time she met Babbage.
5. A linking verb connects the grammatical subject of a sentence to a noun or adjective that follows it. Linking verbs are not usually used in the progressive form, but when used, the meaning changes. Linking verbs: *be, seem, appear*.	5. Byron **was** intelligent. Byron **was being** helpful.
6. An active verb makes a statement about an action. The grammatical subject of an active verb is the "doer" of the action. The grammatical object is the "receiver" of the action.	doer active verb receiver of the action 6. Byron **wrote** the first computer program.

CHART 1-2 | Present Tenses (Active)

Simple Present

Forms: verb or verb + *-s* / *do* or *does* + (*not*) + verb

Can be used to express:

1. General truths or scientific facts	1. Computers **control** the power grid.
2. Customs and habits	2. A computer normally **boots up** in seconds.
3. Planned and scheduled events in the future	3. Computer upgrades do not **begin** next week.
4. Generalizations that begin a paragraph	4. Computers **are** electronic devices.

Used with these common time expressions: *always, often, normally, sometimes, usually*

Present Progressive

Forms: *is / are* + (*not*) + verb + *-ing*

Can be used to express:	
1. Single actions occurring at this moment or during a longer period of time the writer considers present	1. A large number of students **are studying** computer science these days.
2. Temporary activities; changing events	2. Computer sales **are growing** at an unprecedented rate nowadays.
3. Events that will occur in the near future	3. The programmers **are leaving** soon.

Used with these common time expressions:
now, this year, nowadays, these days, at the moment, soon, tomorrow, next week, next year

Exercise 1 Identifying Present Tense Verbs

With a partner, underline the present tense verbs in the following passage.
1 Name each tense underlined and discuss what it expresses.
2 Explain why *seeks*, *requires*, and *continues* end with *-s*.

Artificial intelligence is the field of computer science that seeks to build autonomous machines—machines that can carry out complex tasks without human intervention. This goal requires that machines be able to perceive and reason. Such capabilities fall within the category of commonsense activities that, although natural for the human mind, are proving difficult for machines. The result is that work in the field continues to be challenging.[3]

Exercise 2 Choosing Simple Present or Present Progressive

For each verb in parentheses, work with a partner to indicate whether the simple present or present progressive should be used and explain what it expresses. Write the correct form.

1. A smartphone application normally _____ (*cost*) less than five dollars.

2. Sales of word processing programs _____ (*decline*) these days.

3. In addition to being telephones, smartphones _____ (*include*) a great number of capabilities.

4. Laptops and tablets _____ (*replace*) desktop computers at the moment.

5. The technical support department _____ (*upgrade*) all office computers tomorrow.

CHART 1-3	Future Tenses (Active)

Future

Forms: *will* + (*not*) + base verb

Can be used to express:

1. Future events	1. Computers **will not run** the data tomorrow.
2. Willingness	2. The IT department **will help** you.
3. Certainty	3. The conference **will be** an event to remember.
4. Predictions about formal events	4. The conference **will begin** at noon.

Will is used most often in formal writing.

Forms: *be* + (*not*) + *going to* + base verb

Can be used to express:

1. Predictions	1. The computer **is going to change** drastically.
2. Plans and scheduled events	2. The lab **is going to install** new computers next Monday.

Used with these common time expressions: *someday, tomorrow, next week, soon, in five years*

Future Progressive

Forms: *will* + (*not*) + *be* + verb + *-ing*

Can be used to express:

1. Events that occur continuously from now into the future	1. Computers **will be changing** for years.
2. Events that will occur at a specific time in the future	2. At this time next year, we **will be thinking** about purchasing new computers.

Forms: *be* + (*not*) + *going to* + *be* + verb + *-ing*

Can be used to express:

(With emphasis) the continuous nature of predicted events	Computers **are going to be changing** for years.

Used with these common time expressions: *for years, at this time tomorrow, next week, next year*

Future Perfect

Forms: *will* + (*not*) + *have* + past participle

Can be used to express:

Events that will happen between now and a time in the future	Computers **will have changed** by 2020.

Used with these common time expressions: *by, by the time, before*

Future Perfect Progressive

Forms: *will* + (*not*) + *have* + *been* + verb + *-ing*

Can be used to express:	
(With emphasis) the continuous nature of a future perfect event	By 2020, engineers **will have been working** to miniaturize smartphones for many years.
In a sentence with an independent (main) clause and a dependent (subordinate) clause, future, future perfect, future progressive, and future perfect progressive can be used only in the independent clause. Present or present perfect must be used in the dependent clause	dependent clause [When miniaturization techniques **improve**,] computers **will become** smaller. dependent clause Computers **will have changed** enormously [by the time this class **graduates** in 2020.]

Exercise 3 **Choosing the Correct Form**

For each verb in parentheses, indicate whether the simple future, future progressive, future perfect, or future perfect progressive should be used and explain why. Write the correct form.

1. Some people predict that someday computers _____ (*take over*) society.

2. Some believe that computers _____ (*perform*) many human jobs at this time next year.

3. Computers always _____ (*be*) essential to humans.

4. A few people say that by the year 2050, machines _____ (*replace*) people in all manufacturing jobs.

5. Certainly, computer engineers _____ (*work*) to develop faster and more intelligent computers by the time any of these predictions prove true.

Exercise 4 **Matching Tenses with a Rule**

1 With a partner, underline the verbs in the following passage.
2 Find the sentences that are examples of the following rule from Chart 1-3: "In a sentence with an independent (main) clause and a dependent (subordinate) clause, future, future perfect, future progressive, and future perfect progressive can be used only in the independent clause. Present or present perfect must be used in the dependent clause."

The automation of computer graphics will certainly progress as technology improves. Programmers will have fully automated the way computer programs create 3-D animations by the time that the next generation of computers comes on the market. Three-dimensional graphics will be changing TV as well as the motion picture industry until a new technology is discovered. Computer graphics is a field that is constantly improving.

CHART 1-4 | **Present Perfect**

Present Perfect

Forms: *has / have* + (*not*) + past participle

Can be used to express:	
1. Unfinished events that started in the past, continue into the present, and perhaps continue into the future	1. The computer industry **has grown** since the 1970s.
2. Events that happened at an unspecified time in the past (we don't know exactly when)	2. Programming **has become** a popular profession.
3. Events that happened repeatedly in the unspecified past	3. These companies **have not released** new devices for years.
4. A generalization that begins a paragraph	4. The release of a new product **has** always **been** risky for computer companies.

Used with these common time expressions: *since, for, lately, these days, often, always, generally, never, scarcely, rarely, hardly ever*

Present Perfect Progressive

Forms: *has / have* + (*not*) + *been* + verb + *-ing*

Can be used to express:	
1. Unfinished events that started in the past, continue into the present, and perhaps continue into the future. This form emphasizes the continuous nature of the event.	1. The value of the stock of companies that manufacture typewriters **has been falling** steadily since the computer was introduced.
2. A temporary situation or action	2. The company **has been losing** market share this year, but that is unlikely to last.

Used with these common time expressions: *since, for, lately, these days, all day, all week, all year*

Exercise 5 | Identifying Present Perfect Tense

With a partner, underline the seven examples of the present perfect in the following passage. Explain
1 why four of the examples do not have auxiliary verbs (*have* or *has*)
2 why the author chose the present perfect in this passage
3 why *has altered* and *has repeatedly challenged* include *has* and not *have*.

The miniaturization of computers and their expanding capabilities have brought computer technology to the forefront of today's society. Computer technology is so prevalent now that familiarity with it is fundamental to being a member of modern society. Computing technology has altered the ability of governments to exert control; had enormous impact on global economies; led to startling advances in scientific research; revolutionized the role of data collection, storage, and applications; provided new means for people to communicate and interact; and has repeatedly challenged society's status quo.[4]

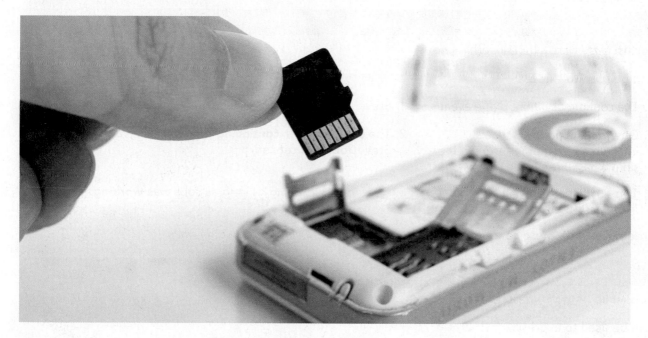

Exercise 6 | Choosing the Correct Form of the Verb

For each verb in parentheses, indicate whether the present perfect or present perfect progressive—or both forms—should or could be used. Write the correct form(s) and explain what each expresses. More than one form may be possible.

1. Computers _____ (*revolutionize*) the world.

2. One computer company _____ (*grow*) since the early 1970s.

3. That best-selling word processing program _____ (*add*) new features every year.

4. Programmers in California _____ (*develop*) many new products for decades.

5. Search engines _____ (*alter*) the way people search for information on the Internet lately.

CHART 1-5 **Past Tenses**

Simple Past

Forms: verb + -ed | did + (not) + verb OR irregular past form of verb | did + (not) + verb

Can be used to express:

1. Finished events or actions at a specific time in the past	1. Steve Jobs **died** in 2011. Jobs **did not have** a chance to complete his work.
2. How many times something happened in the past	2. Steve Jobs **invented** a new device every year during his career.

Often used with these common time expressions: *last year, yesterday, ago, in 1955, for three years, during*

Past Progressive

Forms: *was | were* + (*not*) + verb + *-ing*

Can be used to express:

1. The continuous nature of the event	1. Steve Jobs's company **was increasing** in value during 2000.
2. One event in progress that is interrupted by another event in the simple past tense (used with *when*)	2. The company **was continuing** to increase in value when Steve Jobs **got** cancer.
3. Two simultaneous actions in progress in the past (used with *while, as*)	3. The stock **was rising** as long as Jobs **was working**.

Often used with these common time expressions: *while, as, as long as, during, when*

Past Perfect

Forms: *had* + (*not*) + past participle

Can be used to express:

An event that occurred before another event in the past	Babbage **had built** his Difference Engine before he designed the Analytical Engine.

Often used with these common time expressions: *by the time, by 1930, before*

Past Perfect Progressive

Forms: *had* + (*not*) + *been* + verb + *-ing*

Can be used to express:

The continuous nature of an event in the past perfect	Babbage **had been working** on the design for several years, but he never built it.

Often used with these common time expressions: *by the time, by 1930, before, for several years, for a long time*

Exercise 7 Identifying Meanings of Verbs

Read the following passage. Underline the verbs.

Gottfried Wilhelm Leibniz of Germany and Blaise Pascal of France were developing rather limited computing machines when Charles Babbage of England created a machine that could do a number of different calculations. Babbage, Leibniz, and Pascal had all created complex machines driven by gears, but the technology in those days could not produce them economically. Then, in the early 1900s, a number of advances in electronics brought about the development of new machines every year from 1940 to 1944. In 1940, Bell Laboratories developed an electromechanical machine, and in 1944, Harvard University and IBM created another. Unfortunately, as researchers were building these machines, other researchers were building completely electronic computers based on vacuum tubes. Bell, Harvard, and IBM had been working on ideas that were obsolete.

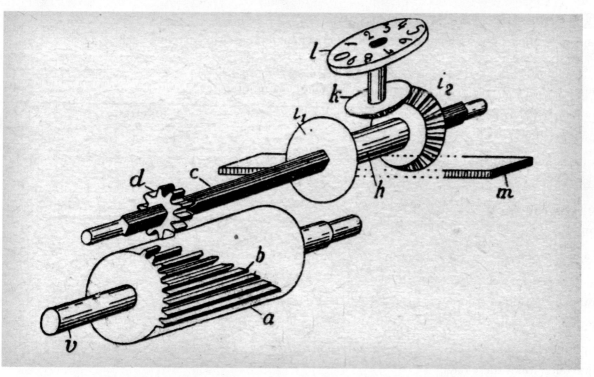

Leibniz wheel and counting wheel © Juulijs

Look back at the passage. Find and write an example of a verb that is used to express the following. State the tense of the verb.

1. Finished events or actions at a specific time in the past: _____

2. How many times something happened in the past: _____

3. One event in progress that is interrupted by another event in the past: _____

4. Two simultaneous actions in progress in the past: _____

5. An event that occurred before another event in the past: _____

6. The continuous nature of an event that occurred before another event in the past: _____

SUMMARY OF VERB TENSES

PAST		NOW		FUTURE
		present perfect		
		present perfect progressive		
past perfect	simple past	simple present	future perfect	future
past perfect progressive	past progressive	present progressive	future perfect progressive	future progressive

Exercise 8 Choosing the Correct Tense

Work in pairs or groups. Choose the best tense of the verbs in parentheses to complete each sentence.

1. An operating system _____ (*is / will be / was*) the software that _____ (*controls / will control / controlled*) the overall operation of a computer.

2. An operating system _____ (*allows / will allow / allowed*) a user to retrieve files and request a program to run.

3. One of the most popular operating systems _____ (*is / will be / was*) Windows®, which _____ (*runs / run / ran*) on PCs.

4. Apple® computers _____ (*operate / operates / had operated*) with the Mac® operating system.

5. After a user _____ (*starts / will start / started*) up his or her computer, the computer _____ (*displays / will display / has displayed*) the desktop.

6. The miniaturization of computers _____ (*results / result / has resulted*) in the development of smartphones.

7. Smartphones _____ (*were becoming / are becoming / become*) more widely used than landline telephones these days.

8. Augusta Ada Byron _____ (*was / had been / will be*) a well-known person because she _____ (*was / is / will be*) Lord Byron's daughter.

9. Charles Babbage _____ (*is designing / has been designing / was designing*) his Analytical Engine at the same time that Joseph Jacquard _____ (*is using / has been using / was using*) holes in cards to program a weaving loom.

10. Jacquard _____ (*has developed / had developed / develops*) his patterns of holes in cards in 1801 before Babbage _____ (*has gotten / had gotten / got*) the idea.

Exercise 9 **Practicing Verb Tenses and Forms**

Write the correct forms of the given verbs to complete each paragraph. Compare your answers with your classmates'.

1. The study of algorithms _____ (*begin*) as a subject in mathematics. Indeed the search for algorithms was a significant activity of mathematicians long before the development of today's computers. The goal _____ (*be*) to find a single set of directions that _____ (*describe*) how all problems of a particular type could be solved.[5]

2. In the past decade mobile phone technology _____ (*advance*) from simple, single-purpose, portable devices to complex, multifunction handheld computers. The first-generation wireless telephone network _____ (*transmit*) analog voice signals through the air, much like traditional telephones but without the copper wire running through the wall.[6]

3. In this section we _____ (*focus*) on an Internet application by which multimedia information is disseminated over the Internet. It is based on the concept of hypertext, a term that originally _____ (*refer*) to text documents that _____ (*contain*) links, called hyperlinks, to other documents. Today, hypertext _____ (*expand*) to encompass images, audio, and video, and because of this expanded scope it is sometimes referred to as hypermedia.[7]

4. Several technologies _____ (*exist*) to produce 3-D imagery in the context of television, but all _____ (*rely*) on the same stereoscopic visual effect—two slightly different images arriving at the left and right eyes are interpreted by the brain as depth. The most inexpensive mechanisms _____ (*require*) special glasses with filter lenses. Older colored lenses (used in cinema in the 1950s) or the more modern polarized lenses _____ (*filter out*) different aspects of a single image from the screen, resulting in different images reaching different eyes.[8]

5. More costly technology _____ (*involve*) "active" glasses that alternately _____ (*shutter*) left and right lenses in synchronization with a 3-D television that _____ (*switch*) quickly between the left and right images. Finally, 3-D televisions have been developed that do not require special glasses or head gear. They _____ (*use*) elaborate arrays of filters or magnifying lenses on the surface of the screen to project the left and right images toward a viewer's head at slightly different angles, meaning that the left and right eyes of the viewer _____ (*see*) different images.[9]

The following passage contains ten errors in active verb tenses. The first error is corrected for you. Work in pairs to find and correct nine more. Compare your answers with your classmates'.

Who Invented the Electronic Digital Computer?

The old saying "Give credit where credit is due" means to acknowledge an accomplishment. In this story it means that the person who first creates a device should receive recognition for that achievement. Sometimes, however, circumstances had *have* prevented the most deserving person from receiving the appropriate credit. John Atanasoff, an American physicist and inventor, is an example of such a deserving person.

After Atanasoff graduates from the University of Wisconsin with a PhD in 1930, he took a job in math and physics at Iowa State University in Ames, Iowa. While he working at ISU, he invented the analog calculator. Then, in 1937, as he was driving to Rock Island, Illinois, he get the idea for a computation machine to do equations. He applied for and received a small grant ($5,000), and with his graduate assistant, Cliff Berry, he built the Atanasoff-Berry Computer (the ABC) between 1939 and 1941. Unfortunately, Iowa State University never patented the ABC.

In 1941, John Mauchly, a physics professor from the University of Pennsylvania, visited Atanasoff at ISU, has stayed with him, saw the ABC, and learned all about it. Mauchly even had the handbook for the ABC in his possession while he is staying with Atanasoff. Mauchly never told his later partner, Presper Eckert, about this visit.

In 1942, Atanasoff went on a wartime assignment (World War II) to work with the navy in Washington DC. While he away, the university dismantled the ABC because the chairman of his department couldn't imagine who would want to use such a device. The ABC was soon forgotten.

Mauchly visited Atanasoff in Washington several times in 1943 but was never telling him that he was working on his own computer. In 1946, John Mauchly and Presper Eckert, an electronics expert, applied for and received patents on the Electronic Numerical Integrator and Computer (ENIAC), which they have designed together in 1943.

The ABC went unrecognized from 1941 to 1973, when U.S. district judge Earl R. Larson made the decision that the ENIAC patents were invalid because the idea for the ENIAC had been derived from John Atanasoff's. The decision was the result of a lawsuit between Honeywell and Sperry Rand over who owned the patents to the ENIAC.

Recently, ISU has replicated the ABC and placed it on display in the lobby of Durham Center (the computer science building). As students going from class to class, they pass the Atanasoff-Berry Computer, the first electronic digital computer. Atanasoff has finally received credit for his creation.

CHART 1-6 | Time Frames

Academic writers and speakers organize their ideas into paragraphs that often follow time frame conventions. Many paragraphs use a single tense. However, time frame conventions allow certain tenses to be used together within a paragraph. For example, the present, present perfect, and future tenses are often used together in one paragraph, while the past tenses are frequently used together in a paragraph. Observe these three basic patterns within the following paragraphs.

Present Time Frame

Simple present	Several technologies **exist** to produce 3-D imagery in the context of television, but all **rely** on the same stereoscopic visual effect—two slightly different images arriving at the left and right eyes **are interpreted** by the brain as depth. The most inexpensive mechanisms **require** special glasses with filter lenses. Older colored lenses (used in cinema in the 1950s) or the more modern polarized lenses **filter out** different aspects of a single image from the screen, resulting in different images reaching different eyes.

Present and Future Time Frame

A combination of simple present, present perfect, future, and future perfect	The computer lab **has** a total of ten computers this year (2014). The university **has promised** that the Instructional Technology Department **will add** ten more computers every year for five years. How many computers **will** we **have received** by the year 2020?

Past Time Frame

Simple past	Conditions such as limited data storage capabilities and intricate, time-consuming programming procedures **restricted** the complexity of the algorithms utilized in early computing machines. However, as these limitations **began** to disappear, machines **were applied** to increasingly larger and more complex tasks. As attempts to express the composition of these tasks in algorithmic form **began** to tax the abilities of the human mind, more and more research efforts **were directed** toward the study of algorithms and the programming process.[10]
A combination of simple past and past perfect	The idea of communicating an algorithm via holes in paper **was not originated** by Babbage. He **got** the idea from Joseph Jacquard (1752–1834), who, in 1801, **had developed** a weaving loom in which the steps to be performed during the weaving process **were determined** by patterns of holes in large, thick cards made of wood. . . . Another beneficiary of Jacquard's idea **was** Herman Hollerith, who **applied** the concept of representing information as holes in paper cards to speed up the tabulation process in the 1890 census. (It **was** this work by Hollerith that **led** to the creation of IBM.)[11]

Exercise 11   Identifying Time Frames

Underline the verbs in the following passages. Identify the time frame(s) by using Chart 1-6. The first one is done for you.

1. The idea of communicating an algorithm via holes in paper <u>was not originated</u> by Babbage. He <u>got</u> the idea from Joseph Jacquard (1752–1834), who, in 1801, <u>had developed</u> a weaving loom in which the steps to be performed during the weaving process <u>were determined</u> by patterns of holes in large, thick cards made of wood (or cardboard). In this manner, the algorithm followed by the loom <u>could be changed</u> easily to produce different woven designs.[12]   *Past time frame*

2. The difficulties involved in measuring software properties in a quantitative manner is one of the reasons that software engineering has struggled to find a rigorous footing in the same sense as mechanical and electrical engineering. Whereas these latter subjects are founded on the established science of physics, software engineering continues to search for its roots.[13]

3. The techniques of problem solving and the need to learn more about them are not unique to computer science but rather are topics pertinent to almost any field. The close association between the process of algorithm discovery and that of general problem solving has caused computer scientists to join with those of other disciplines in the search for better problem-solving techniques. Ultimately, one would like to reduce the process of problem solving to an algorithm in itself, but this has been shown to be impossible. (This is the result of the material in Chapter 12, where we will show that there are problems that do not have algorithmic solutions.) Thus the ability to solve problems remains more of an artistic skill to be developed than a precise science to be learned.[14]

4. The machines designed by Babbage were truly the forerunners of modern computer design. If technology had been able to produce his machines in an economically feasible manner, and if the data processing demands of commerce and government had been on the scale of today's requirements, Babbage's ideas could have led to a computer revolution in the 1880s. As it was, only a demonstration model of his Difference Engine was constructed in his lifetime. This machine determined numerical values by computing "successive differences."[15]

5. A Math Problem: As you step from a pier into a boat, your hat falls into the water, unbeknownst to you. The river is flowing at 2.5 miles per hour, so your hat begins to float downstream. In the meantime, you begin traveling upstream in the boat at a speed of 4.75 miles per hour relative to the water. After 10 minutes you realize that your hat is missing, turn the boat around, and begin to chase your hat down the river. How long will it take to catch up with your hat? (Answer: 10 minutes)

   Most algebra students as well as calculator enthusiasts approach this problem by first determining how far upstream the boat will have traveled in 10 minutes as well as how far downstream the hat will have traveled during that same time. Then, they determine how long it will take for the boat to travel downstream to this position. But, when the boat reaches this position, the hat will have floated farther downstream. Thus, the problem solver either begins to apply techniques of calculus or becomes trapped in a cycle of computing where the hat will be each time the boat goes to where the hat was.[16]

Using the Correct Tenses to Complete a Time Frame

Complete each paragraph with the correct form of the verb(s) in parentheses. Write the name of the time frame(s) at the end of each paragraph.

1. We begin with the most fundamental concept of computer science—that of an algorithm. Informally, an algorithm _____ (*was / is*) a set of steps that defines how a task is performed. . . . For example, there _____ (*were / are*) algorithms for cooking (called recipes), for finding your way through a strange city (more commonly called directions), for operating washing machines (usually displayed on the inside of the washer's lid or perhaps on the wall of a Laundromat), for playing music (expressed in the form of sheet music), and for performing magic tricks. . . .[17] _____

2. Early approaches to software engineering insisted on performing requirements analysis, design, implementation, and testing in a strictly sequential manner. The belief _____ (*is / was*) that too much was at risk during the development of a large software system to allow for variations. As a result, software engineers _____ (*insist / insisted*) that the entire requirements specification of the system be completed before beginning implementation. The result _____ (*is / was*) a development process now referred to as the waterfall model, an analogy to the fact that the development process was allowed to flow in only one direction.[18] _____

3. Artificial intelligence (AI) techniques are increasingly showing up in smartphone applications. For example, Google® has developed Google Goggles™, a smartphone application providing a visual search engine. Just take a picture of a book, landmark, or sign, using a smartphone's camera, and Goggles™ _____ (*performed / will perform*) image processing, image analysis, and text recognition, and then initiate a web search to identify the object. If you are an English speaker visiting in France, you _____ (*took / can take*) a picture of a sign, menu, or other text and have it translated to English. Beyond Goggles™, Google® _____ (*actively worked on / is actively working on*) voice-to-voice language translation. Soon you _____ (*were able to / will be able to*) speak English into your phone and have your words spoken in Spanish, Chinese, or another language. Smartphones _____ (*undoubtedly got / will undoubtedly get*) smarter as AI continues to be utilized in innovative ways.[19] _____

4. Gottfried Wilhelm Leibniz of Germany and Blaise Pascal of France were developing rather limited computing machines when Charles Babbage of England _____ (*create / created*) a machine that could do a number of different calculations. Babbage, Leibniz, and Pascal _____ (*have all created / had all created*) complex machines driven by gears, but the technology in those days was not able to produce them economically. Then, in the early 1900s, there _____ (*have been / were*) a number of advances in electronics that _____ (*had allowed / allowed*) several new machines to be developed between 1940 and 1944. In 1940, Bell Laboratories _____ (*develop / developed*) an electromechanical machine, and in 1944 Harvard University and IBM _____ (*create / created*) another. Unfortunately, as researchers _____ (*had been building / were building*) these machines, other researchers _____ (*are building / were building*) completely electronic computers based on vacuum tubes. Bell, Harvard, and IBM _____ (*have been working / had been working*) on ideas that _____ (*have been / were*) obsolete. _____

Exercise 13 Completing Verbs in Time Frames

Complete each of the paragraphs with the tenses that form a particular time frame or are indicated by other words in the paragraph.

1. In 1833, Charles Babbage (1791–1871) _____ (*invent*) an analytical machine that was designed to read instructions from holes in paper cards. Babbage _____ (*not originate*) this idea. In 1801, Joseph Jacquard (1752–1834) _____ (*develop*) a weaving loom that _____ (*use*) patterns of holes in large, thick wooden cards to determine the steps to be performed.

2. As the twentieth century _____ (*draw*) to a close, the ability to connect individual computers in a worldwide system called the Internet _____ (*revolutionize*) communication. . . . At the same time that desktop computers and laptop computers were being accepted and used in homes, the miniaturization of computing machines _____ (*continue*).[20]

3. In 1981, IBM® _____ (*introduce*) its first desktop computer, called the personal computer, or PC, whose underlying software was developed by a newly formed company known as Microsoft®. The PC _____ (*be*) an instant success and _____ (*legitimize*) the desktop computer as an established commodity in the minds of the business community. Today, the term *PC* is widely used to refer to all those machines (from various manufacturers) whose design _____ (*evolve*) from IBM®'s initial desktop computer, most of which _____ (*continue*) to be marketed with software from Microsoft®. At times, however, the term *PC* is used interchangeably with the generic terms *desktop* or *laptop*.[21]

4. The miniaturization of computers and their expanding capabilities has brought computer technology to the forefront of today's society. Computer technology is so prevalent now that familiarity with it _____ (*be*) fundamental to being a member of modern society. Computing technology _____ (*alter*) the ability of governments to exert control; had enormous impact on global economies; . . . revolutionized the role of data collection, storage, and applications; provided new means for people to communicate and interact; and repeatedly _____ (*challenge*) society's status quo. The result _____ (*be*) a proliferation of subjects surrounding computer science, each of which _____ (*be*) now a significant field of study in its own right. Moreover, as with mechanical engineering and physics, it _____ (*be*) often difficult to draw a line between these fields and computer science itself. Thus, to gain a proper perspective, our study not only _____ (*cover*) topics central to the core of computer science but also _____ (*explore*) a variety of disciplines dealing with both applications and consequences of the science. Indeed, an introduction to computer science _____ (*be*) an interdisciplinary undertaking.[22]

Exercise 14 Apply It to Speaking

Reread the passage about Augusta Ada Byron on page 5. In small groups, discuss the following questions. Use the chapter vocabulary as appropriate. Take notes as you talk; then share your ideas with another group.

1. Who were Augusta Ada Byron and Charles Babbage?
2. How did Byron become interested in "compute science"?
3. What was the connection between Byron and Babbage?
4. According to the passage, why was Babbage interested in Byron's work?
5. How did the relationship between Byron and Babbage affect his fund-raising efforts?

Exercise 15 Apply It to Writing

Write a short summary of the passage about Augusta Ada Byron on page 5. Include information from your discussion in Exercise 14. Be sure to use the correct verb tenses and forms, and incorporate the chapter vocabulary as appropriate. For information about writing a summary, see Appendix B for help.

Exercise 16 Apply It to Speaking

Prepare a presentation about a historical person whom you admire and who was unusual for his or her time. Consider the following questions:

1. Who was the person?
2. Where and when did he or she live?
3. What did he or she do that was unusual?
4. Why do you admire this person?

Incorporate examples and details to make your presentation interesting, using correct verb tenses and forms. For information about preparing an oral presentation, see Appendix B.

Exercise 17 Apply It to Writing

Write a paragraph discussing your opinions about the changing roles of men and women. Address the following questions and support your ideas with examples. Be sure to use the correct verb tenses and forms. See Appendix B for help.

1. How do you think people in the nineteenth century regarded a woman such as Augusta Ada Byron, who was interested in "compute science"?
2. How have men's and women's roles changed since the nineteenth century?
3. How do you think they will change in the future?

Passive Verbs

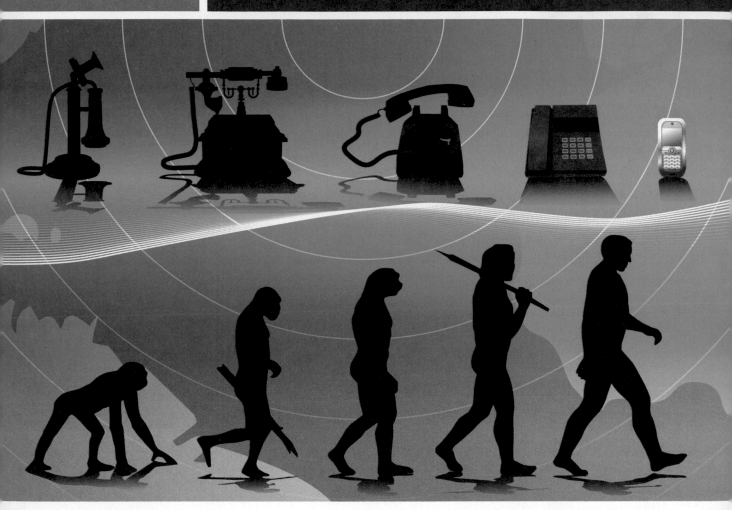

Evolution of the telephone

PREVIEW

VOCABULARY   Here are some words that you will encounter in Chapter 2. How much do you know about each word? Turn to Appendix A to assess and expand your word knowledge.

device	embed	equip	evolve	implement
legitimize	manipulation	potential	stream (v.)	virtual

Prepare to Read

1. How have computers changed since you were born?
2. Do you have a cell phone or a smartphone? How do you use it?

Read the following passage from *Computer Science: An Overview*, 11th Edition, by J. Glenn Brookshear.[1]

Computer Miniaturization

[1]In 1981, IBM introduced its first desktop computer, called the personal computer, or PC, whose underlying software **was developed** by a newly formed company known as Microsoft. The PC was an instant success and legitimized the desktop computer as an established commodity* in the minds of the business community. Today, the term *PC* **is** widely **used** to refer to all those machines (from various manufacturers) whose design has evolved from IBM's initial desktop computer, most of which continue to be marketed with software from Microsoft. At times, however, the term *PC* **is used** interchangeably with the generic terms *desktop* or *laptop*. . . .

[2]At the same time that desktop computers (and the newer mobile laptop computers) were being accepted and used in homes, the miniaturization of computing machines continued. Today, tiny computers are embedded within various devices. For example, automobiles now contain small computers running Global Positioning Systems (GPS), monitoring the function of the engine, and providing voice command services for controlling the car's audio and phone communication systems. . . .

[3]Perhaps the most potentially revolutionary application of computer miniaturization is found in the expanding capabilities of portable telephones. Indeed, what was recently merely a telephone has evolved into a small hand-held general-purpose computer known as a smartphone on which telephony is only one of many applications. These "phones" are equipped with a rich array of sensors* and interfaces* including cameras, microphones, compasses, touch screens, accelerometers (to detect the phone's orientation and motion), and a number of wireless technologies to communicate with other smartphones and computers. The potential is enormous. Indeed, many argue that the smartphone will have a greater effect on society than the PC. . . .[2]

* *commodity*—a product
* *sensor*—a piece of equipment used for discovering the presence of light, heat, sound, movement, and so on, especially in small amounts
* *interface*—something that helps a computer or program work with another program, another piece of electronic equipment, or the person who is using the computer

Review the Ideas

1. How have computers changed over the years?
2. Why are smartphones revolutionary? Name some of the features and capabilities of the smartphone that are mentioned in the article.

Analyze the Grammar

1. Look at the boldfaced verbs in paragraph 1. What tenses and form are they?
2. In paragraphs 2 and 3, underline other verbs similar to the boldfaced ones in paragraph 1. What tenses and form are they?
3. Work in pairs. Discuss the boldfaced verbs. Explain why the author of this passage chose that form.

CHART 2-1	Active Voice vs. Passive Voice

The voice of a verb indicates whether its subject performs or receives the action. The subject of a verb in the active voice is the doer, and the object of the verb is the receiver of the action. In the passive voice, the subject of the sentence receives the action of the verb. The doer—called the *agent*—is expressed in a prepositional phrase beginning with *by*.

Active: (*not*) + simple or progressive verb

subject (doer)   active verb   object (receiver)
The computer **records** information.

Passive: *be* + (*not*) + past participle of verb

subject (receiver)   passive verb   prepositional phrase + *by* + doer (agent)
Information **is recorded** by the computer.

1. Transitive verbs are action verbs that can be followed by objects. Transitive verbs may be active or passive. A sentence with an active verb is an active sentence. A sentence with a passive verb is a passive sentence.

subject   transitive verb (active)   object
1. The computer **records** information.
transitive verb (passive)
Information **is recorded** by the computer.

2. Intransitive verbs do not have objects. Intransitive verbs cannot be passive.

intransitive verb
2. Steve Jobs **died** in 2011.

3. Linking verbs (*be*, *seem*, *appear*, *become*), like intransitive verbs, cannot be used in the passive.

linking verb   adjective
3. Bill Gates **is** famous.

4. The verbs *have* and *get* do not have passive forms.

4. The computer **has** a keyboard and a monitor.

5. When an active sentence changes to a passive sentence, the subject of the active sentence becomes the agent (in a *by* phrase) of the passive sentence. The object of the active sentence becomes the subject in the passive sentence. The passive verb must agree with the "new" subject.

subject   active verb   object
5. **The computer** records data.
new subject   passive verb   agent
Data are recorded **by the computer**.

A computer **controls** the safety features.
The safety features **are controlled** by a computer.

6. When a passive sentence changes to an active sentence, the agent in the passive sentence becomes the subject of the active sentence. When there is no agent, the word *people* or *someone* may be used. The active verb must agree with the "new" subject.

6. Information was recorded **by the computer**.
The computer recorded information.

The program was written in 1990.
Someone wrote the program in 1990.

7. Passive verbs can be followed by infinitives. Infinitives can be active or passive.

active infinitive
7. The term *PC* is used **to refer** to personal computers.
passive infinitive
Personal computers continue **to be referred** to as PCs.

CHART 2-2	Passive Forms of Verbs

Simple Present

be + (*not*) + past participle	Data **are recorded** by the computer.

Present Progressive

be + (*not*) + *being* + past participle	Data **are not being recorded** by the computer.

Future

will + (*not*) + *be* + past participle	An A **will be recorded** by the computer.
be + (*not*) + *going to be* + participle	An A **is going to be recorded.**
Progressive form very rare.	

Future Perfect

will + (*not*) + *have* + *been* + past participle	Something **will have been recorded** by the computer.
Progressive form very rare.	

Present Perfect

has / *have* + (*not*) + *been* + past participle	Information **has been recorded** by the computer.
Progressive form very rare.	

Simple Past

was / *were* + (*not*) + past participle	Information **was not recorded** by the computer.
	Data **were recorded** by the computer.

Past Progressive

was / *were* + (*not*) + *being* + past participle	Information **was being recorded** by the computer.
	Data **were being recorded** by the computer.

Past Perfect

had + (*not*) + *been* + past participle	Information **had been recorded** by the computer.
Progressive form very rare.	

Exercise 1 Identifying Passive Verbs

With a partner, underline the passive verbs. Name each tense underlined and discuss what it expresses. Find the infinitives and underline them. Do they follow passive or active verbs? Are the infinitives active or passive?

1. One recent application on the Internet is known as Internet radio. Internet radio is a type of streaming audio (real-time sound) that is sent out over the Internet in a process called webcasting. A number of popular web radio stations such as Pandora®, Jango®, BBC®, and NPR® have been developed for webcasting.

    The first Internet radio was introduced in 1993 by Carl Malamud, using the Internet Multicasting Company® of Washington. Before 1993, access to traditional radio had been restricted to listeners within a particular broadcast area. Soon after 1993, Internet radio was being broadcast all over the world. Since 1993, the number of Internet radio listeners has been estimated to be about 77 million. Researchers today predict that in the future, the number of listeners will be limited only by the number of people who own smartphones, laptops, or desktop computers.

2. In 1981, IBM® introduced its first desktop computer, called the personal computer, or PC, whose underlying software was developed by a newly formed company known as Microsoft®. The PC was an instant success and legitimized the desktop computer as an established commodity in the minds of the business community. Today, the term *PC* is widely used to refer to all those machines (from various manufacturers) whose design has evolved from IBM®'s initial desktop computer, most of which continue to be marketed with software from Microsoft®. At times, however, the term *PC* is used interchangeably with the generic terms *desktop* and *laptop*.

Exercise 2 Writing Passive Verbs

For each verb in parentheses, write the correct passive form.

1. Hypertext documents _____ (*write*) in HTML (hypertext markup language). HTML looks like regular text, but it includes special symbols (tags) that determine how the document will appear on the computer screen. Links to other web pages or images _____ (*indicate*) with particular symbols.

2. A series of steps indicating how to perform a task _____ (*call*) an algorithm. A program _____ (*represent*) by an algorithm. Programming consists of creating a program, encoding it so that the computer can read it, and then putting it into the computer. Programs _____ (*call*) software, while the computer itself _____ (*refer to*) as hardware.

3. One of the first computing devices was the abacus. The early abacus _____ (*make*) of beads on rods that _____ (*hold*) by a wooden frame. The abacus _____ (*use*) not only by ancient Chinese but also by the Greeks and Romans.

An abacus

Exercise 3 Choosing Active or Passive Voice

Choose the correct form of the verb to complete each sentence.

1. Blaise Pascal (1623–1662) of France, Gottfried Wilhelm Leibniz (1646–1717) of Germany, and Charles Babbage (1792–1871) of England _____ (*experimented / were experimented*) with the technology of gears.

2. Pascal _____ (*built / was built*) a machine that only _____ (*performed / was performed*) addition, but Leibniz's machine _____ (*built / was built*) to perform a number of operations.

3. Babbage's Analytical Engine _____ (*programmed / was programmed*) by Augusta Ada Byron.

4. These days, computers _____ (*operate / are operated*) by the Windows®, Mac®, or Linux® operating system.

5. The word *PC* _____ (*is used / is using*) for machines that _____ (*based / are based*) on IBM®'s desktop computers.

6. Miniature computers _____ (*have embedded / have been embedded*) in all kinds of devices such as automobiles and smartphones.

7. Steve Jobs _____ (*had experimented / had been experimented*) with several pursuits before he and his friend Stephen Wozniak _____ (*started / was started*) Apple Computer, Inc.® in 1976.

Steve Jobs

8. Bill Gates _____ (*was writing / was written*) computer programs at the same time that he and his friend Paul Allen _____ (*were attending / were attended*) Lakeside High School.

9. In the future, Steve Jobs and Bill Gates _____ (*will probably know / will probably be known*) as the greatest programmers of all time.

10. By the year 2020, computers _____ (*will have evolved / will have been evolved*) into completely new kinds of devices.

Exercise 4 Changing Passive Sentences into Active Sentences

Go back to the passages in Exercise 1. Rewrite the sentences with underlined passive verbs as sentences with active verbs. The first one is done for you. There are ten additional sentences.

1. One recent application on the Internet <u>is known</u> as Internet radio.

   People know one recent application on the Internet as Internet radio.

2. _____

3. _____

4. _____

5. _____

6. _____

(continued on next page)

Passive Verbs **27**

7. _____

8. _____

9. _____

10. _____

Exercise 5 **Changing Active Sentences into Passive Sentences**

Rewrite the paragraphs with underlined active verbs as paragraphs with passive verbs.

1. Who should receive the credit for a particular invention? People often <u>credit</u> one individual for an invention while another person <u>has actually created</u> the device. For example, at the same time that other inventors <u>were developing</u> the airplane, the Wright brothers <u>took</u> the credit. As a matter of fact, Leonardo da Vinci <u>had conceived</u> the idea of a flying machine in the 1600s, and he <u>had based</u> his ideas on even earlier ones. In another example, several inventors <u>invented</u> the light bulb at the same time, but people <u>credit</u> only Thomas Edison for it.

2. From time to time, people <u>have made</u> mistakes in giving credit for ideas. The well-known scientist John von Neumann <u>made</u> great contributions to science, but the stored-program concept was not one of them. However, people <u>have given</u> him the credit for developing it because he <u>published</u> the idea first. The real inventors were J. P. Eckert and his team of researchers at the University of Pennsylvania.

3. In order for a computer to perform a task, programmers <u>develop</u> an algorithm for performing that task. Next, the programmer <u>represents</u> the algorithm as a program in a code that the computer <u>can follow</u>. The computer has the correct code, but users <u>need</u> a program on paper or on the computer screen in order to follow it. We <u>call</u> this encoding process "programming." We <u>call</u> the program and the algorithm "software." The computer itself is known as "hardware."

1. _____
_____
_____
_____
_____
_____

2. _____
_____
_____
_____
_____

3. _____
_____
_____
_____
_____
_____

CHART 2-3	When to Choose Passive

Most academic writers favor active voice; however, passive is chosen for particular reasons:

1. Passive is used when the person or thing doing the action (the agent) is not important or not known. In this case no *by* phrase is used.	Your reservations **are confirmed** for next week.
If it is important to include the agent, a *by* phrase may be used.	Your driving record is maintained **by the government** on a computer.
2. Passive is preferred in scientific writing because it sounds objective.	A computer network i**s** often **classified** as being either a local area network (LAN), a metropolitan area network (MAN), or a wide area network (WAN).[3]
3. Passive is used to describe procedures and processes in experiments, research papers, and reports.	In early batch processing systems, each job **was accompanied** by a set of instructions explaining the steps required to prepare the machine for that particular job. These instructions **were encoded**, using a system known as a job control language (JCL), and **stored** with the job in the job queue.[4]
4. Passive is often used to create a smoothly flowing paragraph.	
a. When a paragraph is about one idea, that idea or a synonym should begin many of the subsequent sentences. This may require use of the passive or of a combination of passive and active verbs.	a. The **smartphone** was a revolutionary application of miniaturized computers. **It** <u>evolved</u> (*active verb*) from a portable telephone into a multipurpose computer. **Smartphones** <u>are equipped</u> (*passive verb*) with touch screens, microphones, and cameras, in addition to the traditional telephone function.
b. When a paragraph shifts focus and a new idea is put at the end of one sentence, it is easier to understand the subsequent sentence if the new idea or a synonym appears at the beginning of that sentence. This may require use of the passive or a combination of passive and active verbs. Note that the adjectives *this* and *these* often precede the idea in the second sentence.	b. Animation is achieved by displaying a sequence of images, called **frames**, in rapid succession. **These frames** <u>capture</u> (*active verb*) the appearance of a changing scene at regular time intervals.[5] ... The storyboard is used as a guide in the construction of a three-dimensional **virtual world**. **This virtual world** <u>is</u> then repeatedly "<u>photographed</u>" (*passive verb*) as the objects within it are moved according to the script or the progression of the video game.[6]

Exercise 6 Determining the Reason for Choosing Passive

Read the text and underline the passive verbs. Then, with a small group of classmates, decide why the passive is used in each instance. Choose the reason(s) from the list below. In many instances there may be more than one reason.

1 Agent not important or unknown
2 Sounds scientific
3 Describes a scientific procedure
4 Helps the paragraph flow smoothly

The World Wide Web is an Internet service application that is based on hypertext. Hypertext documents contain hyperlinks that are connected to other documents containing audio, images, or video. A mouse is used to point and click on a hyperlink to move from document to document. Such a hypertext document is called a web page, and a group of related web pages is known as a website.

Firefox®, Safari®, and Chrome® are called browsers. A browser is software that allows users to access hypertext documents on the Internet. A user employs a browser to request the documents from web servers. The documents are then transferred from the web servers to the browser. Each document has been given an Internet address or URL (universal resource locator), which is used to access the appropriate server and obtain the correct document. A typical URL looks like this: http://www.iastate.edu/~hschmidt/homepage.html.

Exercise 7 Completing the Description of a Process

On a separate sheet of paper, use passive voice to complete the following scrambled sentences. Write the sentences in the form of a paragraph. Be sure to write each verb in the correct tense.

1. A word processing program / use / research papers and business letters / to write
   In the past, word processing programs / to the purchaser of a computer / on CDs / give
   they / from the Internet / easily / download / Now
   The purchaser / a special code at the time / give / of the purchase
   When the code / at the word processing website, / enter / the program / download / onto the computer
   After the preferences / choose, / the other settings / adjust / and the program is ready to use
2. In the first computer processing systems, jobs / by instructions / accompany
   First, the instructions / encode / and store / in a job queue
   the jobs / select / for execution / Then
   by the operating system / print / the instructions / at a printer / After that,
   they / read / by the computer operator / there / Finally,

Exercise 8 **Writing Paragraphs That Flow**

Read the four paragraphs below and, working with a partner, determine what the topic of each is. (The topic in one paragraph shifts.) Then, keeping the original topic sentence in each paragraph, decide if other sentences within that paragraph can be rewritten—substituting an active or a passive verb—so that the main idea appears at the beginning of those sentences.

1. The miniaturization of computers has resulted in some valuable inventions. Engineers have developed tiny computers to fit into very small spaces. People use these miniaturized computers in automobiles to operate the Global Positioning System (GPS) and voice-controlled radios and cell phones. You sometimes find a miniaturized computer in the seat and mirror adjustment mechanism.

2. Early computers were large machines requiring entire rooms. Then Microsoft® developed the software, and in 1981 IBM® created the first personal computer. People called this personal computer a PC. The business community considered the PC a great success, and soon it was used everywhere. Currently, we use the word *PC* to refer to all laptops.

3. Fast, lightweight computers have made it possible to build mobile robots. A number of different tasks are being performed by mobile robots, such as assembling automobiles and fighting fires. Mobile robots move around easily, so they have been developed to jump like frogs, hop like rabbits, swim like fish, and fly like bees. In fact, people are developing flying robots as drones to deliver products from manufacturers directly to consumers' homes.

4. Computer graphics is the branch of computer science that applies computer technology to the production and manipulation of visual representations. A wide assortment of topics including the presentation of text, the construction of graphs and charts, the development of graphical user interfaces, the manipulation of photographs, the production of video games, and the creation of animated motion pictures are associated with it. However, people are increasingly using the term *computer graphics* in reference to the specific field called 3-D graphics and most of this chapter concentrates on this topic.[7]

A woman using GPS

Exercise 9 Error Analysis

The following student essay contains ten errors in the use of verbs. The first error is corrected for you. Find and correct nine more.

The Global Positioning System (GPS)

decided
In 1973, it was ~~decide~~ to develop a satellite navigation system based on existing systems of the U.S. Air Force and Navy. This system of twenty-four satellites is knows as the GPS (Global Positioning System). GPS is using in aviation, marine, and onshore navigation to locate one's position on the earth within about 200 feet. Between 1973 and 1983, the system was limit to the government, but in 1983, ordinary people given access to it.

Now GPS is use by millions of people all over the world to find out where they are and where they are going. Nowadays, the miniaturization of computers was allowed tiny GPS units to be placed into all sorts of devices. Airplane, ship, and automobile engines, radios, and phone communication systems contain GPS devices that is controlled by such tiny computers.

It's amazing to think that even when a boat is a thousand miles out to sea and the captain needs to know his or her position, a satellite will pinpoint the position exactly. If a hiker who is carried a cell phone gets lost, others can find him or her by using GPS. Currently, similar systems are been developed by other nations. It's possible that someday GPS units will be implanted directly inside people so that they can always be found. This idea is sure to cause a lot of controversy.

Exercise 10 Apply It to Speaking

Read the following paragraph. In small groups discuss the questions that follow.

Mary Analyst has been assigned the task of implementing a system with which medical records will be stored on a computer that is connected to a large network. In her opinion the design for the system's security is flawed, but her concerns have been overruled for financial reasons. She has been told to proceed with the project, using the security system that she feels is inadequate.[8]

1. What task has Mary Analyst been assigned?
2. What does Mary believe is true about the security system? Why is that dangerous?
3. What happened after Mary expressed her concerns? Why?
4. What has Mary been told to do?
5. What do you think will happen if Mary does not proceed with the project?
6. What could happen if Mary proceeds with the project?

APPLICATION

Exercise 11 Apply It to Speaking

Prepare a two- to three-minute presentation to explain the meaning of the following statement to a small group of classmates:

> Society has been greatly changed by the miniaturization of computers.

Answer these questions in your explanation:

1. What does it mean to say the computer has been miniaturized?
2. How has our society been changed by miniaturization? Give some examples.

See Appendix B for help.

Exercise 12 Apply It to Writing

Write a smoothly flowing paragraph to describe a process or procedure that you know about, such as how a particular item or product is made, how a game or musical instrument is played, or how a popular cell phone app is used. See Appendix B for help.

Modal Auxiliary Verbs

A robot doing household chores

PREVIEW

VOCABULARY   Here are some words that you will encounter in Chapter 3. How much do you know about each word? Turn to Appendix A to assess and expand your word knowledge.

appall	catastrophic	credit	dignity	ethics
expediency	maneuver	mimic	onslaught	uncharted

Prepare to Read

1. How have computers changed in your lifetime?
2. What do you think the future of computers will be?

Read the following passage from *Computer Science: An Overview*, 11th Edition, by J. Glenn Brookshear.[1]

Considering the Consequences

[1]Some view the advancement of technology as a gift to humanity—a means of freeing humans from boring, mundane* tasks and opening the door to more enjoyable lifestyles. But others see this same phenomenon as a curse that robs citizens of employment and channels wealth toward those with power. This, in fact, was a message of the devoted humanitarian Mahatma Gandhi of India. He repeatedly argued that India **would be better served** by replacing large textile mills with spinning wheels placed in the homes of the peasants. In this way, he claimed, centralized mass production that employed only a few **would be replaced** by a distributed mass production system that would benefit multitudes.

[2]. . . History is full of revolutions with roots in the disproportionate distribution of wealth and privilege. If today's advancing technology is allowed to entrench* such discrepancies, catastrophic consequences **could result**.

[3]. . . But the consequences of building increasingly intelligent machines are more subtle—more fundamental—than those dealing with power struggles between different segments of society. The issues strike at the very heart of humanity's self-image. In the nineteenth century, society was appalled by Charles Darwin's theory of evolution and the thought that humans might have evolved from lesser life forms. How then will society react if faced with the onslaught of machines whose mental capabilities challenge those of humans?

[4]We might get a clue to humanity's potential reaction to machines that challenge our intellect by considering society's response to IQ tests in the middle of the twentieth century. These tests were considered to identify a child's level of intelligence. Children in the United States were often classified by their performances on these tests and channeled into educational programs accordingly. In turn, educational opportunities were opened to those children who performed well on these tests, whereas children who performed poorly were directed toward remedial programs of study. In short, when given a scale on which to measure an individual's intelligence, society tended to disregard the capabilities of those who found themselves on the lower end of the scale. How then would society handle the situation if the "intellectual" capabilities of machines became comparable, or even appeared to be comparable, with those of humans? Would society discard those whose abilities were seen as "inferior" to those of machines? If so, what would be the consequences for those members of society? Should a person's dignity be subject to how he or she compares to a machine?[2]

mundane—ordinary
entrench—to firmly establish an attitude, a belief, or a position over time

Review the Ideas

1. What are the two views of technology discussed in the passage?
2. What does the passage suggest about the effect on society of machines that challenge human intellect?

Analyze the Grammar

Work in pairs to answer the following questions about the reading passage.

1. Look at the boldfaced verbs in paragraphs 1 and 2. What do we call the auxiliary verbs used in these verb phrases?

2. Underline other verb phrases in the passage that contain these kinds of verbs. What does each verb phrase express? Discuss the meaning of each one.

3. What verb tenses and forms do you see in this passage?

CHART 3-1	Modal Auxiliary Verbs (Active)

Modal and semimodal auxiliary verbs allow speakers and writers of English to express feelings and attitudes of ability, possibility, certainty, advisability, necessity, and doubt.

Modals: *can, could, may, might, must, ought to, should, will, would*

Semimodals: *be able to, have to, need to, be supposed to, had better*

Modals often combine with semimodals (except *had better*): The new browser **may not be able to** compete with the old one. The programmers **might need to** make changes.

1. Ability

Present: *can (not), be (not) able to*	Computers **can** manipulate data.
Past: *could (not), be (not) able to*	The abacus **could** add and subtract.
Future: *will (not) be able to*	People **will be able to** buy the newest computer every year.

2. Possibility or doubt; speculation

Present: *may (not), might (not), could (not), will (not), would (not)*	Any computer engineer **could** invent a new computer. The on-button **will** be on the keyboard. Any computer engineer **would** like to create a new application.
Past: *may (not) have, might (not) have, could (not) have, would (not) have*	Charles Babbage **may have** asked Lord Byron for financial backing directly. Lord Byron **might have** refused. Augusta Ada Byron **could have** demanded money from her husband. An interested man **would have** given Babbage financial backing.
Future: *may (not), might (not), would (not), could (not)*	The programmers **may** develop an entirely new product. Without power, no computers **would** exist.

3. Advisability / expectation / obligation

Present: *should (not), ought (not) to*	People **should not** buy untested computers. Manufacturers **should** test their products.
Past: *should (not) have, ought (not) to have*	Some form of advanced computing machine **should have** been possible at that time.
Future: *should (not), ought (not) to*	The computers **ought to** arrive tomorrow.

4. Urgent advice / warning

Present and future: *had better (not)*	Companies **had better** pay attention to public opinion.

5. Necessity / obligation

Present and future: *(not) need to, (not) has / have to*	The company **needs to** announce it soon. The engineers **have to** develop a new product soon.
Past: *had to (did not have to)*	Steve Jobs **had to** develop a new product every year.

6. Strong necessity (rules and laws)

Present and future: *must*	Computers **must** pass rigid testing.

7. Logical deduction

Present: *must (not)*	Bill Gates **must** be a generous man, because he gives away so much money.
Past: *must (not) have*	The researchers in those days **must have** had the knowledge to build such a computer.

8. Logical deduction: absolute impossibility

Present: *cannot, could not*	This number **cannot / could not** be the answer to the problem.
Past: *could not have*	Lord Byron **could not have** had much interest in the computing machine.

9. Prohibition

Present and future: *must not*	Computer hackers **must not** continue to break into government computers.

10. Obligation

Past, present, and future: *be (not) supposed to*	Computer programmers **are supposed to** test their programs before selling them.

Exercise 1 Identifying Modals in Context

With a partner, look at the text. Underline the verbs that include modal auxiliary verbs. Explain what each modal expresses. There may be more than one correct response in some cases.

Developing a creative idea has never been easy. Charles Babbage might have built his Difference Engine, but he couldn't raise the money. We can see what the machine would have looked like at the London Science Museum today only because the museum built a model of it in 1991. Babbage couldn't complete his later Analytical Engine either, due to lack of funding, but his son was able to build part of it in 1910. Without the London Science Museum and Charles Babbage's son, there would be no physical models of the first computers.

Exercise 2 Identifying Meanings of Modals

With a partner look at the text. Find one or more examples of verb phrases with modal auxiliaries that express the following meanings. Underline each verb phrase and label it with the number:

1 ability	3 advice	5 logical	6 necessity
2 possibility	4 obligation	deduction	7 impossibility

Steven Jobs and Stephen Wozniak developed a computer, the Apple I™, that ordinary people could use at home. They were able to put it together in their garage without the help of a large corporation that might have given them advice about what they should and shouldn't be doing. They probably had to pay for it themselves because they didn't have financial backers, but later, in 1976, they were able to establish Apple Computer®, then Apple Computer Inc.® Subsequently Apple Computer Inc.® would produce and market the first desktop computers, such as the Apple I™, Apple II™, Apple IIe™, and Macintosh™, and then laptops, iPods™, iPads™, and iPhones™.

Jobs must have been a genius. Almost every year while he was alive, Apple® introduced a new product. The advertising campaign used to begin several months ahead of the release of a new product. The TV commercials can only be described as brilliant. Everything about them was supposed to attract attention. The videos were spectacular; the audios were breathtaking. The consumer couldn't resist!

CHART 3-2	Modal Auxiliary Verbs (Passive)
Present and Future	
modal + (*not*) + *be* + past participle	Safety features **might / can / must not be ignored**. Computers **are supposed to / have to / need to be updated** periodically.
Progressive form very rare.	The information **may / could / should / ought to / be recorded** tomorrow.
Past	
modal + (*not*) + *have* + *been* + past participle Progressive form very rare.	The features **might / could / must have been forgotten**. The computers **were supposed to have been updated**. The information **may / would / should not have been recorded**.

Exercise 3 Identifying Passive Modals in Context

With a partner, look at the text. Underline the verbs that include passive modal auxiliary verbs. Explain what each modal expresses.

The creators of computers had no idea they were designing machines that would change the future. Originally, computers would have been designed as machines that added, subtracted, multiplied, and divided lists of numbers. In other words, they would have been calculators. Today a computer might be developed to be a simple calculator, or it could be designed to execute a number of functions. The smartphone is an example of a computer that can be used in a many ways. Some smartphones can even serve as video cameras and then are able to upload the videos to the Internet. Computer users today shouldn't be surprised if computers of the future include the ability to emit odors.

Look at the sentences and passages. Underline the verbs with modals. With a partner, name the underlined verb tenses and tell whether they are active or passive. Discuss what each modal expresses.

1. A typical smartphone can now be used to text message, browse the web, provide directions, view multimedia content—in short, it can be used to provide many of the same services as a traditional PC.[3]

2. In order to perform the actions requested by the computer's users, an operating system must be able to communicate with the users.[4]

3. A computer network is often classified as being either a local area network (LAN), a metropolitan area network (MAN), or a wide area network (WAN). . . . Computers on a university campus or those in a manufacturing plant might be connected by a LAN.[5]

4. On the surface, Internet radio may not seem to require special consideration. One might guess that a station could merely establish a server that would send program messages to each of the clients who requests them.[6]

5. When using a GUI (graphical user interface), the reader of a hypertext document can follow the hyperlinks associated with it by pointing and clicking with the mouse. For example, suppose the sentence "The orchestra's performance of 'Bolero' by Maurice Ravel was outstanding" appeared in a hypertext document and the name Maurice Ravel was linked to another document—perhaps giving information about the composer. A reader could choose to view that associated material by pointing to the name Maurice Ravel with the mouse and clicking the mouse button. Moreover, if the proper hyperlinks are installed, the reader might listen to an audio recording of the concert by clicking on the name Bolero.[7]

This is an HTML document.

```
<p>A <b>hypertext </b>document
is written this way. Additional
hypertext code symbols can be
found at <a href="http://symbol.
com">code symbols</a>.</p>
<p><img src="pen.gif"></p>
```

This is how it looks on a web page.

A **hypertext** document is written this way. Additional hypertext code symbols can be found at code symbols.

6. . . . humans should be allowed to use a software system as an abstract tool. This tool should be easy to apply and designed to minimize (ideally eliminate) communication errors between the system and its human users. This means that the system's interface should be designed for the convenience of humans rather than merely the expediency of the software system.[8]

7. In the nineteenth century, society was appalled by Charles Darwin's theory of evolution and the thought that humans might have evolved from lesser life forms. . . . In the past, technology has developed slowly, allowing time for our self-image to be preserved by readjusting our concept of intelligence. Our ancient ancestors would have interpreted the mechanical devices of the nineteenth century as having supernatural intelligence, but today we do not credit these machines with any intelligence at all.[9]

Exercise 5 Choosing the Correct Modal Form

Choose the correct form of the verb to complete the sentences.

1. A smartphone _____ (*can perform / can be performed*) a number of functions.

2. Laptop computers _____ (*may be / may have been*) at the top of the list of world-changing inventions.

3. Computers _____ (*should not expose / should not be exposed*) to high temperatures.

4. The microprocessor _____ (*ought to find / ought to be found*) on the motherboard of a computer.

5. The Difference Engine that Charles Babbage created _____ (*could be changed / could have been changing*) to perform several calculations.

6. Babbage imagined computers that _____ (*would be printed / would print*) results of calculations on paper.

7. Babbage's Analytical Engine _____ (*could program / could be programmed*) by means of paper cards with holes punched in them.

8. The numbers on the Difference Engine _____ (*would have located / would have been located*) on the gears.

9. The positions of gears _____ (*have to read / had to be read*) by the computer operator on Blaise Pascal's and Gottfried Wilhelm Leibniz's early machines.

10. The fact that Augusta Ada Byron was the first programmer _____ (*might have amazed / must amaze*) the nineteenth-century world.

Exercise 6 Writing the Correct Modal Form

Work in pairs. Then compare your answers in groups. Complete the sentences. Use the active or passive forms of the given verbs.

1. Sometimes stores have special offers for people who are registered as customers. The registration process _____ (*may / involve*) the issuance of identification cards that _____ (*must / present*) in a form that is compatible with the machine.

2. New automobile engines _____ (*not / have to / design*) every time a new automobile is developed. The company _____ (*can / often / use*) an earlier engine model.

3. In order to design a new laser computer game, the remote _____ (*should / be able to / control*) the laser so that it _____ (*can / aim*) in all directions by all players.

4. Charles Babbage imagined machines that _____ (*would / print*) computation results on paper so that mistakes _____ (*could / minimize*).

5. Blaise Pascal and Gottfried Wilhelm Leibnitz _____ (*might / surprise*) at Babbage's vision, but of course they had died before Babbage was born, so they _____ (*could / never / imagine*) Babbage's creative idea.

6. Babbage had the ideas for some amazing creations that _____ (*should / build*), but he _____ (*could / not / raise*) the money. It _____ (*must / be*) frustrating for him.

Exercise 7 Writing Modal Auxiliaries to Complete Sentences

Add appropriate modal auxiliaries to the following sentences. There may be more than one correct answer.

1. . . . new technologies _____ present uncharted territory in which existing ethical contracts _____ not apply.[10]

2. The premise that our society is different from what it _____ been without the computer revolution is generally accepted.[11]

3. Suppose we were asked to design a program to produce animation for an action computer game. . . . Then the animation _____ constructed by creating multiple activations of this program. . . .[12]

4. Many software engineers argue that testing _____ no longer be viewed as a separate step in software development but instead, it, and its many manifestations, _____ incorporated into the other steps, producing a three-step development process. . . .[13]

5. Most _____ agree that a company or individual _____ be allowed to recoup, and profit from, the investment needed to develop quality software.[14]

6. The quest to build machines that mimic human behavior has a long history, but many _____ agree that the modern field of artificial intelligence had its origins in 1950.[15]

7. Medical treatment has advanced to the point that numerous parts of the human body _____ now be replaced with artificial parts or parts from human donors. It is conceivable that this _____ someday include parts of the brain.[16]

8. We _____ note that the subject of data mining is not restricted to the domain of computing but has tentacles that extend far into statistics. In fact, many _____ argue that since data mining had its origins in attempts to perform statistical analysis on large diverse data collections, it is an application of statistics rather than a field of computer science.[17]

CHART 3-3	Degrees of Certainty

Present and Future Forms

99% positive certainty	*would*	Only a human being **would tell** a lie.
	must	The printer **must be connected**. I'm sure of it.
	should	The On button **should be** near the keyboard.
50% certainty	*may, might, could*	The power **may go off** in a few minutes.
	may / might not	The printer **might not print** the document.
	should not	The On button **should not be** difficult to find.
99% negative certainty	*must not*	The power **must not be** on.
	cannot	The computer **cannot be** broken!
	could not	The computer **could not be** off-line!
	would not	A computer **would not lie**.

Past Forms

99% positive certainty	*would have* + past participle	Scholars **would have deciphered** the meanings of ancient documents.
	must have + past participle	Ancient scholars **must have had** great patience.
	should have + past participle	The On button **should have been** near the keyboard, but it wasn't.
50% certainty	*may / might / could have* + past participle	They **might have moved** the computer to another classroom.
	may / might not have + past participle	Ancient scholars **may not have known** about the universe.
	should not have + past participle	The On button **should not have been** difficult to find.
99% negative certainty	*must not have* + past participle	You **must not have looked** very carefully.
	could not have + past participle	You **could not have missed** the On button!
	would not have + past participle	He **would not have left** the machine on without telling someone.

Exercise 8 **Deciding on the Relative Strength of Modals of Certainty**

With a partner, write the following sentences in order so that they range from nearly absolute positive certainty to nearly absolute negative certainty in descending order. Write the sentences after the percentages given.

1. Byron must have been an extremely intelligent person.

2. The Internet can't be down again!

3. Graphic design software could help architects create better designs.

4. Babbage must not have impressed others with his inventions.

5. In a computer, the software may not be compatible with the hardware.

6. An honest programmer wouldn't hack into government files.

7. Those computer files couldn't have caused the problem.

8. The CPU (central processing unit) in this computer should be in the keyboard.

9. A word processing program might be useful for your project.

10. The headphones should have been in the computer lab, but no one could find them.

11. The monitor would be connected to the keyboard.

12. The size of the file should not make a difference to this computer.

99% positive certainty

_____

_____

_____

_____

50% certainty

_____

_____

_____

99% negative certainty

_____

_____

_____

_____

CHART 3-4 Degrees of Necessity

Present and Future Forms

100% positive necessity = action is obligatory	*must, have to*	All computers on campus **must be registered**. Students **have to pay** tuition.
	need to *be supposed to* *should, ought to*	Students **need to sign up** for classes early. Students **are supposed to take** prerequisites first. Professors **ought to distribute** syllabi on the first day of class.
50% necessity	*might, could*	You **could sign up** for a computer science class.
	not have to *not be supposed to* *should not*	Students **do not have to pay** tuition immediately. Students **are not supposed to use** cell phones in class. Students **should not sleep** during class.
100% negative necessity = action is forbidden	*must not*	Students **must not cheat** during exams.

Past Forms

100% positive necessity = action was obligatory	*had to*	In 2010, students **had to take** an English exam before starting classes.
	was / were supposed to *was / were supposed to have* + past participle	The professor **was supposed to grade** the exams. Students **were supposed to have taken** a makeup test, but they didn't.
50% necessity	*should have* + past participle *should not have* + past participle	The professor **should have handed out** his syllabus on time, but he didn't. The professor **should not have postponed** the test.
	was / were not supposed to *was / were not supposed to have* + past participle	The students **were not supposed to miss** the test. We **were not supposed to have left** early.
100% negative necessity = action was not necessary	*did not have to*	Students **did not have to take** an English exam before 1990.

Exercise 9 Deciding on the Relative Strength of Modals of Necessity

With a partner, write the following sentences in order so that they range from 100% positive necessity to 100% negative necessity in descending order. Write the sentences after the percentages given.

1. University students must not remove computers from the computer labs.
2. Keyboards have to be cleaned frequently.
3. High school students don't have to carry laptops to school.
4. Smartphones should not be dropped on the floor.
5. Computers must be kept cool, or they will not operate properly.
6. Internet users are not supposed to download copyrighted material.
7. Programmers should learn several programming languages.
8. Computer operators are supposed to take good care of their equipment.

100% positive necessity

_____

_____

_____

_____

50% necessity

_____

_____

_____

100% negative necessity

_____

CHART 3-5	Modal Auxiliary Verbs Used to Express Doubt (Hedging)

A **hedge** is a strategy that academic writers use to avoid stating that they are completely certain of a statement. They do this to allow for argument in case other authorities have contrary opinions. A writer who uses this strategy is said to **hedge**.

In the examples below, note that the hedge expresses less than 100% certainty; the statement of fact expresses 100% certainty.

1. Sometimes *can* and *could* are used to hedge.

   1. HEDGE: Absolute certainty **can foster** the inability to change ideas.

      FACT: Absolute certainty **fosters** the inability to change ideas.

      HEDGE: The theory **could have been discussed** in the 1900s.

      FACT: The theory **was discussed** in the 1900s.

2. Sometimes *may* and *might* are used to hedge.

   2. HEDGE: Absolute certainty **may foster** the inability to change ideas.

      FACT: Absolute certainty **fosters** the inability to change ideas.

      HEDGE: The theory **might have been discussed** in the 1900s.

      FACT: The theory **was discussed** in the 1900s.

3. Sometimes *must*, implying a logical deduction, is used to hedge.

   3. HEDGE: The theory **must have been discussed** in the 1900s.

      FACT: The theory **was discussed** in the 1900s.

4. *Will* and *would* together with adverbs such as *likely* and *probably* as well as quantity words such as *some*, *many*, and *most* may be used to hedge.

   4. HEDGE: **Most** computer errors **would likely be caused** by programmer errors.

      FACT: **Every** computer error **is caused** by the programmer.

5. *Should*, implying certainty, is used to hedge.

   5. HEDGE: A power switch **should be located** on the keyboard.

      FACT: A power switch **is located** on the keyboard.

Exercise 10 · Identifying Modals Used to Hedge

With a partner, underline the verbs with modals used to hedge. Match the modals you choose with one of the explanations in Chart 3-5.

Scientists all over the world are working to develop AI (artificial intelligence) in robots. They believe that machine intelligence can probably be increased so that intelligent machines have abilities equal to or greater than human abilities. These scientists hope that humans will be freed from boring, repetitive jobs and be given the opportunity to have more fulfilling lives. Some people are asking if this is a good idea. They say that people could eventually be replaced by intelligent machines, and they wonder what would happen then.

Imagine a world in which all service jobs are filled by machines. When you go into a restaurant, you might be led to your table by a headwaiter robot. Then another server robot may bring you your automated menu, with which you can order your meal. Meanwhile, an auto cook could be cooking food in the fully automated kitchen. After the server robot has brought you your meal, it will likely bring you an automated bill to pay electronically. Finally, an auto busboy / dishwasher might clear away the dishes to wash before taking them to set up a new table.

Is this the future that we want? Many people would worry about what happened to all the people who had those restaurant jobs. They probably would have been unemployed and couldn't have found new jobs in restaurant work. Some must not have been able to find jobs at all. At that point, most people would likely agree that the robots should not have been developed to replace human jobs.

Exercise 11 · Practicing Modals and Hedging

Choose the best forms of the verbs to hedge in the following passages. How do they express the attitude of the writer? Discuss your answers in small groups.

1. Data mining consists of techniques for discovering patterns in collections of data. . . . Data mining techniques even have applications in what _____ (*seems / might seem*) unlikely settings as exemplified by their use in identifying the functions of particular genes encoded in DNA molecules and characterizing properties of organisms.[18]

2. We close this section by introducing some of the approaches to ethics that have been proposed by philosophers in their search for fundamental theories that lead to principles for guiding decisions and behavior. Most of these theories _____ (*can classify / can be classified*) under the headings of consequence-based ethics, duty-based ethics, contract-based ethics, and character-based ethics. You _____ (*wish / may wish*) to use these theories as a means of approaching the ethical issues presented in the text. In particular, you _____ (*will find / may find*) that different theories lead to contrasting conclusions and thus expose hidden alternatives.[19]

3. The human mind has an amazing ability to retrieve information that is associated with a current topic of consideration. When we experience certain smells, we _____ (*will readily recall / might readily recall*) memories of our childhood. The sound of a friend's voice _____ (*conjures / might conjure*) an image of the person or perhaps memories of good times. Certain music _____ (*will generate / might generate*) thoughts of particular holiday seasons. These are examples of associative memory—the retrieval of information that is associated with, or related to, the information at hand.[20]

(continued on next page)

4. At first glance utilitarianism appears to be a fair way of resolving ethical dilemmas. But, in its unqualified form, utilitarianism leads to numerous unacceptable conclusions. For example, it _____ (*allows / would allow*) the majority of a society to enslave a small minority.[21]

5. The human-machine interface has become an important concern in the requirements stage of software development projects and is a growing sub-field of software engineering. Indeed some _____ (*argue / would argue*) that the study of human-machine interfaces is an entire field in its own right.[22]

6. ... humans _____ (*must be allowed / should be allowed*) to use a software system as an abstract tool. This tool _____ (*must be easy / should be easy*) to apply and designed to minimize (ideally eliminate) communication errors between the system and its human users. This means that the system's interface _____ (*has to be designed / should be designed*) for the convenience of humans rather than merely the expediency of the software system.[23]

Exercise 12 Expressing Uncertainty

Complete the following sentences so that they hedge. Use the verbs given.

1. ... new technologies _____ (*present*) uncharted territories in which existing ethical contracts may not apply.[24]

2. You _____ (*argue*) that much of this section borders on science fiction rather than computer science.[25]

3. If today's advancing technology is allowed to entrench such discrepancies, catastrophic consequences _____ (*result*).[26]

4. In fact, some _____ (*argue*) that the study of human-machine interfaces is an entire field in its own right.[27]

5. Most smartphone users _____ (*argue*) that there is plenty of room for further innovation.[28]

6. It is unlikely that many _____ (*be*) willing to undertake the task of producing the software our society desires.[29]

7. The quest to build machines that mimic human behavior has a long history, but many _____ (*agree*) that the modern field of artificial intelligence had its origins in 1950.[30]

8. The fact that a particular convenience store has sold a high number of winning lottery tickets _____ (*not consider*) significant to someone planning to buy a lottery ticket, but the discovery that customers who buy snack food also tend to buy frozen dinners _____ (*constitute*) meaningful information to a grocery store manager.[31]

Exercise 13 **Expressing Certainty**

Rewrite the following sentences on a separate sheet of paper so that they no longer hedge.

1. Most would agree that a company or individual should be allowed to recoup, and profit from, the investment needed to develop quality software.[32]

2. The quest to build machines that mimic human behavior has a long history, but many would agree that the modern field of artificial intelligence had its origins in 1950.[33]

3. At first glance utilitarianism appears to be a fair way of resolving ethical dilemmas. But, in its unqualified form, utilitarianism leads to numerous unacceptable conclusions. For example, it would allow the majority of a society to enslave a small minority.[34]

4. The human-machine interface has become an important concern in the requirements stage of software development projects and is a growing sub-field of software engineering. Indeed some would argue that the study of human-machine interfaces is an entire field in its own right.[35]

5. Medical treatment has advanced to the point that numerous parts of the human body can now be replaced with artificial parts or parts from human donors. It is conceivable that this might someday include parts of the brain.[36]

6. The human mind has an amazing ability to retrieve information that is associated with a current topic of consideration. When we experience certain smells, we might readily recall memories of our childhood. The sound of a friend's voice might conjure an image of the person or perhaps memories of good times. Certain music might generate thoughts of particular holiday seasons. These are examples of associative memory—the retrieval of information that is associated with, or related to, the information at hand.[37]

7. We should note that the subject of data mining is not restricted to the domain of computing but has tentacles that extend far into statistics. In fact, many would argue that since data mining had its origins in attempts to perform statistical analysis on large diverse data collections, it is an application of statistics rather than a field of computer science.[38]

Exercise 14 **Writing Sentences That Hedge**

Read the following passage on robotics. On a separate sheet of paper, answer the related questions in complete sentences that hedge about your ideas regarding the past, present, and future of robots. Use Chart 3-5 for help and vary your hedging strategies.

Robotics

[1] Robotics is the study of physical, autonomous agents that behave intelligently. As with all agents, robots must be able to perceive, reason, and act in their environment. Research in robotics thereby encompasses all areas of artificial intelligence as well as drawing heavily from mechanical and electrical engineering.

[2] To interact with the world, robots need mechanisms to manipulate objects and to move about. In the early days of robotics, the field was closely allied with the development of manipulators, most often mechanical arms with elbows, wrists, and hands or tools. Research dealt not only with how such devices could be maneuvered but also with how knowledge of their location and orientation could be maintained and applied. (You are able to close your eyes and still touch your nose with a finger because your brain maintains a record of where your nose and finger are.) Over time robots' arms have become more dexterous* to where, with a sense of touch based on force feedback*, they can handle eggs and paper cups successfully.

(continued on next page)

[3]Recently, the development of faster, lighter-weight computers has led to greater research in mobile robots that can move about. Achieving this mobility has led to an abundance of creative designs. Researchers in robot locomotion* have developed robots that swim like fish, fly like dragonflies, hop like grasshoppers* and crawl like snakes.

[4]Wheeled robots are very popular since they are relatively easy to design and build, but they are limited in the type of terrain* they can traverse*. Overcoming this restriction, using combinations of wheels or tracks to climb stairs or roll over rocks, is the goal of current research. As an example, the NASA Mars rovers used specially designed wheels to move on rocky soil.

[5]Legged robots offer greater mobility but are significantly more complex. For instance, two-legged robots, designed to walk as humans, must constantly monitor and adjust their stance or they will fall. However, such difficulties can be overcome, as exemplified by the two-legged humanoid robot named Asimo developed by Honda, that can walk up stairs and even run.[39]

* *dexterous*—skillful and quick in using hands or body
* *force feedback*—the return of information to the computer
* *locomotion*—movement or the ability to move
* *grasshopper*—an insect that has long back legs for jumping
* *terrain*—a particular type of land
* *traverse*—to move across, over, or through something

1. Why do you suppose researchers became interested in robotics?
2. How would robots likely have looked and behaved in the past?
3. Why do you think researchers wanted to make robots that looked like people?
4. Why do you think researchers are developing robots that can swim, fly, hop, and crawl?
5. What do you think the future of robots will be?

Error Analysis

The following student essay contains ten errors in the use of modal auxiliary verbs. The first error is corrected for you. Find and correct nine more.

Computer Intelligence

Researchers have been working for the past fifty years to build more and more intelligent machines. The goal has been to build an artificial intelligence (AI) that ~~should~~ *can* challenge the intellectual power of a human. In the past, progress on such a goal would have been rather slow. People could have adjusted slowly to the idea of a smart machine. They might have alarmed at first, but eventually would probably have learned to live with the machines. Nowadays, however, the goal of a superintelligent machine is approaching faster than most people can imagine. We can see machines that is able to beat experts in chess, give medical advice, and manage investments. These machines soon may perform better than their human counterparts. What would the consequences be to the humans who could replaced by such intelligent machines? No one knows for sure, but it is likely that the humans' self-image would be severely damaged.

On the other hand, some disagree. They would argued that machines can never be approach the human decision-making ability because they are mechanical and humans are biological. That means the process of making a decision would be completely different. Even if a final decision were the same, it must have been made by a machine, not a human, and many believe that it would not be ethical to follow what machines tell us to do.

Most ethical people think that even though intelligent machines can to do a number of tasks better than their human counterparts, they should not be allowed to make decisions related to human life. Imagine what might happen when a machine acting as a judge decides that someone is guilty of a terrible crime or when a medical machine decides a person has a dangerous mental illness. Could a machine be permitted to sentence a person to death or send someone to a locked mental hospital?

The question of how much power humans ought give intelligent machines will probably be debated for many years. It is really a question of ethics, what is right and what is wrong, and humans must make hard choices in order to stay in control of their lives.

Exercise 16 Apply It to Speaking

Reread the essay in Exercise 15. In small groups, discuss the questions below. Make notes as you talk. Then report your group's conclusions to your classmates. See Appendix B for help.

1. What can computers do better than humans? Give some examples.

2. Discuss what would happen if computers replaced human workers in one or more of the following settings: schools, factories, retail businesses, medical facilities, investment companies, or governments. What would be the positive and negative effects?

3. Conclude by addressing these questions: What kinds of tasks should computers be given? What kinds of tasks should they not be given?

Exercise 17 Apply It to Writing

Write a paragraph summarizing your own conclusions based on your discussion and notes in Exercise 16. How much power should we give to intelligent machines? What limits ought we to place on their use? Provide reasons and examples and use modal verbs to express your ideas. See Appendix B for help.

Putting It All Together

CHOCOLATE CAKE

Preheat oven to 350°F. Grease and flour two 8-x-8-inch round cake pans.

Ingredients:
- ⅓ **cup cocoa**
- 1 ½ **cups cake flour**
- 1 **cup sugar**
- 1 **tsp baking powder**
- ½ **tsp baking soda**
- 1 ½ **sticks of soft butter**
- 2 **eggs**
- 2 **tsp vanilla**
- ⅔ **cup sour cream**

Put all the ingredients into a food processor and mix until smooth.

Scrape batter into the pans and spread evenly.

Bake until toothpick comes out clean (25–35 minutes).

Cool on rack for 10 minutes.
Invert cake and remove it. Cool.

Frost with fudge frosting.

Serve.

A flowchart for making chocolate cake

Preheat oven to 350°F
↓
Prepare cake pans
↓
Mix ingredients
↓
Pour into pans and spread
↓
Bake at 350°
↓
Test with a toothpick
↓
Not Ready   Ready

Remove from oven
↓
Cool
↓
Remove from pan
↓
Frost
↓
Serve

An algorithm is a set of steps that defines how a task is performed. The recipe and flowchart are algorithms for chocolate cake.

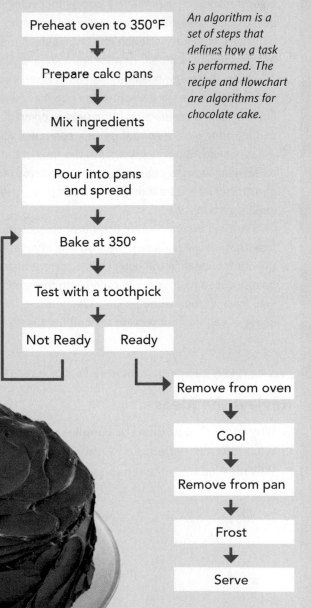

Read the following passage from *Computer Science: An Overview,* 11th Edition, by J. Glenn Brookshear.[1]

The Science of Algorithms

[1]Conditions such as limited data storage capabilities and intricate, time-consuming programming procedures restricted the complexity of the algorithms utilized in early computing machines. However, as these limitations began to disappear, machines were applied to increasingly larger and more complex tasks. As attempts to express the composition of these tasks in algorithmic form began to tax* the abilities of the human mind, more and more research efforts were directed toward the study of algorithms and the programming process.

[2]It was in this context that the theoretical work of mathematicians began to pay dividends. . . . Mathematicians had already been investigating those questions regarding algorithmic processes that advancing technology was now raising. With that, the stage was set for the emergence of a new discipline known as *computer science*.

[3]Today, computer science has established itself as the science of algorithms. The scope of this science is broad, drawing from such diverse subjects as mathematics, engineering, psychology, biology, business administration, and linguistics. Indeed, researchers in different branches of computer science may have very distinct definitions of the science. For example, a researcher in the field of computer architecture may focus on the task of miniaturizing circuitry and thus view computer science as the advancement and application of technology. But a researcher in the field of database systems may see computer science as seeking ways to make information systems more useful. And, a researcher in the field of artificial intelligence may regard computer science as the study of intelligence and intelligent behavior.

[4]Thus, an introduction to computer science must include a variety of topics, which is a task that we will pursue in the following chapters. In each case, our goal will be to introduce the central ideas in the subject, the current topic of research, and some of the techniques being applied to advance knowledge in the area. With such a variety of topics, it is easy to lose track of the overall picture. We therefore pause to collect our thoughts by identifying some questions that provide a focus for this its study.[2]

* *tax*—to make someone have to work hard or make a strong effort

Review the Ideas

1. Why couldn't algorithms be complex in early computing machines?
2. What different definitions of computer science do researchers in different branches have?
3. Why must an introduction to computer science include a variety of topics?

Exercise 1 Analysis of the Reading Passage

1 Complete the chart by filling in the tenses and time frames used in each paragraph of the reading passage.

Paragraph	Tenses Used	Time Frame
1		
2		
3		
4		

2 Find the two passive verbs in paragraph 1 and write them here. Explain why the writer chose each one.

_____

_____

3 Find the modal auxiliaries in paragraph 3 and write them here. Explain why the writer chose to use modals.

_____ _____

_____ _____

_____

_____

4 Find the verb that includes a modal auxiliary verb in paragraph 4. Write it here. Is it considered a strong or weak modal?

_____

Exercise 2 Identifying Time Frames

Place each of the boldfaced verbs in this sentence from the reading passage into the correct time frame by completing the time line provided.

It was in this context that the theoretical work of mathematicians **began** to pay dividends. . . . Mathematicians **had already been investigating** those questions regarding algorithmic processes that advancing technology **was not raising**. With that, the stage **was set** for the emergence of a new discipline known as *computer science.*

```
←─────────────┬───────────────────────┬───────────────────────┬──────────────→
            Past                   Present                  Future
```

The following student essay contains ten errors in verb tenses and forms. The first error is corrected for you. Find and correct nine more.

Social Media

In November 2011, one of the social media companies ~~registers~~ *registered* more than 721 million active users, more than twice the population of the United States (314 million). This and other social media have easily outdistanced even e-mail in popularity. People who use social media say that they have been changed the way they communicate. They can actually see their families while they chat online and share information to keep up with family and friends on various social media such as Skype®. However, social media have definite disadvantages compared to traditional means of communication that may outweigh the advantages.

While it is true that social media have changed the way people communicate, the illusion of privacy is puts users at risk. First, young people may post photos that attract stalkers or worse. Or people share personal information such as dates of birth, Social Security numbers, and medical information that identity thieves steal. In addition, employees may talk negatively about employers on social media and then lose their jobs. For example, in 2010, several of the students at my school were suspended after a teacher discovered that they have been writing negative comments about their teachers and other students on Facebook®. They had been forwarding copies of e-mails that are sent to them about other students and that made nasty comments about them on the site. Someone told the director, and of course they are reprimanded.

Another problem with social media is that instead of bringing people together, it may be isolate them. Many people spend so much time developing long-distance friendships online that they don't develop personal relationships with the people around them and in some cases had lost their friends completely. It is sad that some students are as addicted to social media as other addicts are to drugs and alcohol.

A final disadvantage of social media is that it is unreliable. Anyone can post anything online, and there is no way to prove whether or not it is true. Bad or fake products may advertise by unscrupulous businesses; identity thieves and other criminals can pose as professionals or friends to rob or kidnap victims. Politicians and other activists have started rumors about their opponents that spread instantly all over the world.

In sum, social media is one of the great developments of technology, but it has some serious disadvantages. People should therefore be careful when using social media and always remember that everyone everywhere can see and hear everything that put on social media sites.

WHAT DID YOU LEARN?

A Review the forms and functions of verbs in Part 1. Decide if the grammar in the following sentences is correct. Write *C* for correct and *I* for incorrect. Correct the errors. Then check your answers in Appendix D.

_____ 1. History tells us that the abacus had its roots in ancient China and used in the early Greek and Roman civilizations.

_____ 2. For control of an algorithm's execution, the machine is relies on the human operator.

_____ 3. As desktop computers were being accepted and used in homes, the miniaturization of computing machines continued.[3]

_____ 4. The algorithm followed by the loom could changed to produce different woven designs.

_____ 5. John Atanasoff from Iowa State University and Clifford Berry, his assistant, has finally received credit for creating the first electronic digital computer.

_____ 6. Once an algorithm for performing a task has been found, the performance of the task no longer requires an understanding of the principles on which the algorithm is based.[4]

_____ 7. Pascal has already designed a computing machine by the time that Babbage created his Difference Engine.

_____ 8. In the field of artificial intelligence, autonomous machines were being built that can operate without human intervention.

_____ 9. Thomas Edison is credited with inventing the incandescent lamp, but other researchers were developing similar lamps and in a sense Edison was lucky to be the one to obtain the patent.[5]

_____ 10. Computer scientists want to develop their knowledge about artificial intelligence—knowledge that allowed them to create new intelligent machines.

B On a separate sheet of paper, describe the time frame of each paragraph.

1. The machines designed by Charles Babbage were truly the forerunners of modern computer design. If technology had been able to produce his machines in an economically feasible manner and if the data processing demands of commerce and government had been on the scale of today's requirements, Babbage's ideas could have led to a computer revolution in the 1880s.[6]

2. The old adage "an ounce of prevention is worth a pound of cure" is certainly true in the context of controlling vandalism over network connections. A primary prevention technique is to filter traffic passing through a point in the network, usually with a program called a firewall. For instance, a firewall might be installed at the gateway of an organization's intranet to filter messages passing in and out of the region.[7]

C On a separate sheet of paper, explain why the passive is used in the following paragraphs.

1. When a user sends e-mail from his or her local machine, it is first transferred to the user's mail server. There it is forwarded to the destination mail server where it is stored until the recipient contacts the mail server and asks to view the accumulated mail.[8]

2. As for the ability to follow an algorithm, we can see a progression of flexibility in these machines. Pascal's machine was built to perform only addition. Consequently, the appropriate sequence of steps was embedded into the structure of the machine itself. . . . Babbage's Difference Engine . . . could be modified to perform a variety of calculations, but his Analytical Engine . . . was designed to read instructions in the form of holes in paper cards.[9]

(continued on next page)

D Do the following two sentences hedge? On a separate sheet of paper, explain your answer.

1. A researcher in the field of database systems sees computer science as seeking ways to make information systems more useful.[10]

2. Some may argue that the study of human-machine interfaces is an entire field in its own right.

How did you do? Are there topics you need to review?

Exercise 4 Apply It to Speaking

Prepare a brief presentation (two to three minutes) about the effects of advancing technology on students' skill levels. See Appendix B for help.

1 Begin by reading the paragraph below, which raises some interesting questions about this topic.

As technology advances, our education system is constantly challenged to reconsider the level of abstraction at which topics are presented. Many questions take the form of whether a skill is still necessary or whether students should be allowed to rely on an abstract tool. Students of trigonometry are no longer taught how to find the values of trigonometric functions using tables. Instead they use calculators as abstract tools to find these values. Some argue that long division should also give way to abstraction. What other subjects are involved with similar controversies? Do modern word processors eliminate the need to develop spelling skills? Will the use of video technology someday remove the need to read?[11]

2 Next, discuss with a small group of classmates how important you think it will be for schools to continue teaching basic skills. Consider the following questions, which relate to points raised in the paragraph above, and take notes as you talk.

a. When you are typing a paper on a computer, what happens when you misspell a word? Should you have to know and remember the correct spelling?

b. In math classes, students are now allowed to use calculators. Is it important that they know how to do calculations without a calculator?

c. Every store checkout line has an electronic cash register, and most have scanners. What would happen if these machines suddenly stopped working?

d. Would you prefer to watch a movie or read a book about a given topic? What could happen if people no longer read books?

3 Now, on the basis of your discussion, prepare your comments to present to the class. Answer this question: Should the teaching of basic skills be modified or eliminated because of the availability of modern technology? Illustrate your ideas with one or more examples, and be sure to accurately use the verb tenses, forms, and modals that you have been reviewing.

4 Give your presentation to the class.

Read the passage below about the GPS capabilities of smartphones. Then, on a separate sheet of paper, write two paragraphs discussing the questions it raises about the advantages and the disadvantages of GPS capabilities.

> Most smartphones are able to identify the phone's location by means of GPS. This allows applications to provide location-specific information (such as the local news, local weather, or the presence of businesses in the immediate area) based on the phone's current location. However, such GPS capabilities may also allow other applications to broadcast the phone's location to other parties. Is this good? How could knowledge of the phone's location (thus your location) be abused?[12]

Follow these steps before you begin to write:

1 Think about how a GPS could broadcast your location to other people and what could happen as a result. Note down your ideas.

- Who might be interested in where you are? How could it be helpful for someone to have this information?
- How could someone "abuse" the knowledge of where you are?
- Make a list of verb tenses, forms, and modals you can use to discuss the possible effects of a smartphone's GPS capabilities.

2 Prepare an outline of your ideas, clearly laying out the (1) advantages and (2) the disadvantages of identifying a smartphone's location.

Now write and then double-check your paragraphs. Remember to begin your paragraphs with a topic sentence. See Appendix B for help.

Check Your Writing

Which of the following tenses, verb forms, and modals did you use in your paragraph? Did you use them correctly?

☐ Simple present tense	☐ Past perfect
☐ Present progressive	☐ Correct word order in verb phrases
☐ Present perfect	☐ Active verbs
☐ Future tense	☐ Passive verbs
☐ Simple past tense	☐ Modals for hedging
☐ Past progressive	

Nouns and Noun Phrases:
Adding Variety and Detail

OBJECTIVES

In Part 2 of the *Advanced Grammar* course you will

- review noun functions.
- review the elements of noun phrases.
- understand and use modifiers that precede nouns (premodifiers).
- understand and use modifiers that follow nouns (postmodifiers).

Nouns and noun phrases are used to add important information and colorful details to academic writing.

Academic texts about culture serve to illustrate how writers pack a great deal of important, interesting, and descriptive information into sentences in formal English. Becoming proficient in using nouns and noun phrases will help prepare you to read textbooks efficiently and to communicate effectively in speaking and writing at the university level.

Portrait of Tzu-hsi. The dowager empress of China, Tzu-hsi died on November 15, 1908, after ruling China for almost fifty years.

Noun Functions

English businessmen in the nineteenth century

A blue-collar worker today

PREVIEW

VOCABULARY   Here are some words that you will encounter in Chapter 4. How much do you know about each word? Turn to Appendix A to assess and expand your word knowledge.

adornment	component	denote	diversity	image
indicator	nature	practice (n.)	status	tight

Prepare to Read

1. Look at the picture of the Chinese empress on the Part 2 opening page. How do we know, from her clothing and other details, that she is a person of very high social status?

2. Look at the hands of the Chinese empress. What do you notice about them? What do you learn about her?

3. Look at the picture of the English businessmen on the previous page. What do you notice about their clothing? What does that tell you about them?

4. Look at the photo of the contemporary blue-collar worker. What do you notice about his clothing? What does that tell you about him?

Read the following passage from *Individuality in Clothing Selection and Personal Appearance*, 7th Edition, by Suzanne G. Marshall, Hazel O. Jackson, and M. Sue Stanley.[1]

What Do Clothing and Adornment Communicate about Culture?

An infinite **number** of diverse **cultures** exist around the **world**; yet, certain **universals** exist in all **cultures**. Clothing and adornment **practices** communicate the culture's **components** and the interactive **nature** of these **components** as well as the **uniqueness** of each **culture**. . . . Both quality and quantity of possessions are indicators of economic position. For example, in ancient times, the wealthy Chinese grew their fingernails to inordinate lengths, thus affirming to all that they did not perform lowly manual tasks. To further enforce the inactivity of their hands, they wore robes with very long sleeves that completely covered the fingernails. Any work involving the hands was impossible.

Likewise, at the end of the nineteenth century, rich and powerful English businessmen wore a high, tight white collar with their heavy, stiff Edwardian* suits. Physical exertion of any kind was inhibited and probably would have caused difficulty in breathing. Thus the term *white-collar worker* came into use. This term as well as the clothing practice, denoted both economic success and status above that of the manual laborer, who usually wore a soft-collared blue shirt.[2]

Edwardian—relating to the time of King Edward VII of Great Britain (1901–1910)

Review the Ideas

1. In ancient times, how did the wealthy in China dress? Why?

2. In the nineteenth century, how did rich Englishmen dress? Why?

3. How did the clothing of rich businessmen differ from the clothing of manual workers in nineteenth-century England?

Analyze the Grammar

Work in pairs to answer the following questions about the reading passage.

1. Look at the boldfaced words in the first two sentences. What parts of speech are they?

2. What is the function of the boldfaced words? Underline other examples of words like these in the rest of the passage.

CHART 4-1 | Types of Nouns

Nouns can be divided into the following categories:

1. Proper nouns and common nouns

   a. Proper nouns are individual names of people, places, and things. Proper nouns are capitalized and usually singular.

   b. Common nouns are all other nouns. Common nouns refer to people, places, and things, but not the individual names.

   a. **Empress Tzu-hsi** lived in **China**.

   b. The **women** wear **pants**.

2. Count nouns and noncount nouns

   a. Count nouns are nouns that can be singular or plural. *A*, *an*, or *one* can be used before singular count nouns.

   b. Noncount nouns cannot be counted. They are almost always singular.

   a. **one** shirt, two shirts

   A blue shirt was **an** indicator of low status.

   b. **Exertion** was impossible.

3. Gerunds (verbs ending in *-ing*) and infinitives (*to* + base verb)

   They function as noncount nouns.

   Wearing comfortable clothes was essential for blue-collar workers.

   To dress well is important.

Exercise 1 Identifying Types of Nouns

Write the following words from the vocabulary list and the reading passage under the correct category. Note that some words will appear in more than one category.

> breathing, businessmen, century, Chinese, clothing, collar, component, culture, difficulty, diversity, end, English, exertion, fingernail, hand, inactivity, indicator, kind, laborer, length, nature, number, position, possession, practice, quality, quantity, robe, sleeve, status, success, suit, task, term, uniqueness, use, worker, world

1. Proper nouns: _____

2. Common nouns: _____

   _____

   _____

   _____

3. Count nouns: _____

   _____

   _____

   _____

4. Noncount nouns: _____

   _____

CHART 4-2   Nouns, Gerunds, and Infinitives as Subjects and Objects

1. A **sentence** has a subject and a verb. The **subject** is the person or thing that acts. The subject does the action of the verb. Adjectives may precede a noun subject.

    subject   *verb*
    Cultures change slowly.

    adjective
    Prehistoric cultures changed slowly.

2. Some verbs are followed by **direct objects**. The object is the thing or person that receives the action of the verb.

    verb   *direct object*
    Each individual has a cultural **history**.[3]

3. Certain verbs (*give*, *teach*, *write*) may also have **indirect objects**. The indirect object is the person or thing that receives the direct object itself or the benefit of the direct object.

An indirect object preceded by *to* or *for* can also follow the direct object.

    verb   *indirect object*   *direct object*
    Anthropologists give **students** knowledge.

    verb   *direct object*   *indirect object*
    Anthropologists give knowledge **to students**.

4. In some sentences there are nouns following **prepositions**. These are **prepositional phrases**. The noun in a prepositional phrase is the **object of the preposition**.

    prepositional phrase
    Certain universals exist **in all cultures**.[4]

5. Gerunds are used in the same way that nouns are. Gerunds can be the following:

   a. Subjects

   b. Objects of prepositions

   c. Objects of certain verbs

    subject
   a. Inhibited **breathing** causes difficulty.

    object of a preposition
   b. Tight collars cause difficulty in **breathing**.

    direct object
   c. Tight collars restrict **breathing**.

6. Infinitives are used in some of the same ways that nouns are. Infinitives can be the following:

   a. Subjects

   b. Direct objects of certain verbs

    subject
   a. **To breathe** easily is necessary.

    subject
   It is necessary **to breathe** easily. (preferred form for a subject infinitive)

    direct object
   b. Workers need **to breathe** easily.

7. Pronouns can take the place of nouns and gerunds.

   a. Subject pronouns—*I, you, he, she, it, we, they*

   b. Object pronouns—*me, you, him, her, it, us, them*

   a. Cultures change slowly.

    subject
   They change slowly.

   b. Anthropologists give knowledge to students.

    object pronouns
   Anthropologists give **it** to **them**.

Identifying Subjects and Objects

Write the function of each underlined word (noun, gerund, infinitive, or pronoun) above it.
Use the abbreviations in the box. The first sentence is done for you.

subject = s	direct object = do	indirect object = io	object of a preposition = op

1. The people _(s) with long fingernails _(op) could not write letters _(do) to their friends _(io and op).

   s ... *op* ... *do* ... *io and op*
   1. The people with long fingernails could not write letters to their friends.

2. The study of clothing and culture has a long and rich history.[5]

3. It is important to identify with members of a group by dressing in a certain way.

4. An enormous variety of styles allows people the opportunity for self-expression and individuality in dress.[6]

5. Clothing symbols express meaning and provide information to other people. For example, clothing with special organization logos may have special meaning only to members of the group.[7]

6. During the 1960s, young women grew their hair as long as possible. Waist-length hair parted in the center and hanging was the fashion. Only straight hair could accommodate this style, so straightening or pressing hair (literally with an iron and ironing board) became popular.[8]

CHART 4-3	Complements

1. The linking verbs *be, seem, appear,* and *become* are often followed by nouns, gerunds, infinitives, or adjectives called subject complements.

   a. A **subject complement** has the same meaning as the subject of the sentence when it is a noun, gerund, or infinitive.

subject	subject complement

   a. One quality of appearance is **image**.

   One bodily function is **breathing**.

   One reason is **to succeed**.

   b. A subject complement describes the subject when the complement is an adjective.

subject	subject complement

   b. One quality of appearance is **important**.

   c. Adjectives and other nouns may precede a subject complement.

subject	subject	noun	complement

   c. One quality of appearance is **body image**.

2. Certain verbs (*elect, appoint, designate, name, make, coin, call, consider*) may be followed by a direct object plus a noun, gerund, or phrase that has the same meaning as the direct object, or by an adjective that describes the direct object. These nouns and adjectives are called **object complements**.

   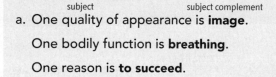

   verb — direct object — object complement
   Experts call the concept **body image**.

   People named that activity **gardening**.

   Experts call the concept **brilliant**.

Exercise 3 Identifying Subject Complements and Object Complements

Write the function of the underlined word above it. Use the abbreviations in the box.
The first sentence is done for you.

subject complement = sc	object complement = oc

1. Scientists coined the term *spacesuit*. (*oc*)

2. The spacesuit is truly a triumph of modern scientific ingenuity.[9]

3. Beginning in the 1980s, sales of hair-care products and services became big business, and sales remained high.[10]

4. Marie Antoinette was so strong that she named her dressmaker, Madame Bertin, her minister of fashion.[11]

5. Both quality and quantity of possessions are indicators of economic position.[12]

6. During the 1960s, young women grew their hair as long as possible. Waist length hair parted in the center and hanging was the fashion.[13]

7. Many theories have attempted to explain the motivations for individuals to cover and decorate all or parts of the body. The basic reasons behind the motivation appear to be the physical, psychological, and sociological needs of all individuals.[14]

8. The identifying name, insignia, or logo makes the item "status" clothing within a small clique, a large group, nationally or internationally.[15]

9. The 1960s civil rights movement, led by Dr. Martin Luther King Jr. and others, inspired the motto "Black is beautiful."[16]

CHART 4-4 | **Appositives**

Sometimes nouns, gerunds, and infinitives follow other nouns in a sentence and have the same meanings. These nouns are called **appositives**. An appositive may be preceded by an adjective or an adverb.

Sometimes *or* introduces the appositive.

Appositives may or may not be separated by commas or dashes. When there are no commas or dashes, the appositive is essential to the meaning of the preceding noun.

appositive
Superstar **Michael Jackson** wore makeup.

Jackson's talents, **singing and dancing**, were legendary.

Jackson's goal, **to entertain** the world, was realized early in his life.

In Bangladesh, a bride wears special clothing, **usually a sari**.

In Iran, Muslim women wear a long piece of cloth, **or** *chador*, over their heads and body when they appear in public.

Exercise 4 Identifying Appositives in Academic Sentences

Underline the appositive(s) in each sentence.

1. Marie Antoinette was so strong that she named her dressmaker, Madame Bertin, her minister of fashion.[17]

2. Manual workers in the nineteenth century had one desire, to survive.

3. In the nineteenth century, concealing the leg was a manifestation of modesty; even the word *leg* was taboo. If one had to refer to "that" part of the body, it was called a limb.[18]

4. After World War II, enthusiasm for sports, especially running, was accompanied by the development of appropriate sports apparel.

5. Parallel to the development of participant sports apparel was the creation of spectator sports clothing—"athleisure"—that evolved into the wardrobe of the post–World War II suburban families' casual lifestyle.[19]

6. At the end of the nineteenth century, rich and powerful English businessmen wore a high, tight white collar with their heavy, stiff Edwardian suits. Physical exertion of any kind was inhibited and probably would have caused difficulty in breathing. Thus the term *white-collar worker* came into use.[20]

7. In some Islamic countries, women wear a veil that covers them from head to toe when they leave their homes. The wearing of this veil, or burka, as it is known in Pakistan, is a condition known as being in purdah.[21]

8. Although about twenty-five of the European member nations have come together around a principle of cooperation, they hold true to their cultural diversity—a culture like a *bouquet de fleurs*, as remarked by Herr, a German native (Reid, 2002).[22]

Exercise 5 Placing Appositives

On a separate sheet of paper, rewrite the following passage, using the appositive phrases in the box. Add them after the nouns they describe. Use the correct punctuation. The first one is done for you.

apples and oranges	to govern the country	her throne	~~Tzu-hsi~~	or robe
a kind of red hat	a lake or river	managing the treacherous people around her		

,Tzu-hsi,

 The dowager empress of China ruled China for almost fifty years. As the leader of China, she

had an extraordinary responsibility. Her secondary occupation was truly hazardous. Others were

always ready to take her place. Looking at her portrait at the beginning of Part 2, one would never

guess that she could have been murdered at any moment. When we look at her, we see her seated

on a chair, holding a painted fan. She is wearing a crown and a long, beautifully decorated coat.

On either side of her are two porcelain bowls of fruit on tall, ornate tables. The scene behind the

empress is filled with green bamboo and pink flowers. A body of water is just visible through the

green plants. The scene in the portrait appears calm and peaceful.

Exercise 6 Identifying Functions of Nouns

Look at the passage below. Find and write down an example of a noun, gerund, pronoun, or adjective from the passage that is used as in the following functions.

1. Subject: _____

2. Direct object: _____

3. Indirect object: _____

4. Object of a preposition: _____

5. Subject complement (noun): _____

6. Subject complement (adjective): _____

7. Object complement (noun): _____

8. Object complement (adjective): _____

9. Appositive: _____

    Clothing has a fascinating history. In ancient China, rich people were never supposed to work with their hands. So these men and women grew their fingernails long and covered them with long sleeves. Long fingernails and long-sleeved robes were the styles for the wealthy.

    In eighteenth- and nineteenth-century Europe, society taught the rich fashion rules. Their tight, heavy clothes and high-heeled shoes made hard work difficult. Working people called wealthy people the idle rich because they did no manual labor. However, manual laborers, blue-collar workers, wore loose blue shirts. These shirts were comfortable for manual work.

Exercise 7 Reordering Scrambled Sentences

Reorder the scrambled sentences to form sentences with the words in the correct order.

1. an official title / Marie Antoinette / her dressmaker / gave

_____

2. wore / at the turn of the century / both men and women / long hair

_____

3. usually had / facial hair, beards, moustaches, and sideburns / men

_____

4. on and off stage / England's Boy George and America's Michael Jackson / full makeup / both wore

_____

5. saw / the World War II era / with crew cuts and whiskerless faces / men

_____

6. is / of recognizing marital status / a common practice / some kind of visible means / among many different cultures

_____

7. after the war / for women / became / wearing pants / a popular way of dressing

_____

8. with long fingernails / it is impossible / manual work / to do

_____

Exercise 8 Using Nouns in Your Writing

Answer the following questions based on some of the ideas in this chapter. Answer in complete sentences. Use the nouns and functions in parentheses in your answers. The first one is done for you.

1. How did the wealthy in China dress in earlier times?
   (*robes*—direct object; *sleeves*—object of the preposition)
   The wealthy in China wore <u>robes</u> *with long* <u>sleeves</u>.

2. Why was any work involving the hands impossible for the wealthy Chinese?
   (*fingernails*—direct object)
   _____

3. What did the nineteenth-century Englishmen's clothes inhibit?
   (*exertion*—direct object)
   _____

4. In the nineteenth century, what word was taboo?
   (*leg*—appositive)
   _____

5. Where does "blue-collar worker" come from?
   (*blue-collar worker*—appositive)
   _____

6. In the 1980s, what happened to sales of hair-care products and services?
   (*big business*—subject complement)
   _____

7. In the 1960s, what was the hair fashion?
   (*fashion*—subject complement; *1960s*—object of a preposition)
   _____

8. What did Marie Antoinette name her dressmaker, Madame Bertin?
   (*minister of fashion*—object complement)
   _____

9. What motto did the civil rights movement inspire in 1960?
   ("*Black is beautiful*"—object complement)
   _____

10. Who wears a veil that covers them from head to toe?
    (*women*—subject; *veil*—direct object)
    _____

Exercise 9 **Error Analysis**

The following student essay contains ten errors in the use of nouns, adjectives, gerunds and infinitives as subjects, objects, appositives, and complements. The first error is corrected for you. Work in pairs to find and correct eight more. Compare your answers with your classmates'.

Are High Heels for Women Only?

indicators

Historically, shoes have always been ~~indicate~~ of gender and status. High-heeled shoes have been associated with upper-class men and women from ancient times. Early Egyptians of the lower classes walked on their bare feet, but the upper classes wore an early type of shoe. The wear of heels by both men and women was depicted on murals. Later, ancient Greeks and Romans wore platform sandals. The higher the soles, the higher the social status.

In the Middle Ages, both men and women wore wooden soles, forerunning of high heels. These soles attached to expensive shoes so that people could keep their shoes out of the mud. In the fifteenth century, chopines, tall platform shoe, were popular with women throughout Europe. Then shoe designers developed a two-piece shoe with a soft upper part and an inflexible sole. The two-piece shoe made an attached heel possibly. These heels were well-liked by both men and women for riding because they were like modern cowboy boots. They allowed riders keeping their feet in the stirrups.

In the sixteenth century, Catherine de Medicis (1519–1589), who was quite short, made high, thin heels fashionably. In the eighteenth century, France's King Louis XIV wore heels 5 inches high that were painted with tiny scenes of battles. The king declared that only nobles could wear red heels, but none could be taller than his. During that century, heels became higher, thinner, and more delicate, and people began to associate them with an attractive and sexually desirable style.

During the nineteenth and twentieth centuries, high heels went through periods of popularity and unpopularity. Platform shoes became popularity again in the 1970s. Today, all kinds of footwear are available for men and women, but women are the one who choose extremely high heels.

Write original sentences to practice the vocabulary in this chapter. Use some of the given nouns to write at least one sentence for each of the functions listed below. Use Charts 4-2, 4-3, and 4-4 for help.

apparel	appearance	adornment	body image
clothing	conceal	denote	diversity
hair	hair-care products	indicator	individuals
makeup	motivations	nature	position
possession	practices	quality	quantity
status	style	tasks	tight
wearing	to wear	uniqueness	world

1. Gerund as subject:

_____

2. Noun as direct object:

_____

3. Noun as indirect object:

_____

4. Noun as subject complement:

_____

5. Noun as object complement:

_____

6. Noun as object of a preposition:

_____

7. Noun as an appositive:

_____

8. Infinitive as a direct object:

_____

Exercise 11 **Apply It to Speaking**

1 Read the two questions below and decide how you would respond to each one, using specific examples. Jot down nouns from the chapter vocabulary list in Exercise 10 that you can use in making your points.

A. How have men's and women's hairstyles and makeup changed since your grandparents' lifetime? (Include beards and moustaches for men.)

EXAMPLE:

Men's hairstyles have changed since my grandparents' days. For example, men used to wear very short hair and no moustache or beard. Then, when my parents were young, men often wore long hair and beards. Today, young men . . .

B. How do hairstyles and makeup indicate a person's social position or lifestyle in your country or a country you know about?

EXAMPLE:

In my country, social class is indicated by hairstyles. For example, working-class men often wear their hair long, but middle-class men wear their hair short. Women . . .

2 Now present your ideas to a small group of your classmates. Take brief notes as each person speaks. What similarities and differences do you notice in their responses? Are there any additional points that could be made? Take turns sharing and discussing your conclusions with your classmates.

Exercise 12 **Apply It to Writing**

Write two paragraphs based on your discussion in Exercise 11. In your first paragraph summarize your classmates' ideas about changes in hairstyles and makeup and note your conclusions. In your second paragraph, address the question about the relationship between hairstyles and makeup and a person's social position and lifestyle, again, drawing appropriate conclusions. See Appendix B for help.

EXAMPLE:

In a recent discussion of the changes in men's and women's hairstyles since our grandparents' lifetime, we agreed that styles have changed a great deal. For example, . . .

A second topic of discussion compared social class and hairstyles in different countries. In China, for instance, . . .

Elements of Noun Phrases: Premodifiers

Balinese men wearing traditional sarongs

VOCABULARY   Here are some words that you will encounter in Chapter 5. How much do you know about each word? Turn to Appendix A to assess and expand your word knowledge.

attire	distinctive	fan	flamboyantly	garment
intricate	masculine	pattern	trousers	wrapped

Prepare to Read

1. Describe the clothes the Balinese men in the photo on the previous page are wearing.

2. Do men in your culture wear similar clothing? If not, how do men's clothes differ?

3. Do men and women wear different garments in your culture? Explain your response.

Read the following passage from *Individuality in Clothing Selection and Personal Appearance,* 7th Edition, by Suzanne G. Marshall, Hazel O. Jackson, and M. Sue Stanley.[1]

Gender and Garments

[1]**Cultural customs or traditions** establish **the gender of a garment**. In the Western world, people have learned to think of pants as masculine and skirts as feminine because **distinct dress differences for males and females** have been based on role differences.

[2]By the 1920s, women's dress and women's suffrage* had undergone revolutionary changes. During World War I* as women filled the wartime needs of industry, they wore trousers like the workmen they replaced. Pants were then considered highly appropriate work and play garments for women. Women's pantsuits were introduced into European high fashion in the middle of the 1960s.

[3]During this same time a change in attire developed for men. The flamboyantly dressed rock-and-roll stars of the 1960s were the male fashion leaders. Their young fans adopted these styles and soon men of all ages and socioeconomic levels were caught up in the fashion-forward style.

[4]First came color. The standard businessmen's white dress shirt became colored and patterned, worn first by those in artistic fields. Bell-bottomed trousers came next. As the popularity of jeans for everyone spread, new designs developed. The universal use of body-conforming jeans made tight pants fashionable for men. Because the close fit of these trousers eliminated pockets, some men began to carry an attaché case or purse.[2]

* *women's suffrage*—the right to vote in national elections
* *World War I (WWI) (1914–1918)*—a war fought in Europe between France, the UK, Russia, and the United States on one side and Germany, Austria-Hungary, and Turkey on the other

Review the Ideas

1. Why were pants for men and skirts for women in the Western world?

2. How did clothing styles for women change after World War I? Why did this change occur?

3. How did men's clothing change during the 1960s? Why did these changes occur?

Analyze the Grammar

Work in pairs to answer the following questions about the reading passage.

1. Look at the boldfaced phrases in the first two sentences of the passage. What parts of speech (word forms) are in them?

2. Sometimes nouns modify (describe) other nouns. Find four examples in paragraphs 1 and 2 of the passage. How does each of these descriptive nouns modify the other noun?

CHART 5-1 | Elements of Noun Phrases

A **noun phrase** is a group of words that functions as a single noun. The most important word in a noun phrase is the **head noun**, which is usually the last noun in the phrase.

article adjective   noun head noun (hn)
a beautiful cotton **skirt**

adjective   noun   hn
their cotton **skirts**

A noun phrase includes the head noun and other words that modify it, such as an article, quantifier, adverb, adjective, or other noun. All the words preceding the head noun are called **premodifiers**.

quantifier   adjective   hn
several wrapped skirts

—————— PREMODIFIERS ——————
article number   adverb   adjective   noun   hn
the ten extraordinarily beautiful cotton skirts

Exercise 1 Identifying Head Nouns in Noun Phrases

Write parentheses around each noun phrase and underline the head noun.

1. The East Indian woman is adorned with a red or saffron tika mark on her forehead.[3]

2. At the end of the nineteenth century, rich and powerful English businessmen wore a high, tight white collar with their heavy, stiff Edwardian suits. Physical exertion of any kind was inhibited and probably would have caused difficulty in breathing. Thus the term *white-collar worker* came into use. This term as well as the clothing practice denoted both economic success and status above that of the manual laborer, who usually wore a soft-collared blue shirt.[4]

CHART 5-2 | Determiners as Premodifiers

Determiners are words such as articles, quantifiers, possessive adjectives, possessive nouns, and demonstrative adjectives. These are premodfiers that begin a noun phrase.

1. Articles

a. Indefinite articles *a, an* Used with singular count nouns	**A** businessman wore **a** suit and carried **an** attaché case.
b. The definite article *the* Used with previously mentioned nouns and with specific nouns known to the reader	**The** attaché case was usually made of leather.
c. No article (Ø) Used with proper nouns Used with noncount nouns and plural count nouns	**Empress Tzu-hsi** had long fingernails. **Breathing** was inhibited by tight collars. **Women** wore **trousers**.

2. Quantifiers

a. Used with singular count nouns: *one, each, every*	**Each** person has his or her own style.
b. Used with plural count nouns: *two, both, a couple of, several, a few, few, many, a great many, a number of*	**A great many** fans dressed flamboyantly.

c. Used with noncount nouns: *a little, little, much, a great deal of*	**Little** exertion was required of an empress.
d. Used with both count and noncount nouns: *no, any, some, enough, a lot of, lots of, plenty of, most, all*	Nineteenth-century men wore **no** jewelry. Today **most** people wear jewelry.

3. Possessives

a. Possessive adjectives: *my, your, his, her, our, their* Used with all nouns	After 1949, women wore **their** hair short.
b. Possessive nouns: *Gandhi's, the professor's* Used with all nouns	**Charles Darwin's** theory of evolution was appalling to some people. A **person's** dignity should not be at risk.

4. Demonstrative adjectives

a. *this, that* Used with singular count nouns and noncount nouns	Fashion is important to young people. **This** fact is crucial to the clothing business. In the South Pacific, some men wear skirts. **That** attire would not be fashionable in the United States.
b. *these, those* Used with plural count nouns *This* and *these* indicate nearness to the speaker in space or time. *That* and *those* indicate distance from the speaker in distance or time.	High-heeled shoes are quite fashionable. **These** shoes can be worn by anyone. Pants were garments for men in the nineteenth century. **Those** garments would soon be worn by women.

Exercise 2 Identifying Determiners

With a partner, underline the determiners in the following sentences and label them. Use the abbreviations in the box. Find the noun phrases with no articles and insert Ø before them.

indefinite article = iart	definite article = dart	quantifier = q
possessive adj = pa	possessive noun = pn	demonstrative adjective = da

1. At the end of the nineteenth century, rich and powerful English businessmen wore an extremely high, tight white collar with their heavy, stiff Edwardian suits.[5]

2. The Amish women wear somber-colored, body-concealing dresses.[6]

3. During the 1970s, many high school and college students paid high prices for recycled, faded, patched, and embellished jeans.[7]

4. The faded, used, worn look was achieved by laundering the indigo-dyed fabric a minimum of four times.[8]

5. Classic clothes were designed with clean, uncluttered, body-conforming lines.[9] *(continued on next page)*

6. By the 1920s, women's dress and women's suffrage had undergone revolutionary changes.

7. . . . some men began to carry an attaché case or purse.

8. Those purses had a long strap and were carried over the shoulder like a book bag today.

CHART 5-3	Adjective, Adverb, and Noun Premodifiers

Adjectives, adverbs, and other nouns may precede the head noun in a noun phrase. Like determiners, they can function as premodifiers.

1. Adjective modifiers of nouns

a. Adjectives modify (describe) nouns. One or more adjectives may be placed before a noun.	adjective adjective hn **distinctive Indonesian** skirts
b. Present and past participles may also be used as adjectives.	past participle a **wrapped** skirt
c. Common adjective endings: *-able*, *-al*, *-ary*, *-ent*, *-ful*, *-ic*, *-ious*, *-ive*, *-like*, *-less*, *-ing*, *-ed*, and *-en*	comfort**able**, loc**al**, ser**ious**, distinc**tive**
A few adjectives end in *-ly*.	kind**ly**, friend**ly**

2. Adverb modifiers of adjectives

a. Adverbs can modify adjectives in a noun phrase. Adverbs may express the idea of intensity (how much), time, or manner.	adverb adjective hn **incredibly** intricate patterns **newly** discovered cultures
b. Common adverb endings: *-ly*, *-ward*	high**ly**, fashionab**ly**, home**ward**

3. Noun modifiers of nouns and head nouns

a. Nouns can describe other nouns in the same way that adjectives do. We call these nouns noun modifiers. In a noun phrase that contains noun modifiers, it is important to distinguish between the noun modifier and the head noun, which is usually the last noun in the phrase. Noun modifiers are always singular.	adjective noun modifier hn distinctive **dress** differences noun modifier hn noun modifier hn **Work garments** differ from **play garments**.
b. Common noun endings include endings for	
• abstract nouns: *-ance*, *-ence*, *-ency*, *-er*, *-ity*, *-ics*, *-ism*, *-ist*, *-logy*, *-ment*, *-ness*, *-sion*, and *-tion*.	resembl**ance**, independ**ence**, consist**ency**, feminin**ity**, econom**ics**, happi**ness**
• nouns referring to people: *-ist*, *-er*, and *-or*.	scient**ist**, labor**er**, profess**or**

4. Compound modifiers

Adjectives, adverbs, and nouns may be combined with other adjectives, adverbs, nouns, participles, or prepositional phrases. Compound modifiers are usually hyphenated.

adjective noun   hn
two-tone colors

adjective adjective   hn
dark-colored dresses

adverb adjective   hn
well-known researchers

noun   present participle   hn
body-conforming jeans

noun adjective   hn
tentlike garments

compound modifier   hn
top-of-the-line attire

Exercise 3   Identifying Premodifiers

Underline and label the determiners (det), adjectives (adj), adverbs (adv), noun modifiers (nm), and compound modifiers (cm) in the sentences. The head nouns are boldfaced.

1. During World War I, as women filled the wartime **needs** of industry, they wore trousers like the **workmen** they replaced.

   Pants were then considered highly appropriate work and play **garments** for women.

   Women's **pantsuits** were introduced into European high **fashion** in the **middle** of the **1960s**.[10]

2. During this same **time** a **change** in attire developed for men.

   The flamboyantly dressed rock-and-roll **stars** of the **1960s** were the male fashion **leaders**.

   Their young **fans** adopted these **styles** and soon men of all **ages** and socioeconomic **levels** were caught up in the fashion-forward **style**.[11]

3. First came color. The standard businessmen's white dress **shirt** became colored and patterned, worn first by those in artistic **fields**.

   Bell-bottomed **trousers** came next. As the **popularity** of jeans for everyone spread, new **designs** developed.

   The universal **use** of body-conforming **jeans** made tight **pants** fashionable for men.

   Because the close **fit** of these **trousers** eliminated pockets, some **men** began to carry an attaché **case** or purse.[12]

Exercise 4 Using Adverbs and Adjectives

Decide which form to use in the following noun phrases—adjective or adverb. Use Chart 5-3 for help. Circle the correct form.

1. A review of (*current / currently*) fashion magazines such as *Bazaar*, *Officiel*, and *Vogue* reveals a variety of designs available to the fashion consumer.[13]

2. A (*rich / richly*) brocaded sari and (*heavily / heavy*) gold jewelry express the (*economically / economic*) wealth of a Bengali bride in Bangladesh.[14]

3. In Japan, the color of the kimono was used to show age. Young children and marriageable young women wore (*bright / brightly*) colored and (*gay / gaily*) patterned kimonos. Dark kimonos of a solid color were for the mature, including married women.[15]

4. Barber (1999) described the well-preserved mummies found in the Tarim Basin of China. "One of these was a 1,000-year-old man who was about 6' 6" tall, with light brown hair; he wore white deerskin boots and (*bright / brightly*) colored woolen pants, shirt and felt leggings."[16]

5. Each person is a composite of many qualities. One's personality is influenced by abilities, temperament, talents, (*physical / physically*) structure, (*emotional / emotionally*) tendencies, ideas, ideals, skills, motives, memories, goals, values, moods, attitudes, feelings, beliefs, habits, and behavior. These (*high / highly*) individualized qualities make up a personality. The influences of heredity, social and cultural contacts, education, and experience also contribute significantly to one's personality.[17]

CHART 5-4 Order of Premodifiers in Noun Phrases

Most noun phrases include no more than three or four premodifiers. Different categories, or types, of modifiers usually appear before the head noun in the order shown below. Adjectives in the same category may be separated with commas or the word *and*. Colors are usually separated by *and* or dashes.

Determiners	Adverb(s)	Adjectives			Nouns	
		Number(s)	General	Physical description	Noun modifier(s)	Head noun
		1. ordinal 2. cardinal		1. size 2. shape 3. age 4. color	1. possessive nouns 2. origin 3. material 4. other nouns	
a			passing			*fad*
the		first two	ethnic			*groups*
some					member	*nations*
that	magnificently		creative	embroidered		*skirt*
his			tattered	black-and-white		*jacket*
					Ana's French silk	*dress*

Identifying Word Order in Noun Phrases

Underline the noun phrases in the following sentences. Then enter each noun phrase into the appropriate column of the chart below, using Chart 5-4 as a model.

1. The bright red-orange silk garment of Afghanistan has tiny knife pleats.[18]
2. The interior of a sixteenth-century Dutch room shows the use of predominantly horizontal lines.[19]
3. . . . Portuguese women continue to wear a vertically striped woven skirt with a heavily embroidered border.[20]
4. Spanish men will continue to wear . . . a well-fitted short jacket with trousers and a wide-brimmed sombrero.[21]
5. The saffron-robed monks of the Buddhist faith wear a specially draped garment of an intense yellow-orange color. [22]

Determiners	Adverb(s)	Adjectives			Nouns	
		Number(s)	General	Physical description	Noun modifier(s)	Head noun
		1. ordinal 2. cardinal		1. size 2. shape 3. age 4. color	1. possessive nouns 2. origin 3. material 4. other nouns	
1.						
2.						
3.						
4.						
5.						

Exercise 6 Completing Sentences with Noun Phrases

Reorder the words in parentheses to complete the sentences.

1. At the end of the twentieth century, _____ (young / university / artistic / some / students) wore _____ (pants and / leather / black) (green and red / long / hair).

2. _____ (blue / close-fitting / jeans and) (red / sneakers / high-top / bright) were popular in _____ (twenty-first / early / the / century).

3. _____ (international / fashionable / a few / students) carry _____ (shiny / backpacks / pink).

4. _____ (designers / several / fashion) are showing _____ (floor-length / sequined / dresses / extravagantly).

5. _____ (American / T-shirts / popular / many) are made in (countries / different / a number of).

Exercise 7 Error Analysis

The following passage contains ten errors. The first error is corrected for you. Work in pairs to find and correct nine more. Compare your answers with your classmates'.

Fashion before the Civil War

Before the Civil War*, wealthy gentlemen in the South often wore suits with patterned trousers, plain-colored vests, brightly ~~coloring~~ *colored* ties, and long velvet-collared jackets. On their heads they wore tallest black, silk top hats, and for travelling they wore overcoats with a kind of cape around their shoulders. Men also were likely to carry a cane.

Women in the South wore hoop skirts wide with stiffly crinoline petticoats underneath. Around the waist a decorate belt or sash often ran to the hem of the skirt. A Southern woman of that era might have worn a colorfully embroider satin hoop skirt or an elegantly layer lace skirt. The Civil War–era hoop skirt was an extraordinary difficult skirt to move around in because it was such an enormously wide piece of clothing. The hoop skirt was also tricky to sit in due to its well-know tendency to fly up over the woman's head just as she was sitting down. Greatly care had to be taken to control the round hoops and hold the skirt firmly in place. Women of the Civil War–era spent much of their time standing up.

Women wearing Civil War–era hoop skirts

*The American Civil War (1861–1865) was a war fought between the Northern states and the Southern states. It is sometimes referred to as the War between the States.

Exercise 8 Using Noun Phrases to Improve Your Writing

Work in pairs to combine the short sentences into one sentence that contains a noun phrase. Make sure the modifiers in the noun phrase are in the correct order.

1. The man wore boots and pants. The boots were deerskin. The boots were white. The pants were brightly colored.

   The man wore white deerskin boots and brightly colored pants.

2. By the 1920s, women's dress and women's suffrage had undergone changes. The changes were revolutionary.

3. The universal use of jeans made pants fashionable. The jeans were body-conforming. The pants were tight.

4. The shirt became colored and patterned. The shirt was standard. The shirt was a businessman's shirt. The shirt was white. The shirt was a dress shirt.

5. A sari and jewelry express the economic wealth of the bride. The sari is richly brocaded. The jewelry is heavy. The jewelry is gold.

6. Pantsuits were introduced into fashion in the middle of the 1960s. The pantsuits were women's pantsuits. The fashion was European. The fashion was high fashion.

7. The performers of the 1960s were leaders. The performers were flamboyantly dressed. The performers were rock-and-roll performers. The leaders were popular. The leaders were fashion leaders.

Exercise 9 **Writing Sentences with Noun Phrases**

Work in pairs. Use the vocabulary from this chapter—see the following suggestions—and your own words to write five original sentences about the clothing of the people shown in the photos. Include in your sentences noun phrases containing combinations of determiners, adverbs, adjectives, noun modifiers, and head nouns. You can refer to the charts in this chapter for help. Take turns sharing and commenting on each others' sentences in small groups.

ADVERBS

brightly	extremely	highly	incredibly	inordinately	newly	richly

ADJECTIVES

artistic	body-conforming	brocaded	close	colored	dark-colored
decorative	distinct	distinctive	fashionable	feminine	heavy
high	intricate	long	manual	masculine	patterned
physical	revolutionary	short	similar	socioeconomic	soft-collared
standard	stiff	tight	universal	well-known	woolen
wrapped					

NOUN MODIFIERS

attaché	clothing	cotton	English	European	fashion	female
gold	male	play	top-of-the-line	wool	work	

HEAD NOUNS

attire	body	boots	case	color	exertion	fabric
fad	fashion	feature	femininity	garment	gender	hairstyle
hem	jeans	levels	masculinity	men	pants	pantsuit
pattern	personality	pockets	popularity	practice	purse	qualities
shirt	shoes	skirt	stars	suit	symbol	tradition
trousers	waist	women				

Exercise 10 Apply It to Speaking

In small groups, discuss the questions below. To prepare, jot down some noun phrases that you can use to make your points and give examples.

1. How are your clothing styles different from the clothes your parents wore?
2. How do celebrities (actors, musicians, athletes, and other famous people) influence fashion today?

Exercise 11 Apply It to Speaking

Give a brief presentation to a small group in which you describe an article or style of clothing that is worn to show gender, age, or marriageability in your culture or another culture that you know about. Use noun phrases to provide detail in your description, and support it with specific examples. See the example below for the beginning of a presentation. See Appendix B for help.

EXAMPLE:

> In Japan, the color of the kimono was used to show age. Young children and marriageable young women wore brightly colored and gaily patterned kimonos. Dark kimonos of a solid color were for the mature, including married women. . . .

Exercise 12 Apply It to Writing

Write a brief paragraph that describes a clothing fashion that interests you. Explain who wears it, when it is worn, and how it looks. Use noun phrases to "paint a picture with words." You can refer to the example that follows. See Appendix B for help.

EXAMPLE:

> One of the most interesting fashions in clothing to me is the pajama bottoms and slippers that many university students wear to class instead of blue jeans and athletic shoes. This sloppy style always makes me think that the student probably didn't have time to get dressed before leaving his or her room, but I know that it is a style choice, not a necessity. . . .

Elements of Noun Phrases: Postmodifiers

Traditional Portuguese dress

VOCABULARY   Here are some words that you will encounter in Chapter 6. How much do you know about each word? Turn to Appendix A to assess and expand your word knowledge.

accessories	apparel	austere	designate	elaborate
excess	magnificent	opulent	striped	sweeping

Prepare to Read

The member states of the European Union (EU) each have their own, traditional forms of dress. Does your culture have clothing that is worn only on special occasions? What are the occasions? Describe the clothing worn for these events.

Read the following passage from *Individuality in Clothing Selection and Personal Appearance*, 7th Edition, by Suzanne G. Marshall, Hazel O. Jackson, and M. Sue Stanley.[1]

Sumptuary Laws and Clothing

[1]A study **of historical and cultural dress** reveals an aspect **of clothing** that is related to legal code. By regulating style and personal expenditure **of dress**, sumptuary laws **in many societies** have perpetuated distinctions **in social class**.

[2]Many examples of sumptuary laws were found in Western Europe before the European unification. As the business classes gained wealth, they were able to challenge the status of royalty by purchasing the opulent apparel of the royal courts. Sumptuary laws were enacted to restrict individual clothing choices in color, motif, and style that designated rank, class, and position within the society. These laws maintained class distinctions. Sumptuary laws have often promoted extreme excesses and exaggerations before the style dies. During the 1300s, French court dress was rich and opulent. Footwear was used to show social status. Shoes, **known** as *poulaines*, had long, pointed toes.

[3]Commoners found ways to circumvent* sumptuary laws. Magnificent, creative stitchery appeared on many regional peasant costumes. The cut and cloth of these garments were decreed by law, but the surface enrichment did not break the law and yet expressed individuality. Other examples can be found in the paintings of the Dutch masters **showing** wealthy businessmen and their families. The clothing is austere, but elegant petticoats peep out from under skirts, and beautiful ermine and mink pelts adorn capes and tunics. . . .

[4]Most of the **recorded** history of Japan includes the use of sumptuary laws such as that affecting the development of the Japanese kimono. . . . A series of sumptuary laws were passed that prescribed dress for the various classes. The penalty for violation of these laws was death. These sumptuary laws brought **sweeping** change in the decoration of the kimono.[2]

circumvent—to avoid or evade

Review the Ideas

1. How have many societies perpetuated distinctions in social class?
2. What are sumptuary laws? Why were they enacted?
3. How did commoners circumvent sumptuary laws?
4. What was the punishment for disobeying the sumptuary laws in Japan?

Analyze the Grammar

1. Look at the boldfaced phrases in paragraph 1. What are they called?
2. What kinds of words do you see in the phrases in paragraph 1?
3. What general statement can you make about the position of these phrases in relation to the nouns they modify?
4. Look at the boldfaced words in paragraphs 2, 3, and 4. What are they called?
5. What general statement can you make about the positions of these words in relation to the nouns they modify?

CHART 6-1 — Postmodifiers: Nouns and Adjectives

Nouns, adjectives, and phrases that follow the nouns they modify are called postmodifiers.

As we saw in Chart 4-3

1. nouns often function as subject complements after the linking verbs *be* and *become*;

    subject (noun)   linking verb   subject complement (noun)
1. The men <u>became</u> **businessmen.**

2. adjectives often function as subject complements after certain linking and perception verbs, such as *appear*, *feel*, *seem*, *smell*, *sound*, *taste*, and *look*;

    subject (noun)   perception verb subject complement (adjective)
2. The fashion <u>looked</u> **masculine.**

3. nouns may follow direct objects as object complements after certain verbs, such as *make*, *call*, *name*, and *elect*;

    direct object (noun)   object complement (noun)
3. Men called <u>the hairstyle</u> **the ducktail.**

4. adjectives may follow direct objects as object complements after certain verbs, such as *make*, *wear*, and *cut*.

    direct object (noun)   object complement (adjective)
4. Men wore <u>their hair</u> **long** in the 1980s.

Exercise 1 — Identifying Postmodifiers of Nouns

With a partner, read the following passage.

    During the 1300s, French court dress was rich and opulent. Long, pointed shoes became symbols of wealth. At the same time, the court made up new laws about how common people could dress. The court named the laws sumptuary laws. Sumptuary laws requiring common people to wear only plain material were strict, so commoners made their clothing austere. However, in spite of the laws, commoners wore their petticoats beautifully decorated and their regional costumes handsomely embroidered.

Now, together, find and underline an example of each of the following postmodifiers in the passage. On a separate sheet of paper, write out the sentence in which each one appears.

1. A noun functioning as a subject complement
2. An adjective functioning as a subject complement
3. A noun functioning as an object complement
4. An adjective functioning as an object complement

CHART 6-2 — Prepositional Phrases and Participles

1. Prepositional phrases can follow head nouns to describe them.

a. Prepositional phrases modify the head noun.

    hn   prep phrase
a. the rate **of migration**

b. With successive prepositional phrases, each phrase describes the head noun just before it.

    hn   prep phrase and hn   prep phrase
b. the rate **of migration of people**

2. Participles

a. Present and past participles may appear before or after head nouns.	past participle hn present participle a. an **embroidered** border **running** along the top
b. A participle that precedes a head noun may be preceded by an adverb.	adverb past participle hn present participle b. a **heavily embroidered** border **running** along the top
c. Present participles describe the actions or conditions of the head noun. They are active ideas.	hn present participle hn present participle c. a photograph **showing** a man **leaning** over a bowl
d. Past participles describe actions that happen to or affect the head noun. They are passive ideas.	hn past participle d. the types of clothing **worn** for protection

3. Participles and prepositional phrases can follow a head noun in either order.

a. A participle and a prepositional phrase sometimes follow the head noun.	participle prepositional phrase a. the social values **associated with a fit body**
b. Sometimes the participle follows the prepositional phrase.	hn prepositional phrase b. . . . caverns **in the French Pyrenees** participle **known** as Trois Frères

Exercise 2 Identifying Prepositional Phrases in Noun Phrases

With a partner, find and underline the prepositional phrases used as postmodifiers in the following paragraphs. Draw an arrow that points to the head noun each phrase modifies. Draw a box around the modified head noun. A head noun can be part of a prepositional phrase. The first two are done for you.

Over the years, the rate of migration of people from one geographical area to another has increased dramatically. These ethnic, cultural, and subcultural groups bring with them symbols of community and culture. Migrants may have multiple and complex relationships with both their homelands and their new places of settlement (Haung, Teo, and Yeoh, 2000). Within the context of a particular geographical location these ideas and symbols are borrowed, shared, mixed, blended, and reinterpreted.[3]

On special occasions, Portuguese women will continue to wear a vertically striped woven skirt, in red, with a heavily embroidered border. Spanish males will continue to wear, for special occasions, a well-fitted short jacket and trousers and a wide-brimmed sombrero. French older women may continue to wear the working dress of the fisherman's wife. And so from Germany to Belgium, the Netherlands, Luxembourg, the U.K., Sweden, Finland, Denmark, Austria, and Italy the practice of wearing traditional dress for special occasions will continue.[4]

Exercise 3 Identifying Participles in Noun Phrases

Find and underline the present and past participles in the noun phrases in the following passages.

1. During the Cultural Revolution in China, the clothing commonly worn was known as the Mao suit.[5]

2. During the 1960s, hairstyles were influenced by rock-and-roll stars led by Elvis Presley and the Beatles.[6]

3. Clothing and accessories, such as "cooling" headbands, have also been designed to control body heat when at work or play in hot environments.[7]

4. Two devastating fires, in Edo (1657) and in Kyoto (1661), destroyed the possessions of most Japanese. To replace the kimonos lost in these fires, the weavers and dyers were forced to develop quicker and simpler methods.[8]

5. Over the years the rate of migration of people from one geographical area to another has increased dramatically. Today, the term *diaspora* refers to various ethnic-group communities living outside of their land of origin.[9]

6. Coulson (1999) studied snapshots of daily life as revealed through paintings on rocks at least 4,000 years old in Northern Africa. These included female figures "with tulip-shaped heads and hourglass bodies," approximately 2,500 years old, "drawings of body painting" and a "seven inch photograph named 'the Hairdresser' showing one man leaning over a bowl while another carefully washes his long hair."[10]

7. Today's skiwear follows somewhat the characteristics of types of clothing worn for maximum protection from the cold. Capitalizing on the quality and high performance of fabric made from synthetic fibers and many fiber variants, companies have developed high-fashion and high-quality skiwear that is durable, waterproof, and breatheable.[11]

8. In Japan, the kimono is held together with an obi, a band of decorated cloth about 5 yards long and a foot wide. The way the obi is tied indicates the wearer's marital state. On her wedding day, the bride wears the obi tied in a butterfly bow straight across the back or at an angle as young girls do.[12]

9. On special occasions, Portuguese women will continue to wear a vertically striped woven skirt, in red, with a heavily embroidered border. Spanish males will continue to wear, for special occasions, a well-fitted short jacket and trousers and a wide-brimmed sombrero. French older women may continue to wear the working dress of the fisherman's wife. And so from Germany to Belgium, the Netherlands, Luxembourg, the U.K., Sweden, Finland, Denmark, Austria, and Italy the practice of wearing traditional dress for special occasions will continue.[13]

Exercise 4 Identifying Participles and Prepositional Phrases in Noun Phrases

1 Find and underline the participles and participles plus prepositional phrases used as postmodifiers in the following paragraph. Draw an arrow to show the modified head noun. The first one is done for you.

2 There are also three participles used as premodifiers. Circle each one and draw an arrow to its head noun. Draw a box around the head noun.

Prehistoric cave paintings have preserved the images of the clothing and adornment of early people. One of the oldest depictions is in the caverns in the French Pyrenees known as Trois Frères, dated as being created 20 to 30,000 years ago. The cave paintings show a man wearing animal skins and a headpiece. It appears that he was a hunter disguised as an animal. It has long been assumed that the first clothing was the skin of an animal killed for food. Archaeological evidence for this comes from the Paleolithic period (the Old Stone Age). Prepared skins could be cut and shaped. Pieces of skin are likely to have been stitched together by looping and knotting lengths of sinew (or plant fibre) through holes in the skin, even before the invention of the eyed needle. . . . A recent excavation of a Paleolithic site at Qeqertasussuk in Greenland yielded many fine bone needles and the earliest remains of stitched-skin clothing preserved in permafrost. . . . The use of plant fibres before wool confirms findings from excavations of Swiss Neolithic Lake Dwellings. . . . His [the man depicted in the cave painting] clothing was in layers: under the cape he had a skin jerkin or tunic and under this was a loin-cloth held from the same belt (Ryder, 2000). . . .[14]

Exercise 5 **Error Analysis**

The following excerpt from a student essay contains ten errors. The first error is corrected for you. Work in pairs to find and correct nine more.

Why Do People Wear Clothing?

Many early civilizations lived in tropical or semitropical climates with warm or hot temperatures. People in those regions did not need protection from the weather. They wore clothing ~~shown~~ *showing* wealth and status.

Another function to clothing is psychological protection. People in many places believe that they need protection against illnesses, droughts, and floods caused by evil spirits. Certain beads wearing by women and children in Southeast Asia protect them from evil powers.

A third function of clothing is for modesty. Modesty, meaning the psychological need to cover a part of the body, exists in most societies. However, different societies have differed ideas about which parts of the body need to be covered. Modesty is a culturally determine concept. Children are not born with a sense of modesty. The sense of modesty learning by children as they grow up differs from culture to culture.

It is interesting to note that the sense of modesty about a particular culture may change over time. An example of the changing concept of modesty is the difference between nineteenth- and twenty-first-century attitudes in America. In the nineteenth century, it was considered immodest to show one's legs or even say the word *leg*. In the twenty-first century, showing one's legs is something considering completely normal.

A fourth function of clothing is adornment. Clothing used for adornment is quite different from clothing worn at psychological protection. Adornment may indicate wealth, age, and gender. Bodies adorned with appealing clothing, jewelry, and hairstyles may enhance a person's status or indicate membership in a particular social group. People wearing permanent adornments such as tattoos indicate lasting cultural conventions. The Masai women by Kenya wear shaved heads and beaded ornaments on their heads and around their necks.

CHART 6-3　Forming Sentences with Participles

When short sentences are combined, the repeated noun is omitted, and the verb of the second sentence is changed to a participle.	The cave painting shows **a man**. **The man** is wearing animal skins and a headpiece.
Combine the short sentences:	
a. The first short sentence begins the combined sentence.	a. The cave painting shows a man
b. In the second sentence, the repeated word "man" and the article "the" are deleted. The verb "is wearing" is reduced to the present participle "wearing."	b. ~~the man is~~ wearing animal skins and a headpiece.
c. The two sentences are combined into one.	c. The cave painting shows a man **wearing** animal skins and a headpiece.
When participial phrases are formed, all active verbs change to the *-ing* form (present participle) and all passive verbs lose their auxiliary verbs and use only the past participle. This will be covered extensively in Parts 3 and 4 when reduced adjective and adverb clauses are discussed.	

Exercise 6　Using Participles to Present Information Efficiently

On a separate sheet of paper, combine each pair of short sentences into a sentence with a noun phrase containing a participial phrase.

1. It appears that he was a hunter.
   The hunter was disguised as an animal.

2. It has long been assumed that the first clothing was the skin of an animal.
   The animal was killed for food.

3. Skins could be cut and shaped.
   The skins were prepared.

4. The clothing was stitched-skin.
   The clothing was preserved in permafrost.

5. His clothing was in layers: Under the cape he had a skin jerkin or tunic, and under this was a loincloth.
   The loincloth was held from the same belt.

6. Sumptuary laws brought change.
   The change was sweeping.

7. Waist-length hair was the fashion.
   The hair was parted in the center and was hanging.

Exercise 7 Apply It to Speaking

Discuss the following questions in a small group. Then share your conclusions with the class, backing them up with examples. Use pre- and postmodifiers in your descriptions.

1. How did you dress for school during your high school years? Was there a required uniform or an informal "uniform" or style that was typical?
2. Did typical attire for boys and girls differ?
3. What did students' choices of attire indicate about them?

Exercise 8 Apply It to Speaking

Prepare a brief presentation (two to three minutes) on the following topic. See Appendix B for help.

Some businesses seem to have a dress code (rules about what one can and cannot wear). For example, some businesses forbid women to wear sleeveless blouses in the office. Based on the businesspeople you have seen, how would you describe the dress code for businessmen and businesswomen who work in offices where you live? How do dress codes differ in other professions, such as teaching or medicine?

Follow these steps:

1 Make a list of phrases you can use to describe the clothes worn in these professions. Include as many postmodifiers as you can.
2 Prepare and practice your presentation.
3 Give your presentation and answer any questions your classmates may have.

EXAMPLE:

People in offices in my country wear formal clothes. The clothes worn by both men and women are very similar. For example, I have noticed men wearing three-piece suits with ties. Women usually wear suits or dresses with long skirts.

Exercise 9 Apply It to Writing

Write a paragraph or two that describe a dress code in a place or at an event that you know well. Support your ideas with specific examples. Use as many postmodifiers as you can. Answer the following questions as you plan your paragraphs. See Appendix B for help.

1. What place or event are you going to describe?
2. What kinds of clothes are men expected to wear? Describe them.
3. What kinds of clothes are women expected to wear? Describe them.
4. What clothes would be inappropriate for this place or event?

Use some of the words from this chapter in your paragraphs.

| accessories | apparel | austere | designate | elaborate | excess | faded |
| magnificent | opulent | patched | sloppy | striped | sweeping | |

EXAMPLE:

An event that I know well is a horse show. Horse shows have a definite dress code depending on what kind of horse show they are. A Western horse show requires both male and female participants to wear tight blue jeans and a leather belt covered in elaborate silver decorations, cowboy boots with ornate embossed designs, Western-style shirts in bright colors, and opulent cowboy hats in a neutral color. A person wearing sloppy jeans with stains or patches and old-looking boots will never receive a prize.

Putting It All Together

Traditional business suits

Read the following passages from *Individuality in Clothing Selection and Personal Appearance,* 7th Edition, by Suzanne G. Marshall, Hazel O. Jackson, and M. Sue Stanley.[1]

Traditional Business Dress

[1]According to Stephen S. Roach, economist for Morgan Stanley, 75 percent of America's 12.3 million jobs added between 1994 and 2000 were white-collar occupations (Koretz, 2001). Many of these workers are required to dress formally in a manner that will inspire confidence and will not attract inappropriate attention. . . .

[2]Most professionals describe the traditional man's business suit complete with shirt and tie, and the female version of the business suit as "power clothes," appropriate for professional meetings. However, this same business suit is a power garment only when it is appropriate to the occasion. It would be an inappropriate choice to wear to a job where no one in authority dresses in business suits. Power dressing is achieved only when the outfits worn are accepted by the people in control of the situation and considered by them to be appropriate for the wearer and the occasion. . . .

[3]For men, the dress rules are specific: Traditional business dress consists of matched business suits with a dress shirt and tie and understated accessories in the best quality one can afford. For women, a well-tailored business suit and a silk blouse of good quality is the basic uniform. Women can sometimes vary this look with dresses or a pants suit. For women, the rules still include no plunging necklines or loud colors and no see-through, clingy, or glittery fabrics. . . .

Business Casual Dress

[4]Business casual dress began in the 1990s as a notion called "casual Fridays." By 2001 more than 50% of companies permitted casual wear every day. . . . Companies opting for casual business wear include IBM, once an icon of traditional professional dress; many motion picture production companies; and the big automobile makers. The popular men's uniform for business casual is often khakis, open-collared shirts, and loafers. This look is being nudged aside for a slightly more polished look of well-cut trousers, button-down shirts, or tailored clothing, both worn with polished leather footwear. . . .

[5]Jay Friedman, group president of Hartmarx's HMX sportswear division, calls the sportcoat "the completer" of a business casual wardrobe. He recommends a wardrobe of "seven easy pieces" for men of which the sportcoat is the anchor. . . .

[6]Judith Rasband also recommends clothing clusters for women that center around a small group of coordinated clothing usually five to ten pieces plus coordinating accessories (Dodd, 2000). . . .

Shoes

[7]Businessmen's shoes work best in colors darker than the suit they are worn with, which makes brown or black shoes a good choice for most suits. Brown is more stylishly flexible and has long been the top choice among European men. The classic men's tie shoe is the wingtip or oxford. . . .

(continued on next page)

Ties

[6]Ties focus the attention toward the face. High-quality ties are made of silk so that they add light to the face. . . . Many American men gave up tie-wearing years ago. . . . "Power is being able to dress the way you want," says Marty Staff, CEO of JA Apparel Corporation (Smith, 2008a, A1). Even designer Tom Ford, who designed $195 ties produced in Italy, states that men can wear a tailored suit without a tie and still look appropriate (Smith, 2008b).[2]

Review the Ideas

1. According to the passage, how are many workers in white-collar occupations required to dress?
2. Describe men's and women's traditional business dress.
3. How does business casual dress differ from traditional business dress?

Exercise 1 Analysis of the Reading Passage

1 Paragraph 1: Draw boxes around the head nouns.

2 Paragraph 2: Underline the one example of a past participle (postmodifier) and draw an arrow to the head noun it describes. Draw a box around the head noun.

3 Paragraph 3: Underline four examples of prepositional phrases (postmodifiers) that describe a head noun and draw arrows to the head nouns. Draw boxes around the head nouns.

4 Paragraph 3: Underline four examples of participles (premodifiers) that describe a head noun and draw arrows to the head nouns. Draw boxes around the head nouns.

5 Paragraph 4: Underline and label a subject complement (sc).

6 Paragraph 5: Underline and label a direct object (do) and an object complement (oc).

7 Paragraphs 5 and 6: Underline two appositives and draw an arrow from each appositive to the head noun it modifies. Draw boxes around the head nouns.

8 List five examples of noun phrases that contain pre- and postmodifiers by completing the chart below.

Premodifier	Head Noun	Postmodifier
1.		
2.		
3.		
4.		
5.		

Exercise 2 Identifying Noun Functions

In the following sentences, underline and label these noun functions: subject = s; direct object = do; indirect object = io; subject complement = sc; object complement = oc; appositive = a; and prepositional phrase = pp.

1. For women, a well-tailored business suit and a silk blouse of good quality is the basic uniform.[3]

2. Women can sometimes vary this look with dresses or a pants suit.[4]

3. High-quality ties are made of silk so that they add light to the face.[5]

4. Jay Friedman, group president of Hartmarx's HMX sportswear division, calls the sportcoat "the completer" of a business casual wardrobe.[6]

5. According to Stephen S. Roach, economist for Morgan Stanley, 75 percent of America's 12.3 million jobs added between 1994 and 2000 were white-collar occupations (Koretz, 2001).[7]

6. Today individuals are not bound by narrow standards of dress. An enormous variety of styles allows people the opportunity for self expression and individuality in dress.[8]

Exercise 3 Analyzing Grammatical Structures in a Text

Discuss the following questions with a small group of classmates.

1 In paragraphs 2 and 3 of the reading passage (included below), how does the addition of participles and prepositional phrases that modify head nouns affect the meaning and impact of the sentences they are in? Draw a box around the participles and double lines under prepositional phrases. Then discuss how the sentences would sound without those pre- and postmodifiers.

[2]Most professionals describe the traditional man's business suit complete with shirt and tie, and the female version of the business suit as "power clothes," appropriate for professional meetings. However, this same business suit is a power garment only when it is appropriate to the occasion. It would be an inappropriate choice to wear to a job where no one in authority dresses in business suits. Power dressing is achieved only when the outfits worn are accepted by the people in control of the situation and considered by them to be appropriate for the wearer and the occasion. . . .

[3]For men, the dress rules are specific: Traditional business dress consists of matched business suits with a dress shirt and tie and understated accessories in the best quality one can afford. For women, a well-tailored business suit and a silk blouse of good quality is the basic uniform. Women can sometimes vary this look with dresses or a pants suit. For women, the rules still include no plunging necklines or loud colors and no see-through, clingy, or glittery fabrics. . . .

(continued on next page)

2 In paragraph 4 (included below), how does the addition of adverbs, adjectives, and nouns affect the sentences? Which nouns act as modifiers? Draw a circle around the adverb that modifies a noun phrase, draw a box around each adjective, underline each noun, and draw two lines under each noun modifier. Imagine the sentences without the adjectives and noun modifiers. How interesting and meaningful would they be?

⁴Business casual dress began in the 1990s as a notion called "casual Fridays." By 2001 more than 50% of companies permitted casual wear every day. . . . Companies opting for casual business wear include IBM, once an icon of traditional professional dress; many motion picture production companies; and the big automobile makers. The popular men's uniform for business casual is often khakis, open-collared shirts, and loafers. This look is being nudged aside for a slightly more polished look of well-cut trousers, button-down shirts, or tailored clothing, both worn with polished leather footwear. . . .

Exercise 4 **Error Analysis**

The following excerpt from a student essay contains ten errors. The first error is corrected for you. Work in pairs to find and correct nine more.

Clothing on Campus

Do university students all over the world dress the same? When I first came to this university, I thought that the students here dressed just the same as the students in my country: T-shirts and shorts or blue jeans and colorful sneakers *for* at the men, and shorts, skirts, fashionably stylishly tops, and the latest shoe styles for the women. However, after I was here for a while, I began to notice that there are actually several dress styles on campus correspond to three social groups: "the jocks," "the geeks," and "the Goths."

First are the jocks. The jocks are the athletes. There is a noticeable group of men and women on campus that are either members of the university athletic teams or play intramural sports. This group is always wearing the latest styles in athletic fashions. You can see these students dresses in designer sporting apparel from the best designers. Their careful chosen outfits always look perfectly put together. The jocks look like they've just stepped out of the shower.

The second group, the geeks, are sometimes called "computer nerds." This group wears a uniformly of dark-framed glasses and short-sleeves plaid cotton shirts and beige polyester pants, or plain T-shirts and jeans. A hooded sweatshirt wearing as a jacket is their preferred everyday fashion. Geeks usually carry a heavy black laptop bag and often look like they have just gotten out of bed.

The third group, the Goths, are usually art or theater majors. This group is distinguished to the others by the color of their hair. Wildly arranged shocking pink, fluorescent-green, or purple hair is common. Goths dress in all black attire with net stockings and tall buckled boots. Both men and women wear heavy eye black makeup and sometimes black lipstick as well. Goth jewelry consists of leather-studded collars and many body piercings. Multiple silver nose rings, lip studs, and earrings are the rule.

Of course, there are other groups and probably their dress styles correspond to social groups, too, but the jocks, the geeks, and the Goths have been the most interesting to me since I arrived.

WHAT DID YOU LEARN?

Review the forms and functions of noun phrases in this chapter. Do the exercises below. Then check your answers in Appendix D.

A Noun Functions

Underline the nouns in the following sentences. Write the function of each noun above it. Use these abbreviations: subject = s; direct object = do; indirect object = io; object of a preposition = op; subject complement = sc; object complement = oc; appositive = a.

1. Possessions are indicators of economic position.

2. Experts call the concept body image.

3. They coined the expression *white-collar worker*.

4. During the 1960s, young women grew their hair as long as possible.

5. Spectator sports clothing—athleisure—paralleled development of participant sports apparel.

6. Clothing choices give people information.

7. In the 1980s, hair-care products became big business.

B Elements of Noun Phrases

Label the words in the following noun phrases. Use these abbreviations: determiner = det; adjective = adj; adverb = adv; noun modifier = nm; head noun = hn; preposition = prep; participle = part.

1. some magnificent creative stitchery
2. the increasingly global designer influence
3. body-conforming jeans worn by men
4. rich and powerful English businessmen
5. highly appropriate work and play garments for women
6. flamboyantly dressed rock-and-roll stars
7. the standard businessmen's white dress shirt
8. dark kimonos in a solid color for women

C Order of Elements in a Noun Phrase

Unscramble the following words to form noun phrases with the correct word order.

1. lowly / tasks / manual

_____

2. regional / many / costumes / peasant

_____

3. the / Afghanistan / bright / red-orange / garment / of / silk

_____

4. somber-colored / dresses / body-concealing

_____

5. embroidered / vertically / border / striped / skirt / with / a / woven / heavily / a

_____

6. lines / clean / uncluttered / body-conforming

_____

7. fisherman's / the / dress / of / the / wife / working

_____

8. stitched-skin / in / preserved / permafrost / clothing

_____

How did you do? Are there topics you need to review?

Exercise 5 Apply It to Speaking

With a small group of classmates, prepare a brief presentation (two to three minutes) about clothing trends you've noticed among today's students. Follow these steps:

1 Brainstorm current clothing trends among students. For example, consider trends among: students from China, Japan, Russia, or Malaysia; students who belong to fraternities or sororities; students who admire sports teams; or students who don't care about fashion.

2 Make a list of noun phrases you can use to describe these trends, for example, *colorful high-top shoes*; *long, straight hair*; *status clothing*; *spectator sports apparel*; *body-conforming jeans*; and *dirty white T-shirts*.

3 Prepare and practice your presentation. See Appendix B for help preparing your presentation.

4 Give your presentation.

Exercise 6 Apply It to Writing

Write a paragraph about traditional clothing popular in your country.
Follow these steps:

1 Choose the clothing you will write about.

2 Answer these questions about the clothing:

- What does it look like?
- Who wears it?
- When (on what occasions) is it worn?
- Why do people wear this clothing?

3 Use your answers to the questions to write your paragraph. See Appendix B for help.

4 Check your paragraph to make sure you have included varied noun phrases to make your descriptions interesting and informative.

A woman in a sari

Check Your Writing

Which of the following noun functions and elements of noun phrases did you use in your paragraph? Did you use them correctly? Is the word order in each of your premodifiers and postmodifiers correct?

- ☐ Nouns as subjects and objects
- ☐ Nouns as complements
- ☐ Nouns as appositives
- ☐ Determiners, adverbs, adjectives, and nouns before nouns
- ☐ Correct word order in noun phrases
- ☐ Participles before or after nouns
- ☐ Prepositional phrases after nouns

PART 3

Adjective Clauses and Phrases: Adding Description, Prediction, Historical Explanation, and Emphasis

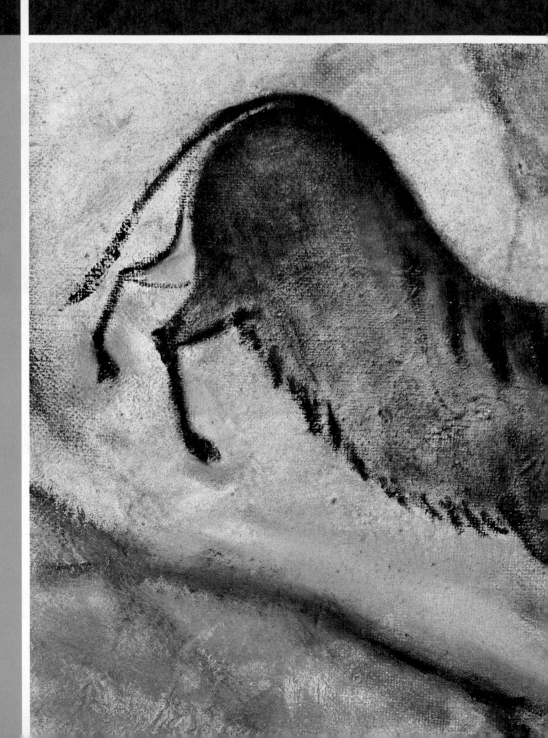

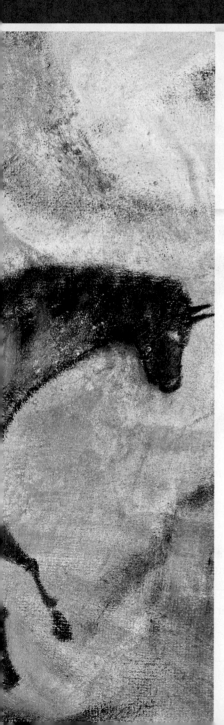

OBJECTIVES

In Part 3 of the *Advanced Grammar* course you will

- review the forms and functions of adjective clauses.

- understand and use adjective clauses, adjective phrases, appositives, and divided (cleft) sentences to emphasize one part of a sentence in academic contexts.

Adjective clauses and related structures add interest, detail, and depth to writing without adding a great deal of extra length.

Academic texts about history serve to illustrate how authors write concisely, including descriptions or background information, for example, within individual sentences, rather than in many separate sentences. Becoming comfortable with adjective clauses will help prepare you to read academic books and to communicate effectively at the university level.

Paleolithic cave art,
Cave of Altamira, Spain

Review of Adjective Clauses

Reconstruction of Ötzi, the 5,000-year-old man found buried in ice in the Ötztal Alps in 1991

VOCABULARY   Here are some words that you will encounter in Chapter 7. How much do you
know about each word? Turn to Appendix A to assess and expand your word knowledge.

blade	contemporary	decade	descendant	nomadic
peasant	remains	sophistication	trait	weapon

What do you imagine life was like for the very early humans who lived thousands of years ago?

Read the following passage from *Civilization in the West,* Volume I, *To 1715,* 6th Edition, by Mark Kishlansky, Patrick Geary, and Patricia O'Brien.[1]

Ötzi, the 5,000-Year-Old Man

[1]The tools, weapons, and clothes found with the remains of a man **who** died five thousand years ago in the Alps show the technological accomplishments of humans before civilization.

[2]Most of us never knew our great-grandparents; thus, it seems all the more incredible that we can visit with an ancestor from three hundred generations past—the dawn of civilization. And yet a discovery in the Italian Alps a decade ago has brought us face to face with Ötzi (so-named for the valley **where** he was found), an ordinary man **who** faced a cruel death more than five thousand years ago. Ötzi's perfectly preserved body, clothing, tools, and weapons allow us to know how people lived and died in Western Europe before it was Europe—before indeed it was the West.

[3]Ötzi was small by modern European standards: he stood at just 5 feet 4 inches. Around 40 years old, he was probably a senior and respected member of his community. Already he was suffering from arthritis, and tattoos on his left wrist, right knee, calves, ankles, and the lumbar region of his spine suggest that, just as in some nomadic societies today, he and his companions used tattooing as a kind of therapy. He probably lived in a village below the mountain **whose** inhabitants lived from hunting, simple agriculture, and goat herding. . . .

[4]Ötzi traveled light, but he had with him all that he needed to provide for himself. He carried an ax, **whose** 60-centimeter yew-wood haft ended in a blade of almost pure copper, and a flint knife with an ash-wood handle secured to his belt in a fiber scabbard. In a pouch he carried a tool made of stag antler and limewood **with which** he could chip new flint tools. He secured his leather backpack on a pack-frame made of a long hazel rod bent into a U shape and reinforced with two narrow wooden slats. Among other things it held birch-bark containers, one filled with materials to start a fire, **which** he could ignite with a flint he carried in his pouch. He also equipped himself with a simple first aid kit consisting of inner bark from the birch tree, a substance with antibiotic and styptic properties.

[5]For so small a man, Ötzi carried an imposing weapon, but unfortunately for him it was not yet finished. Near his body was found a yew-wood bow almost six feet long and a quiver of arrows. He must have been working on the bow and arrows shortly before he died. . . .

[6]For ten years after the discovery of his body scholars and scientists examined, x-rayed, and studied his remains and speculated on why and how he died. Was he caught by a sudden storm and had he succumbed to hypothermia? Did he fall, injure himself, and die of exposure? And what was he doing so high in the mountains—six hours from the valley **where** he had his last meal, without adequate food or water—in the first place? For a decade it was thought that the mystery would never be solved. Then, following yet another x-ray of his frozen corpse, the truth came out. A sharp-eyed radiologist saw the telltale shadow of a stone point lodged in his back. Apparently, Ötzi left the lower villages that fateful spring day frightened and in a great hurry. Alone at an altitude of over 10,000 feet, desperately trying to finish his bow and arrows, he was fleeing

(continued on next page)

for his life, but his luck ran out. Ötzi was shot in the back with an arrow. It pierced his shoulder between his shoulder blade and ribs, paralyzing his arm and causing extensive bleeding. He pulled the arrow out but the flint point remained embedded, and his efforts only increased the pain and the damage. His simple medical kit was of no help. Exhausted, he lay down in a shallow cleft in the snowy rocks. In a matter of hours he was dead and the snows of centuries quietly buried him.[2]

Review the Ideas

1. Who was Ötzi?
2. What is important about the discovery of Ötzi?
3. What was Ötzi carrying when he died?
4. What happened to Ötzi? Why?

Analyze the Grammar

1. Look at the boldfaced words in the passage. What are they?
2. What is the function of the boldfaced words?

CHART 7-1	Overview of Adjective Clauses

There are four types of sentences in English:

- A simple sentence is composed of one independent clause.
- A compound sentence is composed of two simple sentences joined with a conjunction.
- A complex sentence is composed of an independent (main) clause and a dependent (subordinate) clause.
- A compound-complex sentence is a combination of a compound and a complex sentence.

Sentences with an independent clause and an adjective clause, which is a dependent clause, are complex sentences.

1. An adjective clause is a dependent clause that can follow any noun in a sentence to describe or identify it.	1. Ötzi was a man **who lived five thousand years ago**. *adjective clause* The tools **that Ötzi carried** included an ax **that was made of copper**. *adjective clause adjective clause*
2. Adjective clauses can also follow and provide information about certain pronouns (*some, others, someone, something, anyone, anybody, anything, everyone, everybody, everything, that, those*).	2. Everyone **who saw Ötzi** was amazed. *adjective clause*
3. More than one adjective clause is possible after a noun.	3. The bow **that Ötzi carried** and **that was found near his body** was not completely finished. *adjective clause adjective clause*
4. An adjective clause must be placed as close as possible to the noun or pronoun it describes.	4. Hikers found **a man**. **The man** had lived five thousand years ago. Hikers found a man **who had lived five thousand years ago**.

5. Adjective clauses can begin with

- the relative pronouns (subordinating conjunctions) *who*, *whom*, *which*, *that*, *whose*, *when*, *why*, *where*, and *whereby*;

- a preposition + *which*, *whom*, or *whose*;

- a quantity expression + preposition + *which*, *whom*, or *whose*;

- a noun + preposition + *which*, *whom*, or *whose*.

The man **whom** the hikers found was completely frozen.

Hikers found the ice cave **in which** Ötzi had died.

Ötzi carried arrows, **many of which** were unfinished.

Ötzi's ax, the **handle of which** was wood, was 5 feet long.

Exercise 1 Identifying Sentence Types

With a partner, match the sentences with their types.

a. compound-complex
b. complex
c. compound
d. simple

_____ 1. Ötzi was a five-thousand-year-old man who died in the Italian Alps.

_____ 2. Ötzi left his home after a meal in a great hurry to escape someone.

_____ 3. Ötzi traveled light, but he had everything that he needed to provide for himself.

_____ 4. Hikers found Ötzi's body, which scientists transported to Austria.

_____ 5. Scientists considered hypothermia, which means "very low body temperature," as the cause of Ötzi's death, and they tried to prove it.

_____ 6. Scientists x-rayed Ötzi's remains, but they were unable to find the cause of death.

_____ 7. Finally, after ten years an X-ray revealed an arrow point lodged in his back.

_____ 8. Now, Ötzi's story has become a murder mystery, and scientists are eager to identify the murderer.

Exercise 2 Placing the Adjective Clause Correctly

With a partner, mark the sentences *C* for correct or *I* for incorrect. Rewrite the incorrect sentences on a separate sheet of paper, putting the adjective clause in the correct place.

_____ 1. Ötzi died when he was about forty years old, who lived in the Italian Alps.

_____ 2. The man who was buried in the ice and who was found by hikers was five thousand years old.

_____ 3. The man was Ötzi that was found in the ice.

_____ 4. The weapons that were found near the body included some unfinished arrows and a bow without a string.

_____ 5. The ax, who his head was made of copper, showed that Ötzi had high status in his community.

_____ 6. The valley was named Ötzi where he was found.

CHART 7-2 **Relative Pronouns That Introduce Adjective Clauses**

The independent clause and the adjective (dependent) clause in a sentence each have a subject, a verb, and sometimes an object.

1. Adjective clauses beginning with *who* or *that* refer to people. When the relative pronoun functions as the subject in its clause, use *who* or *that*.	1. Ötzi was a man **who** / **that** lived five thousand years ago. Ötzi was an ordinary man **who** / **that** lived five thousand years ago. Those **who** / **that** studied Ötzi were not sure how he died.
2. When the relative pronoun functions as the object in its clause, use *whom* or *that* to refer to people. *Whom* is more formal than *that*. The conjunctions *whom* or *that* used as objects may be omitted.	2. Hikers found a man **whom** scientists named Ötzi. The man (**whom** / **that**) the hikers found had been killed.
3. Adjective clauses beginning with *which* or *that* refer to things. These relative pronouns can function as either a subject or an object in the adjective clause. The relative pronouns *which* or *that* used as objects may be omitted.	3. Ötzi carried fire materials **which** / **that** could be ignited with a flint. Ötzi carried fire materials (**which**) he could ignite with a flint (**that**) he carried in his pocket.
4. Adjective clauses beginning with *whose* + noun show possession. They often refer to people, but they are used primarily with inanimate nouns (things). *Whose* + noun can function as the subject or object in its clause.	4. Ötzi, **whose body** was found in the Italian Alps, was perfectly preserved. Ötzi's bow, **whose ends** were unfinished, was almost ready to use. Ötzi, **whose body** scientists examined closely, has been kept frozen since its discovery.
5. Adjective clauses beginning with *where* refer to places. Adjective clauses beginning with *when* refer to time. Adjective clauses beginning with *why* refer to reasons. *Where*, *when*, and *why* function as adverbs in their clauses. *Where*, *when*, and *why* are informal.	5. Ötzi was named for the valley **where** he was found. No one is sure of the year **when** he died. No one knows the reason **why** he died, either.

With a partner, mark the sentences *C* for correct or *I* for incorrect. Rewrite the incorrect sentences on a separate sheet of paper, using the correct relative pronouns.

_____ 1. Ötzi was found about six hours from the valley where he had his last meal.

_____ 2. Ötzi was a man whom lived five thousand years ago.

_____ 3. The mountains which Ötzi was found were a long way from his home.

_____ 4. The hikers which found Ötzi were Europeans.

_____ 5. Ötzi carried several weapons included an unfinished bow and some arrows that needed arrowheads.

_____ 6. The scientists whose investigated the body tried to find the cause of death.

_____ 7. The mystery scientists finally solved had lasted for more than ten years.

_____ 8. Ötzi was killed by an arrow had been shot by someone behind him.

CHART 7-3	Adjective Clauses after Prepositions, Quantity Expressions, and Nouns

1. Adjective clauses sometimes begin with a preposition + *which, whom,* or *whose.* When short sentences are combined, the preposition in the first sentence becomes part of the adjective clause. In formal English, the preposition is placed in front of the relative pronoun. In informal English, the preposition can remain after the verb. *In which, on which,* and *at which* referring to time or place may be replaced with the less formal *where* or *when.*	1. Ötzi was found **in an area**. The area was remote. The area **in which** Ötzi was found was remote. The period had some basic technology. Ötzi lived **during the period**. The period **during which** Ötzi lived had some basic technology. Ötzi carried a bow **on which** he was working. Ötzi carried a bow **which / that** he was working **on**. The year **in which / when** Ötzi was born is unknown.
2. Adjective clauses sometimes begin with a quantity expression + preposition + *which, whom,* or *whose.* These clauses have commas.	2. Ötzi had a quiver with arrows. **Some of the arrows** were ready to use. Ötzi had a quiver with arrows, **some of which** were ready to use.
3. Adjective clauses sometimes begin with a noun + preposition + *which* or *whom,* or a noun + preposition + *whose* + noun. Examples from this chapter: *the nature of which, the extent to which, the produce of which, the inhabitants of which, an explanation for which, the end of which, the last of whom.*	3. Ötzi's bow was almost 6 feet long. **The ends of the bow** were unfinished. Ötzi's bow, **the ends of which** were unfinished, was almost 6 feet long. The attackers followed Ötzi into the mountains. **The nature of their weapons** was unknown. The attackers, **the nature of whose weapons** was unknown, followed Ötzi into the mountains. Italy differed from other areas in **the extent to which** it was urban.

Identifying Adjective Clauses and the Nouns and Pronouns They Modify

With a partner, underline the adjective clauses, circle the nouns or pronouns they modify, and write *F* for formal or *I* for informal.

_____ 1. The weapons which Ötzi was found with included a copper ax.

_____ 2. The valley where Ötzi had his last meal was six hours from the mountains.

_____ 3. The ax, the blade of which was almost pure copper, was unusual.

_____ 4. Ötzi's arrows, some of which were unfinished, were found near his body.

_____ 5. In a pouch, Ötzi carried several items, among which was a birch-bark container with fire-starting materials.

_____ 6. Ötzi carried a large bow with which he could shoot his arrows. Unfortunately, neither his bow nor his arrows were ready to use.

Exercise 5 **Identifying Adjective Clauses in Context**

With a partner, read the passage and underline the adjective clauses. Discuss what kind of information each adjective clause adds to the meaning of the noun it follows.

The Earliest Humans

[1]Six and a half million years ago was a time when important changes were occurring on Earth. The first species that scientists identified as human appeared. Fossil remains of one of these early human ancestors were found in 1972. The remains of "Lucy," who was named by the discovering scientist, were located in present-day Ethiopia, where she lived by a lake.

[2]Lucy and those with whom she lived were much smaller than modern humans and lacked the large, well-developed brains that humans have today. This group used simple tools, some of which were sticks and bone clubs for hunting and protection. They also worked together to find roots and berries that were used for food. These tiny humans, whose origins remain a mystery, were our first ancestors.

[3]Homo sapiens, who were not quite modern humans, first lived more than one hundred million years ago in Africa, Europe, and Asia. Homo sapiens were called Neanderthals, and they were very similar to people today. The Neanderthals had a society in which people worked together hunting for food and protecting each other. We also know that they created tools that they made from stone and had shelters they made from wood. The Neanderthals' disappearance, an explanation for which has never been found, continues to be a scientific mystery.

[4]Homo sapiens sapiens, which means "thinking thinking man," were modern humans and eventually completely replaced Homo sapiens. All modern humans are descendants of a woman other than Lucy, who, scientists say, passed on no DNA found today. Those who have studied DNA from people all over the world have proven that modern humans all descend from the very same woman, an almost unbelievable idea.

Identifying the Functions of Adjective Clauses

With a partner, look back at the passage in Exercise 5 and find examples of each of the following types of adjective clauses. Look in the paragraph(s) indicated. Write each sentence on a separate sheet of paper, underlining the adjective clause and circling the relative pronoun and any associated preposition or noun.

1. An adjective clause that refers to a person or people and begins with a relative pronoun that functions as the subject in its clause (paragraphs 1 and 3)
2. An adjective clause that refers to people and begins with a relative pronoun that functions as the object in its clause (paragraph 1)
3. An adjective clause that describes a pronoun (paragraphs 2 and 4)
4. An adjective clause that refers to people and a relative pronoun that functions as a possessive (paragraph 2)
5. An adjective clause that refers to a place (paragraph 1)
6. An adjective clause that begins with a preposition (paragraph 2)
7. An adjective clause that begins with a quantity expression (paragraph 2)
8. An adjective clause that begins with a noun (paragraph 3)
9. An adjective clause with the relative pronoun omitted (paragraph 3)

CHART 7-4	Restrictive and Nonrestrictive Adjective Clauses

Adjective clauses are either restrictive (essential or identifying) or nonrestrictive (nonessential or nonidentifying).

1. A restrictive adjective clause is essential to identify the noun that it describes. If a restrictive clause is omitted from a sentence, the sentence does not make much sense. A restrictive clause has no commas around it.	1. Hikers found a man **who** had died in the Alps. Hikers found a man.
2. A nonrestrictive adjective clause does not identify the noun it follows but adds information about the noun. If a nonrestrictive clause is omitted from a sentence, the sentence still makes sense. A nonrestrictive clause has one or two commas, parentheses, or dashes around it. Names of people, places, and things are followed by nonrestrictive adjective clauses.	2. Ötzi, **who lived five thousand years ago**, was killed with an arrow. Ötzi (**who lived five thousand years ago**) was killed with an arrow. Hikers found Ötzi, who lived five thousand years ago. Hikers found Ötzi—who lived five thousand years ago.
3. A nonrestrictive adjective clause should never begin with *that*.	3. INCORRECT: Ötzi, ~~that~~ *who* lived five thousand years ago, was killed with an arrow.
4. A nonrestrictive adjective clause introduced by a comma + *which* sometimes follows a complete sentence to add a comment about the ideas in that sentence.	4. Scientists are mystified by the cause of Ötzi's death, **which seems strange in such a technological age.**
5. An adjective clause introduced by a quantity expression or a noun + a preposition is nonrestrictive. Remember: Commas begin and end a nonrestrictive adjective clause, unless the adjective clause is at the end of the sentence.	5. Ötzi had a quiver with arrows, **some of which** were ready to use. Ötzi's bow, **the ends of which** were unfinished, was almost 6 feet long.

Exercise 7 Identifying Restrictive and Nonrestrictive Adjective Clauses

With a partner, underline examples of the following types of adjective clauses and label them.
- Restrictive adjective clauses (R)
- Nonrestrictive adjective clauses (NR)
- A nonrestrictive adjective clause that adds a comment to an entire sentence (C)

_____ 1. Ötzi, who lived in the Italian Alps, died when he was about forty years old.

_____ 2. The man that was buried in the ice was five thousand years old.

_____ 3. The weapons that were found near the body included some unfinished arrows and a bow without a string.

_____ 4. The ax, whose blade was made of copper, showed that Ötzi had high status in his community.

_____ 5. The valley where he was found was named Ötzi.

_____ 6. Ötzi's arrows, some of which were unfinished, were found near his body.

_____ 7. Scientists are still trying to solve Ötzi's murder, which is a difficult task to accomplish.

Exercise 8 Identifying Restrictive and Nonrestrictive Adjective Clauses in Academic Writing

In pairs, underline the adjective clauses in the following textbook excerpts and write whether they are restrictive or nonrestrictive.

1. The hallmark of Persian rule was a benevolent attitude toward those they conquered.[3]

   _____

2. Rome won a war of attrition against a series of Hellenistic commanders, the last of whom was the Greek king Pyrrhus of Epirus (319–272 B.C.E.).[4] _____

3. Until the middle of the seventh century B.C.E., Corinth and its wealth were ruled in typical Dark Age fashion by an aristocratic clan known as the Bacchiads. There were approximately 200 members of this clan, all of whom claimed descent from the mythical hero Heracles.[5] _____

4. Florence, center of Renaissance culture, was one of the wealthiest cities of Europe before the devastations of the plague and the sustained economic downturn of the late fourteenth century. The city itself was inland and its main waterway, the Arno, ran to the sea through Pisa, whose subjugation in 1406 was a turning point in Florentine history.[6] _____

5. The peasants who engaged in the opening of the internal frontier were the descendants of the slaves, unfree farmers, and petty free persons of the early Middle Ages. . . . While serfs were not slaves in a legal sense, their degraded status, their limited or nonexistent access to public courts of law, and their enormous dependency on their lords left them in a situation similar to that of those Carolingian slaves who settled on individual farmsteads in the ninth century. Each year, peasants had to hand over to their lords certain fixed portions of their meager harvests. In addition, they were obligated to work a certain number of days the demesne, or reserve of the lord, the produce of which went directly to him for his use or sale. Finally, they were required to make ritual payments symbolizing their subordination.[7] _____ _____ _____

Exercise 9 **Choosing the Correct Relative Pronoun**

Write the correct relative pronouns to complete the sentences in the following paragraphs from academic textbooks.

1. Whether they lived inside the city or on the farmland _____ (*where / Ø / who*) it controlled, Mesopotamians formed a highly stratified society _____ (*on which / in which / Ø*) various groups shared unequally in the benefits of civilization. Slaves, _____ (*that / who / Ø*) did most of the unskilled labor within the city, were the primary victims of civilization. Most were prisoners of war, but some were people forced by debt to sell themselves or their children. Most of the remaining rural people were peasants _____ (*whose lives / that lives / Ø*) were little better than those of slaves. Having lost their freedom to the religious or military elite, peasants were reduced to working the land of others and depended on markets and prices out of their control. Better off were soldiers, merchants, and workers and artisans _____ (*whom / who / Ø*) served the temple or palace. At the next level up were landowning free persons. Above all of these were the priests responsible for temple services and the rulers. Rulers included the *ensi*, or city ruler, and the *lugal*, or king, the earthly representative of the gods. Kings were powerful and feared.[8]

2. By 3500 B.C.E., government and temple administrators were using simplified drawings today termed pictograms— _____ (*who / that / Ø*) were derived from the tokens to help them keep records of their transactions. The first tablets were written in Sumerian, a language related to no other known tongue. Each pictogram represented a single sound, _____ (*which / in which / Ø*) corresponded to a single object or idea. In time, the pictograms developed into a true system of writing.[9]

3. Law was not the only area _____ (*to which / in which / Ø*) the Old Babylonian Kingdom began an important tradition. In order to handle the economics of business and government administration, Babylonians developed the most sophisticated mathematical system known prior to the fifteenth century C.E. Although Babylonian mathematicians were not primarily interested in theoretical problems and were seldom given to abstraction, their technical proficiency indicates the advanced level of sophistication _____ (*on which / with which / Ø*) Hammurabi's* contemporaries could tackle the problems of living in a complex society.[10]

4. The founder of the Old Kingdom, King Zoser, _____ (*that / who / Ø*) was a rough contemporary of Gilgamesh*, built the first of the pyramid temples, the Step Pyramid at Sakkara. The pyramid tombs were only part of elaborate religious complexes _____ (*the center of which / at whose center / Ø*) were temples housing royal statues.[11]

5. In the Old Kingdom, _____ (*whose population / which / Ø*) has been estimated at perhaps 1.5 million, more than 70,000 workers at a time were employed in building the great temple-tombs. No smaller work force could have built such a massive structure as the Great Pyramid of Khufu (ca. 2600 B.C.E.), _____ (*in which / which / Ø*) stood 481 feet high and contained almost six million tons of stone.[12]

*Hammurabi—the king of Babylon
*Gilgamesh—a king in a popular legend of the time

Exercise 10 Using Relative Pronouns in Context

Complete each textbook passage with one of the relative pronouns from the box, when appropriate. Some may be used more than once and more than one answer is possible in some instances.

at which	both of whose	from which	from whom	in which	of which
on which	that	when	where	which	who
whom	∅				

1. The Persian conquerors were a new but lasting power in the Fertile Crescent, the heirs of the great imperial systems _____ had gone before them. The Indo-European Persians and the Medes had settled in the Iranian plateau late in the second millennium. Initially they were dominated by Assyrian rulers _____ looked to them for military support. After they had helped destroy the Assyrian Empire, the Medes became a major power in the region.[13]

2. A powerful element in Persian civilization was Zoroastrianism, a monotheistic religion founded by Zoroaster (ca. 630–550 B.C.E.). The center of the faith was the worship of Ahura Mazda (the "Lord Wisdom,") _____ all good things in the universe derive, and the rejection of Angra Mainyu (the "Fiendish Spirit"), the source of all evil. Zoroastrianism places great emphasis on individual responsibility to choose good over evil and announces a last judgment _____ each individual will be granted either paradise or eternal damnation.[14]

3. Greek slaves were not distinguished by race, ethnicity, or physical appearance. Anyone could become a slave. Prisoners of war, foreigners _____ failed to pay taxes, victims of pirate raids— all could end up on the auction blocks of the ancient world. . . . Still, the variety of slave experience was enormous. Rural slaves generally fared worse than urban ones, and those _____ worked the mines led the most appalling lives; they literally were worked to death. Others worked side by side with their masters in craft shops or even set up their own businesses, _____ they were allowed to keep some of their profit to ultimately purchase their freedom. One slave left an estate worth more than 33,000 drachmas (the equivalent of 165 years' salary for an ordinary free man), _____ included slaves of his own![15]

4. Roughly half of Athens's free population were foreigners—*metoikoi*, or *metics*. These were primarily Greek citizens of the tributary states of the empire, but they might also be Lydians, Phrygians, Syrians, Egyptians, Phoenicians, or Carians. The number of metics increased after the middle of the fifth century B.C.E., both because of the flood of foreigners into the empire's capital and because Athenian citizenship was restricted to persons with two parents _____ were of citizen families. Under these rules, neither Cleisthenes, the great reformer of the sixth century B.C.E., nor Themistocles, the architect of the victory against Persia, _____ mothers had been foreigners, could have been Athenian citizens.[16]

5. The earliest was Herodotus (ca. 484–ca. 420 B.C.E.), the first historian. He was one of the many foreigners _____ found in Athens the intellectual climate and audience _____ he needed to write an account of the Persian Wars of the preceding generation. . . . He believed that wars arose from grievances and retribution. Thus the Persian Wars appear rather like large-scale feuds, the origins _____ are lost in myth.[17]

The following excerpt from a student essay contains ten errors. The first error is corrected for you. Work in pairs to find and correct nine more.

How Early Humans Obtained Food

Ancient humans such as Lucy, the Neanderthals, and the early Homo sapiens sapiens lived in hunter-

gatherer groups ~~whom~~ *that* were called nomadic, a word that means they moved from a place where there was

little food to another that they could find enough food to support the group. People whom live as nomads

move when they have depleted the plants and animals in an area and then return at a later time when the

plants and animals have renewed their numbers.

Eventually, people began to settle in one place and grow food. This period is known for the development

of agriculture. Agriculture, that is considered riskier than hunting and gathering, became the dominant way

of life. People concentrated on developing new strains of plants and animals which to increase the food

supply, but at the same time they risked a situation when the new strains might fail. For example, certain

genetic traits who were recessive might have produced hardy plants resulting in an abundant harvest,

but other recessive traits where might have produced less robust plants and increased the risk of a poor

harvest. Nevertheless, new plants, examples of that were barley and lentils, and animals, such as pigs,

sheep, and goats, were grown.

From time to time, people who practiced agriculture suffered from disastrous crop failures and

devastating animal losses due to disease. It is important to understand that the people who lives were

dependent on hunting and gathering faced less risk than those who lived by farming.

Combining with Adjective Clauses to Add Detail to Sentences

On a separate sheet of paper, combine the given sentences into one long sentence containing one or more adjective clauses. Add the appropriate relative pronouns.

EXAMPLE:

1. a. Some wars originated in feuds.

   b. The reasons for the feuds had long been forgotten.

   Some wars originated in feuds, **the reasons for which** *had long been forgotten.*

2. a. The Hittites' gradual expansion south along the coast was checked at the battle of Kadesh around 1286 B.C.E.

   b. Around 1286, they encountered the army of an even greater and more ancient power: the Egypt of Ramses II.

3. a. Like other ancient civilizations, Minoan Crete was a strongly stratified system.

   b. In the system, the vast peasantry paid a heavy tribute in olive oil and other produce.

4. a. From roughly 1200 until 800 B.C.E., the Aegean world entered what is generally termed the Dark Age, a confused and little-known period.

   b. Greece returned to a more primitive level of culture and society during the period.

5. a. Rome won a war of attrition against a series of Hellenistic commanders.

   b. The last of the Hellenistic commanders was the Greek king Pyrrhus of Epirus (319–272 B.C.E.).

6. a. There were approximately 200 members of this clan.

   b. All of this clan claimed descent from the mythical hero Heracles.

Exercise 13 **Writing Adjective Clauses to Add Information about a Person, Place, or Thing**

Complete the independent clauses with adjective clauses. Look for ideas in the exercises in this chapter. Remember that an adjective clause must be placed as close as possible to the noun or pronoun it modifies and that commas are used with nonrestrictive clauses.

1. Ancient humans were nomads _____

2. Lucy was a tiny human _____

3. Two hikers found Ötzi _____

4. Ötzi was named for the valley _____

5. Neanderthals were very much like modern humans _____

6. Anyone could be a slave _____

7. Herodotus wrote about the Persian Wars _____

8. Zoroastrianism was powerful in Persian civilization _____

9. Babylonians developed a mathematical system _____

10. In Mesopotamia, merchants and soldiers were better off than peasants _____

Exercise 14 Apply It to Speaking

Look at the representation of a Neanderthal, and, in small groups, discuss the following statement: "It has been said that a Neanderthal, properly groomed and dressed, could today be lost in the crowd of a European city." Be sure to address the following questions in your discussion, incorporating the chapter vocabulary, as appropriate. Then share your conclusions with the class, backing them up with examples.

1. What do you think the statement means?
2. How would you describe the appearance of the Neanderthal? How would you describe the appearance of a modern man? How are they similar and how are they different?
3. On the basis of your assessment in question 2, do you think the Neanderthal could be "lost" in a modern crowd?

A representation of a Neanderthal

Exercise 15 Apply It to Speaking

Reread the introductory passage about Ötzi, the five-thousand-year-old man; then prepare a brief oral presentation discussing what we have learned from Ötzi about the technical accomplishments of people of his era. Focus on describing the various things found with him (listed below) that enabled him to take care of himself, incorporating adjective clauses into your comments. See Appendix B for help.

- His ax
- His knife
- His tool for chipping flint
- His backpack
- The containers in his backpack and their contents

Exercise 16 Apply It to Writing

Use your imagination to write a story about Ötzi's last hours, using adjectives and adjective clauses in your narrative. Describe what happened to him, summarizing what we know about his final hours, but focusing especially on how he was probably feeling as he tried to save himself and realized that he could not do so. See Appendix B for help.

CHAPTER

8

Reduced Adjective Clauses and Adjective Phrases

Ancient Greek athletes

PREVIEW

VOCABULARY Here are some words that you will encounter in Chapter 8. How much do you know about each word? Turn to Appendix A to assess and expand your word knowledge.

block (n.)	counterpart	defeat	disgrace	dowry
endure	fare (v.)	glorify	inherit	prestigious

Prepare to Read

1. What do you imagine the original Olympic Games were like?
2. Who do you think competed in the original Olympic Games?

Read the following passage from *Civilization in the West,* Volume I, *To 1715,* 6th Edition, by Mark Kishlansky, Patrick Geary, and Patricia O'Brien.[1]

The Agony of Athletics

[1]The Greeks did not play sports. Our word *play* is related to the Greek word *pais* (child), and there was nothing childish about Greek athletics. The Greek word was *agonia,* and our modern derivation, *agony,* hits closer to the mark. From Homeric times, sports were a deadly serious affair. Poets, philosophers, and statesmen placed athletic victories above all other human achievements. "There is no greater glory for a man, no matter how long his life," proclaimed Homer, "than what he achieves with his hands and feet."

[2]Athletic contests took place within a religious context, **honoring** the gods but **glorifying** the human victors. By 500 B.C.E., there were 50 sets of games across the Greek world **held** at regular intervals. Among the most prestigious contests were the so-called Crown Games at Delphi, Corinth, and Nemea; the most important were those **held** every four years as part of the cult of Zeus at Olympia. The most important event of the Olympic Games was the 192-meter race, or *stade,* from which comes the word *stadium.* . . . In time, other events were added to the Olympics—other footraces (including one in which the contestants wore armor), throwing of the discus and javelin, the long jump, horse races, and chariot races. The *pankration* combined wrestling and boxing in a no-holds-barred contest. The pentathlon included five events: discus, jumping, javelin, running, and wrestling.

[3]The serious nature of sport was equaled by its danger. One inscription from a statue **erected** at Olympia reads simply, "Here he died, **boxing** in the stadium, having prayed to Zeus for either the crown or death." The most celebrated pankration hero was Arrichion, who won but died in victory. Although his opponent was slowly strangling him, Arrichion managed to kick in such a way as to horribly dislocate his adversary's ankle. The **excruciating** pain caused the opponent to signal defeat just as Arrichion died, **victorious.** The ultimate disgrace was not injury or even death, but defeat. . . . Greeks did not honor good losers, only winners. As Pindar, the great lyric poet who celebrated victorious athletes, wrote, "As they the losers returned to their mothers no laughter sweet brought them pleasure, but they crept along the backroads, **avoiding** their enemies, **bitten** by misfortune."

[4]If failure was bitter, victory was sweet indeed. Victors received enduring fame and enormous fortune. . . . Thus the best athletes were essentially professionals, traveling from game to game. The Thasian boxer and pankratiast Theogenes claimed to have won more than 1300 victories during a professional career that spanned more than two decades. After his death he received the ultimate accolade: he was worshipped in Thasos as a god. . . .

[5]In keeping with the rest of male-dominated Greece, only men were allowed to participate in or attend the Olympic Games. Separate games dedicated to Zeus's wife, Hera, were held for unmarried women at Olympia. Women competed only in footraces over a shortened track. While men competed naked, their bodies rubbed down with olive oil, in the *Heraia* women wore a short tunic. Victors in the Heraia did not receive the same honors as their male counterparts. . . .[2]

Review the Ideas

1. Why were the ancient Greek Olympic Games not really "games" at all?
2. What were some of the events included in the games? Who competed in them?
3. What was the most important aspect of the Olympic Games?
4. What happened to athletes who won their events?

Analyze the Grammar

Work in pairs to answer the following questions about the reading passage.

1. Look at the boldfaced words in paragraphs 2 and 3 of the passage. What different kinds of words do you see?
2. What is the function of the boldfaced words?

CHART 8-1	Adjective Phrases

Adjective clauses can be reduced to adjective phrases if the relative pronoun is in the subject position. Adjective phrases may be participles (ending in *-ing* or *-ed / -en* or irregular forms), adjectives, nouns, or prepositional phrases. Using adjective phrases can be an efficient way to present information concisely and naturally.

1. Adjective clauses with active verbs in the progressive form are reduced to present participial phrases.	1. Athletic contests **that were taking place** included fifty sets of games. Athletic contests **taking place** included fifty sets of games.
2. Adjective clauses with active verbs in the simple present, future, past, present perfect, and past perfect forms are reduced to present participles (*-ing*). The relative pronoun is deleted.	2. The athletes **who participated** in the Olympic Games were men. The athletes **participating** in the Olympic Games were men.
3. Adjective clauses with passive verbs are reduced to past participles (*-ed* or *-en*). The relative pronoun and the *be* verb are deleted.	3. The games **that were organized every four years** were the most important. The games **organized every four years** were the most important.
4. Adjective clauses with the verb *be* followed by an adjective phrase are reduced to the adjective phrase. The relative pronoun and the *be* verb are deleted.	4. Athletes **who were victorious in their sports** were celebrated. Athletes **victorious in their sports** were celebrated.
5. Adjective clauses with the verb *be* followed by a prepositional phrase are reduced to the prepositional phrase. The relative pronoun and the *be* verb are deleted.	5. The contests **that were at Delphi, Corinth, and Nimea** were the most prestigious. The contests **at Delphi, Corinth, and Nimea** were the most prestigious.

6. Adjective clauses with the verb *be* followed by a noun are reduced to the noun. The relative pronoun and the *be* verb are deleted. When a noun follows another noun in the adjective phrase, it is also called an appositive. (See Chapter 4, Chart 4-4, where appositives are presented.)	6. Separate games dedicated to Zeus's wife, **who was Hera**, were held for unmarried women. Separate games dedicated to Zeus's wife, **Hera**, were held for unmarried women.
7. Single adjectives (including participles) and adverb + adjective phrases usually move in front of the noun.	7. Athletes **who were defeated** were scorned. **Defeated** athletes were scorned. The contests **that were the most prestigious** were called the Crown Games. **The most prestigious** contests were called the Crown Games.
8. Sometimes an adjective phrase appears at the beginning or end of a clause separated by a comma, especially when the noun has other modifying adjective clauses and phrases.	8. **Running from their enemies**, the losing athletes, who feared for their lives, escaped along the back roads. The losing athletes, who feared for their lives, escaped along the back roads, **running from their enemies**.
9. An adjective clause that modifies a complete sentence can also be reduced to a participial phrase. These phrases remain at the ends of sentences.	9. Athletes would rather die than lose, **which probably means that a lot of athletes died**. Athletes would rather die than lose, **probably meaning that a lot of athletes died**.
10. Adjective phrases include commas or no commas just like the adjective clauses from which they are reduced. Sometimes *or* is added before a noun. Sometimes dashes or parentheses are used in place of commas.	10. The Greek word for *athletics*, which was *agonia*, meant *agony*. The Greek word for *athletics*, *agonia*, meant *agony*. The Greek word for *athletics*, **or** *agonia*, meant *agony*. The losing athletes escaped along the back roads—running from their enemies. The losing athletes (running from their enemies) escaped along the back roads.

Exercise 1 Identifying Adjective Phrases in Context

With a partner, go over the following passage from the introductory reading and underline the adjective phrases.

If failure was bitter, victory was sweet indeed. Victors received enduring fame and enormous fortune. . . . Thus the best athletes were essentially professionals, traveling from game to game. The Thasian boxer and pankratiast Theogenes claimed to have won more than 1300 victories during a professional career that spanned more than two decades. After his death he received the ultimate accolade: he was worshipped in Thasos as a god. . . .

In keeping with the rest of male-dominated Greece, only men were allowed to participate in or attend the Olympic Games. Separate games dedicated to Zeus's wife, Hera, were held for unmarried women at Olympia. Women competed only in footraces over a shortened track.

Exercise 2 Reducing Adjective Clauses

Underline the adjective clauses in the passage. Then, on a separate sheet of paper, reduce them.

Athletes who were in ancient Greece took sports more seriously than the athletes who live in the world today. Apparently, Greek athletes preferred death to losing an athletic competition, which is difficult for people to believe in the twenty-first century. Greek men who competed in events such as wrestling, which was a contact sport, continued fighting long after people who compete these days would stop.

The games took place all over Greece. By 500 B.C.E., there were fifty sets of games that were held at regular intervals. The games that were the most prestigious were those that were called Crown Games, which were at Delphi, Corinth, and Nemea. The most important of the Crown Games were those that were held every four years that honored the god who was Zeus at Olympia. The winner of the 192-meter race, which was the stade, was honored by having his name become the basis of the Greek system of calculating dates. For example, a year would be figured from the date a person won the stade in a statement such as this: Two years after so-and-so won the stade . . .

Exercise 3 Identifying and Rewriting Adjective Phrases in Sentences

With a partner, underline the adjective phrase(s) in each sentence. On a separate sheet of paper, rewrite the sentences, changing the phrases to clauses. Underline the rewritten portion, as in the example. The first one is done for you.

1. Most groups of people in the world play sports.

   Most groups of people who are in the world play sports.

2. People living in ancient Greece when the Olympic Games began had a very different idea about sports.

3. For the ancient Greeks, the idea of sports—*agonia*, meaning "agony"—was a life-or-death matter, very different from our idea of sports today.

4. The most serious sports in ancient Greece were the Olympic Games.

5. Male citizens had the opportunity to participate in the Olympic Games.

6. Women born in ancient Greece were not included in public life or allowed into the Olympic Games.

7. However, the *Heraia*, a footrace, was a similar competition for unmarried women.

8. Poets celebrating the winners of the Olympic Games wrote about the losers as well, but they did not write about the Heraia.

9. The seriousness with which the ancient Greeks took the games meant that losing competitors were heavily criticized.

10. Beaten and ashamed, the losers returned to their homes as quietly as possible.

Exercise 4 Identifying the Derivation of Adjective Phrases

With a partner, use the sentences and your rewritten answers for Exercise 3 to find an example of nine of the rules in Chart 8-1. One of the following rules has two examples. Write your answers on a separate sheet of paper and underline the adjective phrases.

1. An adjective phrase reduced from a clause with an active verb in the progressive form

2. An adjective phrase reduced from a clause with an active verb in the simple form

3. An adjective phrase reduced from a clause with a passive verb

4. An adjective phrase reduced from a clause with the verb *be* + adjective phrase

5. An adjective phrase reduced from a clause with the verb *be* + prepositional phrase

6. An adjective phrase reduced from a clause with the verb *be* + noun
7. An adjective clause reduced to one word that has been moved in front of the noun it describes
8. An adjective phrase reduced from a clause and moved to the beginning of a sentence
9. An adjective phrase reduced from a clause that describes a complete sentence

Exercise 5 Using the Correct Participle

Write the present or past participle of the verb in parentheses to complete each sentence with the correct form of a reduced adjective clause.

1. By 3500 B.C.E., government and temple administrators were using simplified drawings—today _____ (*term*) pictograms—that were derived from the tokens to help them keep records of their transactions.[3]

2. Each pictogram represented a single sound _____ (*correspond*) to a single object or idea. In time, the pictograms developed into a true system of writing.[4]

3. As the _____ (*favor*) agent of the gods, the king was responsible for regulating all aspects of Babylonian life, _____ (*include*) dowries and contracts, agricultural prices and wages, commerce and money lending, and even professional standards for physicians and architects.[5]

4. In order to handle the economics of business and government administration, Babylonians developed the most sophisticated mathematical system _____ (*know*) prior to the fifteenth century C.E.[6]

5. No smaller work force could have built such a massive structure as the Great Pyramid of Khufu (ca. 2600 B.C.E.), _____ (*stand*) 481 feet high and _____ (*contain*) almost six million tons of stone.[7]

6. More than half of those _____ (*bear*) into citizen families were entirely excluded from public life. These were the women, _____ (*control and direct*) the vital sphere of the Athenian home but _____ (*consider*) citizens only for purposes of marriage, transfer of property, and procreation.[8]

7. Greek slaves were not distinguished by race, ethnicity, or physical appearance. Anyone could become a slave. Prisoners of war, foreigners _____ (*fail*) to pay taxes, victims of pirate raids—all could end up on the auction blocks of the ancient world.[9]

8. Rural slaves generally fared worse than urban ones, and those _____ (*work*) the mines led the most _____ (*appall*) lives; they literally were worked to death.[10]

9. Most were prisoners of war, but some were people _____ (*force*) by debt to sell themselves or their children. Most of the _____ (*remain*) rural people were peasants whose lives were little better than those of slaves.[11]

10. Better off were soldiers, merchants, and workers and artisans _____ (*serve*) the temple or palace.[12]

11. _____ (*Disgust*) with public life, Plato left Attica for a time and traveled in Sicily and Italy, where he encountered different forms of government and different philosophical schools.[13]

Exercise 6 **Building Sentences with Adjective Phrases**

On a separate sheet of paper, rewrite each group of sentences as a single sentence by changing the second (and third) sentences into an adjective phrase. The first one is done for you.

1. a. In Germanic society, the elite had owed its position to a combination of inherited status and wealth.
   b. The combination of inherited status and wealth was perpetuated through military command.

   In Germanic society, the elite had owed its position to a combination of inherited status and wealth, perpetuated through military command.[14]

2. a. The Thasian boxer and pankratiast Theogenes claimed to have won more than 1,300 victories during a professional career.
   b. The professional career spanned more than two decades.

3. a. Fathers arranged marriages.
   b. The marriages were contracted to produce legitimate children and acquire wealth through dowries.

4. a. One slave left an estate worth more than 33,000 drachmas (the equivalent of 165 years' salary for an ordinary free man).
   b. The estate included slaves of his own!

5. a. Knowledge created curiosity about the present.
   b. The knowledge was bequeathed from the past.

6. a. Families who produced great military commanders were thought to have a special war-luck.
   b. The special war-luck was granted by the gods.

7. a. From roughly 1200 until 800 B.C.E., the Aegean world entered what is generally termed the Dark Age.
   b. The Dark Age was a confused and little-known period during which Greece returned to a more primitive level of culture and society.

8. a. Siddharta abandoned his comfortable life for one of extreme self-deprivation and meditation that culminated in his enlightenment.
   b. Siddharta was profoundly saddened.
   c. His enlightenment was the realization of how to break the endless cycle of sorrow.

Exercise 7 **Error Analysis**

The following passage contains ten errors. The first error is corrected for you. Work in pairs to find and correct nine more.

The Olympics Today

The athletic competitions taking place today are quite similar to those ~~taking~~ *that took* place in ancient Greece.

Much like athletes are competing in the modern Olympics in the twentieth and twenty-first centuries, some

of the athletes who competed in the ancient games were professionals, the best ones were receiving fame

and fortune. The most famous Olympic athletes today spend their lives train for their sports competitions

while someone else, who either a private sponsor or a government, supports them.

The twenty-first-century Olympics, holding them every four years, provide a goal for hopeful athletes in

every sport. During the four years preceding an Olympic event, amateur athletes from all over the country travel from competition to competition hope to gain a position on the short list for their sport, which gives them the best chance to get on their country's Olympic team for that event. Athletes have been chosen for their country's team then travel to the Olympic venue, or location, where they live with their teams and compete for gold, silver, and bronze Olympic medals, and great fame and fortune as well.

The prestige of a gold medal is so high that some athletes will do anything to win, includes sometimes even using performance-enhancing drugs to gain an advantage over their opponents. Of course, such drugs are prohibited, officials are required the athletes to undergo frequent drug tests. It is unfortunate but true that some of those who train athletes and some athletes themselves continue to try to win at any cost.

Exercise 8 Apply It to Speaking

In a small group, discuss what you know about the modern Olympic Games. What sports are included? How often are they held? Who competes? Where do they compete? Then compare the attitudes and practices of the Olympians in ancient Greece to those of modern-day Olympians. Use vocabulary from the box and as many adjective phrases as you can.

athlete	champion	competitor	consistent	contemporary
contestant	event	hold	injure	interval
loser	participate	precede	predominate	rank
sponsor	stadium	training	winner	

Exercise 9 Apply It to Writing

Write a paragraph comparing the attitudes and practices surrounding sports competitions in ancient Greece and modern times. Use some of the vocabulary from Chapter 8 and as many adjective phrases as you can.

Exercise 10 Apply It to Writing

In ancient Greece, athletes were prepared to die rather than lose. In today's Olympics, some athletes take performance-enhancing drugs or cheat in other ways in order to win. Write a paragraph describing what you know about these contemporary athletes and their motivation. Use as many adjective phrases as you can. Conclude by addressing these questions: How do you feel about athletes who compete this way? What do you think should be done about them? See Appendix B for help.

Academic Uses of Adjective Clauses, Phrases, and Cleft Sentences

A Roman atrium

VOCABULARY   Here are some words that you will encounter in Chapter 9. How much do you know about each word? Turn to Appendix A to assess and expand your word knowledge.

column	courtyard	dwelling	elegant	flow
luxurious	marble	mosaic	painting	wealth

Prepare to Read

1. The image on the previous page shows the atrium of an ancient Roman house. What features do you notice?
2. What do you imagine the differences were between houses for the rich and houses for other people?

Read the following passage from *Civilization in the West,* Volume I, *To 1715,* 6th Edition, by Mark Kishlansky, Patrick Geary, and Patricia O'Brien.[1]

The Roman Domus, the Family House

[1]The center of everyday life for the Roman family was the *domus*, **the family house, whose architectural style had developed from Etruscan traditions**. Early Roman houses, even of the wealthy and powerful, were simple, low buildings **well suited to the Mediterranean climate, constructed around an open courtyard, or atrium**. Cato the Elder described the home of the great general Manius Curius, **who had driven Pyrrhus from Italy**, as a small, plain dwelling; that simplicity predominated throughout the second century B.C.E. The house looked inward, **presenting nothing but blank walls to the outside world.** Visitors entered through the front door into the atrium, **a central courtyard containing a collecting pool into which rainwater for household use** flowed from the roof through terra-cotta drains. Originally, the atrium not only provided sunlight but allowed smoke from the hearth to escape. In niches or on shelves stood wax or terra-cotta busts of ancestors and statues of the household gods. The walls, **constructed of blocks of stone**, were often painted in bands of different colors **in imitation of polychrome marble**. Around the atrium, openings gave onto workrooms, storerooms, bedrooms, offices, and small dining rooms. . . .

[2]Homes grew in size, wealth, and complexity for those who participated in the wealth of empire. With increasing prosperity, the atrium became more elegant, intended to impress visitors with the wealth of the family and its traditions. The water basin became a reflecting pool, often endowed with a fountain and surrounded by towering columns. In many cases a second open area, or peristyle, appeared behind the first. The wealthy surrounded the atrium and peristyle with glass-enclosed porticoes and decorated their walls with frescoes, mosaics, and paintings looted from Hellenistic cities of the east. Furniture of fine inlaid woods, bronze, and marble, and eastern carpets and wall hangings increased the exotic luxury of the patrician domus.

[3]Not every Roman family could afford its own domus, and in the aftermath of the imperial expansion, housing problems for the poor became acute. In Rome and other towns of Italy, shopkeepers lived in small houses attached to their shops or in rooms behind their workplaces. Peasants forced off their land and crowded into cities found shelter in multistory apartment buildings, an increasingly common sight in the cities of the empire. In these cramped structures, families crowded into small, low rooms about ten feet square. All the families shared a common enclosed courtyard. The apartment buildings and shops were not hidden away from the homes of the wealthy. In Roman towns throughout Italy, simple dwellings, luxurious mansions, shops, and apartment buildings existed side by side. The rich and the poor rubbed shoulders every day, producing a friction that threatened to burst into flame.[2]

Review the Ideas

1. What was the *domus*?
2. How did early Roman houses look?
3. Describe the atrium.
4. How did the atrium change as people became wealthier?
5. How were shopkeepers' houses different from houses of the wealthy?

Analyze the Grammar

1. Look at the boldfaced clauses and phrases in paragraph 1 of the passage. What kind of clauses and phrases are they?
2. What is the function of these clauses and phrases?

CHART 9-1	Purposes of Adjective Clauses and Adjective Phrases in Academic Writing

Adjective clauses and adjective phrases are used not only to describe appearance, but also to define, identify, and give the history and purpose of nouns and noun phrases in a description. They are used for the following specific reasons:

1. To describe the appearance or composition of a noun or noun phrase	1. He carried an ax, **whose 60-centimeter yew-wood haft ended in a blade of almost pure** [adjective clause] **copper,** and a flint knife **with an ash-wood** [adjective phrase] **handle** [**secured to his belt in a fiber scabbard**].[3] [adjective phrase]
2. To describe the use or purpose of a noun or noun phrase	2. There were frequently group and individual sports, such as soccer or wrestling, **which served to channel aggressions.**[4] [adjective clause]
3. To give examples of a noun or noun phrase	3. Most domestic activities, **of which cooking, eating, and sleeping were dominant**, took place close to the ground. . . .[5] [adjective clause]
4. To identify a noun, noun phrase, or pronoun	4. Roughly half of Athens's free population were foreigners—**metoikoi, or metics.**[6] [adjective phrase] Art Hobson, **physicist and author**, wrote *Physics: Concepts and Connections.* [adjective phrase] Those **participating in the events** were honored. [adjective phrase]
5. To define a noun or noun phrase	5. The ducat and florin, **two Italian coins**, were universally accepted. . . .[7] [adjective phrase]
6. To predict a future event regarding a noun or noun phrase	6. Around 1450 B.C.E., a wave of destruction engulfed all of the Cretan cities except Knossos, **which finally met destruction around 1375 B.C.E.**[8] [adjective clause]
7. To describe an action or event occurring at the same time as the action in the main clause	7. Early Homo sapiens sapiens lived in small kin groups of 20 or 30, **following game and seeking shelter in tents, lean-tos, and caves.**[9] [adjective phrase]

8. To provide a historical perspective on a noun, noun phrase, or an entire statement	8. Ottoman expansion on the southern and eastern frontiers of the Continent, however, threatened access to the goods of the East *adjective clause* **on which Europeans had come to rely**.[10]
9. To provide the comment of the writer or speaker about a noun, noun phrase, or an entire statement	9. The courtyards of the wealthy were luxurious compared to the courtyards of the poor, *adjective phrase* **a situation similar to that of the rich and poor today.**
10. To indicate the date of an event or action	10. The Cretan period of destruction ended with *adjective phrase* the devastation of Knossos (**ca.* 1375 B.C.E.**).

**ca.* = circa (approximately, around)

CHART 9-2	Summary: Punctuation of Adjective Clauses and Adjective Phrases

Writers of academic English use adjective clauses and adjective phrases to pack large amounts of information into single sentences in the following ways:

1. With and without commas (See Chapter 7, Chart 7-4, Restrictive and Nonrestrictive Adjective Clauses.)	1. The ducat and florin, **which were two Italian coins**, were universally accepted. The ducat and florin, **two Italian coins**, were universally accepted. Those **who participated in the events** were honored. Those **participating in the events** were honored.
2. With dashes	2. Since the late nineteenth century, archaeologists have discerned three fairly distinct late Bronze Age cultures—**the Cycladic, the Minoan, and the Mycenaean—that flourished in the Mediterranean prior to the end of the twelfth century B.C.E.**[11]
3. With parentheses	3. The two greatest pan-Hellenic (**meaning "all Greek," from** *Hellas*, **the Greek word for** *Greece*) sanctuaries were Olympia and Delphi.[12]
4. With adjective clauses and phrases that follow one another	4. The 40 men **that Columbus left on Hispaniola, almost half his company,** disappeared without a trace.[13]

Identifying the Purposes of Adjective Clauses and Adjective Phrases in Academic Writing

1 With a partner, underline the adjective clauses and adjective phrases in the following passages. Indicate the function of each one by selecting an option from the box. Write the function(s) after each passage.

author's comment	definition	description of appearance or composition
description of use or purpose	event occurring at the same time as the action in the main clause	example
historical perspective on a past event	identification	prediction of a future event (future in the past)
to indicate the date		

1. By 3500 B.C.E., government and temple administrators were using simplified drawings—today termed pictograms—that were derived from the tokens to help them keep records of their transactions.[14]

   _____

2. A powerful element in Persian civilization was Zoroastrianism, a monotheistic religion founded by Zoroaster (ca. 630–550 B.C.E.).[15] _____

3. The drugs of the East, the nature of which we can only guess at, helped soothe chronic ill health.[16]

   _____

4. Printing was not invented. It developed as a result of progress made in a number of allied industries, of which papermaking and goldsmithing were the most important.[17]

   _____

5. Fathers arranged marriages, which were contracted to produce legitimate children and acquire wealth through dowries. A wife had no control over her dowry, which passed to her son.[18]

   _____

6. Some women, perhaps in imitation of their more liberated Hellenistic sisters, began to take a more active role in public life. One example is Cornelia, a daughter of Scipio Africanus, who bore her husband 12 children, only three of whom survived to maturity.[19] _____

7. A typical family could keep all of its belongings in the chest, which could then be buried or carried away in times of danger. The chest could also serve as a table or bench or as a sideboard on which food could be placed.[20] _____

8. Maximinus rose quickly through the ranks and in 235 was proclaimed emperor at Mainz by a mutinous army, which had overthrown the grandson of Septimius Severus.[21]

   _____

9. Although some contemporary historians have suggested that the Paleolithic era (ca. 600,000–10,000 B.C.E.) was a peaceful golden age in which women played a dominant role in social organization, no evidence substantiates this theory.[22] _____

10. The hinterland population were steady consumers of grain, cloth, and the new manufactured goods—glass, silk, jewelry, and cottons—that came pouring onto the market in the Later Middle Ages.[23]

   _____

11. Metalworkers fashioned gold and silver into valuable items of adornment and prestige. They also began to cast bronze, an alloy of copper and tin, which came into use for tools and weapons about 3000 B.C.E.[24]

   _____

2 Look at the adjective clauses and phrases that you have underlined in part 1 of this exercise. Write the numbers of the sentences that use the following punctuation marks to indicate these clauses or phrases.

   1. no punctuation: _____

   2. commas: _____

   3. parentheses: _____

   4. dashes: _____

Exercise 2 Finding Examples of Adjective Clauses and Adjective Phrases with Specific Purposes

With a small group of classmates, find in the introductory reading passage at least one example of an adjective clause or an adjective phrase used for each of the purposes specified below. (Provide an additional example for the first entry, where one example is done for you.) Write the complete sentences on a separate sheet of paper, underlining the adjective clause(s) and adjective phrase(s) in each one. Share your group's responses with the class as a whole.

1. To describe the appearance or composition of a noun

   The walls, <u>constructed of blocks of stone</u>, were often painted in bands of different colors <u>in imitation of polychrome marble</u>.

2. To describe the use, purpose, or origin of a noun

3. To identify a noun or pronoun

4. To define a noun

5. To predict a future event regarding a noun

6. To provide a historical perspective on a noun

CHART 9-3	Cleft Sentences

Cleft sentences are used in academic writing to focus particularly on a time, place, person, purpose, or reason.

1. A cleft sentence looks very much like other sentences with adjective clauses, but the cleft sentence begins with *It + be + (not)* + emphasized word, phrase, or clause + adjective clause with *who / whom / that / Ø*.

   The cleft sentence emphasizes the word, phrase, or clause that follows *be*.

   emphasized noun
   1. It was **Rembrandt** who had created the paintings. (not someone else)

   emphasized prepositional phrase
   It was **in Italy** that the paintings were found.

   emphasized clause
   It was **because the taxes were so high** that many individuals took to a life of banditry.

2. A cleft sentence can be rewritten as a simple sentence, but the emphasis is lost.

2. Rembrandt created the paintings.

The paintings were found in Italy.

Many individuals took to a life of banditry because the taxes were so high.

3. The adjective clause in a cleft sentence can omit the relative pronoun if the relative pronoun is the object in the clause: *It* + *be* + noun phrase + (*that / whom*) + subject + rest of the adjective clause.

Commas are not used with the adjective clauses in cleft sentences.

3. It was the Greek athletes (**that / whom**) the public admired.

Exercise 3 Identifying Cleft Sentences in Context

Underline the cleft sentences used for emphasis in the passages. Then circle the words that are being emphasized. There may be more than one cleft sentence in a passage.

1. The technology associated with commerce achieved no breakthroughs to compare with the great transformations of the fifteenth century, when new techniques of navigation made transatlantic travel possible. It is certainly true that there continued to be improvements. . . . It was the Dutch who made the single most important innovation in shipbuilding. To gain maximum profit from their journeys to the Baltic, the Dutch designed the so-called flyboats. Flyboats sacrificed speed and maneuverability, but they were cheap to build and could be manned by small crews.[25]

2. In India it was the military brilliance of a young cavalry officer, Robert Clive, that eventually led to British dominance and the expulsion of the French in the 1760s. . . . As if he were a local ruler, Clive was offered the *dirwani*—the right to collect local taxes from the entire population. It was an offer he could not refuse. The yield from the dirwani changed the balance of trade in Asia dramatically. Now it was the British who were exporting bullion and creating a drain on the local Indian economy. . . . After the American War of Independence, it was in India that British imperial interest and efforts were focused, forging a relationship quite different than the trading partnership with which it had begun.[26]

3. Coal had been in use as a fuel for several centuries, and the coal trade between London and the northern coal pits had been essential to the growth of the capital. . . . As canals and roadways improved, more inland coal was brought into production for domestic use. Yet it was in industry rather than in the home that coal was put to its greatest use. There again Britain was favored, for large seams of coal were also located near large seams of iron.[27]

4. Youth culture was created by outside forces as much as it was self-created. . . . Anthropologists and sociologists in the 1960s began studying youth as if they were a foreign tribe. The "generation gap" appeared as the subject of hundreds of specialized studies. Adolescent behavior was examined across cultures. Sexual freedom and the use of drugs were subjected to special scrutiny. But, above all, it was the politics of the young that baffled and enraged many observers.[28]

Exercise 4 Writing Cleft Sentences

On a separate sheet of paper, use the information in the parentheses to write a cleft sentence that emphasizes the boldfaced word or words. The first one is done for you.

1. (**The need to ship increasing amounts of coal** to foundries and factories provided the spur for the development of a new form of transportation.)

   It was the need to ship increasing amounts of coal to foundries and factories that provided the spur for the development of a new form of transportation.

2. The greatest of all English scientists was the mathematician and physicist Sir Isaac Newton (1642–1727). (**Newton** brought together the various strands of the new science.)

3. The microscope served to advance medical science in a number of areas. While it had probably been invented in Holland, (**Galileo** was able to improve its function so that it could be used for experimentation).

4. The relationship between artist and social context was all the more important in the Renaissance, when artists were closely tied to the crafts and trades of urban society and to the demands of clients who commissioned their work. Although (**the elite** patronized art, **skilled tradesmen** produced it).

5. (**Leonardo da Vinci** attempted to apply a theory of mechanics to Renaissance warfare), and he made drawings for the creation of war machines such as tanks and flying machines such as airplanes, though, of course, neither were produced during his lifetime.

6. Marriage involved more than just the union of bride and groom. . . . Many couples were engaged long before they were married, and in many places (**the engagement** was most important to the individuals and **the wedding** was most important to the community).

Exercise 5 Error Analysis

The following passage contains ten errors. The first error is corrected for you. Work in pairs to find and correct nine more.

The Roman Family

The basic unit of Roman society, ~~was~~ the family, was also the basic unit of the Roman state. Rome was a patriarchal society, which was a major reason for its success.

The Roman family consisted of the father (who *paterfamilias*), his wife, children, and slaves. It was the paterfamilias had the power of life and death over his entire family for his whole life. A son was the heir but could not be independent of his father. There was only at the death of the paterfamilias that his son attained legal and financial independence.

Women lived in Rome had no power in society. An unmarried Roman girl was completely dominated by her father. The father chose the girl's husband base on economic reasons. As soon as the girl was married, her father's authority passed to her husband, resulting in her complete separation from her original family. A husband had the power to divorce his wife at any time which resulted in the return of the wife to her original family. There was little chance that a wife could divorce her husband.

A Roman woman had some power, however, consisted of authority over the household and the teaching of morality to her children. Otherwise, the children were completely under the control of the father, who could even kill or abandon unwanted children. If a family had no sons, the father could adopt boys or young men, who received the same rights as natural sons.

Other members of the family included the slaves, considered property with no rights of their own. Slaves lived and worked together with the free members of the family. Slaves, were like other family members, were under the complete domination of the paterfamilias, who could even sell his own children as slaves. A slave might be freed, but he or she owed the paterfamilias lifelong respect, meant he or she could never oppose him in any way.

Exercise 6 Apply It to Speaking

Read the following passage from this chapter's introductory reading about early Roman houses. Focus on how it is organized. Notice the adjective clauses and adjective phrases and think about how they help to guide the reader through the house in an orderly way and describe its main features. Then, with a small group of classmates, discuss the following questions. Be prepared to summarize and share your conclusions with students in other groups.

1. What essential point does the first sentence make about the Roman house? How do the second and third sentences provide additional related information? What does the reader learn in these sentences?

2. How does the writer organize the rest of the text in order to guide the reader to and through the house?

   The center of everyday life for the Roman family was the *domus*, the family house, whose architectural style had developed from Etruscan traditions. Early Roman houses, even of the wealthy and powerful, were simple, low buildings well suited to the Mediterranean climate, constructed around an open courtyard, or atrium. Cato the Elder described the home of the great general Manius Curius . . . as a small, plain dwelling; that simplicity predominated throughout the second century B.C.E. The house looked inward, presenting nothing but blank walls to the outside world. Visitors entered through the front door into the atrium, a central courtyard containing a collecting pool into which rainwater for household use flowed from the roof through terra-cotta drains. Originally, the atrium not only provided sunlight but allowed smoke from the hearth to escape. In niches or on shelves stood wax or terra-cotta busts of ancestors and statues of the household gods. The walls, constructed of blocks of stone, were often painted in bands of different colors in imitation of polychrome marble. Around the atrium, openings gave onto workrooms, storerooms, bedrooms, offices, and small dining rooms.

Exercise 7 Apply It to Speaking and Writing

Work with a small group of classmates to describe the image of a Roman atrium at the beginning of the chapter. Follow the steps outlined below to prepare and then to write up your description. Be sure to use adjective clauses and adjective phrases and to incorporate this chapter's vocabulary as appropriate. Some useful words are included in the box. See Appendix B for help.

1 Begin by deciding how you will organize your description, focusing on one or more different areas of the structure. For example, you might choose to describe the courtyard and then the walls of the house.

2 Prepare a well-organized oral description, with everyone participating and helping to fine-tune.

3 Take turns reading your description aloud to the class, or post it online.

architectural style	atrium	block of stone	bronze	column
elegant	fountain	fresco	luxury	marble
mosaic	open courtyard	painting	rainwater	reflecting pool
statue	sunlight	work of art		

PART
3

Putting It All Together

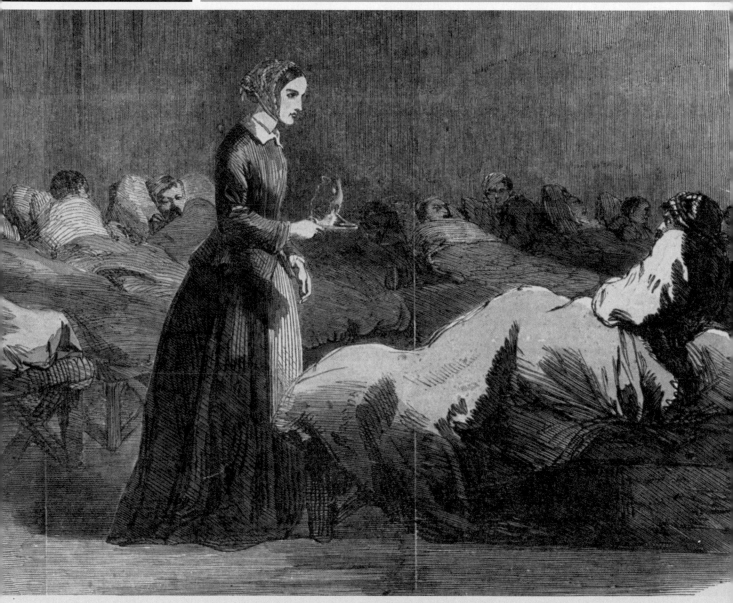

Florence Nightingale nursing soldiers during the Crimean War

Read the following passage from *Civilization in the West*, Volume II, *Since 1555*, 6th Edition, by Mark Kishlansky, Patrick Geary, Patricia O'Brien.[1]

A Closer Look: A Working Woman

[1]Women have always worked, but how society has valued women's work has changed over time. After 1850, women were expected to retire from the workplace upon marrying. Woman's proper role was that of wife and mother in the home, caring for her husband and family, watching over her children. Young women worked before they married to help their parents and to save for dowries. There is no doubt that many women continued to work for wages because they had to; they were too poor to live by society's norms. But mid-nineteenth-century European culture reinforced the idea that woman's place was in the separate domestic sphere of private pleasures and unpaid labor. To be a "public" man was a valued trait. The same adjective applied to a woman meant that she was a harlot. Yet it is this culture that immortalized Florence Nightingale, a woman who valued what she called "my work" above home and family. She was a single woman in an age when more and more women were making the choice to remain unmarried; but it was also an age in which *spinster* was a term of derision and a sign of failure. Miss Nightingale, as she was known, received the British Empire's Order of Merit for her achievements. Queen Victoria, the most maternal and domestic of queens, hailed her as "an example to our sex." Nightingale was widely regarded as the greatest woman of her age, among the most eminent of Victorians. A highly visible and outspoken reformer, Nightingale deviated from woman's unpaid role as nurturer in the private sphere. How could she be an example to the women of her time? Florence Nightingale was hailed as a national heroine because of her work during the Crimean War in organizing hospital care at Scutari, a suburb outside Constantinople on the Asiatic side of the Bosporus. In the Crimea, she entered her own field of battle, attacking the mismanagement, corruption, and lack of organization characteristic of medical treatment for British soldiers. She campaigned for better sanitation, hygiene, ventilation, and diet, and in 1855 the death rate plummeted from 42 percent to 2 percent thanks to her efforts. The London *Times* declared, "There is not one of England's proudest and purest daughters who at the moment stands on as high a pinnacle as Florence Nightingale."

[2]It was a pinnacle not easily scaled. Blocked by her family and publicly maligned, Nightingale struggled against prevailing norms to carve out her occupation. She was the daughter of a wealthy gentry family, and from her father she received a man's classical education. Women of her milieu were expected to be educated only in domestic arts. The fashion of the day emphasized woman's confinement to the home: crinolines, corsets, and trains restricted movement and suggested gentility. That was the life of Nightingale's older sister, a life that "the Angel of the Crimea" fiercely resisted. Nightingale railed at the inequity of married life: "A man gains everything by marriage: he gains a 'helpmate,' but a woman does not." Her memoirs are filled with what she called her "complaints" against the plight of women. Nightingale was not a typical working woman. She struck out on her career as a rebel. Because of her wealth, she did not need to work, yet she felt driven to be useful. Her choice of nursing much alarmed her family, who considered the occupation to be on a level with domestic service. For them, nursing was worse, in

fact, because nurses worked with the naked bodies of the sick. Thus nurses were either shameless or promiscuous, or both. Nightingale shattered those taboos. She visited nursing establishments throughout Europe, traveling alone—another feat unheard of for women in her day—and studied their methods and techniques. She conceived of her own mission to serve God through caring for others. As with any exceptional individual, character and capabilities must figure in an explanation of achievements. Nightingale was a woman of drive and discipline who refused to accept the limited choices available to Victorian women. She possessed, in her sovereign's words, "a wonderful, clear, and comprehensive head." Yet her unique talents are not enough to explain her success. In many ways, Nightingale was not a rebel, but rather an embodiment of the changing values of her age. In 1860, she established a school to train nurses, just as similar institutions were being created to train young women.

[3]Florence Nightingale spent a good part of the last 45 years of her life in a sickbed suffering from what she called "nervous fever." During that period she wrote incessantly and continued to lobby for her programs, benefiting, one of her biographers claimed, from the freedom to think and write provided by her illness. It may well be true that her invalidism protected her from the claims on her time made by her family and by society. It may also be true that she, like many of her middle-class female contemporaries, experienced debilitation or suffered from hypochondria in direct proportion to the limitations they experienced. New occupations labeled "women's work" were essential to the expansion of industrial society. A healthy and literate population guaranteed a strong citizenry, a strong army, and a strong work force. As helpmates, women entered a new work sector identified by the adjective *service*. Women were accepted as clerical workers, performing the "housekeeping" of business firms and bureaucracies. After midcentury, gender differences, socially defined virtues for men and women, became more set. Individualism, competition, and militarism were the values of the world of men. Familial support, nurturance, and healing were female virtues. Those were the separate and unequal worlds created by the factory and the battlefield. The virtues of the private sphere were extended into the public world with the creation of new forms of poorly paid female labor. In that sense, Florence Nightingale was not a rebel. The "Lady with the Lamp," whom fever-ridden soldiers called their mother, was another working woman.[2]

Review the Ideas

1. How was Florence Nightingale different from most women of her time? Why did she feel the need to work?

2. What were her achievements?

3. What happened during the last forty-five years of Florence Nightingale's life? Why does the author of this passage think this was so?

Exercise 1   Analysis of the Reading Passage

Underline the adjective clauses and adjective phrases in the reading passage. Then indicate how each is used by supplying the information requested below. Write your answers on a separate sheet of paper.

Paragraph 1

1. Two adjective phrases that describe a noun's function
2. Two adjective phrases (appositives) that describe two nouns
3. An adjective phrase that describes a noun
4. An adjective phrase (appositive) that begins a sentence
5. An adjective phrase that describes action occurring at the same time as the subject's action in the main clause
6. An adjective phrase that expresses the author's opinion about the success of Florence Nightingale's campaign
7. Two adjective clauses that express time
8. A cleft sentence that expresses emphasis

Paragraph 2

9. An adjective phrase that begins a sentence
10. Two adjective phrases used as adjectives in front of nouns
11. An adjective phrase (appositive) followed by an adjective clause
12. A nonrestrictive adjective clause
13. An adjective phrase + adjective phrase (appositive) + adjective phrase with special punctuation
14. A restrictive adjective clause
15. An adjective phrase (appositive) expressing the author's comment

Paragraph 3

16. Six restrictive adjective phrases
17. Three nonrestrictive adjective phrases
18. A nonrestrictive adjective clause with relative pronoun deleted, giving an author's comment
19. A restrictive adjective clause with the relative pronoun deleted

Exercise 2   Error Analysis

The following excerpt from a student essay contains ten errors. The first error is corrected for you. Find and correct nine more.

Simón Bolívar

        whose
     Simón Bolívar (who his full name was Simón José Antonio de la Santísima Trinidad Bolívar y Palacios

Ponte y Blanco) is widely called the George Washington of South America. His military victories over

Spanish colonial forces brought independence to Venezuela, Colombia, Ecuador, Peru, and Bolivia. It was

these stunning victories what earned him the title of *El Libertador,* or the Liberator.

     Borned in Nueva Granada (now Venezuela) in 1783 to a wealthy family that made its fortune in gold and

copper mines, Bolívar was privileged, his family be originally from Spain and his ancestors including the

governor of Santo Domingo. He became an orphan at a young age, inherited the family fortune, and was able to travel mostly in Europe, where he also lived for extended periods.

He befriended Emperor Napoleon of France, but then, after invading the Iberian Peninsula and deposing the king of Spain, Napoleon appointed his older brother, was Joseph Bonaparte, king of Spain and its colonies. Bolívar's Venezuela was one of these colonies, and that offended his nationalist sentiment. Bolívar returned to his native land and joined the resistance against the "usurped" Spanish rule.

Bolívar had a vision for a United States of South America modeling on the United States of North America which had recently come together and shown great promise. He managed to create an independent republic calling Gran

Simón Bolívar in Peru

Colombia included the territories of today's Bolivia, Colombia, Venezuela, Ecuador, Panama, the Caribbean coast of Costa Rica and Nicaragua, the Mosquito Coast of Central America, Guayana Esequiba in Guyana, northern Peru, and northwest Brazil. This short-live nation lasted only from 1819 to 1831 and fell to the political ambitions and growing nationalism of the individual territories and powerful regional interests.

Bolívar took power as dictator in several of the newly independent countries as internal divisions and ambitions caused his union to start crumbling. He imposed the principles of the Bolivian Constitution, which made him president for life. This offended the regional leaders. After a failed assassination attempt, Bolívar began to slide.

Probably his most famous final pronouncement was the discouraged comment that "all who served the revolution have plowed the sea." His dream of a unified South America that could rival the United States to the north was in pieces.

In 1830, Bolívar, who on his way to European exile, died in Santa Marta, Colombia, after a battle with tuberculosis. He was only forty-seven when he died.

WHAT DID YOU LEARN?

Review the forms and functions of adjective clauses, adjective phrases, and cleft sentences in Part 3. Complete the exercises below. Then check your answers in Appendix D.

A Is the grammar in these sentences correct? Write *C* for correct and *I* for incorrect. Correct any errors.

_____ 1. The five-thousand-year-old man who found was named Ötzi.

_____ 2. Several hikers, many of whom were German, found Ötzi.

_____ 3. Scientists were mystified by Ötzi's death, the reason for that they were unable to discover.

_____ 4. The earliest human, named Lucy by the scientists who found her, lived in Ethiopia.

_____ 5. The Neanderthals, whose disappearance has never been explained, looked much like modern humans.

_____ 6. The Olympic Games were the most prestigious athletic events holding in Greece.

_____ 7. Some of the athletes racing in the games had prepared for many years.

_____ 8. One Greek athlete, was Theogenes, competed for more than twenty years.

_____ 9. Women did not compete in the male-dominated Greek Olympics.

_____ 10. It was the ancient Greeks what focused the most attention on athletes.

B Is each statement above the sentence that follows it correct? Write *C* for correct and *I* for incorrect.

_____ 1. The adjective phrase identifies the noun that it precedes.

A highly visible and outspoken reformer, Florence Nightingale deviated from woman's unpaid role as nurturer in the private sphere.

_____ 2. The adjective phrase defines the noun phrase that it follows.

After midcentury, gender differences, socially defined virtues for men and women, became more set.

_____ 3. The adjective clauses are punctuated correctly.

The earliest Roman villages were found on the Palatine—from whose heights the accompanying photograph was taken—which remained throughout Rome's history the favored residential area.[2]

_____ 4. The cleft clauses express emphasis.

There can be no question that it was the rich who commissioned works of art and that it was the highly skilled male craftsmen who executed them.[3]

_____ 5. The adjective clause describes the noun it follows.

Nightingale was a woman of drive and discipline who refused to accept the limited choices available to Victorian women.

_____ 6. The adjective clause tells about the future of the noun.

Nightingale was an exceptional woman who would change society's view of working women.

_____ 7. The adjective clause tells the purpose of the noun.

The temples, which housed a statue of the god, were otherwise largely empty.[4]

_____ 8. The cleft sentence tells about the purpose of something.

It was the Roman women who controlled the house and taught the children about morality.

_____ 9. The adjective clause expresses emphasis.

The most famous of the bandits was Bulla the Lucky, who headed a band of more than 600 men and plundered Italy during the reign of Septimius Severus.[5]

How did you do? Are there topics you need to review?

Exercise 3 Apply It to Speaking and Writing

In this chapter, you have read about Florence Nightingale and Simón Bolívar, both people who had an impact on the world. Now choose and discuss another person who has had an impact on the world, and then follow up by writing a paragraph about him or her.

1 Choose a person (living or dead) who has had an impact on the world, and do an Internet search to learn more about him or her. Take notes.

• Find very brief biographical information about the person (when the person was born and died, where he or she grew up and spent his or her active years, etc.).

• Find what the person did to have an impact on the world; note some specific examples.

• Decide, for your conclusion, why the person is still remembered—or influential—today.

2 With a small group of classmates, take turns reporting what you have found about the person you chose and providing feedback to each other. Ask and answer questions about points that are not clear. Take notes during the discussion in order to improve your presentation.

(continued on next page)

3 On the basis of your research and your classmates' feedback, write a paragraph or two describing the person you chose. Use some of the vocabulary from Part 3 in the box and as many adjective clauses, adjective phrases, and cleft sentences as you can.

contemporary	counterpart	decade	defeat	descend
disgrace	elegant	endure	fare	inherit
prestigious	sophistication	wealth		

EXAMPLE:

George Washington (1732–1799), the first president of the United States, came from a prestigious, wealthy family who were tobacco farmers in Virginia. Washington, chosen to be commander in chief of the Continental army, spent nearly a decade fighting the Revolutionary War against his more powerful counterparts in the British army. After the British were defeated, Washington struggled to build a new nation based on federalist principles.

It was Washington's commitment to democratic ideals and his opposition to dictatorship that lead him to resign the presidency after one term. Washington was so loved by the citizens that they would have elected him president for life. He understood that such a situation could lead to dictatorship. Although Washington was only president for one term, his democratic ideals and dedication to them have contributed to his legacy today as "the father of his country."

George Washington

_____

_____

_____

_____

_____

_____

_____

_____

_____

Check Your Writing

Which of the following grammar structures did you use in your paragraph(s)? Did you use them correctly?

- [ ] Adjective clauses with *who, whom, that, which, whose* + noun, *where*, and *when*
- [ ] Adjective clauses with prepositions (*in which, on which*, etc.)
- [ ] Adjective clauses with quantity expressions (*some of which*, etc.)
- [ ] Adjective clauses with nouns + prepositions (*the top of which*, etc.)
- [ ] Adjective clauses with the relative pronoun omitted
- [ ] Restrictive and nonrestrictive adjective clauses and adjective phrases (with commas or without commas)
- [ ] Adjective phrases with present participles (*-ing*) and past participles (*-ed, -en,* or irregular)
- [ ] Adjective clauses and phrases that describe, identify, define, exemplify, or tell future or historical actions
- [ ] Appositives
- [ ] Cleft sentences to emphasize something or someone

PART

4

Adverb Clauses, Adverb Phrases, and Other Structures That Express Complex Relationships

ACADEMIC DISCIPLINE
ANTHROPOLOGY

OBJECTIVES

In Part 4 of the *Advanced Grammar* course you will identify, understand, and use the following structures that express time, cause and effect, purpose, manner, concession, opposition, and condition:

- adverb clauses.
- conjunctions.
- adverb phrases and absolute constructions.

Adverb clauses and phrases, absolutes, and simple and compound sentences are used to show, in a concise way, time, cause, effect, purpose, manner, contrast, and condition relationships between ideas. They also express background, acknowledge the opinions of other people, and make persuasive arguments in academic writing.

Academic texts about anthropology serve to illustrate how academic writers express these complex relationships between ideas.

Anthropology: the study of human beings

Adverb Clauses and Other Structures That Express Time, Cause / Effect, Purpose, and Manner

Aborigines were the original people who lived in Australia.

PREVIEW

VOCABULARY   Here are some words that you will encounter in Chapter 10. How much do you know about each word? Turn to Appendix A to assess and expand your word knowledge.

| betrothed | ceremony | courtship | feast | forager |
| game | immunity | kin | survive | yield |

Prepare to Read

1. What do you think the Australian aborigines did on a typical day before the arrival of Europeans?
2. How do you think the Australian aborigines got their food?

Read the following passage from *Anthropology,* 13th Edition, by Carol R. Ember, Melvin Ember, and Peter N. Peregrine.[1]

Australian Aborigines

[1]Before Europeans came to the Australian continent, all the aboriginal people who lived there depended on foraging. Although the way of life of Australian aborigines is now considerably altered, we consider the life of the Ngatatjara, as described by Richard Gould in the 1960s, when they still lived by gathering wild plants and hunting wild animals in the Gibson Desert of western Australia (based on Gould 1969). (We mostly use the present tense in our discussion because that is the custom in ethnographic* writing, but readers should remember that we are referring to aboriginal life in the 1960s.)

[2]The desert environment of the Ngatatjara averages less than 8 inches of rain per year, and the temperature in summer may rise to 118°F. The few permanent water holes are separated by hundreds of square miles of sand, scrub, and rock. Even before Europeans arrived in Australia, the area was sparsely populated—fewer than one person per 35 to 40 square miles. Now there are even fewer people, because the aboriginal population was decimated* by introduced diseases and mistreatment after the Europeans arrived.

[3]On a typical day, the camp begins to stir just before sunrise, while it is still dark. Children are sent to fetch water, and the people breakfast on water and food left over from the night before. In the cool of the early morning, the adults talk and make plans for the day. When the women decide which plants they want to collect, and where they think those plants are most likely to be found, they take up their digging sticks and set out with large wooden bowls of drinking water on their heads. Their children ride on their hips or walk alongside. Meanwhile, the men have decided to hunt emus, six-foot-tall ostrich-like birds that do not fly. The men go to a creek bed where they will wait to ambush any game that may come along. They lie patiently behind a screen of brush they have set up, hoping for a chance to throw a spear at an emu or even a kangaroo. They can throw only once, because the game will run away if they miss.

[4]By noon, the men and women are usually back at camp, the women with their wooden bowls each filled with up to fifteen pounds of fruit or other plant foods, the men often with only some small game such as lizards* and rabbits. The daily cooked meal is eaten toward evening, after an afternoon spent resting, gossiping, and making or repairing tools.[2]

ethnographic—relating to scientific study of different races of people
decimated—destroyed
lizard—a type of reptile with four legs and a long tail

Review the Ideas

1. How did the aborigines in the Gibson Desert live during the 1960s?
2. Describe the Gibson Desert environment.
3. What do the aborigines in the Gibson Desert do on a typical day?
4. Why can the men throw a spear at an animal only once?

Analyze the Grammar

1. Look at the underlined words in the first paragraph. Are they phrases or clauses? How do you know? What ideas do they add to the sentence they are in? Underline other examples of word groups like these in the rest of the passage.
2. Look at the underlined group of words in the last sentence of the passage. What is the difference between this underlined group of words and the ones you have just found? (Hint: Is it a clause or a phrase? How do you know?)

CHART 10-1	An Overview of Connectors

Connectors join different kinds of sentences and clauses.

1. A subordinating conjunction connects an independent clause with an adverb clause that modifies it, telling when, where, how, why, or under what condition the action in the independent clause takes place.

before, after, because, since	**Before** the women cook, they gather plants. The women gather plants **before** they cook. The men hunt game **after** they eat breakfast. **After** they eat breakfast, the men hunt game. Europeans have lived in Australia **since** they arrived in the seventeenth century.

2. A coordinating conjunction connects two independent clauses and is preceded by a comma.

for, and, nor, but, or, yet, so	The women walked a long way, **but** they did not find much vegetation. They continued to search, **so** they eventually found some edible plants.

3. A conjunctive adverb connects two independent clauses and is preceded by a semicolon and followed by a comma.

meanwhile, therefore, thus, consequently, however	The women collected plants; **meanwhile**, the men hunted game. Both groups found food; **therefore**, they were able to return to the camp.

4. A transition usually connects two simple sentences and is followed by a comma. Transitions are sometimes preceded by a semicolon and followed by a comma.

as a result, in contrast	The hunt was successful. **As a result**, the evening meal was satisfying for everyone.

The main difference between the connectors is the kinds of sentences and clauses they connect and their punctuation. You will learn more about connectors in the following charts.

CHART 10-2 | Adverb Clauses of Time

1. An adverb (dependent) clause is used with a main (independent) clause to form a complex sentence. Adverb clauses of time are introduced by subordinating conjunctions that express the following time relationships between events in the sentence:

   • *before*—happening earlier in time

   • *after*—happening later in time

   • *since*—happening after a time in the past

   • *when*—happening at the same time or after something else happens

   • *whenever*—every time that something else happens

   • *as soon as / once*—immediately after something else happens

   • *as long as*—happening for a specified length of time

   • *while / as*—during the time that something else happens

   • *just as*—happening at exactly the same time that something else happens

   • *until*—happening up to a particular point in time and then stopping; signals the end of the action in the independent clause

   • *by the time that*—happening before something else happens

Before the women leave, they discuss the best places to gather food.

After the women have discussed their plans, they leave the camp.

The men have hunted the same areas **since** they moved there.

They are sure to find prey **when** they plan carefully.

Whenever the aborigines find food, they gather it.

The aborigines gather food **as soon as / once** they make plans for the day.

They continue searching for food **as long as** they can.

While / As the women are collecting plants, the men hunt game.

The people began to eat **just as** the sun rose.

The aborigines gather food **until** they find enough for the meal.

The people have eaten their meal **by the time that** the sun sets.

2. The order of the independent clause and the dependent adverb clause may be reversed. When the dependent clause comes first, it is followed by a comma.

Before the chief begins a journey, he obtains beads from each family.

The chief obtains beads from each family **before** he begins a journey.

3. In future time sentences, the dependent (time) clause is in the present tense and the independent clause is in the future tense.

When food **is** plentiful, the population **will** grow.

(continued on next page)

4. The sequence of actions and events in sentences with adverb time clauses is generally as follows:

- *before* + dependent clause: second action or event

  independent clause: first action or event

  second   first
  Before Europeans arrived, the area was sparsely settled.

- *after* + dependent clause: first action or event

  independent clause: second action or event

  first   second
  After the people settled, the population grew.

- *Since* + dependent clause signals the beginning of the action in the independent clause. In a dependent clause beginning with *since*, the verb is usually in the simple past tense. The verb in the independent clause is usually in the present perfect.

  The population **has grown** since the Europeans **arrived**.

- *when / whenever / as soon as / once* + dependent clause: first action or event

  independent clause: second action or event

  first
  When / Whenever / As soon as / Once food is second plentiful, the population grows.

- *while / as / as long as*

  In sentences with these subordinating conjunctions, actions or events in both clauses occur at the same time. *While*, *as*, and *as long as* are often followed by the progressive form of the verb.

  While / As / As long as the men were hunting, the women gathered wild plants.

  While / As the women **are gathering** grain, the men meet to discuss the hunt.

Exercise 1 Identifying Adverb Clauses of Time

With a partner, underline examples of adverb clauses of time and discuss what time relationship they express between the events presented.

1. There were people in Australia before Europeans arrived.
2. After the Europeans landed, the original inhabitants experienced a great change in their lives.
3. Once the Europeans settled in Australia, the aborigines moved to the desert regions of the continent.
4. Native people suffer whenever more economically developed people move into their territory.
5. As the native people were trying to adjust to their new circumstances, the invaders began to mistreat them.
6. Newly introduced diseases begin to decimate native populations as soon as they encounter outsiders.

Choosing Subordinating Conjunctions

Choose the correct subordinating conjunctions to complete the sentences.

1. A new species emerges (*when* / *before*) changes in traits or geographic barriers result in the reproductive isolation of the population.[3]

2. (*While* / *Until*) Darwin was completing his book on the subject, naturalist Alfred Russell Wallace (1823–1913) sent him a manuscript that came to conclusions about the evolution of species that matched Darwin's own.[4]

3. (*After* / *While*) Darwin's revolutionary work was published, the Neanderthal find aroused considerable controversy.[5]

4. The presumed place of origin of the first modern humans has varied over the years (*as* / *until*) new fossils have been discovered.[6]

5. In anthropology, as in any discipline, there is a continual ebb and flow of ideas. One theoretical orientation will arise and may grow in popularity (*until* / *as long as*) another is proposed in opposition to it.[7]

CHART 10-3	Adverb Time Clauses with Special Meanings
1. In some sentences, *when* means "if" or "every time that" and signals a definition. This usage is common in academic writing.	1. **When** scientists talk about populations, they mean groups of people.
2. *Only when* means "never except when." At the beginning of a sentence, *only when* requires question word order with the addition of the appropriate auxiliary verb for the tense in the independent clause. This form is used for emphasis.	2. The population grows **only when** the food is plentiful. Only when the food is plentiful **does** the population grow.
3. *Even when* signals that the idea expressed in the dependent clause is unusual or seems to be impossible and the action or event in the independent clause is unexpected.	3. Scientists try to solve the most challenging problems **even when** they seem impossible to solve.
4. *Not until* signals the moment when something finally happens. At the beginning of a sentence, *not until* requires question word order with the addition of the appropriate auxiliary verb for the tense in the independent clause. This form is used for emphasis.	4. The girl does **not** meet her husband **until** she is married. (The girl is married before she meets her husband.) It is **not until** the girl is married that she meets her husband. Not until the girl is married **does** she meet her husband.

Exercise 3 **Identifying Adverb Clauses with Special Meanings**

With a partner, underline examples of adverb clauses of time and discuss what they mean.

1. Only when the newly introduced diseases are under control will a native population recover.

2. Not until European Australians changed their behavior toward the aborigines did the native population stabilize.

3. When an anthropologist uses the word *aborigine*, he or she means a person or animal that has lived in a place from early times.

4. Scientists will continue to work to eradicate diseases even when they face the worst difficulties.

5. Anthropologists do not stop studying aboriginal populations until they discover their origins and beliefs.

Exercise 4 Choosing Subordinating Conjunctions with Special Meanings

Choose the correct subordinating conjunctions to complete the sentences.

1. (*Only when / Until*) we compare ourselves with people in other societies may we become aware of cultural differences and similarities.[8]

2. The Shavante inhabit the Mato Grosso region of Brazil. Right into the middle of the twentieth century, they were hostile to Brazilians of European ancestry who tried to move into their territory. (*Not until / When*) the 1950s was peaceful contact with the 2,000 or so Shavante achieved.[9]

3. (*Only when / When*) we say that an exchange is balanced, we do not mean to imply that the things exchanged are exactly equivalent in value or that the exchange is purely economic.[10]

4. We may not realize that we are different from another culture (*even when / only when*) we study it.

Exercise 5 Using Adverb Clauses of Time to Create More Substantial, Interesting Sentences

On a separate sheet of paper, combine each pair of sentences into a single sentence using one of these conjunctions: *when, while, after, as, once, only when, even when*. Make any necessary changes. Be careful of punctuation.

1. a. In our society, children may live away.
   b. They go to college.

2. a. We contrast horticulture and intensive agriculture.
   b. The physical environment appears to explain some of the variation.

3. a. Anthropologists speak of marriage.
   b. They do not mean to imply that couples everywhere must get marriage certificates or have wedding ceremonies, as in our own society.

4. a. Someone discovers or invents something.
   b. There is still the question of whether others will adopt the innovation.

5. a. Archaeologists find other substantial differences, as in house size and furnishings.
   b. We can be sure the society had different socioeconomic classes of people.

6. a. The climate of what is now the American Southwest became drier.
   b. The animals and the cultural adaptations changed somewhat.

7. a. We know that an economic transformation occurred in widely separate areas of the world beginning after about 10,000 years ago.
   b. People began to domesticate plants and animals.

8. a. Humans colonized the Americas.
   b. They established a way of life very similar to that of their Upper Paleolithic cousins in the Old World, a life generally based on big game hunting.

CHART 10-4	Other Structures That Express Time Relationships

1. Simple sentences

| Time relationships may be expressed in simple sentences that begin or end with a prepositional phrase introduced by *before, after, since, while, until, once, by* (= not later than), or *during* (= within the limit of a period of time). | . . . the camp begins to stir just **before** sunrise. . . . |
| A conjunctive adverb between two simple sentences can express a time relationship. *Meanwhile* means "at the same time." | **By** noon, the men and women are usually back at camp. . . .
 Their children ride on their hips or walk alongside. **Meanwhile**, the men have decided to hunt emus. . . . |

2. Compound sentences

| A conjunctive adverb can join two simple sentences to form a compound sentence that expresses a time relationship. | Their children ride on their hips or walk alongside; **meanwhile**, the men have decided to hunt emus. . . . |

Exercise 6 Identifying Simple and Compound Sentences with Expressions of Time

With a partner, underline the expressions of time. Discuss which ones are in simple sentences and which one is in a compound sentence. Explain what time relationships they convey. See Chart 10-4.

The Gibson Desert in Australia is extremely hot during the summer. The inhabitants of a typical aboriginal camp in the desert wake up before dawn. After eating breakfast, the men and women plan their day. The morning is spent gathering food and collecting water. The women bring plant foods to the camp; meanwhile, the men bring game such as rabbits. Once home again, they spend the early afternoon resting. The women prepare and cook the food until late afternoon. By evening, everyone is ready to eat. During the meal, everyone laughs and talks about the day.

Exercise 7 Choosing the Correct Conjunction or Preposition

Fill in each blank with one of these conjunctions or prepositions: *when, after, during, before, once, until, meanwhile, by, as*. Punctuation and word order may provide clues.

1. _____ we discuss each school of thought, we will indicate what kinds of information or phenomena it emphasizes (if it does) as explanatory factors. Some of these orientations have passed into history _____ now; others continue to attract adherents.[11]

2. In the United States, there is a tendency to equate "work" with a job earning income. _____ relatively recently, being a "homemaker" was not counted as an occupation.[12]

3. Evidence from a few societies suggests that the degree of sharing may actually increase _____ the period of food shortage.[13]

4. _____ the 1950s, the Yanomamö had only stone axes, so felling trees was quite difficult.[14]

5. _____ the ground is cleared, the Yanomamö plant plantains, manioc, sweet potatoes, taro, and a variety of plants for medicine, condiments, and craft materials. . . . _____ two or three years, the yields diminish and the forest starts growing back, making continued cultivation less desirable and more difficult, so they abandon the garden and clear a new one.[15]

6. The Yanomamö men do the work of clearing the land. _____, the women plant the crops.

CHART 10-5	Adverb Clauses of Cause / Effect (Reason / Result), Purpose, and Manner

1. Cause / effect ideas can be expressed in adverb (dependent) clauses introduced by the subordinating conjunctions *as*, *since*, *because*, and *inasmuch as* (formal), which express the reason something happens. The following subordinating conjunctions also express causality:

- *now that* = since, because

- *as (so) long as* = since (used to introduce a condition that will make something happen)

The following subordinating conjunctions, which also express causality, are very formal:

- *on account of* (*the fact that*) = because

- *due to* (*the fact that*) = because

- *owing to* (*the fact that*) = because

- *in view of* (*the fact that*) = because

1. **As / Since / Because / Inasmuch as** vaccines have been developed, some diseases may disappear entirely.

Now that vaccines are available, everyone should be vaccinated.

These diseases will continue to be rare **as (so) long as** people keep being vaccinated.

In view of the fact that we have effective vaccines, we need to be sure to use them.

2. Purpose is expressed in an adverb clause introduced by the subordinating conjunction *so that* or *in order that*. The verb in the adverb clause often includes a modal auxiliary verb such as *will*, *would*, *can*, or *could*. These clauses follow the sequence-of-tense rule: If a past tense is used in the main (independent) clause, a past tense should be used in the subordinate (dependent) clause.

2. Scientists develop vaccines **so that** / **in order that** people can develop immunity to disease.

Scientists **developed** vaccines so that people **could develop** immunity to disease.

3. Manner (how something is or was done) is expressed in an adverb clause introduced by the subordinating conjunction *as*.

3. The "pox," **as** it was called in the past, was a popular name for smallpox.

Exercise 8 — Identifying Adverb Clauses of Cause / Effect, Purpose, and Manner

With a partner, underline the adverb clauses of cause / effect, purpose, and manner in the following passage. Discuss their meanings.

Isolated native populations are at risk because they are not immune to many diseases. Inasmuch as previously exposed populations already have immunity to such diseases, they are likely to carry the diseases into new areas. Smallpox is a good example. The first European explorers to the Americas introduced smallpox to the native populations. In view of the fact that the Native Americans had never encountered smallpox, they were immediately infected. Many of them died as medicines were largely ineffective. Eventually, vaccines were developed so that diseases like smallpox could be eradicated. As historians have noted, this chain of events was repeated throughout American history.

Using Adverb Clauses of Cause / Effect and Purpose to Create Richer Sentences

On a separate sheet of paper, combine each pair of sentences into a single sentence using one of these conjunctions: *so that, as, because, since, inasmuch as, now that*. Make any necessary changes. Be careful of punctuation.

1. a. Language is an open system.
   b. We can make up meaningful utterances that we have never heard before.
2. a. The Monte Verde site has been reliably dated.
   b. We know that there were people south of Canada before the Clovis people were in New Mexico.
3. a. It seems as if people go to war to protect themselves ahead of time from disasters.
   b. The victors in war almost always take resources (land, animals, other things) from the defeated, even when the victors have no current resource problems.
4. a. . . . taro patches can produce a few crops before they must be allowed to revert to bush.
   b. Soil fertility can be restored.
5. a. . . . in describing the Netsilik Inuit, Asen Balikci said, "Whenever game was abundant, sharing among nonrelatives was avoided."
   b. "Every family was supposedly capable of obtaining the necessary catch."

CHART 10-6	**Other Structures That Express Cause / Effect, Purpose, and Manner**

1. Simple sentences

a. Cause / effect is expressed in simple sentences with an adverb phrase (*because of, due to, on account of, owing to,* and *in view of*) + a noun.	a. Many native people died **because of / due to** disease. **Because of / Due to** disease, many native people died. **On account of / Owing to / In view of** their lack of immunity, many natives died of European diseases. Many natives died of European diseases **on account of / owing to / in view of** their lack of immunity.
So introduces a simple sentence that is the <u>effect</u> / <u>result</u> of the sentence before it.	^{cause} Both parents take care of the children. **So** it ^{result} is easy for them to feed themselves and their children.
For introduces a simple sentence that is the <u>cause</u> of the sentence before it.	^{result} It is easy for parents to feed themselves and their children. **For** both parents take care of them. ^{cause}
Therefore, thus, consequently, as a result, and *hence* introduce simple sentences of effect / result. *Therefore, thus, consequently,* and *as a result* are followed by a comma. A sentence showing cause precedes a sentence showing effect / result.	^{cause} Both parents take are of the children. ^{effect / result} **Therefore, / Thus, / Consequently, / As a result, / Hence,** it is easy for them to feed themselves and their children.

(continued on next page)

b. Purpose is expressed in simple sentences with the phrase *in order to* at the beginning or at the end of the sentence.	purpose b. **In order to** combat diseases, vaccines were developed. Vaccines were developed **in order to** combat diseases.
c. Manner is expressed in simple sentences with a phrase beginning with *as* + past participle or a noun phrase. (Note that adverb phrases will be treated more fully in Chapter 12.)	c. Some people use plants **as** medical treatment.

2. Compound sentences

Compound sentences expressing cause / effect are connected with coordinating conjunctions (*for* and *so*):	
So introduces a result.	Both parents take care of the children, **so** it is easy for them to feed themselves and their children.
For introduces a cause. A comma precedes *so* and *for*.	It is easy for parents to feed themselves and their children, **for** both parents take care of them.
Compound sentences expressing cause / effect may also be constructed with conjunctive adverbs (*therefore*, *thus*, *consequently*, *hence*) or a transition (*as a result*). A semicolon precedes *therefore*, *thus*, *consequently*, and *as a result*. A comma follows.	Both parents take care of the children; **therefore, / thus, / consequently, / hence / as a result,** it is easy for them to feed themselves and their children.
Hence may follow *and* or a comma. *Therefore* may follow *and*.	Both parents take care of the children, and **hence / therefore** it is easy for them to feed themselves and their children.
A semicolon can replace any of the conjunctions or conjunctive adverbs.	Smallpox is rare; we have a vaccine against it.
Because, *because of*, *since*, *so*, and *as a result* are common in formal and informal English.	
Therefore, *thus*, *consequently*, *hence*, and *for* are primarily formal.	

3. Compound-complex sentences

Compound-complex sentences are combinations of simple, complex, and compound sentences. They are common in academic writing. The minimum compound-complex sentence contains two independent clauses connected with a coordinating conjunction or a conjunctive adverb + one dependent clause.	independent clause dependent clause Families need help, **and when** children are born, independent clause they will probably need even more help. dependent clause independent clause **When** families need help, it is important to independent clause provide it; **however,** parents must also contribute.

Exercise 10 Identifying Types of Sentences

With a partner, match each lettered description to the appropriate sentence. (Some descriptions will have more than one match.) The part of each sentence that identifies it as the specified type is underlined.

a. Simple sentence expressing cause
b. Simple sentence expressing effect
c. Compound sentence expressing cause

d. Compound sentence expressing effect
e. Complex sentence expressing purpose
f. Complex sentence expressing manner

_____ 1. Native Americans became infected with smallpox, <u>for they had never encountered it</u>.

_____ 2. European explorers carried smallpox to the New World, <u>so many natives became infected</u>.

_____ 3. Native populations are not immune to some diseases; <u>therefore, they easily become infected</u>.

_____ 4. <u>Due to recent technological discoveries</u>, scientists can help people with viral diseases.

_____ 5. Most people today are immune to smallpox; <u>scientists created an effective vaccine</u>.

_____ 6. Vaccines have been developed <u>so that people will not become infected with diseases like smallpox</u>.

_____ 7. New vaccines have not always performed <u>as researchers expected</u>.

_____ 8. Most people have been vaccinated. Thus, many diseases <u>have nearly disappeared</u>.

Exercise 11 Choosing the Correct Conjunction

Choose the correct words to complete the following passages.

1. Food appears in markets or supermarkets already processed by other specialists. It comes in paper or plastic packages, looking far different from how it originally looked in the field or on the feedlot. _____ (*Thus,* / *By the time*) most of us are "market foragers," collecting our food from stores.[16]

2. Bronislaw Malinowski noted that people in all societies are faced with anxiety and uncertainty. They may have skills and knowledge to take care of many of their needs, but knowledge is not sufficient to prevent illness, accidents, and natural disasters. The most frightening prospect is death itself. _____ (*However,* / *Consequently,*) there is an intense desire for immortality (Malinowski 1939; Malinowski 1954).[17]

3. It seems clear that the Egyptian aristocracy and royalty indulged in father-daughter and brother-sister marriages. Cleopatra was married to two of her younger brothers at different times (Middleton 1962). The reasons seem to have been partly religious—a member of the family of the pharaoh, who was considered a god, could not marry any "ordinary" human—and partly economic, _____ (*for* / *because of*) marriage within the family kept the royal property undivided. In Egypt, between 30 B.C. and A.D. 324, incest was allowed not just in the royal family; an estimated 8 percent of commoner marriages were brother-sister marriages (Durham 1991).[18]

4. There is no disagreement that humans were living south of Canada around 11,000 years ago. The Clovis people, _____ (*as* / *because of*) they are called (after an archaeological site near Clovis, New Mexico), left finely shaped spear points in many locations in North America. And we have human skeletal remains from _____ (*during* / *after*) 11,000 years ago. _____ (*Before* / *Now that*) the Monte Verde site has been reliably dated, we know that there were people south of Canada _____ (*before* / *, for*) the Clovis people were in New Mexico.[19]

(continued on next page)

5. We imagine that establishments like McDonald's promote fast eating. But Japan has long had fast food—noodle shops at train stations, street vendors, and boxed lunches. Sushi, which is usually ordered in the United States at a sit-down restaurant, is usually served in Japan at a bar with a conveyor belt—individuals only need to pluck off the wanted dish _____ (*since / as*) it goes by. Observations at McDonald's in Japan suggest that mothers typically order food for the family _____ (*consequently, / while*) the father spends time with the children at a table, a rare event _____ (*before / since*) fathers often work long hours and cannot get home for dinner often.[20]

6. Most theories about the development of money and market exchange assume that producers have regular surpluses they want to exchange. But why do people produce surpluses in the first place? Perhaps they are motivated to produce extra _____ (*so that / only when*) they want to obtain goods from a distance and the suppliers of such goods are not well known to them, making reciprocity less likely as a way to obtain those goods. _____ (*Because of / So*) some theorists suggest that market exchange begins with external, or intersocietal, trade; kin would not likely be involved, _____ (*once / so*) transactions would involve bargaining, and therefore are market exchange, by definition. Finally, some argue that, _____ (*not until / as*) societies become more complex and more densely populated, social bonds between individuals become less kinlike and friendly, and _____ (*when / therefore*) reciprocity becomes less likely (Pryor 1977). Perhaps this is why traders in developing areas are often foreigners or recent immigrants (B. Foster 1974).[21]

Exercise 12 Using Adverb Clauses to Show Cause / Effect Relationships between Ideas

On a separate sheet of paper, rewrite the following passages, using the given conjunctions. Make any necessary changes. Pay special attention to punctuation. The first one is done for you.

1. In the competition for land between the faster-expanding food producers and the foragers, the food producers may have had a significant advantage: They had more people in a given area. The foraging groups may have been more likely to lose out in the competition for land. (*thus*)

   In the competition for land between the faster-expanding food producers and the foragers, the food producers may have had a significant advantage: They had more people in a given area. Thus, the foraging groups may have been more likely to lose out in the competition for land.[22]

2. In the 19th century, Western missionaries in all parts of the world encouraged natives to wear Western clothing. In Africa, the Pacific Islands, and elsewhere, native peoples can be found wearing shorts, suit jackets, shirts, ties, and other typically Western articles of clothing. (*hence*)

3. Higher-status individuals give directions and solutions; they do not seek directions or solutions. Asking for directions is like acknowledging lower status. (*so*)

4. In most horticultural societies, simple farming techniques have tended to yield more food from a given area than is generally available to foragers. Horticulture is able to support larger, more densely populated communities. (*consequently*)

5. But the practical advantages of the kula ring are not the only gains. There may be purely social ones. Goods are traded with ease and enjoyment. (*for*)

6. As we will see in the next section, people do behave differently in social groups in ways that they might not even imagine ahead of time. Mob behavior is an extreme, but telling example. We think we should look at behavior as well as rules or ideas in people's heads in describing a culture. (*therefore*)

7. The horticultural Trobriand Islanders, who live off the eastern coast of New Guinea, worked out an elaborate scheme for trading ornaments, food, and other necessities with the people of neighboring islands. The exchange of goods between far-flung islands is essential. Some of the islands are small and rocky and cannot produce enough food to sustain their inhabitants, who specialize instead in canoe building, pottery making, and other crafts. (*for*)

8. When enough individuals change their behavior and beliefs, we say that the culture has changed. It is possible for culture change to occur much more rapidly than genetic change. (*therefore*)

Exercise 13 Writing Sentences with Adverb Clauses

Complete the sentences based on information from Exercise 11.

1. People everywhere have a desire for immortality due to

_____

_____

_____.

2. Ancient Egyptian royalty married within their own families because

_____

_____

_____.

3. We can be described as "market foragers," for

_____

_____

_____.

An ancient Egyptian scroll

4. At McDonald's, Japanese fathers sit with their children as

_____

_____

_____.

5. The Clovis people were in New Mexico after

_____

_____

_____.

6. According to Pryor (1977), people produce surpluses so that

_____

_____

_____.

The following student essay contains ten errors. The first error is corrected for you. Work in pairs to find and correct nine more.

The Old World and the New World

Anthropologists have been studying the effects of interaction between isolated native populations and the populations that invade them. As soon ~~as~~ the outside culture moves into the native culture's territory, the natives experience a variety of problems, some of which may threaten their very survival. Researchers have found that the greatest problems occurred due to the Old World moved into the New World. A threat to survival was experienced by the Native Americans when the Europeans first arrived in the New World. The explorers and colonists brought not only measles and smallpox but also cholera, yellow fever, and other even more destructive diseases. In Europe, those diseases had existed in the population for centuries. The Europeans were periodically infected and many died. Thus, a few survived before they had developed immunity to the diseases. Survivors passed along this immunity to their children, and, before several generations, many people were immune. Consequently, they might have become ill, but most of them survived. However, until some of those slightly infected Europeans had contact with a vulnerable community that lacked immunity, such as the Native American tribes, much of that population succumbed. In fact, entire villages were destroyed.

Later, the Europeans brought African slaves to the New World. Hence the Africans arrived, a variety of tropical diseases added to the reduction of the Native American population. The Europeans were also vulnerable to the African infections, as long as they did not succumb in such great numbers. Historians have estimated that up to 90 percent of the native population of the New World was destroyed because the diseases brought by the Europeans and their slaves.

Exercise 15 Apply It to Speaking

Read the two passages on the following page, each of which deals with marriage customs in another culture. Then, with a classmate, follow the steps outlined to study the organization of each paragraph.

1 Referring to Appendix B, identify and underline the topic sentence—the sentence that introduces the main idea—of each paragraph.
2 Put parentheses around the time clauses, phrases, and other words that indicate time in each paragraph. Discuss how these help the reader to understand the order of events that take place before and during the marriage ceremony.
3 Be prepared to share your conclusions with the class.

APPLICATION

Marriage Customs

Many societies have ceremonies marking the beginning of marriage.
. . . Among those societies that have ceremonies marking the onset
of marriage, feasting is a common element. It expresses publicly the
unification of two families by marriage. The Reindeer Tungus of Siberia
set a wedding date after protracted negotiations between the two
families and their larger kin groups. Go-betweens assume most of the
responsibility for the negotiating. The wedding day opens with the two
kin groups, probably numbering as many as 150 people, pitching their
lodges in separate areas and offering a great feast. After the groom's gifts

An Indonesian wedding

have been presented, the bride's dowry is loaded onto reindeer and carried to the groom's lodge. There, the
climax of the ceremony takes place. The bride takes the wife's place—that is, at the right side of the entrance
of the lodge—and members of both families sit in a circle. The groom enters and follows the bride around the
circle, greeting each guest, while the guests, in their turn, kiss the bride on the mouth and hands. Finally, the go-
betweens spit three times on the bride's hands, and the couple are formally husband and wife. More feasting and
revelry bring the day to a close (Service 1978).[23]

The Kwoma of New Guinea practice a trial marriage followed by a ceremony that makes the couple husband
and wife. The girl lives for a while in the boy's home. When the boy's mother is satisfied with the match and
knows that her son is too, she waits for a day when he is away from the house. Until that time, the girl has been
cooking only for herself, and the boy's food has been prepared by his womenfolk. Now the mother has the girl
prepare his meal. The young man returns and begins to eat his soup. When the first bowl is nearly finished, his
mother tells him that his betrothed cooked the meal, and his eating it means that he is now married. At this
news, the boy customarily rushes out of the house, spits out the soup, and shouts, "Faugh! It tastes bad! It is
cooked terribly!" A ceremony then makes the marriage official (J.W.M. Whiting 1941)[24]

Exercise 16 Apply It to Speaking

In small groups, describe the marriage customs in your country or in a country you know about.
Address the following questions in your discussion, supporting your ideas with specific details and examples.

1. How do a future bride and groom usually meet? Are they introduced by their parents? Or do they find
   each other?
2. Is there a courtship period? If so, what is it like?
3. What are the first "official" steps for a couple who plans to get married? An engagement? Other traditions?
4. Describe typical wedding festivities. Who is involved? What events are associated with a wedding, and in
   what order do they take place?

Exercise 17 Apply It to Writing

Write a paragraph or two about marriage customs in your country. Be sure to include a good topic sentence
to introduce the main idea of each paragraph. Then use sentences expressing time, cause / effect, purpose,
and manner and some of the vocabulary from the box in your paragraph(s). See Appendix B for help.

bride	ceremony	clothing	couple	courtship
feast	groom	kin	wedding	

Adverb Clauses and Other Structures That Express Concession, Opposition, and Condition

A couple taking a "selfie," or self-portrait

PREVIEW

VOCABULARY   Here are some words that you will encounter in Chapter 11. How much do you know about each word? Turn to Appendix A to assess and expand your word knowledge.

aggression	assertiveness	behavior	compliant	constraint
dating	gender	misinterpret	sample	strive

Prepare to Read

1. Describe courtship customs in your culture.
2. How are your customs different from other customs you know about?

Read the following passage from *Anthropology,* 13th Edition, by
Carol R. Ember, Melvin Ember, and Peter N. Peregrine.[1]

Courtship and Marriage

[1]Using observation and interviewing, anthropologists discover the customs and the ranges of acceptable behavior that characterize the society under study.

[2]Similarly, anthropologists interested in describing courtship and marriage in our society would encounter a variety of behaviors*. Dating couples vary in where they go (coffee shops, movies, restaurants, bowling alleys), what behaviors they engage in on dates, how long they date before they split up or move on to more serious relationships. **If they decide to marry**, ceremonies may be simple or elaborate and involve either religious or secular rituals*. Despite this variability, the anthropologists would begin to detect certain regularities* in courting practices. **Although couples may do many different things on their first and subsequent dates**, they nearly always arrange the dates by themselves; they try to avoid their parents when on dates; they often manage to find themselves alone at the end of a date; they put their lips together frequently; and so forth. After a series of more and more closely spaced encounters, a man and woman may decide to declare themselves publicly as a couple, either by announcing that they are engaged or by revealing that they are living together or intend to do so. Finally, if the two of them decide to marry, they must in some way have their union recorded by the civil authorities.

[3]In our society, a person who wishes to marry cannot completely disregard the customary patterns of courtship. If a man saw a woman on the street and decided he wanted to marry her, he could conceivably choose a quicker and more direct form of action than the usual dating procedure. He could get on a horse, ride to the woman's home, snatch her up in his arms, and gallop away with her. In Sicily, until the last few decades, such a couple would have been considered legally married, even if the woman had never met the man before or had no intention of marrying. But in North American society, any man who acted in such a fashion would be arrested and jailed for kidnapping and would probably have his sanity challenged. Although individual behaviors may vary, most social behavior falls within culturally acceptable limits.[2]

* *behaviors*—kinds of behavior (*Behavior* is usually a noncount noun with no plural form; however, the social sciences use it as a count noun.)
* *ritual*—a ceremony that is always performed in the same way in order to mark an important religious or social occasion
* *regularities*—repeated actions

Review the Ideas

1. What behaviors might an anthropologist interested in courtship and marriage in America discover?
2. What are some of the regularities of courtship the anthropologist will discover?
3. What behavior was common in Sicily decades ago? What would happen to a man who did that in America today?

Analyze the Grammar

1. Look at the boldfaced groups of words in the second paragraph of the passage. Are they phrases or clauses? How do you know? What words introduce them?

2. Why do we use these clauses? Hint: In the first sentence, what has to happen in order for the ceremonies to take place? In the second sentence, are the two clauses about the same ideas or do they express slightly different ideas?

3. Underline other clauses in the passage similar in function to the two clauses in boldface.

CHART 11-1	Adverb Clauses of Concession and Opposition

1. An adverb clause of concession (dependent clause) expresses an idea that is followed by an unexpected result in the independent clause.

<table>
<tr><td>

The following subordinating conjunctions have the same meaning and are associated with adverb clauses of concession.

- *although* (most common)
- *though* (least formal)
- *even though* (more formal)

Though may be placed at the end of a simple sentence that expresses concession.

REMEMBER: When the adverb clause comes first, it is followed by a comma.

</td><td>

Although / **Even though** / **Though** chimpanzees are fruit eaters**,** they eat meat.

Chimpanzees eat meat **although** / **even though** / **though** they are fruit eaters.

Chimpanzees will eat meat. They are fruit eaters, **though.**

</td></tr>
</table>

2. An adverb clause can express the idea of contrast or opposition.

<table>
<tr><td>

The subordinating conjunctions *while* and *whereas* appear at the beginning of adverb clauses of opposition. These clauses express an idea that is opposite to the idea in the independent clause.

A comma follows the adverb clause when that clause is first. A comma also precedes *while* and *whereas* when the adverb clause comes second.

While and *whereas* are used in formal writing and speech.

</td><td>

While / **Whereas** males disperse, the females stay together.

The females stay together, **while** / **whereas** the males disperse.[3]

Whereas sociologists study the social behavior of large groups of people**,** anthropologists study the past and present culture and language of smaller groups.

Anthropologists study the past and present culture and language of small groups**,** **whereas** sociologists study the social behavior of large groups of people.

</td></tr>
</table>

Exercise 1 Identifying Clauses of Concession and Opposition

With a partner, underline each adverb clause of concession once and each adverb clause of opposition twice. Discuss their meanings. Explain why the result in each concession sentence is unexpected. Explain how the concession sentences differ from the opposition sentences.

1. Although all societies have marriage, courtship customs may differ.

2. While some couples enjoy playing sports together, others may prefer quieter activities like playing board games.

3. Even though some cultures don't practice courtship in the same way our society does, they all have marriage.

GRAMMAR

ANTHROPOLOGY

4. Younger couples may go to the movies together, whereas older couples may go to the theater.

5. Although they are very young, girls in some cultures may marry at the age of twelve.

6. In American society, young couples go out on dates. They don't always engage in the same activities, though.

Exercise 2 Identifying Clauses of Concession and Opposition in Context

With a partner, find and underline the dependent clauses of concession and opposition once and underline the independent clauses twice.

1. Why do women have few rights and little influence in some societies and more of each in other societies? . . . There are many theories about why women have relatively high or low status. . . . What does predict higher status for women in many areas of life? Although the results are not that strong, there is some support in Whyte's study for the theory that women have somewhat higher status where kin groups and marital residence are organized around women. The Iroquois are a good example. Even though Iroquois women could not hold political office, they had considerable authority within and beyond the household.[4]

2. Herbert Barry, Irvin Child, and Margaret Bacon cross-culturally investigated the possibility that child-training practices are adapted to the economic requirements of a society. Such requirements, they theorized, might explain why some societies strive to develop "compliant" (responsible, obedient, nurturant) children, whereas others aim more for "assertiveness" (independence, self-reliance, and achievement) (Barry et al. 1959). The cross-cultural results indicated that agricultural and herding societies are likely to stress responsibility and obedience, whereas hunting and gathering societies tend to stress self-reliance and individual assertiveness.[5]

Exercise 3 Selecting the Correct Subordinating Conjunction

Select the best subordinating conjunctions to complete the passages.

1. _____ (*If* / *Although*) giving things to others may be expected in some societies, this does not necessarily mean that everyone does so willingly or without some social pressure. For example, the !Kung call "far-hearted" anyone who does not give gifts, and they express their disapproval openly.[6]

2. Claude Lévi-Strauss (1908–2009) was the leading proponent of an approach to cultural analysis called structuralism. Lévi-Strauss's structuralism differs from that of Radcliffe-Brown.
_____ (*Even though* / *Whereas*) Radcliffe-Brown concentrated on how the elements of a society function as a system, Lévi-Strauss concentrates more on the origins of the systems themselves. He sees culture, as expressed in art, ritual, and the patterns of daily life, as a surface representation of the underlying structure of the human mind.[7]

3. The islands of Samoa, which are about 2,300 miles south of the Hawaiian Islands, are volcanic in origin, with central ridges and peaks as high as 6,000 feet. _____ (*Conversely,* / *Though*) the land is generally steep, the islands have a lush plant cover watered by up to 200 inches of rain a year (about five times the amount of rain that falls on New York City in a year).[8]

4. . . . people may make mistakes in judgment, especially when some new behavior seems to satisfy a physical need. Why, for example, have smoking and drug use diffused so widely _____ (*even though* / *nevertheless*) they are likely to reduce a person's chances of survival? Second, even if people are correct in their short-term judgment of benefit, they may be wrong in their judgment about long-run benefit.[9]

Exercise 4 Writing the Correct Subordinating Conjunction

Fill in the blanks with *although*, *though*, *even though*, *while* or *whereas*. There may be more than one correct answer.

1. _____ many primates are omnivores, eating insects and small reptiles in addition to plants—some even hunt small mammals—only hominids hunt very large animals.[10]

2. Languages may show similarities _____ they do not derive from a common ancestral language and _____ there has been no contact or borrowing between them.[11]

3. _____ anthropology may have been born out of its largely colonialist background, anthropologists are now overwhelmingly inclined to support the value of other ways of life and try to support the needs of peoples formerly colonized or dominated by powerful nation-states.[12]

4. Some variations in music may be explained as a consequence of variation in childrearing practices. For example, researchers are beginning to explore childrearing as a way to explain why some societies respond to, and produce, regular rhythm in their music, _____ others enjoy free rhythm that has no regular beat.[13]

CHART 11-2	Other Structures That Express Opposition
1. The ideas of concession and opposition can also be expressed in two simple sentences with a conjunction (*but*, yet, *however*, *nevertheless*, or *nonetheless*) at the beginning of the second sentence. The transitions *in contrast*, *conversely*, or *on the other hand* may also be used to show opposition.	1. The males disperse. **But / Yet / However, / Nevertheless, / Nonetheless,** the females stay together. The females stay together. **In contrast, / Conversely, / On the other hand,** the males disperse.
2. Contrasting ideas may also appear in compound sentences. Note punctuation: a comma before *but* and *yet*; a semicolon before *however*, *nevertheless*, *nonetheless*, *in contrast*, *conversely*, and *on the other hand* followed by a comma. All the conjunctions have the same meaning. Sometimes a semicolon is used alone and the contrasting meaning is understood.	2. The males disperse**, but** the females stay together. The males disperse**, yet** the females stay together. The males disperse**; however,** the females stay together. The males disperse**; nonetheless,** the females stay together. The males disperse**;** the females stay together.

Exercise 5 Rewriting Simple Sentences as Compound Sentences

Work with a partner. On a separate sheet of paper, rewrite the simple sentences as compound sentences. Be careful with punctuation.

1. Some couples decide to marry. However, others do not.

2. Some couples might play a strenuous game of tennis. Yet others may prefer a quiet walk in the park.

3. Young teenagers in the United States often go out in groups. Nevertheless, many individual teens would probably prefer to be with just one other person.

4. Music majors may enjoy going to the symphony on a date. On the other hand, science majors would probably rather visit a museum.

5. Couples may do many different things when they go out on dates. But they usually arrange the dates by themselves.

6. Until recently, a man in Sicily could marry a woman without her agreement. In contrast, nowadays that behavior is against the law.

Exercise 6 **Choosing the Correct Conjunction**

Complete the sentences with *nevertheless*, *nonetheless*, or a semicolon. Add any other appropriate punctuation. More than one answer may be correct.

1. Vervet monkeys in Africa are not as closely related to humans as are African apes. _____ scientists who have observed vervet monkeys in their natural environment consider at least three of their alarm calls to be symbolic because each of them means (refers to) a different kind of predator—eagles, pythons, or leopards—and monkeys react differently to each call. For example, they look up when they hear the "eagle" call [14]

2. The major source of animal protein in the Samoan diet is fish, caught inside and outside the reef. Younger men may swim in the deep sea outside the reef and use a sling to spear fish _____ older men are more likely to stand on the reef and throw a four-pointed spear at fish swimming inside the reef.[15]

3. All living primates, including humans, evolved from earlier primates that are now extinct. _____ by observing how humans and other primates differ from and resemble each other, we may be able to infer how and why humans diverged from the other primates.[16]

CHART 11-3	A Few Rules about Conjunction Usage
1. A subordinating conjunction and a coordinating conjunction, one at the beginning of each clause, may not be used in the same sentence.	1. INCORRECT: Although the males disperse, ~~but~~ the females stay. CORRECT: **Although** the males disperse, the females stay. CORRECT: The males disperse, **but** the females stay.
2. A coordinating conjunction and a subordinating conjunction may be used together to begin either a simple sentence or the second clause of a compound sentence.	2. The females stay together. **But although** the males disperse, they find other groups of females. The females stay together, **but although** the males disperse, they find other groups of females.
3. Two subordinating conjunctions may be used together at the beginning of a simple sentence. Note that the first subordinating conjunction connects the two sentences in a meaningful way.	3. The females stay together. **Although when** the males disperse, they find other groups of females.

Exercise 7 | Identifying Correct Sentences

With a partner decide which of the sentences are correct and which are incorrect. Discuss the reasons why.

1. Young couples need parental approval to date. Nevertheless, a young couple must get permission to date from their parents.
2. The couple is too young to marry. But since they want to date, their parents must agree.
3. Although the young couple is too young to marry, but it will be acceptable for them to date.
4. The couple is too young to marry even though it will be acceptable for them to date.
5. A young couple may want to date; nonetheless, they must get parental approval.

Exercise 8 | Writing Complex and Compound Sentences

Combine the following sentences in two ways, writing the alternatives on a separate sheet of paper. First, use a subordinating conjunction to create a single sentence containing an adverb clause of concession or contrast. Second, using one of the other conjunctions, rewrite each sentence as a compound sentence. Use the conjunctions from the boxes. See Charts 11-1, 11-2, and 11-3 for help. Pay attention to punctuation. The first one is done for you.

SUBORDINATING CONJUNCTIONS

although	even though	though	whereas	while

OTHER CONJUNCTIONS

but	however	nevertheless	nonetheless	yet

1. Radcliffe-Brown concentrated on how the elements of a society function as a system.

   Lévi-Strauss concentrates more on the origins of the systems themselves.

   a. *Whereas Radcliffe-Brown concentrated on how the elements of a society function as a system, Lévi-Strauss concentrates more on the origins of the systems themselves.* (also possible: *while*)

   b. *Radcliffe-Brown concentrated on how the elements of a society function as a system; however, Lévi-Strauss concentrates more on the origins of the systems themselves.* (also possible: *nevertheless* and *nonetheless, but* and *yet* preceded by a comma)

2. Chimpanzees are primarily fruit eaters.
   Chimpanzees show many similarities to their close relative, the gorillas.

3. A needle in a haystack is hard to find.
   One may be sure that the needle is there.

4. Most mutations may not be adaptive.
   Those that are will multiply in a population relatively quickly, by natural selection.

5. Our songs sometimes have single lines of nonwords.
   It is rare for an entire song to be made of them.w

6. Many primates have opposable thumbs that enable them to grasp and examine objects.
   The greater length and flexibility of the human thumb allows us to handle objects with more firmness and precision.

7. Other societies clearly and actively encourage aggression.
   The Semai communicate nonviolence in more subtle ways.

8. Anthropology may have been born out of its largely colonialist background.
   Anthropologists are now overwhelmingly inclined to support the value of other ways of life and try to support the needs of peoples formerly colonized or dominated by powerful nation-states.

CHART 11-4 | **Adverb Clauses of Condition: Real (True) Conditions**

If introduces adverb (dependent) clauses of condition. Conditional sentences may involve real (true or possible) conditions or unreal (contrary-to-fact or impossible) conditions.

1. Meaning and use

In real conditional sentences, the *if*-clause expresses a real or possible condition. The independent clause expresses a real or possible result of that condition. *If* has the meaning of *when* in these sentences.	**If** monkeys hear a call, they look up. = **When** monkeys hear a call, they look up.
Whenever is also used to mean "every time."	**Whenever** monkeys hear a call, they look up.
Either the *if-* (conditional) clause or the result clause may be first in the sentence. When the *if*-clause is first, it is followed by a comma.	**If the monkeys hear a call**, they look up. The monkeys look up **if they hear a call**.
When *should* is used in the *if*-clause, it expresses an unexpected action (the idea "happens to").	**If** monkeys **should** hear a call, they look up.

2. Forms: Present and future time

Active

If + subject + (*not*) + present verb, subject + (*may / can / will*) + (*not*) + verb	**If** you **attend** many football games, you **will observe** many activities. If a man **hunts** with his family, they (can / may) **share** the meat equally.
When the meaning is future, the present tense is used in the *if*-clause. The independent clause is in the future tense.	If the man **does not share** meat, the villagers **will not share** with him in the future.

Passive

If + subject + *is / are* + (*not*) + past participle, subject + (*may / will*) + (*not*) + *be* + past participle	If the call **is heard**, the monkeys **may not be attacked**.
One or both clauses can be passive.	If the call **is heard**, the monkeys **escape**.

3. Forms: Other tenses

The *if*-clause in real conditional sentences may be in the present, present perfect, or a past tense. They may use simple or progressive forms. The modals *can*, *may*, *would*, *should*, *could*, *might*, and *must* are possible in the independent clause. The meanings of the tenses are the same as in other English sentences. Any logical combination of tenses can be found.	If people **are living** in an area, they **are** probably **working** there. If people **have lived** in a place for a long time, they **know** the area well. If a man **hunted** with his family, they **shared** the meat equally. If people **were loved** as children, we can be sure they **are** well-adjusted today.

Exercise 9 **Identifying Real Conditionals**

With a partner underline the conditional clauses in the sentences. Discuss whether each conditional clause expresses past, present, or future time.

1. If a couple gets married, they must register the marriage with an official office.
2. The official office of registry will add the marriage to the records if the couple reports it correctly.
3. The records can get out of order if the couple has filled out the forms incorrectly.
4. If the couple should make a mistake, it's important to correct the error immediately.
5. If a couple has made the correction in time, the office corrects the records instantly.
6. Whenever the marriage registration office found a mistake in its records, an official was notified.
7. If the mistake had been made when the couple had filled out the forms, the official could correct it, but it was not a simple process.
8. The records are being checked more often when a mistake has been found.
9. Marriage records are being transferred to computers whenever it is possible because of the difficulty of finding mistakes in paper records.
10. New registrations may be entered directly into computer records when couples fill out their forms online.

CHART 11-5	Adverb Clauses of Condition: Unreal (Contrary-to-Fact) Conditions

1. Unreal (contrary-to-fact) conditionals in the present

	conditional (*if*) clause ⟶ independent (result) clause
a. In unreal conditional sentences in the present, *if* introduces an untrue condition in present time. The independent clause expresses a possible or desired result that will not happen.	a. If we had permission, we would study the culture.
Present forms: Active *If* + subject + (*not*) + past tense verb, subject + *would / could / might* + (*not*) + base verb	If we **wanted** to arrive at a cultural rule, we **could study** a sample.
Present forms: Passive *If* + subject + *be* + (*not*) + past participle, subject + *would / could / might* + (*not*) + *be* + past participle Either clause can be active or passive.	If we **were trained**, we **might be considered** for the job.
b. *Were* is used for all forms of *be* in present tense unreal *if*-clauses. When the *if*- (dependent) clause is first, it is followed by a comma.	b. If Margaret Mead **were** alive today, she would still do research. If the community **were** settled, we would call it a village.

2. Unreal (contrary-to-fact) conditionals in the past

In unreal (contrary-to-fact) conditional sentences in the past, *if* introduces an untrue or imaginary past condition. The independent clause expresses a result that did not happen.	If we **had wanted** to arrive at a cultural rule, we **could have studied** a sample.

Past forms: Active *If* + subject + *had* + (*not*) + past participle, subject + *could | might | would* + (*not*) + *have* + past participle	If we **had asked** her, she **would have helped** with our research.
Past forms: Passive *If* + subject + *had* + (*not*) + *been* + past participle, subject + *could | might | would* + (*not*) + *have* + *been* + past participle	If she **had been interested**, she **would have been chosen** immediately.

3. Other unreal conditional forms

Mixed time conditionals are used when the conditional clause takes place at a different time from the result clause:	
a. Past condition with a present result	a. If Mead **had not studied** anthropology, we **would not have** the results of her research today.
b. Progressive forms in either clause	b. If we **had wanted** a cultural rule, we **could be studying** a sample now. If Mead **had been using** different techniques, we **would have** them today as well.
There may be multiple result clauses.	If we **were** confident in our results, we **might write** up the results. We **could** also **publish** them, and as a result, the world **would know** about our research.

Exercise 10 **Identifying Unreal Conditionals**

With a partner, identify the sentence that contains the conditional described. Discuss your choices.

1. An unreal conditional
   a. If I were you, I would study harder.
   b. If they were tired, they took a rest.
   c. They are successful if they are careful.
   d. If you should need help, you can call me.

2. An unreal conditional expressing present time
   a. We should work longer hours if we plan to finish the project.
   b. We could leave early if the work has been done.
   c. If we wanted to finish the project, we would work longer hours.
   d. The members of the committee were pleased if everyone was on time.

3. An unreal conditional expressing past time
   a. If you have finished your work, would you like to leave early?
   b. If we plan to finish early, we could stop immediately.
   c. We might finish early if we worked harder.
   d. If we had wanted to finish early, we would have started this morning.

(continued on next page)

4. An unreal conditional expressing mixed time

    a. They would be finished now if they had started earlier.

    b. If they started earlier, they could leave earlier.

    c. They could have left the meeting if they had wanted to.

    d. The committee could have been meeting at 9 A.M. if they had been willing to come to work early.

CHART 11-6	Other Structures That Express Conditions

In Complex Sentences:

1. Real conditions

A conditional clause that begins with *unless* expresses the idea *if not*.	**Unless** a man hunts with his family, they will not share the meat equally. **If** a man does **not** hunt with his family, they will not share the meat equally.
Only if = there is only one condition that will give this result. When *only if* is first, the verb and the subject are reversed in the independent clause.	You will pass the test **only if** you study. **Only if** you study, **will you pass** the test.
On condition that, *provided that*, *providing that*, *in the event that*, *in case*, *given that*, and *assuming that* may also be used in place of *if*. The meanings are the same. These expressions are more formal than *if*.	**Providing that** she calls, ask for a message. **In the event that** she calls, ask for a message. **Given that** she plans to call, ask for a message. **Assuming that** she calls, ask for a message.
The conditional clause may begin with *should*. This structure is quite formal.	**Should** she call, ask for a message.

2. Unreal conditions

Conditional clauses may begin with *were* or *had*. These structures are very formal.	**Were** I the president, I would resign. I would resign **were** I the president. **Had** we known the truth, we would have stopped him. We would have stopped him **had** we known the truth.
As if, *as though*, and *even if* are conjunctions that can be used to introduce either real or unreal conditions.	
As if, *as though* (real) = as it is because something is actually true.	He looks **as if / as though** he **is** sick. (He is sick.)
As if and *as though* (unreal) = as it would be if something were actually true.	He looks **as if / as though** he **were** sick. (He isn't sick.)
Even if (real) = the condition does not matter. The result will remain the same.	**Even if** you are rich, you will not be treated as special.
Even if (unreal) = the condition would not matter. The result would be the same.	**Even if** she were the president, she would not have complete power.

3. In simple and compound sentences

Otherwise = if something does not happen.	Anthropologists live in cultures to analyze them. **Otherwise**, they **will misinterpret** behavior. = Anthropologists live in cultures to analyze them. **If they don't**, they **will misinterpret** behavior.
Otherwise can introduce a simple sentence.	Societies teach their members certain ways of behaving. **Otherwise,** their children will not know how to behave in their culture.
Otherwise can introduce a real result.	Semai society encourages aggressive behavior; **otherwise,** their children will have difficulty living in that group.
Otherwise can introduce a hypothetical result.	The anthropologists lived in the culture to analyze it; **otherwise,** they **would have misinterpreted** behavior.

Exercise 11 Identifying Conditionals without *If*

With a partner, underline the conditionals without *if* and then rewrite them, using *if*.

1. Given that cultures have different marriage customs, it's not surprising that the bride does not see the groom until the wedding.

   _____

2. Were those cultures more alike, it would be easier to analyze their customs.

   _____

3. We would have finished the project by now had we begun earlier.

   _____

4. The villagers will return providing that we leave them alone.

   _____

5. Anthropologists will be able to identify similarities in marriage customs, assuming that all cultures have such similarities.

   _____

6. Should there be a problem with communications, researchers can usually obtain a satellite phone.

   _____

7. Anthropologists publish their findings on a regular basis; otherwise, students would not receive the latest information.

   _____

Exercise 12 Identifying the Meanings of Conditional Sentences

With a partner, match the list of ideas and structures to the sentences. One choice is used twice.

a. *If not*

b. The result will remain the same. The condition will not matter.

c. There is one condition that will give the result.

d. *As it would be if* or *like something was actually so*

e. *Happens to occur*

____ 1. Please let us know should you need some help.

____ 2. It's unlikely that we will be able to completely understand that culture even if we live in it for a long time.

____ 3. We might not succeed unless the members of the village help us.

____ 4. The members of the family will eat only if the father has a successful hunt.

____ 5. The village looked as if it had been abandoned.

____ 6. It's important for researchers to interpret data correctly; otherwise, mistakes are made.

Exercise 13 Identifying Clauses of Concession, Contrast, and Condition in Context

With a partner, underline the adverb clauses of concession, contrast, and condition in the following passages once. Underline the independent clauses twice. Discuss which conditional sentences are real and which are unreal. Passages 1 and 3 each contain a sentence that begins with *but if*. Explain why the writer used those two words together. See Chart 11-3 for help.

1. Cultural constraints are of two basic types, direct and indirect. Naturally, the direct constraints are the more obvious. For example, if you choose to wear a casual shorts outfit to a wedding, you will probably be subject to some ridicule and a certain amount of social isolation. But if you choose to wear nothing, you may be exposed to a stronger, more direct cultural constraint—arrest for indecent exposure.[17]

2. Although indirect forms of cultural constraint are less obvious than direct ones, they are no less effective. Durkheim illustrated this point when he wrote, "I am not obliged to speak French with my fellow-countrymen, nor to use the legal currency, but I cannot possibly do otherwise. If I tried to escape this necessity, my attempt would fail miserably" (Durkheim 1938 / 1895). In other words, if Durkheim had decided he would rather speak Icelandic than French, nobody would have tried to stop him. But hardly anyone would have understood him either. And although he would not have been put into prison for trying to buy groceries with Icelandic money, he would have had difficulty convincing the local merchants to sell him food.[18]

3. Peter J. Ucko and Andree Rosenfeld have identified three principal locations of paintings in the caves of Western Europe. . . . The subjects of the paintings are mostly animals. . . . Perhaps like many contemporary peoples, Upper Paleolithic men and women believed that the drawing of a human image could cause death or injury. If that were indeed their belief, it might explain why human figures are rarely depicted in cave art. Another explanation for the focus on animals might be that these people sought to improve their luck at hunting. But if hunting magic was the chief motivation for the paintings, it is difficult to explain why only a few show signs of being speared.[19]

4. We have no way of knowing if Homo erectus had fur like other primates, but we think probably not, because we think they may have worn clothing, as we discuss later. The brain in Homo erectus may also have already expanded enough that Homo erectus infants, like modern human infants, could not adequately support their heads even if they could hold onto their mother's fur. [20]

Exercise 14 **Choosing the Correct Conjunction**

Choose the correct conjunction to complete the sentences. Notice the punctuation before you decide.

1. _____ (*If / Whereas*) kinship is important, there is still the question of which set of kin a person affiliates with and depends on. After all, _____ (*if / although*) every single relative were counted as equally important, there would be an unmanageably large number of people in each person's kinship network. [21]

2. Perhaps early humans thought their hunting could be made more successful _____ (*if / even though*) they drew images depicting good fortune in hunting. [22]

3. _____ (*If / Unless*) the society is very small, it is usually not practical to use the whole society as the sampling universe. [23]

4. _____ (*If / Otherwise*) chimpanzees and other primates have the capacity to use nonspoken language and even to understand spoken language, then the difference between humans and nonhumans may not be as great as people used to think. [24]

5. The vast majority of the societies in a recent cross-cultural study had at least occasional wars when they were first described, _____ (*otherwise / unless*) they had been pacified or incorporated by more dominant societies (M. Ember and Ember 1992). [25]

6. What, then, might be the advantages of light-colored skin? Presumably, there must be some benefits in some environments; _____, (*if / otherwise*) all human populations would tend to have relatively dark skin. [26]

Exercise 15 **Expressing Real and Unreal Conditions**

Complete the following passages with the correct forms of the verbs to express real or unreal conditions. Use modals when it is appropriate.

1. In order to study the patterning of sounds, linguists who are interested in phonology have to write down speech utterance as sequences of sound. This would be almost impossible if linguists _____ (*restrict*) to using their own alphabet. [27]

2. In rank societies, chiefs are often treated with deference by people of lower rank. Among the Trobriand Islanders of Melanasia, people of lower rank must keep their heads lower than a person of higher rank. So, when a chief is standing, commoners must bend low. When commoners have to walk past a chief who happens to be sitting, he may rise, and they will bend. If the chief _____ (*choose*) to remain seated, they must crawl. [28]

3. If the early primates ate mostly plant foods rather than speedy insects, why _____ they _____ (*become*) more reliant on vision than on smell? Robert Sussman suggests it was because the early primates were probably nocturnal (as many prosimians still are): if they _____ (*be*) to locate and manipulate small food items at the ends of slender branches in dim light, they would need improved vision. [29]

4. Although it may seem surprising, some recent hunter-gatherers have starved when they had to rely on lean meat. If they could have increased their carbohydrate or fat intake, they _____ (*be*) more likely to get through the periods of lean game. So it is possible that some foragers in the past thought of planting crops to get them through the dry seasons when hunting, fishing, and gathering did not provide enough carbohydrates and fat for them to avoid starvation. [30]

(continued on next page)

5. Members of food-collecting societies generally do not have private ownership of land. If there is collective ownership, it _____ (be) always by groups of related people (kinship groups) or by territorial groups (bands or villages). Land is not bought and sold. The reason is probably that land itself generally has no intrinsic value for foragers; what is of value is the presence of game and wild plant life on the land. If game moves away or food resources _____ (become) less plentiful, the land _____ (be) less valuable.[31]

6. In their pioneering work, Beatrice T. and R. Allen Gardner raised a female chimpanzee named Washoe and trained her to communicate with startling effectiveness by means of American Sign Language hand gestures. After a year of training, she was able to associate gestures with specific activities. For example, if thirsty, Washoe would make the signal for "give me" followed by one for "drink." As she learned, the instructions grew more detailed. If all she _____ (want) was water she _____ (signal) for "drink." But if she _____ (crave) soda pop, as she did more and more, she _____ (preface) the drink signal with the sweet signal—a quick touching of the tongue with her fingers.[32]

7. . . . In Chuuk society, the owner of a canoe has first use of it; the same is true for farming implements. Yet, if a close relative needs the canoe and _____ (find) it unused, the canoe _____ (may take) without permission. A distant relative or neighbor must ask permission to borrow any tools, but the owner may not refuse. If owners _____ (be) to refuse, they would risk being scorned and refused if they _____ (be) to need tools later.[33]

8. . . . North Americans would never even think of the possibility of eating dog meat if they _____ (not know) that people in some other societies commonly do so. They would not realize that their belief in germs was cultural if they _____ (be) not aware that people in some societies think that witchcraft or evil spirits cause illness. They might not become aware that it is their custom to sleep on beds if they _____ (be) not aware that people in many societies sleep on the floor or on the ground. Only when we compare ourselves with people in other societies may we become aware of cultural differences and similarities.[34]

Exercise 16 Completing Sentences

On a separate sheet of paper, complete the sentences using the conditionals you have learned in this chapter. Pay attention to punctuation.

1. We would not have had the results of Margaret Mead's studies . . .
2. Anthropologists do not always understand diverse cultures . . .
3. Researchers may misinterpret what they see in a culture . . .
4. Students of anthropology could learn a great deal from Mead . . .
5. If Mead's results had been published . . .
6. If anthropologists had been more thorough in their research . . .
7. If Mead had not published . . .
8. If Mead had employed different observation techniques . . .

The following student essay contains ten errors. The first error is corrected for you. Work in pairs to find and correct nine more.

Magic and Disease

Most people in the developed world would say that they believe that diseases are caused by bacteria and viruses. ~~In~~ *On the* other hand, many believe that diseases are caused by supernatural forces. Supernatural forces may be defined as unnatural, unearthly, and mysterious forces such as gods or spirits. Magic is the belief that one's actions can coerce or influence supernatural forces to act in a certain way, either for good or for evil. Two types of individuals use magic to cause a supernatural act—sorcerers and witches. Sorcerers use materials, objects, and medicines to provoke supernatural ill will, if witches accomplish the same thing by using thoughts and emotions alone. People who use sorcery and witchcraft appeal to the spirits to do harm to others. Whereas sorcerers and witches have low status in their societies, people fear them because they are believed to be able to cause sickness and death. Sorcerers and witches will harm a person only he or she offends them in some way.

In a study of 139 societies, researchers found that people in only two of the societies did not believe that sickness was due to gods or spirits. In other words, people in many societies believe that the supernatural is responsible for illness even the illness may come from different aspects of the supernatural. For example, the people in Truk, an island in the Pacific Ocean, believe that disease and death are caused by spirits, however the Ojibwa people (a Native American tribe) believe that serious sickness results from doing something bad to an animal or other person and that medicine will be ineffective if not one reflects on one's wrongdoing. The Hopi (another Native American tribe) believe that we cause our own illness because of wrongdoing or bad thoughts and anxiety. They also believe that witches can cause illness, however, only in depressed or anxious people. While a witch has caused illness, it means that the sick person was depressed or anxious. If that person had had good thoughts, he or she will not get sick. Anthropologists have studied many such societies, otherwise they cannot explain why they hold different beliefs.

Exercise 18 Apply It to Speaking

APPLICATION

1 In small groups, discuss the information in the chart entitled "Gender Profile of News Audiences."[35] Answer the following questions in your discussion.

  a. Who published the chart?

  b. What does *gender* mean?

  c. What is a profile?

  d. What are news audiences?

  e. What does the chart compare?

  f. What does it tell us about the differences between the genders in general?

2 Conclude by evaluating the information the chart presents. Address the questions below, using adverb clauses and other structures of concession and contrast to express your ideas. Use some of the words in the box. Be prepared to share your conclusions with the class.

  a. What are some of the most interesting specific differences?

  b. What is your reaction to the data in the chart?

although	but	conversely	even if	even though	however
if	in contrast	nevertheless	nonetheless	on the other hand	otherwise
though	unless	whereas	while	yet	

GENDER PROFILES OF NEWS AUDIENCES		
	Percent who are...	
	MEN	WOMEN
Of those who closely follow:	%	%
Sports news	74	26
Science / technology	69	31
Business / finance	65	35
International	63	37
Washington news	59	41
Local government	55	45
Consumer news	51	49
National Population:	**48**	**52**
The weather	47	53
Crime news	46	54
Culture and arts	42	56
Community news	42	58
Entertainment news	39	61
Health news	37	63
Religion	36	64

Source: "Online Papers Modestly Boost Newspaper Readership," Pew Research Center for the People & the Press, July 30, 2006.

Exercise 19 | Apply It to Writing

On a separate sheet of paper, write a paragraph summarizing the findings in the chart "Gender Profile of News Audiences" on the previous page. Use the outline below to help you organize your paragraph. Use as many of the conjunctions and transitions from the box in Exercise 18 as you can. See Appendix B for help.

I. Topic sentence (main idea for the paragraph)

"According to the Pew Research Center, _____."

II. Second sentence to explain the topic sentence further. This sentence should mention the difference in numbers between men and women in the total U.S. population.

III. First supporting detail

   A. Specific example from the top half of the chart

   B. Another specific example from the top half of the chart

IV. Second supporting detail

   A. Specific example from the bottom half of the chart

   B. Another specific example from the bottom half of the chart

V. A concluding sentence with your reactions to the data

Add any other sentences you need to improve your paragraph.

Reduced Adverb Clauses and Absolute Constructions

SOURCE: Adapted from P. Bohannan 1954

A lineage is a set of kin descended from a common ancestor. The Tiv of northern Nigeria have four levels (segments) of lineage, which are represented in this figure as triangles. Starting from the top, I represents the common ancestor. From I descend lineages A and B. A divides into lineages 1 and 2, and B into lineages 3 and 4. Each of these is further divided into lineages a, b, c, d, e, f, g, and h. Each of these is connected to a separate area of territory (land), shown at the bottom of the figure. We can see that the lineages live next to each other and are all linked into a single tribe, the Tiv.[1]

The Dinka of Southern Sudan, a tribe that neighbors the Tiv

PREVIEW

VOCABULARY   Here are some words that you will encounter in Chapter 12. How much do you know about each word? Turn to Appendix A to assess and expand your word knowledge.

engage (in combat)	exercise (leadership)	hierarchical	inclusive	integrate
labor	lineage	role	segment	tribe

Prepare to Read

1. Look at the image and chart and read the related explanation on the previous page. What does the Tiv lineage chart represent?

2. What do the triangles represent?

3. What are the curving lines leading down from the letters connecting to?

Read the following passage from *Anthropology,* 13th Edition, by Carol R. Ember, Melvin Ember, and Peter N. Peregrine.[2]

The Tiv People

[1]The Tiv of northern Nigeria offer a classic example of a segmentary lineage system, one that happens to link all the Tiv into a single genealogical structure or tribe. The Tiv are a large society, numbering more than 800,000 [The chart on the previous page] is a representation of the Tiv lineage structure as described by Paul Bohannan. In the figure, there are four levels of lineages. Each of the smallest lineages, symbolized by *a* through *h*, is in turn embedded in more inclusive lineages.

[2]The segmentary lineage system was presumably very effective in allowing the Tiv to intrude into new territory and take land from other tribal societies with smaller descent groups. Individual Tiv lineage segments could call on support from related lineages **when faced** with border troubles. Conflicts within the society— that is, between segments—especially in border areas, were often turned outward, "**releasing** internal pressure in an explosive blast against other peoples" (Sahlins 1961).

[3]Segmentary lineage systems may have military advantages even when they do not unite the entire society. A classic example is the Nuer of the Upper Nile region, who had tribal, but not society-wide, organization because of their segmentary lineages. In the early 1800s, the Nuer had a territory of about 8,700 square miles, and the neighboring Dinka had ten times that much. But by 1890, the Nuer had cut a 100-mile swath through Dinka territory, increasing Nuer territory to 35,000 square miles. Even though the Nuer and Dinka were culturally very similar, the segmentary lineage organization of the Nuer seems to have given them a significant military advantage in their incursions* into Dinka territory (R. C. Kelly 1985).

[4]A segmentary lineage system may generate a formidable military force, but the combinations of manpower it produces are temporary, forming and dissolving as the occasion demands (Sahlins 1961). Tribal political organization does not make for a political system that more or less permanently integrates* a number of communities.[3]

incursion—an invasion, entering without permission
integrate—to mix, combine

Review the Ideas

1. Who are the Tiv? Who are the Nuer?

2. What do the Tiv have in common with the Nuer?

3. According to the passage, what is the advantage of a segmentary lineage system?

Analyze the Grammar

1. Look at the boldfaced words in the second paragraph of the passage. What grammatical forms are they?

2. What do these forms express?

3. Underline similar forms in paragraphs 3 and 4, and indicate what they express.

CHART 12-1 — Reducing Adverb Clauses to Phrases: Time and Cause Phrases

Adverb clauses of time and cause can be reduced to phrases beginning with the adverbs *before*, *after*, *when*, *while*, *as*, *once*, *until*, and *upon*. *As* is changed to *while* or omitted in a reduced phrase.

1. Reducing time clauses to participial phrases

Adverb clauses of time may be reduced to participial phrases when the subjects of the dependent and independent clauses are the same. When an adverb phrase is used, the subject noun must be moved from the adverb clause to the independent clause. In active sentences, the active verb becomes a present participle (verb + *-ing*).

In passive sentences, the passive verb becomes a past participle.

Phrases with *before*, *after*, *when*, and *while* may include *being*.

Having + past participle means the action occurred at an earlier time. *When*, *before*, *once*, and *after* may be included or omitted in this pattern. There is no difference in meaning.

While is used when the two actions occurred at the same time. The phrase may appear after the independent clause. No comma separates the phrase at the end of the sentence. When the phrase introduces the sentence, *while* may be omitted. *While* + present or past participle are the forms.

Until signals the end of the action in the independent clause. *Until* + past participle is the usual reduced form.

When meaning "after" may be reduced to *upon* or *on*. *Upon* or *on* + present participle or *being* + past participle are the forms.

---

dependent clause   independent clause
After the child left school, he walked home.

phrase   independent clause
After leaving school, the child walked home.

independent clause   phrase
The child walked home **after leaving school.**

When an applicant is chosen for a job, she signs a contract.

When chosen, an applicant signs a contract.

After having left work, the nurse drove home.

Having left work, the nurse drove home.

While she was driving, she listened to the radio.

(While) driving, she listened to the radio.

She listened to the radio **while driving**.

Driving, she listened to the radio.

The truck driver drove **until exhausted**.

When the women decided where to collect food, they left.

Upon / On deciding where to collect food, the women left.

2. Reducing time clauses to other phrases

Clauses of time that use *when*, *while*, and *once* with a *be*-verb may be reduced to noun phrases, adjective phrases, or prepositional phrases. *Being* is not used in these phrases.	**When / Once the women are ready**, they leave for the day. **When / Once ready**, the women leave for the day.

3. Reducing cause clauses to participial phrases

When clauses that use *because* or *as* are reduced, the words *because* and *as* are omitted. The subjects of the dependent and independent clauses must be the same.	**Because / As the villagers hunt all day**, they are often tired. **Hunting all day**, the villagers are often tired.
Any form of *be* in the passive may change to *being* or may be omitted.	**Because the villagers were tired**, they went to bed. **Being tired**, the villagers went to bed. **Tired**, the villagers went to bed.
An adverb clause with a past perfect verb may be reduced to *having* + past participle.	**Because / As he had driven so far**, the driver was exhausted. **Having driven so far**, the driver was exhausted. The driver was exhausted **having driven so far**.
An adverb clause with a past perfect passive verb may be reduced to *having* + *been* + past participle.	**Because / As the chief had been given a great deal of support**, he won the election. **Having been given a great deal of support**, the chief won the election.
Reduced phrases can be placed at the beginning or end of the independent clause. A phrase at the beginning of a sentence is set off with a comma.	

Exercise 1 Identifying Time and Cause Phrases

With a partner, underline the reduced adverb clauses in the following passage and discuss their meanings.

A lineage system is a set of kin that descend from a common ancestor. Anthropologists are experts at researching lineage. Once found, a lineage can be followed to its beginning. Sources of information about each lineage are investigated until exhausted. While researching lineages, the researcher may discover previously unknown connections that further knowledge about previously misunderstood groups of people. Having searched for all possible connections, the anthropologist is ready to put the information into some kind of order. Upon deciding who is related to whom, the researcher will develop a graphic representation of the direct and indirect connections between and among the groups involved. When fairly sure of the accuracy of the graphic, he or she will consult selected members of the group to see if they recognize the connections and have any information to add. Finally, after having investigated all aspects of the connections, the anthropologist can be satisfied that the lineage system is established. Having conducted such careful research, the anthropologist will probably be asked to publish the results in a professional journal. Having been published, the results of the research will become established in the field.

Exercise 2 Reducing Time and Cause Clauses to Phrases

With a partner, decide which of the sentences containing adverb clauses of time and cause can be reduced and reduce them. Write the reduced sentences on a separate sheet of paper.

1. Once the anthropology of the Tiv lineage system was understood, anthropologists drew a graphic representation.
2. Before the Nuer took the Dinka's land, the Dinka had ten times as much land as the Nuer.
3. After the territory was taken, the land belonged to the Nuer.
4. Because the Tiv had a segmentary lineage system, they had an advantage over other groups.
5. The segmentary lineage system makes it possible to raise a large military force until it is no longer needed.

Exercise 3 Choosing the Correct Participle

Complete the sentences by choosing the correct form of the participle. With a partner, indicate which rule in Chart 12-1 applies.

1. Archaeologists and physical anthropologists feel ethical responsibilities that can be in conflict when _____ (*dealt / dealing*) with human remains.[4]

2. Once _____ (*initiated / initiating*), a boy has become a man, one with a clearly defined status and the ultimate certainty of exercising full authority together with his set partners.[5]

3. After _____ (*discovered / discovering*) which sounds are grouped into phonemes, linguists can begin to discover the sound sequences that are allowed in a language and the usually unconscious rules that predict those sequences.[6]

4. Not so long ago in the United States, fathers were excluded from the birth, hospitals whisked the baby away from the mother and only brought the baby to her infrequently, and visitors (but not attending nurses and doctors) had to wear masks when _____ (*hold / holding*) the baby. Rationalizations were given for those practices, but _____ (*looked / looking*) back at them, they do not appear to be based on scientific evidence. Many medical anthropologists now argue that the biomedical paradigm (the system in which physicians are trained) itself needs to be understood as part of the culture.[7]

5. Woven goat hair provides an exceptionally versatile cloth. For winter use, it retains heat and repels water; in the summer, it insulates against heat and permits free circulation of air. Lambskin hides also serve many purposes. When _____ (*plucked and turned inside out / plucking and turning inside out*), they are made into storage bags to hold water, buttermilk, sour milk, and other liquids.[8]

6. Anthropology is a comparatively young discipline. Anthropologists only began to go to live with people in far-away places in the late 1800s. _____ (*Compared / Comparing*) to our knowledge of the physical laws of nature, we know much less about people, about how and why they behave as they do.[9]

CHART 12-2

Reducing Adverb Clauses to Phrases: Result, Concession, and Condition Phrases

1. Reducing simple and compound sentences that express result to phrases

Simple and compound sentences with the conjunctions *thus*, *therefore*, and *because of that* can be reduced to phrases beginning with *thus* or *thereby*, indicating result. An active verb in the original clause becomes a present participle. *Thereby* is preceded by a comma; *thus* may or may not be preceded by a comma.	The hunter was tired; **thus / therefore / because of that**, he **failed** to catch prey. The hunter was tired **(,) thus / , thereby failing** to catch prey.

2. Reducing adverb clauses in complex sentences

Adverb clauses of concession beginning with *although*, *even though*, or *though* can be reduced to phrases, especially with the past participle. **Note:**	**Although the hunter was tired**, he finished the work. **Although tired**, the hunter finished his work.
• *Albeit* is sometimes used to mean *although* in a phrase. *Albeit* is very formal.	**Although he was tired,** the hunter continued his hunt. **Albeit tired,** the hunter continued his hunt.
• When a concession clause has the same subject as the independent clause and a *be*-verb, the subject and *be*-verb can be deleted and the clause can be reduced to a noun phrase, adjective phrase, or prepositional phrase.	**Although the hunter was successful,** he continued to hunt. **Although successful**, the hunter continued to hunt. **Although he was in trouble**, the hunter continued to run. **Although in trouble**, the hunter continued to run.
Adverb clauses of condition can be reduced to phrases, especially with the past participle. **Note:**	**If I am asked,** I will serve. **If asked**, I will serve.
• *When* meaning "if" or "because" may be omitted when it begins a sentence.	I will serve **when asked**. **(When) asked**, I will serve.
• *If* is not usually used with the *-ing* form.	

Exercise 4 **Identifying Adverb Phrases of Result, Concession, and Condition**

With a partner, underline the phrases of result, concession, and condition in the following passage. Explain their meanings.

The Tiv tribe of northern Nigeria has a complicated relationship system that connects all the Tiv in one tribe albeit not integrating communities in any permanent way. This system makes the Tiv a huge interrelated group that is able to combine manpower to take over new territory and defend it if faced with border disputes. In this way, any disagreements within the group are aimed at others, resulting in a release of tension among the Tiv. Another group, the Nuer, who lived in the Upper Nile region, had a similar system. In the early nineteenth century, they controlled an area of about 8,700 square miles next to the territory owned by the Dinka, another tribe that had much more land. Though lacking land, by the end of the century, the Nuer had taken over a huge amount of Dinka territory, thereby increasing their land to 35,000 square miles. The Neur's system of tribal organization was flexible, thus ensuring military success. Although powerful, this system is also temporary; it develops only if needed.

Exercise 5 Reducing Adverb Clauses of Concession, Time, and Condition

With a partner decide which of the adverb clauses in the sentences can be reduced to phrases and reduce them.

1. Although the Tiv segmentary lineage system is advantageous, it is not permanent.
2. If Tiv are asked about lineage, their answer might surprise the anthropologists.
3. When the Nuer were successful, the Nuer's neighbors were not.
4. The Nuer took much of the Dinka's territory even though Dinka land was originally larger.
5. The Tiv have a segmentary lineage system; therefore, they have an advantage over their neighbors.

Exercise 6 Choosing Correct Adverb Phrases

Complete the sentences with the best choice. Indicate which rule in Chart 12-2 applies.

1. Societies that have open class systems vary in the degree to which members of the society recognize that there are classes, _____ (*thereby* / *albeit*) somewhat open classes.[10]

2. Fossils, although rare, are particularly informative about human biological evolution. Fossils may be impressions of an insect or leaf on a muddy surface that now is stone. A fossil may also consist of the actual hardened remains of an animal's skeletal structure. . . . If the remains are buried under such circumstances, the minerals in the ground may become bound into the structure of the teeth or bone, _____ (*hardened* / *hardening*) the remains and thus _____ (*make* / *making*) them less likely to deteriorate.[11]

3. Society specifies what is considered property and the rights and duties associated with that property (Hoebel [1954] 1968). These specifications are social in nature, for they may be changed over time. For example, France declared all its beaches to be public, thereby _____ (*state* / *stating*), in effect, that the ocean shore is not a resource that an individual can own.[12]

4. In many societies, women are brought up to be submissive. But when possessed, women are taken over by spirits and they are not responsible for what they do or say—therefore, they can unconsciously do what they are not able to do consciously (Bourguignon 2004). Although _____ (*intrigue* / *intriguing*), these suggestions need to be tested on individuals in field situations.[13]

5. One might think that floods, of all disasters, are the least influenced by social factors. After all, without a huge runoff from heavy rains or snowmelt, there cannot be a flood. But consider why so many people have died from Hwang River floods in China. (One such flood, in 1931, killed nearly 4 million people, _____ (*made* / *making*) it the deadliest single disaster in history.) The floods in the Hwang River basin have occurred mostly because the clearing of nearby forests for fuel and farmland has allowed enormous quantities of silt to wash into the river, _____ (*raised* / *raising*) the riverbed and _____ (*increased* / *increasing*) the risk of floods that burst the dams that normally would contain them.[14]

Exercise 7 Using Adverb Phrases

Complete the sentences with adverbials from Chart 12-2.

1. Hunters may start a hunt _____ doubtful of success.
2. _____ extremely hungry, hunters carefully track their prey.
3. Hunters will stop and rest _____ tired.

4. _____ rested, they will continue the pursuit.

5. Hunters follow their prey relentlessly, _____ exhausting it.

6. Experienced hunters use strategies to find prey, _____ succeeding in their search.

CHART 12-3	Reducing Purpose, Cause, Concession, and Conditional Clauses to Prepositional Phrases

Adverb clauses of purpose, cause, concession, and condition can be reduced to prepositional phrases when the subjects of the dependent and independent clauses are the same. A prepositional phrase can be used at the beginning or end of a simple sentence to show purpose, cause, concession, or condition. A prepositional phrase at the beginning of a sentence is set off with a comma.

1. Purpose clauses with *so that* can be reduced to phrases with *in order to*. Purpose clauses often include *can* or *could*, which must be deleted.	The hunter rested **so that he could** hunt. The hunter rested **in order to** hunt.
2. When a cause or concession clause changes to a prepositional phrase, the verb in the clause becomes a noun in the phrase.	
• *because, as, since* (in the clause)	**Because / As** the hunter **was fatigued**, he was unsuccessful. *(verb)*
• *because of, due to, on account of, as a result of* (in the phrase)	**Because of / Due to his fatigue**, the hunter was unsuccessful. *(noun)* The hunter was unsuccessful **because of / due to his fatigue**.
• *although, even though, though, in spite of the fact that, despite the fact that* (in the clause)	**Although** the hunter **was fatigued**, he continued his hunt. *(verb)*
• *in spite of, despite, regardless of* (in the phrase)	**In spite of / Despite fatigue**, the hunter continued his hunt. *(noun)* The hunter continued his hunt **in spite of / despite fatigue**.
3. Conditional clauses (real or unreal) with the verb *have* (possession) can be reduced to phrases that use *with* or *without*. To form the phrase, *if* and *have* are replaced:	
• *if + have = with*	**If** a hunter **has** enough meat, he can feed his family. **With** enough meat, a hunter can feed his family.
• *if + not + have = without*	**If** a hunter **doesn't have** enough meat, he cannot feed his family. **Without** enough meat, a hunter cannot feed his family. A hunter cannot feed his family **without enough meat**.

Exercise 8 Identifying Adverb Clauses Reduced to Prepositional Phrases

With a partner, underline the prepositional phrases used to express purpose, cause, concession, and condition. Then rewrite on a separate sheet of paper the sentences with clauses in place of the phrases.

1. The Tiv lineage segments call on related lineages in order to deal with border problems.
2. The Dinka were unsuccessful despite ownership of a large territory.
3. Segmentary lineage systems have military advantages because of their efficient organization.
4. Without segmentary lineage systems, societies like the Dinka are at a disadvantage.
5. The Dinka continued to move into territories in spite of their small numbers.

Exercise 9 Choosing the Correct Prepositions

Choose the best prepositions to complete the sentences. Indicate which rule in Chart 12-3 applies.

1. _____ (*With / Without*) language, the transmission of complex traditions would be virtually impossible, and each person would be trapped within his or her own world of private sensations.[15]

2. The "push" out of the rural areas and the "pull" of the cities are hard to resist, _____ (*despite / because of*) the enormous political problems of urban living.[16]

3. _____ (*Because / Because of*) the work involved in clearing a garden, the Yanomamö prefer to make use of forest patches that have little thorny brush and not too many large trees (Chagnon 1983).[17]

4. For most people in our society, getting food consists of a trip to the supermarket. Within an hour, we can gather enough food from the shelves to last us a week. Seasons don't daunt us. Week after week, we know food will be there. But we do not think of what would happen if the food were not delivered to the supermarket. We wouldn't be able to eat, and _____ (*due to / without*) eating for a while, we would die.[18]

5. Archaeological evidence suggests that major changes in food-getting, such as the domestication of plants and animals, have been independently invented in at least several areas of the world. Yet, _____ (*despite / although*) these comparable inventions and their subsequent spread by diffusion and migration, there is still wide diversity in the means by which people obtain food.[19]

6. What happened to the Neandertals*? Three answers have generally been considered. First, they interbred with modern humans and the unique Neandertal characteristics slowly disappeared from the interbreeding population. Second, they were killed off by modern humans. Third, they were driven to extinction _____ (*due to / in spite of*) competition with modern humans.[20]

Neandertal is the spelling used in this passage. *Neanderthal* is more common.

Exercise 10 **Choosing the Correct Prepositions**

Complete the passage with the correct prepositions according to Chart 12-3.

Human beings cannot survive _____ sleep. Some hunters attempt to hunt _____ fatigue. They will certainly stay awake _____ obtain enough meat to feed a starving family. Unfortunately, these people soon find their performance suffers _____ sleep deprivation. And _____ continued efforts, their ability to focus deteriorates _____ the lack of sleep. Finally, a sleep-deprived hunter will fall asleep _____ his or her intentions to remain awake. _____ a few hours of sleep, the hunter will be alert and ready to hunt again.

CHART 12-4	Absolute Constructions

Absolute constructions, or absolutes, are phrases that modify entire clauses or sentences. The meaning of absolute constructions is often a combination of time and cause. Absolute constructions are very formal.

Cause and time clauses with different subjects from the independent clause may be reduced to absolute constructions. These clauses may become participial phrases, noun phrases, prepositional phrases, or adjectives or adverbs with a subject. In the reduced clause, the original subject is kept and the original verb is reduced. If the verb in the clause contains a form of *be*, *be* is deleted.	*dependent clause* Because the children were crying, *independent clause* the family left the meeting. *absolute construction* *independent clause* **The children crying**, the family left the meeting. The family left the meeting, **the children crying**.
If the original verb is *be*, it can be deleted or changed to *being*. Absolutes with *being* mean "because."	*dependent clause* Because the guests **were** in a hurry, *independent clause* the hosts hurried to help them. *absolute construction* The guests **(being) in a hurry**, *independent clause* the hosts hurried to help them.
If the original verb is in the simple past, present perfect, or past perfect, it is replaced with *having* + past participle. The original subordinating conjunctions (*after, because, since*, etc.) are not included in the absolute construction.	After the guests **arrived**, the hosts served the meal. The guests **having arrived**, the hosts served the meal. The hosts served the meal, **the guests having arrived**.
The absolute construction may introduce the sentence or come after the independent clause. In both cases, the absolute is set off with a comma.	Because the chief had been selected, the village celebrated. **The chief having been selected**, the village celebrated. The village celebrated, **the chief having been selected**.
Absolutes are sometimes introduced by the word *with*.	Since the train was late, researchers took the bus. **(With) the train (being) late**, the researchers took the bus. The researchers took the bus, **(with) the train (being) late**.

Exercise 11 **Identifying Absolute Constructions**

With a partner, find the one absolute construction in each of the groups of sentences. Discuss the meaning of each absolute construction.

1. a. Lineages having disappeared in many places, large kin groups remain important to some Chinese, Africans, and Pacific Islanders.
   b. Lineages have disappeared in many places, but large kin groups remain important to some Chinese, Africans, and Pacific Islanders.
   c. Having disappeared in many places, large kin groups remain important to some Chinese, Africans, and Pacific Islanders.
   d. Large kin groups remain important to some Chinese, Africans, and Pacific Islanders. Lineages have disappeared in many places.

2. a. People sometimes migrate to other countries, and kinship is especially useful for them when they move.
   b. People sometimes migrate to other countries, yet kinship is especially important for them when they move.
   c. People sometimes migrate to other countries, with kinship being especially useful for them when they move.
   d. People sometimes migrate to other countries; kinship is especially useful for them when they move.

3. a. The most common use of kinship connections is for help; the migrants need to work in the new country.
   b. The most common use of kinship connections is for help since the migrants need to work in the new country.
   c. The most common use of kinship connections is for help due to the migrants' need to work in the new country.
   d. The most common use of kinship connections is for help, the migrants needing to work in the new country.

4. a. Some wives, children, and elders remain at home, and the migrant fathers and husbands send money home and visit from time to time.
   b. Some wives, children, and elders remain at home, the migrant fathers and husbands sending money home and visiting from time to time.
   c. Some wives, children, and elders remain at home, so the migrant fathers and husbands send money home and visit from time to time.
   d. Some wives, children, and elders remain at home while the migrant fathers and husbands send money home and visit from time to time.

5. a. In time, the wives may join their husbands, with the children following close behind.
   b. In time, the wives may join their husbands, and the children follow close behind.
   c. In time, the wives may join their husbands, yet the children follow close behind.
   d. In time, the wives may join their husbands before the children follow close behind.

6. a. The friends and other relatives are established there, whereas the elders usually prefer to stay in the home country.
   b. The friends and other relatives are established there; the elders usually prefer to stay in the home country.
   c. The elders usually prefer to stay in the home country, for their friends and other relatives are established there.
   d. The elders usually prefer to stay in the home country, their friends and other relatives established there.

Exercise 12 Completing Sentences with Absolutes

Write the best form of the verb given to complete the passages with absolutes.

1. The period of cultural history known as the Upper Paleolithic in Europe, the Near East, and Asia or the Later Stone Age in Africa dates from about 40,000 years ago to about 14,000 to 10,000 years ago. During this time, the world was locked in an ice age, with glaciers _____ (*cover*) much of northern Europe and North America, and annual temperatures as much as 50 degrees Fahrenheit (10 degrees Celsius) below today's temperatures.[21]

2. Papermaking was introduced as a commodity in Europe by Arab trade through Italian ports in the 12th century. The Moors built the first European paper mill in Spain about 1150. The technical knowledge then spread throughout Europe, with paper mills _____ (*build*) in Italy in 1276, France in 1348, Germany in 1390, and England in 1494.[22]

3. One of the new cultures, now known as Aluku, emerged when slaves fled from coastal plantations in Suriname to the swampy interior country along the Cottica River. After a war with the Dutch colonists, this particular group moved to French Guiana. The escaped slaves, originating from widely varying cultures in Africa or born on Suriname plantations, organized themselves into autonomous communities with military headmen (Bilby 1996). They practiced slash-and-burn cultivation, with women _____ (*do*) most of the work.[23]

4. Some scholars recently have suggested that the type of family people are raised in predicts the degree of political participation in a society. A large extended family with multiple generations tends to be hierarchical, with the older generations _____ (*have*) more authority.[24]

Exercise 13 Rewriting Sentences with Adverb Phrases or Absolutes

On a separate sheet of paper, rewrite the sentences so that they contain adverb phrases or absolutes.

1. Archaeologists must always be concerned with the ethics of their work when they undertake or report the results of their research.
2. The most obvious, and universal, example of a song made entirely of repetition is the relaxed lullaby of a mother repeating a comforting syllable to her baby while she improvises her own tune.
3. When violence occurs within a political unit in which disputes are usually settled peacefully, we call such violence *crime*, particularly when it is committed by an individual.
4. After Charles Darwin (1809–1882) studied changes in plants, fossil animals, and varieties of domestic and wild pigeons, he rejected the notion that each species was created at one time in a fixed form.
5. To many women of European ancestry, short hair was a symbolic statement of their freedom. To Native American women, who traditionally cut their hair short when they were in mourning, it was a reminder of death (Trouillot 2001).
6. Bands are typically small, with less than 100 people usually, often considerably less. Each small band occupies a large territory, so population density is low. Band size often varies by season. The band breaks up or recombines according to the food resources available at a given time and place.
7. Most medical anthropologists use the term *biomedicine* to refer to the dominant medical paradigm in Western cultures today. The *bio* part of the word emphasizes the biological emphasis of this medical system.

The following student essay contains ten errors. The first error is corrected for you. Work in pairs to find and correct nine more.

Borrowing from Other Cultures

Societies borrow from other cultures in a process known as diffusion. Most of us don't realize that much of what we have in modern Western culture has been borrowed from others. Anthropologist Ralph Linton (1853–1953) published a piece titled "One Hundred Per-Cent American" in *American Mercury* (vol. 40 [1937]: 427–29) satirizing the mistaken belief of most U.S. citizens that every aspect of their lives originated in the United States. Linton describes the typical morning of a U.S. businessman approximately as follows. (Notice that he uses the term "American" to apply only to people in the United States.)

While ~~sleep~~ *sleeping*, the good American wears pajamas, which originally come from eastern India, and lies in a bed similar to those invented in Persia. Upon awakened, the American goes to the bathroom, in which almost everything has a foreign origin—the glass been from ancient Egypt, porcelain from China, and tiles from the Middle East. If asking, the American would tell you that every part of his surroundings is 100 percent American. He then returns to the bedroom after having showering and shaved and dresses in clothing derived from the clothing worn by ancient nomads in Asia. While having dressing, he uses buttons first used by Stone Age people to close his shirt and pants and puts on shoes, which were invented by the ancient Greeks.

When dressed, the American has his breakfast. Being uninform about all this history, the American continues to believe that everything he eats and drinks is purely American—French roast coffee from Arabia, orange juice from the Mediterranean, and waffles from Scandinavia. With breakfast finished, he runs to catch a train for work. Before being boarding the train, he buys a newspaper, paying for it with a few coins. Despite settled in his seat, he reads the news printed through a process invented by Germans on paper invented in China. Because his complete disregard for antiquity, the American remains oblivious to the origins of his great American institutions.

Exercise 15 **Apply It to Speaking and Writing**

1 In small groups, take turns explaining the following table, comparing and contrasting the labor roles of men and women worldwide. Take notes as you talk.

EXAMPLE:

> Although perfectly capable of doing so, men never care for infants. I think this is probably because of their primary role as hunters.

Worldwide Patterns in the Division of Labor by Gender[25]					
Type of activity	**Males almost always**	**Males usually**	**Either gender or both**	**Females usually**	**Females almost always**
Primary subsistence activities	Hunt and trap animals, large and small	Fish Herd large animals Collect wild honey Clear land and prepare soil for planting	Collect shellfish Care for small animals Plant crops Tend crops Harvest crops Milk animals	Gather wild plants	
Secondary subsistence and house activities		Butcher animals	Preserve meat and fish	Care for children Cook Prepare vegetable foods, drinks, and dairy products Launder Fetch water Collect fuel	Care for infants
Other	Cut lumber Mine and quarry Make boats, musical instruments, and bone, horn, and shell objects Engage in combat	Build houses Make nets and rope Exercise political leadership	Prepare skins Make leather products, baskets, mats, clothing, and pottery	Spin yarn	

2 With a partner, create statements explaining why you think this role division exists. Use at least five of the introductory phrases and five of the concluding phrases provided. Write your statements. Then share them with the group as a whole.

Introductory phrases

- Despite having plenty of leadership ability . . .
- After studying the animals in the area . . .
- Because of the difficulty of the work . . .
- Having caught fish . . .
- Both men and women . . .
- When dealing with hostile invaders . . .
- Although interesting, this table of the patterns of division of labor by gender . . .
- Compared to men . . .
- Without women . . .
- Upon entering a new environment . . .
- Having . . .
- Due to . . .

Concluding phrases

- . . . with women preserving the meat and fish afterward.
- . . . because of their role as hunters.
- . . . until the harvest.
- . . . when faced with a difficult task.
- . . . after an afternoon spent preparing the food.
- . . . with women doing much of the cooking.
- . . . thus making the food digestible.
- . . . despite the problems.
- . . . increasing the rate of success.
- . . . their husbands having already cleared the land.
- . . . while preparing the soil for planting.
- . . . due to their great physical strength.

3 Conclude by preparing a two-paragraph written summary incorporating (1) your initial discussion of labor roles and (2) a logical, integrated selection of the explanatory statements that you have prepared. Include adverb phrases and absolutes in your paragraphs. See Appendix B for help.

Putting It All Together

Following a volcanic eruption, rain evaporates on a lava field in Goma, Democratic Republic of Congo.

Read the following passage from *Anthropology*, 13th Edition, by Carol R. Ember, Melvin Ember, and Peter N. Peregrine.[1]

Natural Disasters as Social Problems

[1]Natural events such as floods, droughts, earthquakes, and insect infestations are usually but not always beyond human control, but their effects are not (Aptekar 1994). We call such events accidents or emergencies when only a few people are affected, but we call them disasters when large numbers of people or large areas are affected. . . . Climatic and other events in the physical environment become disasters because of events or conditions in the social environment.

[2]If people live in houses that are designed to withstand earthquakes—if governing bodies require such construction and the economy is developed enough so that people can afford such construction—the effects of an earthquake will be minimized. If poor people are forced to live in deforested floodplains to be able to find land to farm (as in coastal Bangladesh), if the poor are forced to live in shanties built on precarious hillsides (like those of Rio de Janeiro), the floods and landslides that follow severe hurricanes and rainstorms can kill thousands and even hundreds of thousands.

[3]Thus, natural disasters can have greater or lesser effects on human life, depending on social conditions. And therefore disasters are also social problems, problems that have social causes and possible social solutions. Legislating safe construction of a house is a social solution. The 1976 earthquake in Tangsham, China, killed 250,000 people, mostly because they lived in top-heavy adobe houses that could not withstand severe shaking, whereas the 1989 Loma Prieta earthquake in California, which was of comparable intensity, killed 65 people.

[4]One might think that floods, of all disasters, are the least influenced by social factors. After all, without a huge runoff from heavy rains or snowmelt, there cannot be a flood. But consider why so many people have died from Hwang River floods in China. (One such flood, in 1931, killed nearly 4 million people, making it the deadliest single disaster in history.) The floods in the Hwang River basin have occurred mostly because the clearing of nearby forests for fuel and farmland has allowed enormous quantities of silt to wash into the river, raising the riverbed and increasing the risk of floods that burst the dams that normally would contain them. The risk of disastrous flooding would be greatly reduced if different social conditions prevailed—if people were not so dependent on firewood for fuel, if they did not have to farm close to the river, or if the dams were higher and more numerous.[2]

Review the Ideas

1. According to the passage, what is the difference between an accident and a disaster?
2. What causes disasters?
3. What are some examples of social conditions that can cause disasters?

Exercise 1 Analysis of the Reading Passage

Find examples in the reading passage of some of the specified structures presented in Part 4 and write them on a separate sheet of paper.

Paragraph 1

1. Two compound sentences with conjunctions expressing contrast
2. Two adverb clauses defining something
3. One adverb phrase expressing cause

Paragraph 2

1. Four real conditional clauses
2. One adverb clause of purpose

Paragraph 3

1. Two simple sentences with a conjunction expressing result
2. One adverb clause expressing cause
3. One adverb clause expressing contrast

Paragraph 4

1. One adverb phrase meaning "if not having"
2. Three adverb phrases expressing result
3. One adverb clause expressing cause
4. Four unreal conditional clauses

Exercise 2 Analyzing Individual Sentences

Answer the questions about sentences from the reading passage.

1. This sentence is a compound-complex sentence. Underline the independent clauses and put parentheses around the dependent clauses. Then explain why the sentence is called compound-complex.

   We call such events accidents or emergencies when only a few people are affected, but we call them disasters when large numbers of people or large areas are affected.

2. What is the function of the dashes in the following sentence?

   If people live in houses that are designed to withstand earthquakes—if governing bodies require such construction and the economy is developed enough so that people can afford such construction—the effects of an earthquake will be minimized.

3. Underline the independent clause and put parentheses around the dependent clauses of the following sentence. How is this sentence different from most sentences? (Hint: Note the number of dependent clauses and their positions relative to the independent clause.)

   The 1976 earthquake in Tangsham, China, killed 250,000 people, mostly because they lived in top-heavy adobe houses that could not withstand severe shaking, whereas the 1989 Loma Prieta earthquake in California, which was of comparable intensity, killed 65 people.

4. What is unusual about the following sentence?

   The risk of disastrous flooding would be greatly reduced if different social conditions prevailed—if people were not so dependent on firewood for fuel, if they did not have to farm close to the river, or if the dams were higher and more numerous.

Error Analysis

The following excerpt from a student essay contains ten errors. The first error is corrected for you. Work in pairs to find and correct nine more.

Disaster and Traditional Cultures

If
~~After~~ asked, many people would say that isolated traditional cultures are helpless when a natural disaster strikes. They think that volcanic eruptions or devastating floods are explained by traditional cultural groups as punishment by a god or spirit thereby the group might be able to please the angry spirit with some type of sacrifice and thus avoid retribution. In addition, it is said that the traditional culture believed that the group had ignored the god's wishes or annoyed the spirits, thereby ensuring a disaster. People also believe that before a disaster has occurred, such a group experiences enormous difficulty recovering from it. Despite a lack of reliable information, this belief in the extreme vulnerability of traditional cultural groups is widespread.

In fact, anthropologists have found that it is not the isolated traditional cultural group that is vulnerable but the group that has received outside aid following a disaster. Apparently, followed a disaster, an isolated group will go through a natural grieving process for lost community and family members whereas gradually rebuilding their villages and lives. They may recover slowly, but have been through disasters before, the victims have traditional ways of coping with them.

In contrast, outside aid agencies often require the victims of disasters to relocate. So the victims suffer even greater trauma, lost long-held connections with their homes and meaningful community places as well as their loved ones. As a result, the victims of disaster must grieve for loss of place on top of loss of family and friends. Researchers have reported that the trauma experienced by the groups receiving such aid is far more devastating than the natural disaster itself. However, anthropologists suggest that domestic and international aid teams consider their actions carefully so that relocating the victims of natural disasters.

WHAT DID YOU LEARN?

Review the forms and functions of adverb clauses, simple and compound sentences, adverb phrases, and absolute constructions in Part 4. Complete the following exercises. Then check your answers in Appendix D.

A Is the grammar in these sentences correct? Write *C* for correct and *I* for incorrect. Correct the sentences with errors.

_____ 1. The bride's family may provide the dowry; meanwhile, the groom's family may plan a special gift for the couple.

_____ 2. Many newly married couples may live with the groom's family at first even they would prefer their own apartments.

_____ 3. Women in some cultures are expected to marry; nonetheless, some decide not to marry at all.

_____ 4. Although matchmakers are used in some cultures, but in other cultures they are not.

_____ 5. Marriage provides happiness and security to a couple unless the relationship is a good one.

_____ 6. In the past, if a hunter had been successful, his family will have enough to eat.

_____ 7. Given that a hunting and fishing community is dependent upon the supply of meat and fish, the people there know that they need to care for the environment.

_____ 8. The Dinka and the Nuer were neighbors, but the Nuer had the advantage, moved into Dinka territory with little difficulty.

_____ 9. When facing with invasion, the Dinka were unable to defend themselves.

_____ 10. Having taken over Dinka land, the Nuer military force dissolved.

_____ 11. Research results being important, anthropologists study lineage systems carefully.

_____ 12. Albeit needing immediate results, the anthropologist took the time to double-check the data.

_____ 13. The anthropologist was extra careful, thereby discovered a few errors in the results.

14. The results showed some errors in the data despite of the researcher's efforts.

_____ 15. Without further research, the results cannot be verified.

B Are the following statements about the sentences correct? Write *C* for correct and *I* for incorrect. Be prepared to explain why the incorrect statements are wrong.

_____ 1. The adverb clause expresses an opposite (contrasting) idea.

Although dating couples often vary their activities, they nearly always plan the dates without help from parents.

_____ 2. The adverb phrase expresses concession.

If asked, the researcher would do it again in the same way.

_____ 3. The adverb clause is punctuated correctly.

After a couple has been dating a while, they may decide to marry.

_____ 4. The adverb clause expresses an unreal condition.

If there weren't enough food, the community would suffer from hunger.

_____ 5. The sentence is punctuated correctly.

Some couples live with the bride's family, whereas the majority live with the groom's family.

_____ 6. The sentence is punctuated correctly.

Lineage systems are studied extensively by anthropologists, thus, connections are found.

_____ 7. The absolute construction means "because."

With the data proving inaccurate, the anthropologist began the research project again.

_____ 8. The adverb phrase means "if there is further research."

With further research, the results will improve.

_____ 9. The adverb phrase expresses purpose.

The researcher kept precise records of the study in order to review it periodically.

_____ 10. The adverb clause expresses a condition.

In many societies, the future groom must ask the future bride's parents for permission to marry before the engagement is announced.

How did you do? Are there topics you need to review?

Exercise 4 Apply It to Speaking

1 Read the following passage about a natural disaster, along with the related questions.

2 Think about points you would like to make in response to the questions and how you can discuss them using adverbial clauses and phrases such as those in the box.

after	although	because	before	but	consequently
despite	due to	even though	given	however	if
in spite of	meanwhile	nevertheless	nonetheless	since	so
thereby	therefore	thus	yet		

3 Discuss your ideas with a small group of classmates, determining points of agreement and possible disagreement. Take notes.

In 2005, Hurricane Katrina made a direct hit on New Orleans, Louisiana. New Orleans is extremely vulnerable to hurricanes because it is 8 feet below sea level in some places and has a large, relatively poor population. Approximately eighteen hundred people died during Hurricane Katrina and total damage amounted to $80 billion.

After the hurricane passed, large areas of New Orleans remained under 20 feet of water. New Orleans was so hard-hit because the city has been slowly sinking for decades. This is the result of soil under the city slowly compacting and not being replaced by silt from the Mississippi River during yearly flooding as it was before development of the area. To keep the river back from the city, high levees* have been built between the neighborhoods and the river. When the hurricane hit, the levees were broken in places by the storm surge and water flowed into the city. At this point the levees kept the water inside the city, not allowing it to escape.

After the storm, thousands of people from the traditional cultural areas of New Orleans were dead and many more were homeless. Various disaster relief groups came into New Orleans to help. One of the solutions they came up with was to relocate large numbers of the poor from their flooded neighborhoods to other areas of the country. Experts estimate that as many as 398,000 people were evacuated and moved to surrounding states, most of them to Texas.

*levee—a dam built of soil to keep a flooding river out of neighborhoods in a city

1. Why is New Orleans vulnerable to hurricanes?

2. How did the neighborhoods get flooded with up to 20 feet of water during Hurricane Katrina?

3. After the hurricane, relief groups came into New Orleans to help. What was their solution in many cases?

4. How many people did they relocate?

5. Using what you learned in Exercise 3 about how traditional cultures cope with disaster, discuss what you think the groups of victims of Hurricane Katrina experienced.

6. What suggestions would you make to disaster relief groups that come up with evacuation and relocation solutions in the future?

Exercise 5 Apply It to Writing

Present your group's conclusions from Exercise 4, including points of agreement and disagreement, in a two-paragraph essay. Remember to use adverb clauses, adverb phrases, and absolute constructions. Incorporate as much vocabulary from the box as possible. See Appendix B for help.

construction	cope	destruction	dispute	grieve
labor	massive	relocation	self-sufficient	shelter
survive	trauma	victim	vulnerable	

Check Your Writing

Which of the following kinds of adverb clauses and phrases and absolute constructions did you use in your paragraphs? Did you use them correctly? Double-check your work.

☐ Adverb clauses of time (*before / after / when / while / as / since*)

☐ Adverb clauses of purpose (*so that*)

☐ Adverb clauses of cause / effect (*because / since / now that*)

☐ Adverb clauses of concession (*although / even though / though*)

☐ Adverb clauses of contrast (*while / whereas*)

☐ Adverb clauses of condition (*if / if not / unless*)

☐ Adverb clauses of condition (*even if / as if / as though*)

☐ Simple and compound sentences that express result (*so / thus / therefore / thereby*)

☐ Simple and compound sentences that express concession and contrast (*but / however*)

☐ Adverb phrases with present participles and past participles (*-ing* and *-ed* or *-en*)

☐ Adverb phrases with prepositions (*in order to / due to / because of / in spite of / despite / during*)

☐ Absolute constructions to express ideas of time or cause

PART

5

Noun Clauses

202

OBJECTIVES

In Part 5 of the *Advanced Grammar* course you will identify, understand, and use noun clauses

- as objects, subjects, complements, and appositives.
- to hedge or qualify statements.
- in reported speech.

Noun clauses are used to reduce the number of words needed in academic writing by summarizing information concisely. Noun clauses clarify ideas, express a point of view indirectly, express and refute others' ideas, report information from a source, and make writing objective. Noun clauses add a professional voice to your writing.

Academic texts about physics and related sciences serve to illustrate how academic writers use noun clauses effectively.

Noun Clauses Used as Objects

The ancient Greeks' concept of the universe, with the sun, moon, and planets attached to transparent spherical shells centered on Earth

PREVIEW

VOCABULARY   Here are some words that you will encounter in Chapter 13. How much do you know about each word? Turn to Appendix A to assess and expand your word knowledge.

axis	fluctuate	horizon	hypothesize	matter (n.)
spherical	spin	stipulate	symmetry	transparent

1. What do you suppose people who lived many thousands of years ago thought about the stars?
2. How do you think ancient people imagined the universe and the place of the earth, the sun, and the planets in it?

Read the following passage from *Physics: Concepts & Connections,* 5th Edition, by Art Hobson.[1]

The Scientific Method

[1]The "scientific method" or, as I will call it, the scientific process, is often described as several activities that scientists sometimes practice: observing, hypothesizing, testing, and so forth. But such a cookbook prescription doesn't capture how science works in real life. In fact, you use aspects of the scientific process whenever you use your own experience to reason through a problem. Science is simply a careful application of experience (often called observation and experimentation) and reason (often called hypothesis, theory, principle, and scientific law) to answer questions. For perspective on how science really operates, we'll study a historical example: the early history of astronomy. Astronomy, the scientific study of the stars and other objects in space, has usually been closely associated with physics. . . .

[2]In these high-technology times, we sometimes fail to see the stars. On some clear night, get away from city lights and take an hour or two to track the stars across the sky. If you're in the Northern Hemisphere, find the moon, the Big Dipper*, the North Star, any group of stars on the eastern horizon, and a group of stars on the western horizon . . . . Observe all of these every 15 minutes for one or more hours. What happens? You should be able to see that the moon and stars move westward, that stars rise in the east and set in the west, that different stars maintain their positions relative to one another while moving as a group across the sky, that the North Star remains fixed, and that stars near the North Star move in circles around the North Star.

[3]There are several small and unusually bright starlike objects that do not keep pace with the stars. If you observe them for a week or more, you'll see that they slowly shift their positions relative to the stars. These objects are called planets ("wanderers" in Greek). Five planets are visible without a telescope. The moon and the sun also move at a different pace from the stars.

[4]From such observations, most people would conclude that the stars, sun, moon, and planets travel in circles around Earth, with their axis of rotation fixed in the direction of the North Star. . . . This is the conclusion most observers drew centuries ago, and it's surely the conclusion that observers draw today unless they learn differently in school. Such observations and conclusions are typical of science's two main processes: observation and rational thought. Science is not really different from a lot of other human endeavors. Whenever you observe your surroundings and develop ideas based on what you observe, you are acting scientifically. . . .

(continued on next page)

This composite image combines multiple time exposures to record the night sky. The North Star, Polaris, can be seen at the center of the star trails.

[5]Because the stars all keep pace with one another, the Greeks supposed that they were all attached to the inside surface of a single transparent (invisible) spherical shell centered at Earth's center and rotating around Earth once a day, carrying the stars with it. The Greeks imagined that each of the other seven objects—sun, moon, and five visible planets—was attached to this transparent spherical shell centered on Earth, one sphere for each object.[2]

*the Big Dipper—a group of seven stars that looks like a big spoon in the Northern Hemisphere

Review the Ideas

1. According to the passage, what is the "scientific process"?
2. If you're in the Northern Hemisphere, find the moon, the Big Dipper, the North Star, any group of stars on the eastern horizon, and a group of stars on the western horizon. What will you see if you observe all of these every fifteen minutes for one or more hours?
3. What does the reference to "acting scientifically" at the end of the fourth paragraph mean?
4. How did the Greeks imagine Earth and the stars?

Analyze the Grammar

1 Look at the underlined clauses in paragraphs 1 and 2 of the passage. What do you think they are called?
2 What kinds of words do they follow?
3 How do they function in sentences?
4 Underline similar clauses in paragraphs 3, 4, and 5.

CHART 13-1	Noun Clauses as Objects Overview

<table>
<tr>
<td>A noun phrase functioning as a direct object is called a noun phrase object.</td>
<td>noun phrase object
Early Greeks believed **the theory**.</td>
</tr>
<tr>
<td>A noun clause is a dependent clause that functions as a noun. Noun clauses used as objects begin with the subordinating conjunctions *that, who, whom, what, how, how much, how many,* and *which*.

Noun clauses function as objects of the following:</td>
<td>noun clause object
Early Greeks believed **that the theory was logical**.</td>
</tr>
<tr>
<td>1. Certain verbs</td>
<td>verb
1. Early Greeks <u>thought</u> **that the theory was logical**.

Early Greeks <u>wondered</u> **what the theory meant**.

Early Greeks <u>asked</u> **whether the theory was logical**.</td>
</tr>
<tr>
<td>2. Gerunds</td>
<td>gerund
2. <u>Imagining</u> **that the world was flat** frightened ancient people.

Ancient people continued <u>asking</u> **what made the sun and moon move**.</td>
</tr>
<tr>
<td>3. Infinitives</td>
<td>infinitive
3. People wanted <u>to believe</u> **that the earth was the center of the universe**.

<u>To learn</u> **how the earth could move**, scientists observed the planets and stars.</td>
</tr>
</table>

GRAMMAR

PHYSICS

4. Prepositions	preposition 4. Regardless <u>of</u> **what scientists claimed**, most people did not believe them. Early Greeks talked <u>about</u> **whether the theory was true**.
5. Participles	participle 5. <u>Thinking</u> **that the world was flat**, ancient people were afraid of traveling far out to sea. <u>Convinced</u> **that the world was flat**, ancient people remained within sight of land.

Exercise 1 Identifying Noun Clauses as Objects

Underline the noun clauses used as objects in the following passages. Then with a partner decide which kind of word each noun clause follows. Write the numbers from Chart 13-1 at the ends of the paragraphs.

1. Weight is measured in newtons . . . while mass is measured in kilograms. An object's weight depends on its environment; for instance, an object's weight is less when it is on the moon than when it is on Earth, because the force of gravity is smaller on the moon than on Earth. But an object's mass is a property of the object alone and . . . so its mass is the same on the moon as on Earth. For example, a kilogram has a mass of 1 kilogram regardless of whether it is on Earth or on the moon or in distant space, but its weight is about 10 N . . . on Earth, only 1.6 N on the moon, and essentially zero in distant space.[3] _____

2. Plato (428 B.C.E.) joined a group of Pythagoreans after his mentor Socrates was executed in 399 B.C.E. Plato and his students discussed how they could construct a hypothesis that was more elaborate than Pythagoras's. Around 300 B.C.E., another Greek, Aristarchus, explained what was actually at the center of the universe, the sun. He tried to show how Earth and the five planets circled the sun. Other Greeks could not imagine how much force it would take to push Earth and keep it moving. Since they were not interested in learning how Earth could move, they rejected Aristarchus's idea. You are probably wondering what happened to Aristarchus's hypothesis. _____

3. Ptolemy, antiquity's greatest astronomer, pointed out that Earth was at the center of the universe. However, Copernicus (1473–1543) was interested in knowing whether Earth was actually at the center of the universe or not. Unfortunately, Copernicus was misled by how inaccurate his calculations were. Another astronomer, Brahe (1546–1601), figured out that both Ptolemy's and Copernicus's theories were inaccurate. Working for Brahe, Johannes Kepler (1571–1630), who had been a convinced Copernican, created what is now accepted as the theory of sun-focused ellipses. _____

4. In 500 B.C.E. the Greek astronomer Pythagoras and his group "the Pythagoreans" were mathematical mystics who believed that many features of the natural world could be described mathematically. They wanted to find a geometric plan for the universe because they were convinced that the idea of a circle was pure and eternal. Feeling that the sphere was the only perfectly symmetrical shape in space, it was natural for them to hypothesize that the universe was made of eight transparent spheres inside each other with Earth, a sphere, at its center. _____

CHART 13-2 **Noun Clauses as Objects Introduced by *That***

A noun clause object is a dependent clause introduced by a subordinating conjunction.

1. Certain transitive verbs, infinitives, gerunds, and a few verbs + prepositions in an independent clause can be followed by a noun clause introduced by the subordinating conjunction *that*.

   That may or may not be expressed.

   verb
   Aristotle **believed** (that) the earth was spherical.

   infinitive
   Aristotle intended **to prove** (that) the earth was spherical.

   gerund
   He continued **believing** (that) the earth was spherical.

   verb + preposition
   People **figured out** (that) Aristotle was correct.

2. A noun clause is formed by adding *that* to a statement.

   statement
   The earth is spherical.

   independent clause   noun clause
   People believe **(that) the earth is spherical.**

   Formal usage:
   The verb in the noun clause is in a past tense when the independent clause verb is in a past tense.

   independent clause   noun clause
   Aristotle believed **(that) the earth was spherical.**

3. Introductory participial and infinitive phrases can contain a noun clause object.

   introductory present participle phrase
   Believing (that) the earth was spherical, Aristotle explained his proof.

   introductory infinitive phrase
   To prove (that) the earth was spherical, the Greeks sailed as far as possible.

4. Verbs followed by *that*-clauses:

   a. Reported speech verbs:

   agree, answer, argue, assume, claim, comment, confide, declare, demonstrate, observe, hypothesize, remark, reply, report, note, predict, show, reveal, suggest, explain, convince, say, state, imply, hold, follow, tell

   b. Mental activity and emotion verbs (active and passive):

   anticipate, believe, hope, know, notice, find, realize, think, amaze, please, annoy, surprise, astonish, bother, delight, frighten, understand, worry, wonder, remember, see, imagine, conclude, prove, comprehend, matter, learn, suppose, doubt

   a. They **claim (that)** the world is round.

   b. The Greeks **hoped (that)** Aristotle was correct.

      The world **was surprised (that)** he was correct.

Exercise 2 Identifying the Noun Clauses and the Verbs That Precede Them

Work with a partner to identify and underline the noun clauses. Then write what kind of verb each noun clause follows: a reported speech verb, or a mental activity and emotion verb.

1. Pythagoras believed that certain groups of elements have similar properties.[4] _____

2. The transparent spheres hypothesis predicted that each planet moved at a uniform rate around the Earth. But careful observation showed that they did not.[5] _____

3. Because the stars all keep pace with one another, the Greeks supposed that they were all attached to the inside surface of a single transparent (invisible) spherical shell centered at Earth's center and rotating around Earth once a day, carrying the stars with it. _____

4. Furthermore, since humans are entirely made of atoms, it follows that every thought or feeling that enters your head is reducible to the motion of atoms within your brain and elsewhere. . . .[6] _____

5. The Greeks noticed that during a planet's retrograde motion it appeared brighter than at other times, as though it were closer to Earth during this time. Yet Plato's hypothesis, with each planet on an Earth-centered sphere, implied that each planet maintained a fixed distance from Earth.[7] _____

6. Observation shows that you are surrounded by an invisible substance, air. You know it's there because you can feel the wind. The atomic theory tells us every material substance, anything you can pick up or touch, is made of atoms. It's reasonable to suppose that air is a material substance, too, because you can feel it blow on you. A careful measurement would show that air has weight, further confirming our hypothesis. We conclude, from the atomic theory, that air is made of atoms. As you know from the Brownian motion experiment, the atoms in a liquid move all the time, even when the liquid appears to be motionless. So it's reasonable to suppose that air molecules are in constant motion, too, even in still air.[8] _____

Exercise 3 Combining Sentences with Statements

On a separate sheet of paper, write one sentence composed of the two clauses given.

1. a. Aristotle hypothesized
   b. All of the material that contributes to the growth of a plant comes from the soil.

2. a. Pythagoras believed
   b. The most perfect ideas were mathematical because they could be stated so precisely yet abstractly.

3. a. One Greek thinker, Aristarchus, proposed
   b. The sun and not Earth was at rest at the center of the universe, that Earth and the five planets circled the sun, and that Earth spun on its axis.

4. a. In the future, astronomers might discover
   b. The planets have begun severely deviating from their elliptical paths, as could happen if, for example, another star passed close to our sun.

5. a. It's a misconception to think
   b. A scientific theory is mere guesswork. . . .

6. a. Pythagoras believed
   b. Certain groups of elements have similar properties.

7. a. The dictionary explains
   b. A quantum is the smallest unit that can be used to measure something such as light or energy.

(continued on next page)

8. a. It goes on to say

   b. A quantum of light is a photon.

9. a. Did you know . . . ?

   b. Quantum theory is a scientific theory that describes the behavior and forces of elementary particles, which is based on the idea that energy, like matter, exists in very small separate pies, not in a continuous form.

10. a. Have you learned . . . ?

    b. An electromagnetic field (EM) is the effect that electrically charged objects have on the surrounding space.

CHART 13-3	Subjunctive Noun Clauses

1. Certain verbs that request, require, demand, or advise, or that express urgency are followed by noun clauses introduced with *that*. The verbs in these noun clauses must be in the subjunctive form. The subjunctive form is the base form of the verb, the form that is found in the dictionary.

   Verbs:
   ask, suggest, demand, urge, advise, require, insist, propose, stipulate, request, prefer

1. The experiment **requires** (that) the researcher

   base form of the verb
   be especially careful.

2. Adjectives that express a request, a requirement, a demand, advice, or urgency are followed by subjunctive noun clauses.

   Adjectives:
   essential, urgent, advisable, important

2. base form of the verb
   It is **essential** (that) the researcher **follow** the appropriate protocol.

3. Nouns that express a request, a requirement, a demand, advice, or urgency can also be followed by subjunctive noun clauses.

   Nouns:
   suggestion, demand, advice, requirement, proposal, stipulation, request, preference

3. base form of the verb
   The **requirement** (that) the researcher **read** the instructions is to avoid accidents.

(Note that subjunctive noun clauses will be treated more fully in Chapter 14.)

Exercise 4 Identifying Subjunctive Noun Clauses

Underline the subjunctive noun clauses in the sentences. Then indicate whether they follow a verb, adjective, or noun.

1. To ancient Greeks, it was important that the earth remain the center of the universe. _____

2. Copernicus could not accept the proposal that he consider the sun to be the center. _____

3. Quantum theory demands that an object's position and velocity have uncertainties Δx and Δv whose product is roughly h/m.[14] _____

4. Even today Pythagoras is known for the Pythagorean theorem. This theorem stipulates that a triangle have a 90-degree angle. _____

5. EM (electromagnetic) fields and other fields extend even into regions containing no matter. Quantum uncertainties require that the energies of all these fields at any point in space fluctuate, over short time-spans, around its long-time average value.[15] _____

6. At the instant the photon appears, the entire spread-out field vanishes. Physicists often describe this as the "collapse" of the field. But . . . the energy doesn't collapse to a true mathematical point having zero volume. Quantum physics demands that it be spread out over at least a certain minimal volume, a volume that is usually of atomic dimensions.[16] _____

Exercise 5 Completing Sentences with Subjunctive Noun Clauses

Complete each sentence with one of the verbs from the box. One verb is used twice. Do not use the other verbs more than once.

accept / accepts	believe / believes	create / creates	have / has
be / is / are	observe / observes	support / supports	travel / travels

1. Pythagoras insisted that everyone _____ the perfection of mathematics.

2. Kepler advised that Brahe _____ the theory of sun-focused ellipses.

3. Plato proposed that his student _____ a new hypothesis.

4. The theory stipulated that the sun _____ at the center of the universe.

5. Does the principle of relativity require that every observer _____ the same laws of physics?[17]

6. Even today Pythagoras is known for the Pythagorean theorem. This theorem stipulates that a triangle _____ a 90-degree angle.

7. The Pythagoreans' requirement that the area of a circle _____ pure and eternal was part of their beliefs about the world.

8. For the ancient Greeks, it was important that no one _____ close to the edge of the world.

CHART 13-4 **Noun Clauses as Objects Introduced by *Wh-* Words**

1. Certain verbs, infinitives, gerunds, and prepositions can be followed by noun clauses introduced by *wh-* words (subordinating conjunctions): *who, whom, what, when, where, which, how, how much, how many,* and *why*.

1. People wonder **what** quantum theory is.
   (verb)

   Try to explain **why** moving charged objects exert forces on magnets.
   (infinitive)

   People are interested in learning **who** created the theory.
   (gerund)

   People argued about **how** the earth was formed.
   (preposition)

2. Noun clauses introduced by *wh-* words are formed from *wh-* questions that are changed into statement word order and added to an independent clause.

   Wh- question:
   Independent clause + noun clause in statement word order

2. Who is that scientist?
   (question)

   People wonder **who that scientist is**.
   (independent clause) *(noun clause)*

   What is quantum theory?
   (question)

   People ask **what quantum theory is**.
   (independent clause) *(noun clause)*

   Who created the theory?
   (question)

   People asked about **who created the theory**.
   (independent clause) *(noun clause)*

   Formal usage:
   The verb in the noun clause is in a past tense when the main verb is in past tense. This is called the sequence of tense rule.

   People **wondered** who that scientist **was**.

3. When the independent clause is a question, a question mark should be placed at the end of the sentence.

3. Did people ask who that scientist was**?**

4. Introductory participial and infinitive phrases can also contain a noun clause object.

   The verbs, infinitives, gerunds and participles followed by *wh-* clauses express ideas of thinking, believing, knowing, or understanding: *think, believe, wonder, know, understand, ask, learn, report, predict, show, reveal, note, suggest, explain, say, state, notice, realize*.

4. Wondering **why the earth was spherical**, Aristotle studied his data.
   (present participle phrase)

   To understand **what shape the earth was**, the Greeks made many calculations.
   (infinitive phrase)

Exercise 6 Choosing a Subordinating Conjunction

Choose the best *wh-* words to complete the sentences.

1. Galileo sought only to describe _____ (*how / what*) things behave, not _____ (*why / which*) they behave as they do.[18]

2. Newtonian physics can predict precisely _____ (*how / what*) far a freely moving object will fall during any specified time.[19]

3. As part of understanding _____ (*how / what*) science is, we need to understand _____ (*how / what*) it's not. Because science is so widely accepted today, it has become common for all manner of charlatans to hawk their wares by alleging some scientific basis for them.[20]

4. Energy conservation says that a system's energy remains the same no matter at _____ (*what / when*) time you view it. In fact all conservation principles can be traced to symmetries in nature.[21]

5. Consider the odor of violets. Among a violet's various molecules, there must be some that make it smell the way it does. Chemists have learned _____ (*how / why*) the violet's odor molecule is strung together. Scientifically, at least, that's what the smell of violets is—those molecules.[22]

6. The "scientific method" or, as I will call it, the scientific process, is often described as several activities that scientists sometimes practice: observing, hypothesizing, testing, and so forth. But such a cookbook prescription doesn't capture _____ (*that / how*) science works in real life. . . . For perspective on _____ (*that / how*) science really operates, we'll study a historical example: the early history of astronomy.[23]

7. . . . the Newtonian view is that the universe itself is just such a collection of atoms. Thus, the future is entirely determined by _____ (*what / when*) all the atoms of the universe are doing right now or at any other time.[24]

Exercise 7 Combining Sentences with *Wh-* Questions

Work with a partner. Combine each pair to form one sentence with a noun clause object. Remember to pay attention to the word order. Write your answers on a separate sheet of paper.

1. a. Scientists found
   b. What kind of wave is light?
2. a. Light is all around us, yet it's not easy to say
   b. What is light?
3. a. Have you ever heard
   b. Why can a magnet make other metal objects move toward it?
4. a. It is difficult to imagine
   b. How does a magnet work?
5. a. A scientific theory is a well-confirmed framework of ideas that explains
   b. What do we observe?
6. a. Aristotle, a careful observer of living organisms, wondered
   b. Where does the material that contributes to the growth of a plant come from?
7. a. A big difficulty for the sun-centered astronomy proposed by Copernicus around 1550 was the problem of
   b. How could Earth keep moving with nothing to push it?
8. a. U.S. oil production illustrated
   b. What happens when a finite resource is consumed exponentially?

CHART 13-5 | **Noun Clauses as Objects Introduced by *If* or *Whether***

1. Certain verbs, infinitives, and gerunds can be followed by noun clauses introduced by *whether* (*or not*) or *if*. Prepositions can be followed by noun clauses introduced by *whether* (*or not*).

                verb

1. Aristotle **asked** whether / if the earth was spherical or flat.

          infinitive

We need **to know** whether / if Aristotle learned the truth (or not).

              gerund

People insist on **knowing** whether / if Aristotle was correct.

              preposition

Greeks wondered **about** whether (or not) the sun orbits the earth.

---

2. Noun clauses introduced by *whether* (*or not*) or *if* are formed from *yes / no* questions that are changed into statement word order and added to an independent clause.

          yes / no question

2. Is the earth spherical?

    independent clause   noun clause

People want to know **whether (or not) / if the earth is spherical**.

          yes / no question

Does the sun orbit the earth?

 independent clause   noun clause

People ask **whether / if the sun orbits the earth (or not)**.

The words *or not* may be placed after *whether* or at the end of the noun clause.

Yes / No question:
Independent clause + noun clause in statement word order

          yes / no question

Were the Greeks impressed by the new theory?

    independent clause   noun clause

Many people wonder **whether (or not) / if the Greeks were impressed by the new theory**.

Formal usage:
The verb in the noun clause changes to past tense when the main verb is in past tense. This is called the sequence-of-tense rule.

Aristotle **wondered** whether (or not) / if the earth **was** spherical.

---

3. When the independent clause is a question, a question mark should be placed at the end of the sentence.

3. Do you know whether / if the Greeks were impressed by the new theory (or not)**?**

---

4. Introductory participial and infinitive phrases can also contain a noun clause object.

The verbs, infinitives, gerunds and participles followed by *whether* (*or not*) or *if* express ideas of thinking, believing, knowing, or asking: *ask, wonder, understand, decide, remember, doubt, calculate, discover, consider*.

         present participle phrase

4. Wondering **whether the earth was spherical**, Aristotle studied his data.

         infinitive phrase

To understand **whether (or not) the earth was round**, the Greeks made many calculations.

Work with a partner to write sentences with noun clauses introduced with *whether (or not)* or *if*, using the information given. Remember to pay attention to the word order and make sure the verb tenses of the noun clauses are correct. Write your answers on a separate sheet of paper.

1. a. From earliest times, astronomers have wondered
   b. Is Earth or the sun at the center of the universe?

2. a. Pythagoras wanted to know
   b. Were his mathematical calculations correct?

3. a. Aristotle, a Greek philosopher, asked himself
   b. Is Earth round or not?

4. a. Aristotle had also noted the circular form of the shadow of Earth on the moon during an eclipse, so he doubted
   b. Is Earth flat? *whether Earth is flat or not*

5. a. An Egyptian astronomer, Ptolemy, living and working in Greece during the second century C.E., wondered
   b. Is the earth-centered model of the universe correct?

6. a. How can we tell
   b. Is a body exerting a force on another body?

7. a. Describe a simple way to determine, in a lab,
   b. Do two objects have equal masses?

8. a. How do we know
   Is light a wave or a particle?

9. a. In 1801, Thomas Young solved the problem of finding two sources with identical vibrations by using a single light source that he split into two parts. He then recombined these parts to see
   b. Did they interfere?

10. a. You would feel weightless in an orbiting satellite for the same reason that you would feel weightless in a freely falling elevator. As you saw in the preceding section, the satellite falls freely around Earth. You are falling freely around Earth too, regardless of
    b. Are you inside the satellite or outside in space? Since both you and the satellite are just falling around Earth, you have the sensation of weightlessness.

Exercise 9 Writing Sentences with *Wh*- and *Yes / No* Questions

On a separate sheet of paper, write sentences with independent clauses made from some of the verbs in the box, noun clauses made from statements, and noun clauses made from *wh*- questions and *yes / no* questions. Write a total of nine sentences. Use Charts 13-1 through 13-5 for help.

advise	ask	believe	calculate	explain
insist	know	learn	notice	predict
propose	realize	remember	report	request
reveal	say	show	state	think
understand	wonder			

Exercise 10 Error Analysis

The following excerpt from a student essay contains ten errors in noun clauses. The first error is corrected for you. Find and correct nine more.

Copernicus's Theory

Polish astronomer Nicolaus Copernicus (1473–1543) felt ~~what~~ *that* Ptolemy's theory of an Earth-centered system was too complicated and too far from Pythagoras's ideas. And so Copernicus devised how became a sun-centered system of the universe. There was resistance to this idea because the people at the time believed whether Earth was at the center and that all of the planets moved around Earth. The question of that the sun was at the center caused a great deal of controversy. A sun-centered theory went against everything that Pythagoras and the other astronomers maintained. Only Aristarchus had imagined if the sun could be at the center.

At the same time, Copernicus assumed what the motions of the planets and stars were circular. He did, however, notice how the moon circled Earth, while Earth and other planets circled the sun. The objections to the new theory were like those that had plagued Aristarchus. People asked that such a large body as Earth could move. They wanted to know what objects weren't thrown off as Earth moved. But Copernicus asked them how much those problems weren't even more evident with Ptolemy's theory of spinning spheres than in his theory of a small spinning Earth. It was a matter of how had the most logical theory. It took decades for the controversy to be settled by Galileo's telescope observations seventy years after Copernicus died.

Exercise 11 Apply It to Speaking

1 Read again the following paragraphs, which are taken from this chapter's introductory reading. Study also the related figure showing the earliest Greek conception of the universe.
2 With a classmate, write on a separate sheet of paper responses to the questions about the paragraphs and the figure, including a noun clause in each of your answers.
3 In small groups, compare your responses. Make sure that everyone has provided the correct information, and identify the noun clause used in each answer.

In these high-technology times, we sometimes fail to see the stars. On some clear night, get away from city lights and take an hour or two to track the stars across the sky. If you're in the Northern Hemisphere, find the moon, the Big Dipper, the North Star, any group of stars on the eastern horizon, and a group of stars on the western horizon. . . . Observe all of these every 15 minutes for one or more hours. What happens? You should be able to see that the moon and stars move westward, that stars rise in the east and set in the west, that different stars maintain their positions relative to one another while moving as a group across the sky, that the North Star remains fixed, and that stars near the North Star move in circles around the North Star.

There are several small and unusually bright starlike objects that do not keep pace with the stars. If you observe them for a week or more, you'll see that they slowly shift their positions relative to the stars. These objects are called planets ("wanderers" in Greek). Five planets are visible without a telescope. The moon and the sun also move at a different pace from the stars.

From such observations, most people would conclude that the stars, sun, moon, and planets travel in circles around Earth, with their axis of rotation fixed in the direction of the North Star. . . . This is the conclusion most observers drew centuries ago, and it's surely the conclusion that observers draw today unless they learn differently in school. Such observations and conclusions are typical of science's two main processes: observation and rational thought. Science is not really different from a lot of other human endeavors. Whenever you observe your surroundings and develop ideas based on what you observe, you are acting scientifically. . . .

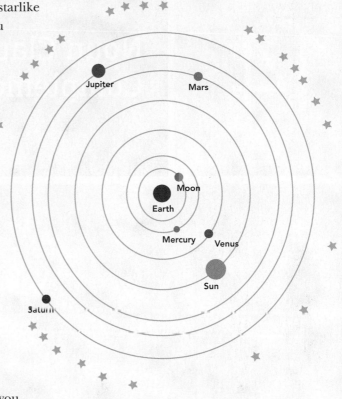

The earliest Greek conception, around 500 B.C.E., of the layout of the universe [31]

1. What would you see if you looked at the stars and their positions in the night sky for several hours?
2. What would you observe about the planets?
3. What might you conclude about the relationship of the heavenly bodies and Earth?
4. Why is it natural that the ancient Greeks thought that the stars and planets were each on separate spheres?
5. Why do you think the Greeks believed that Earth was at the center of the universe?
6. How were the Greeks acting scientifically when they drew their conclusions about the relationship of the heavenly bodies and Earth?

Exercise 12 **Apply It to Writing**

Discuss another phenomenon about which people have made observations and then provided an explanation. For example, you might choose a topic like global warming or the extinction or near extinction of some animal species. Write a paragraph in which you make statements about what is observed and believed about the phenomenon. Include a concluding statement of your own. Use in your paragraphs the phrases from the box along with noun clauses. See Appendix B for help.

People have observed . . .	Researchers have hypothesized . . .
Some scientists wondered . . .	I doubt whether . . .
It's important to consider . . .	Observers have asked what . . .
Most people assume . . .	It is essential . . .

Noun Clauses as Subjects, Complements, and Appositives

The Intergovernmental Panel on Climate Change (IPCC) is 95 percent confident that humans are the main cause of the current global warming.

PREVIEW

VOCABULARY Here are some words that you will encounter in Chapter 14. How much do you know about each word? Turn to Appendix A to assess and expand your word knowledge.

analogous	CO_2	electromagnetic (EM)	emissions	fossil fuel
galaxy	photon	radiation	skeptical	vapor

Prepare to Read

1. What is global warming?
2. What do you think about the idea that humans are causing global warming?

Read the following passage from *Physics: Concepts & Connections,* 5th Edition, by Art Hobson.[1]

Global Warming

[1]If you took Earth's temperature from space, you would find it to be a chilly –19°C (–2°F). . . . Fortunately for us, Earth's average surface temperature is +14°C, far warmer than the –19°C detected from space. The extra 33 degrees is due to Earth's surrounding blanket of atmospheric gases. . . . This 33 degrees of warming is called the greenhouse effect. Surprisingly, the gases that create the greenhouse effect are not the nitrogen and oxygen that form the bulk of Earth's atmosphere. Rather, the effect is due to certain trace* gases, mainly water vapor and carbon dioxide [CO_2]. . . . The distinguishing feature of these greenhouse gases is that they strongly absorb infrared* radiation.

[2]The natural greenhouse effect has warmed our planet for millions of years, but it has been enhanced recently by human activities. Fossil fuel combustion* creates enormous quantities of carbon dioxide, an important greenhouse gas. . . . This has warmed our planet during the past century. Such human enhancement of the natural greenhouse effect is called global warming. . . .

[3]Water vapor is the biggest contributor to the natural greenhouse effect, followed by CO_2. However, water vapor cannot be a primary cause of human-caused global warming because neither humans nor natural processes can appreciably change the amount of water vapor in the atmosphere. The reason is that air can only hold a certain amount of water vapor, beyond which the vapor condenses and "rains out. . . ."

[4]Global warming caused by CO_2 buildup has been predictable for many decades and was in fact predicted during the nineteenth century but was not taken seriously as long as it lay only in the future. The future has arrived. In 1990, 1995, 2001, and again in 2007, thousands of scientists from some 100 nations evaluated tens of thousands of scientific papers and came to a broad consensus that global warming is happening now and will increase. This effort, known as the Intergovernmental Panel on Climate Change (IPCC), represents our current understanding of global warming. . . .

[5]Some people are understandably skeptical when they learn that the human impact on our environment might lead to temperature increases of several degrees. There's a gut feeling that human actions are too puny* to do this. And it's true that the human energy input to our environment is relatively tiny: nearly all of Earth's energy comes from the sun, with less than 0.0075% from fossil fuels. The answer to this skepticism is that the predicted temperature rise is not caused directly by the human energy input, but by the human contribution to the greenhouse effect. Think of the atmosphere as a blanket that's –19 C on top but +14 C on the bottom because of the greenhouse effect that traps Earth's infrared radiation, just as a blanket on your bed is cold on top but warm on the bottom because it traps your body's radiation. The "insulation" in the greenhouse blanket is a thin trace of water vapor, CO_2, and a few other gases. Some 20% of the natural effect comes from CO_2. As we've seen, human activities have already increased the CO_2 by 40%, so overall we've increased the "greenhouse insulation" in Earth's blanket by 0.2 x 0.4 = 0.08, or 8%. Since the natural greenhouse effect raises Earth's temperature by 33 C, it's not surprising that a detailed calculation predicts a human-caused increase of a few degrees.[2]

* *trace*—present in tiny amounts
* *infrared*—radiation in the range below ultraviolet

* *combustion*—burning
* *puny*—small and insignificant

Review the Ideas

1. According to the passage, what is the natural greenhouse effect?
2. What is global warming?
3. What happened in 2007?
4. Why are people skeptical about the human impact on global warming? Explain.

Analyze the Grammar

1. In paragraphs 1, 3, 4, and 5 of the passage, five clauses are underlined. What kinds of words do they follow? Can you identify the clauses?
2. Underline other similar clauses in paragraph 5.
3. What kinds of words do they follow?
4. What are the functions of these clauses?

CHART 14-1	Noun Clauses as Subjects
1. A noun clause introduced by *that* can function as the subject of a sentence. Such clauses are followed by linking verbs such as *be*, *seem*, *appear*, *remain*, and *become*.	1. **That scientists disagree** has become a problem.
2. A *wh-* clause can be in the subject position with linking verbs such as *be*, *seem*, *appear*, *remain*, and *become*.	2. **How it relates** seems unimportant.
3. A *whether* clause can be in the subject position with linking verbs such as *be*, *seem*, *appear*, *remain*, and *become*. A noun clause beginning with *if* is not possible in the subject position.	3. **Whether global warming is real** is a key point.
4. Noun clauses in the subject position are rare. A more common pattern uses *it*. *It* is the "dummy" subject in this pattern. The noun clause is the "real" subject.	4. **It** has become a problem **that scientists disagree.** **It** seems unimportant **how it relates.** **It** is a key point **whether (or not) global warming is real.**
5. Sentences with the pattern *it* + linking verb + adjective + noun clause can be reversed so that the noun clause becomes the subject of the sentence. *It* is deleted when the reversal occurs.	5. It is obvious **that people disagree.** **That people disagree** is obvious. It wasn't clear **whether the solutions were effective.** **Whether the solutions were effective** wasn't clear.
6. Sentences with the pattern *it* + verb + object + noun clause can be reversed so that the noun clause becomes the subject of the sentence. Typical verbs are *surprise*, *amaze*, *fascinate*, *annoy*, *astonish*, and *make*.	6. It surprised the astronomers **that the sun was the center of the universe.** **That the sun was the center of the universe** surprised the astronomers. It could make a difference **what theory is used.** **What theory is used** could make a difference.

7. As you learned in Chart 13-3, certain verbs that request, require, demand, advise, and express urgency are followed by noun clauses whose verbs must be in the subjunctive form. Similarly, subjunctive noun clauses can follow certain adjectives after linking verbs. Some of these adjectives are forms of the verbs presented in Chart 13-3: *urgent, advisable, essential, imperative, important, critical, necessary, vital*.	7. It is urgent **that the researcher understand the problem.**
These kinds of sentences can be reversed so that the noun clause becomes the subject of the sentence.	**That the researcher understand the problem** is urgent.
8. Subjunctive noun clauses can also follow certain nouns after linking verbs. Some of these are noun forms of the verbs that are followed by subjunctive noun clauses in Chart 13-3: *advice, requirement, necessity*.	8. It is a requirement **that the researcher solve the problem.** **That the researcher solve the problem** is a requirement.
These kinds of sentences can also be reversed.	

Exercise 1 Identifying Noun Clause Subjects

With a partner, underline the noun clauses used as subjects. Some noun clauses used as subjects will have "it" as a "dummy" subject. Match the type of noun clause with an explanation from Chart 14-1.

1. What happens during combustion is the release of a great deal of CO_2.

2. Physics is still in the middle of the post-Newtonian revolution, and it is not clear what new scientific worldview will emerge.[3]

3. Newtonian physics is a remarkable achievement that is incredibly effective in explaining countless observed phenomena. Are its materialistic* philosophical underpinnings then necessarily correct? Is it true that atoms are all there is?[4]

4. "In our view the challenge of climate change is now so serious that it demands a degree of political commitment which is virtually unprecedented. Whether the political leaders of the world are up to the task remains to be seen. . . ." British House of Commons, Environmental Audit Committee, from their 2005 Report.[5]

5. Global warming has already had a wide range of consequences. . . . Snow and ice cover have decreased. For example, only 26 of the original 150 named glaciers in Glacier National Park, Montana, still remained in 2007, and it's expected that they'll all be gone by 2030. . . . In the future, it's expected that climate zones will shift some 500 km northward, resulting in extinctions of 1.25 million plant and animal species, or 25% of all species, by 2050. Also, it's likely that warming will partially disrupt the ocean currents that transport thermal energy around the globe.[6]

materialistic—the idea that matter is the basic substance in nature

Exercise 2 Combining Sentences with Noun Clause Subjects

Combine the pairs of sentences into one sentence by using one sentence as a noun clause subject. In one instance a "dummy" subject is possible. The first is done for you. Write your answers on a separate sheet of paper.

1. a. Who is Steven Weinberg?
   b. This is essential for students of physics to know.

   Who Steven Weinberg is is essential for students of physics to know.

2. a. Who was Sir Isaac Newton?
   b. This is important to know.
3. a. What did Newton discover?
   b. This is the basis of Newtonian physics.
4. a. What is Newton's discovery called?
   b. This is gravity, the force that pulls one object toward another, especially toward the surface of Earth and other planets.
5. a. How did Newton make his great discovery?
   b. This became the famous story of Newton sitting under an apple tree and noticing apples falling.
6. a. Why did Newtonian physics lose its place as the most powerful and accurate?
   b. This was because it failed to explain forces at high speeds, very large gravitation, and microscopic distances.
7. a. How did Albert Einstein and others account for the failures of Newtonian predictions?
   b. This was by inventing the new theories of special relativity, general relativity, and quantum physics.
8. a. What's needed?
   b. It is a joining of relativity and quantum physics into a single theory covering all sizes and speeds.
9. a. As I hope you'll discover throughout this book, it's amazing.
   b. What can careful thought guided by simple observations accomplish?

Exercise 3 Writing Sentences with Noun Clause Subjects

With a partner write sentences with noun clause subjects in response to the numbered questions on the following page. Use the sentence starters and completions in the box. Write your sentences on a separate sheet of paper. The first one is done for you.

SENTENCE STARTERS	SENTENCE COMPLETIONS
It's apparent . . .	. . . is important.
It's interesting . . .	. . . is key to understanding physics.
It's important . . .	. . . is confusing.
It is not clear . . .	. . . seems logical.
It amazed the ancient Greeks . . .	
It has become well known . . .	

1. What is an atom?

   It is not clear to me what an atom is.

2. What is a photon?
3. Why was Newtonian physics abandoned?
4. How are magnets made?
5. Are particles the pieces that atoms are made of?
6. Does an element contain only one type of atom, and can it be changed into a simpler substance?
7. What is matter?
8. Is mass the amount of matter that a physical object contains?
9. Is a photon a particle?
10. Is an atom the smallest part of an element that can exist alone or combine with other substances to form a molecule?

CHART 14-2 Noun Clauses as Complements

1. A noun clause introduced by *that* can follow linking verbs such as *be*, *seem*, *appear*, *remain*, and *become* as the subject complement. *That* may be omitted.	1. The problem is **(that) global warming is real**.
2. A *wh-* clause can follow linking verbs such as *be*, *seem*, *appear*, *remain*, and *become* as the subject complement.	2. Our question is **how greenhouse gases can be reduced**.
3. A *whether-* or *if-* clause can follow linking verbs such as *be*, *seem*, *appear*, *remain*, and *become* as the subject complement.	3. One question is **whether / if we will have time to solve the problem**.
4. Sentences with noun clause subject complements may be reversed so that the noun clauses become the subjects. In this case *that* may not be omitted.	4. **That global warming is real** is a problem. **How greenhouse gases can be reduced** is our question. **Whether we will have time to solve the problem** is one question.
5. Noun clauses can function as adjective complements. Adjective complements are clauses or phrases that follow certain adjectives and add to their meanings. Adjectives that can be followed by noun clauses include *amazing, annoying, surprising, astonishing, frightening, clear, important, aware, sure, certain,* and *uncertain*.	5. The scientists remain **sure** that global warming is real. Scientists are not **certain** what solutions to suggest. They seem **uncertain** whether / if humans can solve the problem.

Exercise 4 Identifying Noun Clauses Used as Complements

With a partner underline the noun clauses used as subject complements and adjective complements. Match the type of noun clause with an explanation from Chart 14-2 and write it after the clause.

1. Here is how the sun and Earth were born.[9] _____

2. The question is not whether the fossil fuel age will soon end; the real question is how it will end.[10]
   _____

3. The pile of atoms that is you has an especially surprising property: it is aware of itself, and in this scientific age it is even aware that it is a pile of atoms. It's something to think about.[11] _____

4. A smooth ball rolls on a smooth table. Initially, no horizontal forces are exerted on the ball. Then you bring a magnet near the rolling ball, but you are unsure whether the magnet actually exerts a magnetic force on the ball. How can you tell whether the magnet is exerting a horizontal force on the ball?[12]
   _____

5. Probabilities are useful whenever the outcome of a particular experiment is uncertain but the overall statistics of many repetitions are predictable. A simple example, having nothing to do with quantum physics, is the flip of a coin. What 50% probability of heads means is that, in a long series of tosses, roughly 50% will be heads.[13] _____

6. It's important to remember that photons aren't really particles. A photon is simply an energy increment of a spread-out EM (electromagnetic) field, analogous to a spread-out liter of water in a bathtub. . . . A photon is nothing like, say, a tiny fast-moving pea. What really happens is that the entire space-filling EM field instantaneously loses one quantum of energy, and at the same instant that quantum of energy shows up at a particular point on the screen.[14] _____

Exercise 5 Combining Sentences with Noun Clauses Used as Complements

On a separate sheet of paper, combine the pairs of sentences to form one sentence with a noun clause complement. The first one is done for you.

1. a. An object that can emit or be affected by an electric charge is known as an electrically charged object.
   b. The first definition students need to know is this.

   The first definition students need to know is (that) an object that can emit or be affected by an electrical charge is known as an electrically charged object.

2. a. Electrically charged objects affect the space that surrounds them, causing an electromagnetic field.
   b. The second piece of information students will find useful is this.

3. a. Electrically charged objects have electromagnetic (EM) energy caused by their positions within an EM field.
   b. Another important point for the study of physics is this.

4. a. An EM field with certain limited amounts of total energy is called a quantized EM field.
   b. An additional piece of important information is this.

5. a. Rather than being tiny points, particles such as electrons are actually tiny loops.
   b. The string hypothesis's key idea is this.

6. a. Particles are loops not points, which has been shown by scientific observations.
   b. It all sounds too amazing to be true, but the truly amazing thing is this.

Completing Sentences with Noun Clause Complements

With a partner, complete in a logical manner the sentences about global warming. Use noun clause complements introduced by *who, what, when, where, why, how, that, whether,* and *if.*

1. Some environmentalists are certain _____.

2. Others are not sure _____.

3. One common question about global warming is _____.

4. A second question might be _____.

5. A well-known fact about greenhouse gases is _____.

6. One hypothesis about global warming is _____.

7. A question people ask about the theory of global warming is _____.

8. It is frightening *when someone is following ya* _____.

9. It isn't clear _____.

10. An explanation for global warming is _____.

CHART 14-3	Noun Clauses as Appositives

1. In Chart 4-4, you learned that sometimes nouns follow other nouns and have the same meanings. These nouns are called **appositives**.

   Noun clauses can also be appositives. Noun clauses used as appositives can be used after a noun in any position: subject, object, or complement.

   subject + noun clause
   1. **The view that the earth was flat** was common.

   direct object + noun clause
   Most people believed [**the view that the earth was flat.**]

   object of a preposition + noun clause
   They talked about **the view that the earth was flat.**

   complement + noun clause
   Our topic is **the view that the earth was flat.**

2. Noun clauses used as appositives begin with *that*. These clauses may follow certain nouns such as *idea, knowledge, belief, assumption, claim, hypothesis, view, agreement, statement, report, anticipation, hope, realization, thought, fact, notion,* and *suggestion*. These nouns are often derived from verbs that take noun clauses.

   The *that* clauses that follow these nouns have the same meaning as the nouns.

   2. We debated the notion **that humans cause global warming**.

   The hypothesis **that matter is actually a wave** surprised Albert Einstein.

3. Remember that an adjective clause beginning with *that* describes the noun it follows.

   A noun clause appositive has the same meaning as the noun it follows.

   adjective clause
   3. The suggestion **that we discussed** will be implemented.

   noun clause
   The suggestion **that she follow the directions** was ignored.

Exercise 7 Identifying Noun Clause Appositives

With a partner, underline the noun clauses used as appositives. Then indicate whether each appositive follows the subject of the sentence or the object of a preposition.

1. The fact that theories are never absolutely certain is a strength, not a weakness, of science.[15] _____

2. The notion that reality is a set of fields . . . is the most important consequence of relativistic quantum field theory.[16] _____

3. There is energy in a light beam, as you can tell from the fact that light (sunlight, for instance) can warm things, and you can get work out of warm things.[17] _____

4. To Copernicus and to scientists since Copernicus, the ancient idea that the universe is centered on Earth seemed narrow-minded, provincial.[18] _____

5. Quantum physics has a well-deserved reputation for being odd. Quantum uncertainty, nonlocality, and the surprising effect of detectors are about as far removed as you can get from the world described by Newtonian physics. The odd results come from the non-Newtonian view that the world is made not of rigid, unchanging, pointlike particles, but rather of continuous fields, and that these fields come in unified parcels or "quanta" of energy.[19] _____

Exercise 8 Writing Sentences with Noun Clauses as Appositives

With a partner, write ten sentences on a separate sheet of paper, using the sentence starters in the box. Be careful, some of the sentences may need the subjunctive; you can review these instances by looking back at Chart 14-1.

the answer	the fact	the hypothesis	the idea	the notion
the possibility	the request	the requirement	the theory	the view

CHART 14-4 Noun Clauses Used for Hedging

As you have learned, academic writers use certain modals (*may, might,* and *could*) to hedge, that is, to avoid claiming that something is certain. Often writers hedge so as not to reduce their own authority in case the statement proves to be wrong. Hedging gives other researchers the chance to express opposing views.	Reducing CO_2 **could** stop global warming.
Noun clauses can also be used to hedge. The following types of noun clauses show a lack of certainty about and a hesitation to commit to a claim:	
1. *That* clauses introduced with verbs such as *assume, estimate, suggest, speculate, indicate, assert,* and *claim*	1. Aristarchus **suggested** that Earth circled the sun.
2. *There* + linking verb + noun + *that* clause following certain nouns such as *assumption, assertion, belief, claim, possibility, probability, estimation, suggestion,* and *indication*	2. In America, there is a high **probability** that many people believe in astrology.

3. *That* clauses introduced by *it* + linking verb + adjective + *that* clause following linking verbs such as *be*, *seem*, and *appear*, and certain adjectives such as *conceivable*, *possible*, *probable*, *believable*, and *likely*

3. It **appears likely** that human actions cause global warming.

4. *That* clauses introduced by *it* + (adverb) + the passive form of certain verbs such as *suggest*, *say*, *believe*, *assume*, *indicate*, *think*, and *be*. Adverbs are common in hedging noun clauses.

4. It **was conventionally assumed** that Earth was the center of the universe.

NOTE: Certain verbs, nouns, and adjectives are used to show commitment to an idea, which is the opposite of hedging. **Verbs**: *prove*, *show*, *demonstrate*, *verify*, *attest*, *substantiate*, *ascertain*, *corroborate*, *uphold*, *support*, *sustain*, *establish*, *confirm*, *provide evidence*. **Nouns**: *evidence*, *proof*, *a fact*. **Adjectives**: *certain*, *true*.

The Greeks **established** that Earth was a sphere.

The **proof** that Earth circled the sun was clear.

Exercise 9 Identifying Noun Clauses Used for Hedging

With a partner, underline the noun clauses that hedge and the verb or phrase that introduces each one. How could you change them so that they show commitment to an idea?

1. The obvious parallels between electroweak and strong forces suggest that there should be a single grand theory that unites the electroweak and strong forces, although such a theory has not yet been found.[20]

_____

2. It seems likely that the Newtonian worldview remains active, even (or perhaps especially) among people who have never heard of Isaac Newton.[21]

_____

3. In the future, astronomers might discover that the planets have begun severely deviating from their elliptical paths, as could happen if, for example, another star passed close to our sun. It is always possible that new data will contradict any general theory.[22]

4. _____

In fact, even if an extra dimension were as large as 1 millimeter, it's possible that it would not yet have been detected experimentally because it's difficult to detect variations in the gravitational force acting over such small distances.[23]

_____

5. It's thought that the sun and some 50 or more other stars all formed at roughly the same time from a single huge region of gas and dust within our Milky Way Galaxy (our galaxy was already some eight billion years old by then).[24]

_____

6. Astronomers have now identified about 20 similar objects within our galaxy that are thought to be black hole remnants of collapsed stars, and they suspect that there might be around one billion of them in our galaxy.[25]

_____

Error Analysis

The following student essay contains ten errors. The first error is corrected for you. Find and correct nine more.

Astrology

       that
Ancient Babylonians believed ~~what~~ the sun, moon, and planets existed for the benefit of humans. They believed that happened on Earth was influenced by the positions of the planets, the moon, and the sun. Their basic belief was where the sun's, moon's, and planets' relative positions at the moment of a child's birth would affect his or her entire life. However, according to Art Hobson, the author of *Physics: Concepts & Connections*, "Astrology is scientifically implausible, to say the least." That the sun, moon, and stars are cannot influence our personalities or lives.

From the scientists' point of view, the planets influence us through gravity and electromagnetism, but not much else. "It's hard to imagine what these effects at birth could influence our lives," continues Hobson. Researchers have studied the horoscopes (diagrams of the sun's, moon's, and stars' positions at the time of someone's birth) of thousands of people and have been unable to find how much they had any predictive value at all. Astrologers apparently guess when certain events will occur or that people will have certain personality traits, but their deductions are no better than anyone else's.

However, no matter how unscientific the researchers claim astrology is, half of the American public remains convinced if astrology is a valid way to make decisions. For example, astrological predictions can be found every day in the newspaper and people love to read them. In addition, it's amazing to think who Ronald Reagan, fortieth president of the United States, was influenced by astrology. According to Donald Regan, chief of staff to former President Reagan, before the Reagans made any plans, they consulted an astrologer in San Francisco who drew up horoscopes to make certain how many the planets were in a favorable alignment for the enterprise. Thoughtful people must ask themselves that humans will ever be able to use technology wisely when half of us are still so superstitious.

Apply It to Speaking

With a partner study the two charts at the top of the following page and discuss the related questions. When possible and appropriate, use noun clauses and modal verbs to hedge as you draw conclusions about the information that is presented.

1. What does each chart illustrate? What trend does each chart show?

2. The information in each chart does not extend to the present time. What would each chart probably show if the information were updated? What would you surmise about the state of the Arctic sea ice? For example, do you think that Earth's temperature would continue to rise, or would it fall?

3. What might you conclude about the relationship between the two charts? Why do you think they are shown together?

APPLICATION

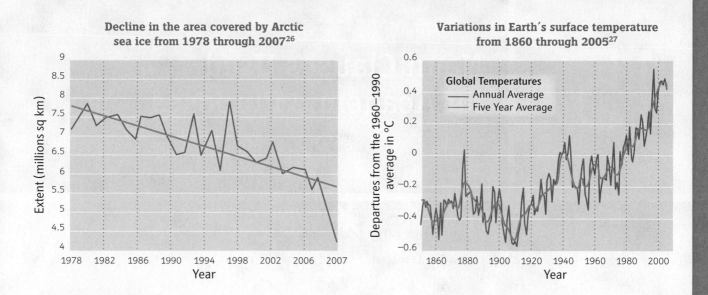

Decline in the area covered by Arctic sea ice from 1978 through 2007[26]

(graph — Extent (millions sq km) vs Year)

Variations in Earth's surface temperature from 1860 through 2005[27]

Global Temperatures
— Annual Average
— Five Year Average

(graph — Departures from the 1960–1990 average in °C vs Year)

Exercise 12 **Apply It to Writing**

Now take a look at the two charts below and write a paragraph interpreting the information they present. Answer the following questions in your analysis, hedging in your comments when you are not completely certain about your conclusions.

1. What does the graph showing world annual carbon emissions illustrate? What do you think the graph will illustrate in 2015? Why?

2. What does the second graph show about CO_2 emissions in the world? Which countries are the worst offenders? Why do you think this might be so? Given that this chart goes back to 2002, do you think some of the information might look different today? How?

3. Looking at the information in both graphs, what conclusions would you draw about world emissions of carbon dioxide? Would you assume this will be a continuing problem? Who, in your opinion, should address this problem? See Appendix B for help.

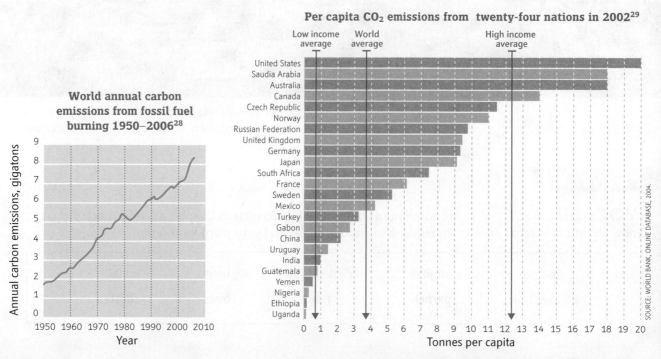

World annual carbon emissions from fossil fuel burning 1950–2006[28]

(graph — Annual carbon emissions, gigatons vs Year)

Per capita CO_2 emissions from twenty-four nations in 2002[29]

Low income average   World average   High income average

United States
Saudia Arabia
Australia
Canada
Czech Republic
Norway
Russian Federation
United Kingdom
Germany
Japan
South Africa
France
Sweden
Mexico
Turkey
Gabon
China
Uruguay
India
Guatemala
Yemen
Nigeria
Ethiopia
Uganda

Tonnes per capita

SOURCE: WORLD BANK, ONLINE DATABASE, 2004.

Noun Clauses Used for Academic Purposes

A traveler from the Middle Ages discovers the new mechanical universe of Nicolaus Copernicus and Isaac Newton.

PREVIEW

VOCABULARY   Here are some words that you will encounter in Chapter 15. How much do you know about each word? Turn to Appendix A to assess and expand your word knowledge.

analog	digital	disdainfully	inert	initial
microscopic	particle	tide	trace	vibrate

Prepare to Read

1. What do you think happened to ancient Greek ideas about the universe?
2. Who was Isaac Newton and why was he important?

Read the following passage from *Physics: Concepts & Connections,* 5th Edition, by Art Hobson.[1]

Atomic Materialism: Atoms and Empty Space

[1]From 1550 to 1700, the revolutionary ideas of Copernicus and others became widespread, and educated people no longer viewed Earth as the central focus of the universe. Humans became passengers on one planet among many, inhabitants of a less personal universe. . . . The new view stimulated an advancing scientific tide whose high point was Newtonian physics, the remarkably effective ideas about motion, force, and gravity developed by Isaac Newton (1642–1727) and others. During 1700 to 1900, its cultural influence spread far beyond science, affecting the way people thought about themselves, their society, and their place in the universe. Today, the Newtonian worldview still dominates our culture.

[2]In summing up his scientific career, Isaac Newton once stated, "If I have seen farther than others, it is by standing on the shoulders of giants." Two such giants, René Descartes (1596–1650) and Galileo Galilei (1564–1642), helped establish the philosophy behind Newton's physics. Descartes, Galileo, and Newton were the leading founders of science as we know it today.

[3]Although in Newton's time there was very little evidence for atoms, the atomic idea underlies much of Newtonian physics. It was an idea that went pretty deep, a philosophical idea. As Democritus put it:

By convention sweet is sweet, bitter is bitter, hot is hot, cold is cold, and color is color. But in reality there are only atoms and empty space. That is, the objects of sense are supposed to be real, and it is customary to regard them as such, but in truth they are not. Only the atoms and empty space are real.

[4]This goes far beyond the atomic theory. Democritus is saying that not only matter but everything is made of atoms and that atoms are all there is. So when you say "the water is hot" or "the shirt is red," you really mean that the atoms in the water and shirt are moving in a certain way. There really is no such thing as hot or red—there are only atoms.[2]

Review the Ideas

1. According to the reading passage, what happened to the Greek idea of Earth as the center of the universe? How did this view of the universe change science?
2. How did Isaac Newton fit into this change?
3. Who were René Descartes and Galileo Galilei?
4. What did Democritus say about reality?

Analyze the Grammar

1. In paragraphs 2 and 3 of the passage, what are the underlined sentences called?
2. Why are they written in a different way in the two paragraphs?
3. In paragraph 4, there is an underlined sentence. How is it different from the underlined sentences in paragraphs 2 and 3?
4. Is there a difference between the sentences with quotation marks in paragraph 4 and the one in paragraph 2?

CHART 15-1 | Punctuation of Direct Speech

Direct quotations (also called *direct speech*) are used to write a person's exact words. Punctuation is important. Commas, periods, question marks, and exclamation points in the quotation are usually written inside the quotation marks.	The professor asked, "Do you think before you speak?"
1. If a question mark or exclamation point applies to the whole sentence, it should be placed outside the quotation marks.	1. Did the professor always say, "Think before you speak"**?**
2. A reporting verb such as *ask* or *say* has a comma between it and the quotation.	2. He said**,** "There are several explanations." "There are several explanations**,**" he said.
3. If the reporting verb is in the middle of a sentence, there is a comma before and after the reporting phrase.	3. "There are**,**" he said**,** "several explanations."
4. If there are two sentences (statements) in the quote with the reporting verb between them, the reporting verb ends with a period.	4. "There are several explanations," he said**.** "So study them all before making a decision."
5. *Wh-* and *yes / no* questions in the quote end with a question mark.	5. "What causes gravity**?**" she asks. She asks, "What causes gravity**?**" "Does Earth move**?**" they asked. They asked, "Does Earth move**?**"
6. An exclamation in the quote ends with an exclamation point.	6. "Imagine it**!**" he cried. He cried, "Imagine it**!**"
7. A quote within a direct quotation is enclosed in single quotation marks.	7. He said, "My professor claimed, 'The Greeks did not consider all the facts.'"
8. A quotation longer than a few lines is written as a separate paragraph in a smaller font with every line indented. There are not quotation marks.	8. As Democritus put it: By convention sweet is sweet, bitter is bitter, hot is hot, cold is cold, and color is color. But in reality there are only atoms and empty space. That is, the objects of sense are supposed to be real, and it is customary to regard them as such, but in truth they are not. Only the atoms and empty space are real.

Exercise 1 | Punctuating Direct Quotations

Punctuate the following imaginary interview with Albert Einstein, the physicist who developed the theory of relativity and is famous for his equation $E=MC^2$.

Excuse me, Dr. Einstein   said the reporter   can you spare a few minutes to answer some questions

I suppose so   replied Einstein   but make it quick. I have important matters to attend to this afternoon.

Of course, I'll make it fast   the reporter said   It is said, sir, that as a young man, you were a poor student. Is that true

Yes, those classes were so boring, you know   answered Einstein   My teachers all said I would never amount to anything

No   exclaimed the reporter   You are the greatest physicist of all time

True   remarked Einstein   but they didn't know it then. Imagine their surprise when little Albert won a Nobel Prize

CHART 15-2 Reported Speech for Authorities' Opinions and Support

Reported speech is a report of what someone said, not the exact words of a speaker. Reported speech is not enclosed in quotation marks.	Albert Einstein said that his classes had been boring.
Reported speech relates what someone said in a noun clause introduced by a reporting verb.	Einstein **said** that he had been a poor student.
To change direct speech to reported speech, omit the punctuation and rewrite the quotations as sentences with noun clauses. Remember to write the noun clauses in statement word order. Note also that the verb in the quotation changes from present tense to past or from past to past perfect tense. Pronouns and time references also change. (See Chart 15-3.)	Einstein said, "Those classes were so boring." Einstein said that those classes had been so boring.

1. Reporting a statement
 	
    Use a *that* clause. *That* may be omitted.
	1. He said, "There are several explanations."
	
	    He said **that there were several explanations**.

2. Reporting a *wh-* question
 	
    Use a *wh-* clause.
	2. Einstein asked, "What is the question?"
	
	    Einstein asked **what the question was**.

3. Reporting a *yes / no* question
 	
    Use *if* or *whether*.
	3. The reporter asked, "Are you busy?"
	
	    The reporter asked **if / whether** he was busy.

4. Reporting an imperative
 	
    Use *tell* + object + a *that* clause (with *should* or *must*).
 	
    Or use *tell* + object + infinitive.
	4. Einstein replied, "Ask the question!"
	
	    Einstein **told him that he should / must** ask the question.
	
	    Einstein **told him to ask** the question.

5. Reporting a quote within a quote
 	
    Use two noun clauses.
 	
    Examples of reporting verbs: *acknowledge, admit, affirm, agree, argue, ask, assert, caution, claim, comment, conclude, confirm, cry, declare, emphasize, estimate, explain, imply, indicate, insist, maintain, note, observe, point out, propose, quip, recommend, remark, reply, report, respond, retort, say, sneer, state, suggest, tell* (someone), *warn, write*
	5. He said, "The professor claimed, 'The Greeks did not consider all the facts.'"
	
	    He said **that the professor claimed that the Greeks did not consider all the facts**.

Exercise 2 Identifying Direct and Reported Speech in Context

In the following paragraphs, underline direct speech once and reported speech twice. Note that in some instances quotation marks are used for a purpose other than a direct quotation.

1. How do we know that things are made of atoms? Science's power comes from its "show-me" attitude, its insistence on evidence. So I will frequently ask, "How do we know?" The ancient Greeks had no direct microscopic evidence for atoms, but Democritus had some ingenious indirect evidence. He argued that since we can smell a loaf of bread from a distance, small bread particles must break off and drift into our noses. This is still an acceptable explanation of odors today.[3]

2. . . . German social scientist Max Weber (1864–1920) spoke of the "disenchantment of the world" brought about by Newtonian science. Poet and painter William Blake (1757–1827) wrote disdainfully in a poem "May God us keep / From Single vision / and Newton's sleep!" Nevertheless, from the seventeenth into the twentieth century, these ideas influenced many educated people.[4]

3. In science it often happens that scientists say, "You know that's a really good argument; my position was mistaken," and then they would actually change their minds and you never hear that old view from them again. They really do it. It doesn't happen as often as it should because scientists are human and change is sometimes painful. But it happens every day. I cannot recall the last time something like that happened in politics or religion. —Carl Sagan, astronomer and science writer[5]

CHART 15-3	Reported Speech Verb Tense and Other Changes

As noted, the change from direct speech to reported speech requires some changes in verb tense as well as in pronouns and time words.

1. The reporting verbs *say*, *claim*, *comment*, and *ask* may be in present or past tense in the direct quotation. They usually change to past tense in reported speech.	1. Albert Einstein **says**, "School was boring." Einstein **said** (that) school had been boring.
2. The verb in the quotation changes from present tense to past when it becomes reported speech. The sequence-of-tense rule requires that a past tense reporting verb be followed by a past tense verb in the noun clause in formal English.	2. "There **are** several explanations," he says. He said that there **were** several explanations. "What **causes** gravity?" she asks. She asked what **caused** gravity.
3. Scientific facts can be reported in simple present tense although past is preferred in formal writing.	3. Newton said, "The moon **falls** around Earth." Newton said that the moon **falls** around Earth. Newton said that the moon **fell** around Earth.
4. Present perfect and past tenses in the direct quotation change to past perfect in the reported speech.	4. "**Has** Earth **moved**?" they asked. They asked if / whether Earth **had moved**. "There **were** several explanations," he said. He said that there **had been** several explanations.

5. In the reported speech, change a present or future modal auxiliary to a past form: *can* to *could*, *may* to *might*, and *will* to *would*. *Should* does not change.	5. "Anyone **can** understand quantum theory," she claimed. She claimed that anyone **could** understand quantum theory.
6. Pronouns and time words also change: *I* to *he / she*, *we* to *they*, *my* to *his / her* (a noun is also possible), *this* to *that*, *these* to *those*, *today* to *that day*, *now* to *then*, *this week* to *that week*.	6. The professor admitted, "**I** don't have the answer **today**." The professor admitted that **she** didn't have the answer **that day**.

Exercise 3 Identifying Changes in Reported Speech

The dialogue between the reporter and Albert Einstein has been changed to reported speech. Work with a partner to find and underline the changes in the reported speech. Then add at the end of each sentence the number(s) of the corresponding rule(s) for the change(s) from Charts 15 2 and 15 3. There may be several rules that apply to a particular change.

1. "Excuse me, Dr. Einstein," asked the reporter, "can you spare a few minutes to answer some questions?"

   The reporter asked Dr. Einstein if he could spare a few minutes to answer some questions. _____

2. "I suppose so," replied Einstein, "but make it quick. I have important matters to attend to this afternoon."

   Einstein replied that he supposed so, but he told the reporter to make it quick. _____ He said that he had important matters to attend to that afternoon. _____

3. "Of course, I'll make it fast," the reporter said. "It is said, sir, that as a young man, you were a poor student. Is that true?"

   The reporter said that of course he would make it fast. _____ The reporter went on to say that it was said that as a young man Einstein had been a poor student. _____ He asked whether that was true. _____

4. "Yes, those classes were so boring, you know," answered Einstein. "My teachers all said I would never amount to anything."

   Einstein answered that yes, those classes had been so boring. _____ He said that his teachers all had said that he would never amount to anything. _____

5. "No!" exclaimed the reporter. "You are the greatest physicist of all time!"

   The reporter exclaimed that no, Einstein was the greatest physicist of all time. _____

6. "True," remarked Einstein, "but they didn't know it then. Imagine their surprise when little Albert won a Nobel Prize."

   Einstein replied that that was true but that they hadn't known it then. _____ He told the reporter to imagine their surprise when little Albert had won a Nobel Prize. _____

Exercise 4 Changing Direct Quotations into Reported Speech

On a separate sheet of paper, rewrite the following interview in reported speech.

1. The reporter asked the astronomer, "How often do you study the sun?"

    The astronomer answered, "We study the sun every day. Astronomers can study the sun at any time."

2. The reporter asked, "Which people are doing the work now?"

    The astronomer replied, "My graduate students are studying the sun this year."

3. "How long have scientists studied the sun?" asked the reporter.

    "Astronomers have studied the sun since the ancient Greeks," answered the astronomer.

4. "Has anyone else studied the sun?" asked the reporter.

    "This astronomer studied the sun last year," the astronomer answered. "Other astronomers will study the sun in the future."

5. The reporter asked, "When are you planning to study the sun personally?"

    The astronomer replied, "I'm going to join my grad students next week."

6. "Why is it important for you to study the sun?" asked the reporter.

    "Astronomers must learn to detect dangerous sunspots soon, so we have to study it constantly," answered the astronomer.

7. The reporter asked, "Is there a danger to Earth from sunspots?"

    The astronomer replied, "Yes, the radiation from a large sunspot may damage our communications satellites."

Exercise 5 Rewriting Academic Quotations as Reported Speech

Some direct quotations in textbooks do not have quotation marks. But they do include the author's name and sometimes his or her profession. Rewrite on a separate sheet of paper the following direct quotations as reported speech. Use as many of the reporting verbs from Chart 15-2 as possible. The first one is done for you. Underline all the additions and changes you made in restating the original quotations.

1. A grain of sand falls as rapidly as a grindstone. —Galileo[6]

    Galileo remarked that a grain of sand fell as rapidly as a grindstone.

2. All who have meditated on the art of governing mankind have been convinced that the fate of empires depends on the education of their youth. —Aristotle[7]

3. Without a scientifically literate population, the outlook for a better world is not promising. —American Association for the Advancement of Science in *Science for All Americans* (1989)[8]

4. For any man to abdicate an interest in science is to walk with open eyes toward slavery. —Jacob Bronowski, philosopher-scientist[9]

5. A philosopher once said, "It is necessary for the very existence of science that the same conditions always produce the same results." Well, they don't! —Richard Feynman[10]

6. The dangers that face the world can, every one of them, be traced back to science. The salvations that may save the world will, every one of them, be traced back to science. —Isaac Asimov, scientist and writer[11]

7. My intellectual development was retarded, as a result of which I began to wonder about space and time (things which a normal adult has thought of as a child) only when I had grown up. —Einstein[12]

8. Attempts have been made to add laws to quantum mechanics to eliminate uncertainty. Such attempts have not only been unsuccessful, they have not even appeared to lead to any interesting results. —Edward Teller[13]

Exercise 6 | Changing Reported Speech to Direct Speech

On a separate sheet of paper, rewrite the interview, which is in reported speech, as direct speech with the correct punctuation. See Chart 15-1 for help.

The interviewer introduced himself and his guest, physicist and author George Smith, who has written extensively about global warming.

1. The interviewer asked what was going to happen in the future regarding global warming.

   Smith replied that scientists predicted that climate zones would move about 500 kilometers to the north, which would result in about 25 percent of all plant and animal species becoming extinct by 2050.

2. The interviewer wanted to know what would happen in the United States.

   Smith answered that the Southwest of the United States might experience more droughts for a period of time.

3. Then the interviewer asked if global warming would affect the Arctic and Antarctic.

   Smith warned that melted sea ice in the Arctic in summer could increase the sea levels. He explained that the same phenomenon could result in even higher sea levels due to parts of the Antarctic ice sheet falling into the ocean.

4. The interviewer asked if there was any more terrible news about sea levels.

   Smith admitted that a warm-up of more than 3 degrees Celsius would melt Greenland completely and raise sea levels up to 7 meters.

5. The interviewer asked what this all meant.

   Smith said warming could change ocean currents and that abrupt changes in the ocean currents had apparently started and ended ice ages in the past.

6. The interviewer asked if other scientists agreed.

   Smith said that many climate scientists had concluded that changes like that would result in a situation unlike any we had experienced in millions of years.

7. The interviewer asked whether anything could be done.

   Smith answered that yes, we needed to reduce emissions by 80 percent in order to stop the concentrations of CO_2 from getting any higher.

8. The interviewer questioned whether that was possible.

   Smith said it would not be easy, and people would have to use extreme methods to deal with the problem. He explained that less had been done about global warming than was done on ozone depletion because of resistance by industry.

9. The interviewer asked if Smith had any hope that the problem would be solved.

   Smith concluded that once global warming had been proven to be an actual problem, government, industry, scientists, and people would work together to solve it.

Exercise 7 Reading and Summarizing Academic Passages

Read the following passages by Art Hobson from *Physics: Concepts & Connections*, 5th Edition. On a separate sheet of paper, write a summary of each, using both reported speech and direct quotations. Begin your summary with "According to Art Hobson in . . . ."

1. About 14 billion years ago, the universe began in a single event called the big bang that created the different forms of energy and matter, causing the "observable" universe (the portion that can be observed with telescopes) to expand from a much smaller initial size. The reality of the big bang is strongly confirmed by several independent lines of observational evidence, but the theoretical understanding of how and why this even occurred is just beginning. . . .[14]

2. The world changed in 1687. In that year, Isaac Newton . . . published his *Mathematical Principles of Natural Philosophy*. . . . Using only a few key principles, Newton was able to give quantitative explanations for all manner of things: planets, moons, comets, falling objects, weight, ocean tides, Earth's equatorial bulge*, stresses on a bridge, and more. It was an unparalleled expansion and unification of our understanding of nature. Newton's influence ranged far beyond physics and astronomy. . . . Newtonian physics worked almost too well. Unchallenged for over two centuries, it was eventually regarded as absolute truth.[15]

* *bulge*—swelling

Exercise 8 Error Analysis

The following excerpt from a student paper contains ten errors. All errors within a given quote count as one single error. The first error is corrected for you. Find and correct nine more.

A Brief Biography of Albert Einstein

Albert Einstein was born in 1879 in Ulm, Germany. As a young child he was considered slow and didn't begin to speak until he was three years old. He did not do well in elementary school and spent a lot of time daydreaming. According to Einstein, "My intellectual development was retarded, as a result of which I began to wonder about space and time (things which a normal adult has thought of as a child) only when I had grown up.["]1 He dropped out of high school in his midteens.

Art Hobson reported Einstein's high school teachers were glad to see him gone, one of them informing Einstein that he would never amount to anything and another suggesting that he leave school because his presence destroyed student discipline." Einstein left happily and spent several months in the Italian Alps enjoying himself.

He then decided to study engineering but failed the entrance exams, with the result that he entered a progressive Swiss high school where he did well. He recalled later that it was here that he had his first ideas leading to the theory of relativity. As Einstein quipped, 'I thought of that while riding my bicycle.'2

After a year at the Swiss school, Einstein was admitted to the Swiss Federal Polytechnic University in Zurich where he spent most of his time in cafés and the physics lab but not doing much in classes. However, he did manage to graduate in 1901. After failed attempts to get an assistanceship and a teaching job, he had to settle for a job in a patent office in 1902. He spent seven years in this eight-hour-a-day job, using the rest of his time to think. He later remarked what this free time after work made it possible for him to invent his theory of relativity in 1905. Years later he said If I were a young man again and had to decide how to make a living, I would not try to become a scientist or scholar or teacher. I would rather choose to be a plumber or a peddler, in the hope of finding that modest degree of independence still available under present circumstances.[3]

Just five years before Einstein's special theory of relativity was announced, the quantum idea was introduced. Quantum physics is what scientists use to study the microscopic world. According to Hobson, its central notion is that, at the microscopic level, some physical quantities such as energy are discontinuous or "quantized" rather than continuous. Using language from our computerized culture, the microscopic world is "digital" rather than "analog. Einstein was never able to accept the quantum idea, which he considered absurd. "I believe in the possibility of a theory which is able to give a complete description of reality, the laws of which establish relations between the things themselves and not merely between their probabilities. . . . Quantum mechanics is very impressive. But an inner voice tells me that it is not yet the real thing. The theory produces a good deal but hardly brings us closer to the secret of the Old One. I am at all events convinced that He does not play dice."[4] The physicist Stephen Hawking remarked God not only plays dice. He also sometimes throws the dice where they cannot be seen.[5] But Einstein and other scientists considered quantum theory "spooky" and thought that quantum uncertainty had to mean the theory was mistaken. Einstein commented, "Marvelous, what ideas the young people have these days. But I don't believe a word of it. He continued, "I cannot seriously believe in [the quantum theory] because it cannot be reconciled with the idea that physics should represent a reality in time and space, free from spooky actions at a distance."[6]

But few other physicists worried about Einstein's objections. They just said whether they didn't have enough understanding of the principles of quantum physics yet. Hobson concluded, "But quantum physics continues to have a perfect record of experimental success, and the quantum predictions that Einstein believed to be absurd have now been tested and found to actually occur."[7]

---

[1] Hobson, A. (2010) *Physics: Concepts & Connections,* Fifth Edition. Upper Saddle River, NJ: Pearson. Page 227. All material cited in this essay is quoted from this text.

[2] page 227

[3] page 289

[4] page 289

[5] page 289

[6] page 299

[7] page 289

Exercise 9 Apply It to Speaking and Writing

1 Select one of the following questions and prepare to present your thoughts about it for two minutes. Support your ideas with examples. See Appendix B for help.

- Americans use the "English" system of measurements, feet and pounds rather than meters and kilograms. Why should the United States change its system of measurement? Explain.
- Why should people learn about physics even if they do not use physics in their professions? Explain.
- Is it a good idea to accept the power of technology without also accepting the responsibility to use that power wisely? Explain.

2 With a partner, take turns presenting your ideas to each other. As your partner speaks, take notes.
3 Write a one-paragraph summary of your partner's ideas in your own words, including some direct quotations and reported speech. Conclude, in a second paragraph, by indicating whether you agree or disagree with his or her conclusions and why.

Exercise 10 Apply It to Writing

1 Read the following passage, underlining the main ideas and most important details.
2 Prepare a one-paragraph summary of these ideas in your own words, incorporating some direct quotes as appropriate. See Appendix B for help.

A Near Disaster

Without the courage of a handful of curious researchers in the mid-1970s, the world would have learned too late of the deadly hidden dangers associated with rapidly expanding use of CFCs. The now legendary hypothesis of Sherwood Rowland and Mario Molina . . . initially unleashed a firestorm of criticism and controversy. . . . They were vindicated* by the 1995 Nobel Peace Prize in Chemistry. . . .[16]

The story begins in 1928 when the General Motors Corporation first synthesized chlorofluorocarbons (CFCs), molecules made from atoms of chlorine, fluorine, and carbon for its Frigidaire refrigerators. . . . CFCs soon became a universal coolant. Production soared. In the 1940s CFCs were found to be useful as pressurized gases to propel* aerosol sprays. In the 1950s, they created the air-conditioning revolution. . . .

CFCs created a lot of business and little fuss until 1974 when scientists began to ask where all these inert gases might be drifting. . . .

In 1974, two university chemists suggested an alarming possibility. Mario Molina and Sherwood Rowland . . . discovered that because CFC molecules are inert and gaseous, they are not chemically broken down or rained out in the lower atmosphere. Instead, they drift slowly into the upper atmosphere or stratosphere, 10 to 50 kilometers overhead, where they may remain intact for decades or centuries. Molina and Rowland theorized that high-energy solar ultraviolet radiation should eventually split CFC molecules apart, releasing large quantities of chlorine [Cl]. This was alarming because chlorine reacts strongly with O_3, known as ozone. . . . Scientists found that a single Cl atom destroyed about 100,000 ozone molecules. . . .

But stratospheric ozone is essential to most life on Earth. Because ozone molecules vibrate naturally at ultraviolet frequencies and so absorb much of the sun's ultraviolet radiation, they protect us from this biologically harmful radiation.[17]

*vindicate—to prove to be correct
*propel—to push forward

Read the following passage from *Physics: Concepts & Connections*, 5th Edition, by Art Hobson.[1]

Special Relativity and Quantum Physics

[1]Special relativity and quantum physics extend Newtonian physics in different directions. One extends it up to lightspeed, and the other extends it down to at least the smallest dimensions yet measured, 10^{-19} meters, 10,000 times smaller than an atomic nucleus. But there's a problem with these two theories. Special relativity doesn't contain the quantum principles so it doesn't work at small sizes, and quantum physics doesn't contain the relativity principles so it doesn't work at high speeds. Thus neither theory describes small-scale high-speed phenomena. What's needed is a joining of relativity and quantum physics into a single theory covering all sizes and all speeds.

[2]Such a theory was developed during 1930–1950. It's called quantum field theory. One part of this theory, quantum electrodynamics, is the most accurate scientific theory ever invented. Like most of modern physics, quantum field theory is basically simple but takes some getting used to. Its underlying idea, and an enduring theme of modern physics, is the field view of reality already discussed in connection with Einstein's mass-energy relation—the view that the universe is made entirely of fields. . . . We'll further discuss what this means. . . .

[3]Recall . . . that a field (examples include gravitational, electromagnetic, and matter fields) is spread out over a region of space. This region needn't contain any matter or "things" at all. A field is a condition of space itself, a kind of stress in space, regardless of any matter that might be in it. For example, a magnetic field is the possibility of a magnetic force, regardless of whether anything feels that possible force. Recall also that fields, even when no matter is present, contain energy and this implies that they are physically real and not mere mental constructions.

[4]At the core of quantum field theory is the view that the universe is made only of fields. The table on which this book rests is simply a configuration* of quivering* force fields, similar to the invisible force field surrounding a magnet, and so is this book. The book doesn't fall through the table, however, because the electric force fields in the table repel the electric force fields in the book. And your eye (which is also just fields) sees the book because the book's force fields emit radiation.

[5]It's an odd idea. There is no truly solid or enduring "thing." In this sense, there is "nothing": no thing. Only fields. But this doesn't mean that everything is empty, or nonexistent, or imaginary. Far from it. In fact, the relatively solid table at which you are perhaps sitting right now is made of atoms that are in turn made of fields that exert quite real forces on the atoms (which are also made of fields) in your elbows, which are perhaps leaning on the table. That's why you don't fall through the table.[2]

* *configuration*—the shape or arrangement of the parts of something
* *quivering*—shaking slightly

Review the Ideas

1. How do special relativity and quantum physics differ from Newtonian physics?

2. What don't these theories explain?

3. What theory joined relativity and quantum physics?

4. What is the basic idea of quantum field theory?

Exercise 1 Analysis of the Reading Passage

1 Underline the noun clauses in the reading passage.
2 Then, on a separate sheet of paper, write the sentence or sentences that illustrate each of the following functions:

Paragraph 1

A noun clause functioning as a subject

Paragraph 2

A noun clause functioning as an appositive

Paragraph 3

Three noun clauses functioning as direct objects
A noun clause functioning as the object of a preposition

Paragraph 4

A noun clause functioning as an appositive

Paragraph 5

Two noun clauses functioning as subject complements

Exercise 2 Paragraph Analysis: Noun Clauses Used for Hedging

Read the following passage about quantum field theory. Then underline the three noun clauses used for hedging once and underline the subjunctive noun clause twice.

Quantum field theory paints an odd new view of "empty" space—space that is devoid of matter, commonly called vacuum. As you know, EM [electromagnetic] fields and other fields extend even into regions containing no matter. Quantum uncertainties require that the energies of all these fields at any point in space fluctuate, over short timespans, around its long-time average value. . . . The uncertainty principle implies that the smaller the region of space and the shorter the time interval, the larger these fluctuations must be. This means that at any point in so-called empty space there's a certain likelihood that a photon or a particle-antiparticle pair, including any of the particles discussed in this chapter, will spontaneously pop into and out of existence during short times. So even in empty space there is always some probability of high-energy events occurring in small regions. Empty space is not the quiet, uninteresting place we had imagined. Microscopically, it's a seething soup of creation and annihilation*. It seems that in nothingness, much is possible.[3]

*annihilation—the complete destruction of something

Exercise 3 Paragraph Analysis: Noun Clauses Used for Reported Speech

Read the following paragraph about the discovery of neutrinos*. Then underline the noun clauses that function as reported speech.

Wolfgang Pauli suggested in 1930 that during radioactive beta decay, the nucleus emitted, in addition to a beta particle, another particle of an entirely new type. The hypothesized new particle was dubbed the neutrino, or "little neutral one." . . . Although neutrinos would not be discovered experimentally for another 25 years, Enrico Fermi immediately took Pauli's suggestion seriously and argued that neutrinos indicated a new fundamental force, the weak force, was at work. Fermi was aware of the work in progress on the quantum field theory of the electric force, and he quickly adapted these ideas to the weak force. Fermi's theory succeeded in predicting the half-lives of radioactive nuclei and the range of energies with which beta particles emerged from the nucleus during beta decay.[4]

*neutrino—a subatomic particle (a piece of matter that is smaller than an atom)

The following excerpt from a student essay contains ten errors. The first error is corrected for you. Find and correct nine more.

The Changing Theories of Physics

An atom

The loops known as strings

Truth is stranger than fiction, people say, and nothing is stranger than the changing theories of physics. Since the time of the ancient Greeks, scientists have wondered ~~that~~ *what* matter (material substances such as water, wood, and metal) consists of and what it behaves in nature. Each generation of scientists believed that their new ways of understanding and explaining matter were correct. It's interesting that each new theory has had elements of truth and some are still useful in explaining phenomena today.

In the fifth century B.C.E., ancient Greeks were fascinated by how material was made of. One ancient Greek, Democritus, cut gold into smaller and smaller pieces, trying to imagine the pieces being cut into more and more microscopic pieces until they could be divided no longer. Democritus called the smallest piece of matter that could not be divided further an atom. Democritus's hypothesis was not confirmed until the nineteenth and twentieth centuries.

Scientists' views of the atom have changed throughout history. From the time of the ancient Greeks up to the 1900s, scientists were certain what an atom was a tiny single spherical object. Then in about 1900, studies with electricity indicated that atoms were mostly empty space in which electrons orbit a nucleus containing protons and neutrons. This became known as the planetary model of the atom because it was imagined to resemble the planets orbiting the sun.

That a theory is useful or not determines whether it will be discarded. The old theories have proven useful in explaining certain phenomena, so they have not been discarded completely. Today scientists still use the notion how an atom is the smallest particle of a chemical element and is itself made up of several smaller particles: electrons, protons, and neutrons. Protons and neutrons are in turn made up of quarks and these are presently the smallest particles known. Each pure chemical element is made up of the same kind of atom, and atoms combine into molecules to form substances such as water or air.

During the 1920s a new theory, "the quantum theory of the atom," contradicted previous theories of the atom. But neither Albert Einstein's special theory of relativity ($E=mc^2$) nor quantum theory worked at both small sizes and high speeds, so scientists realized they needed to search for a new unifying theory. As a result, between 1930 and 1950, a new unifying theory, quantum field theory, was developed.

Since 1950, quantum field theory has been accepted by physicists as the structure of all matter and energy at both the macroscopic and microscopic levels. The idea is where the universe is made up of invisible but physically real fields spread out in space, not made of material things. Electromagnetic and gravitational fields are two examples. According to Art Hobson, author of *Physics: Concepts & Connections*, "A field is a condition of space itself, a kind of stress in space, regardless of any matter that might be in it. For example, a magnetic field is the possibility of a magnetic force, regardless of whether anything feels that possible force. . . . Fields, even when no matter is present, contain energy and this implies that they are physically real and not mere mental constructions."[1] He goes on to explain, "The essential reality is a few fields, such as the EM field, that fill the universe and that obey the principles of quantum physics and special relativity. Everything that happens in nature is a result of changes in these fields. Quantization requires that, whenever an interaction occurs, these fields must exhibit themselves as bundles of quanta of field energy. All of nature's particles of radiation and matter are quanta of this sort."[2]

In the last twenty-five years, the string hypothesis has seemed to unify the special theory of relativity and quantum theory. The idea is what every fundamental particle is a tiny vibrating loop, a string, that looks like a rubber band. A string is so small that it appears to be a single point. Each fundamental particle is made up of a string vibrating in a certain way. All fundamental particles are strings; the difference between them is determined by the way that they vibrate. For example, an electron vibrates in one way and a quark vibrates in another. So that we see as a desk or book is actually made of innumerable vibrating microscopic loops of energy. At the same time, our eyes (and our entire bodies) are made up of vibrating loops of energy as well. truth is stranger than fiction is no exaggeration!

Hobson concludes, "When we consider general relativity, quantum physics, the string hypothesis, and other contemporary science, it's clear that the natural universe holds possibilities that, to quote philosopher-scientist John Haldane, 'are not only queerer than we suppose, but queerer than we can suppose.'"[3]

---

[1]Hobson, A. (2010) *Physics: Concepts & Connections*, Fifth Edition. Upper Saddle River, NJ: Pearson. Page 227. All material cited in this essay is quoted from this text.

[2]page 407

[3]page 431

WHAT DID YOU LEARN?

Review the forms and functions of noun clauses in Part 5. Complete the exercises. Then check your answers in Appendix D.

A Is the grammar in these sentences correct? Write *C* for correct and *I* for incorrect. Correct the wording as necessary in the sentences with errors.

_____ 1. The ancient Greeks were certain that the stars were placed in an invisible sphere surrounding Earth.

_____ 2. Ancient Greeks supported the theory what Earth was at the center of the universe.

_____ 3. One false idea is that theories are absolutely certain.

_____ 4. If Earth or the sun is at the center of the universe was debated among philosophers for centuries.

_____ 5. Aristarchus, a Greek astronomer, was the first to claim whether the sun was the center of the universe and Earth and other planets moved around the sun.

_____ 6. Pythagoras believed that the most perfect ideas were mathematical because they could be stated so precisely yet abstractly.[5]

_____ 7. It is surprising that Artistarchus's theory was ignored for so long.

_____ 8. It is always possible if new evidence will contradict an accepted theory.

_____ 9. The notion that Earth circled the sun seemed impossible to ancient Greeks.

_____ 10. A big difficulty for the sun-centered astronomy proposed by Copernicus around 1550 was the problem of how Earth could keep moving with nothing to push it.[6]

B Are the following statements about the sentences correct? Write *C* for correct and *I* for incorrect.

_____ 1. The noun clause functions as the object of the verb.

   The mathematical mystics led by Pythagoras found they could describe many ideas with mathematics.

_____ 2. The noun clause functions as the subject.

   Quantum physics holds that changes in nature occur discontinuously, rather than continuously as Newtonian physics predicts.[7]

_____ 3. The noun clause functions as a subject complement.

   One reassuring thing about philosophy is that, for most good philosophical ideas, there are also good arguments to refute those ideas.[8]

_____ 4. The noun clause in the first sentence functions as the object of a preposition.

   . . . studies show that corn-based ethanol drives up food prices. Thus there's debate about whether any further expansion of food-based biofuels is a good idea.[9]

_____ 5. The noun clause in the second sentence functions as an appositive.

   It sounds simple. But the requirement that the EM field and electron field obey both relativity and quantum theory leads to astonishing results.[10]

_____ 6. The noun clause expresses reported speech.

As physicist Niels Bohr put it, "The hallmark of a profound idea is that its converse is also profound."[11]

_____ 7. The noun clause hedges.

The constancy of light speed suggests something is amiss in our intuitive conceptions of space and time.[12]

_____ 8. The first noun clause is a subjunctive noun clause.

Relativity's requirement that quantum theory be symmetric under time reversal implies that for every existing type of particle, there must be an antiparticle having the same mass but the opposite charge.[13]

_____ 9. The noun clause in each sentence is an adjective complement.

If an object's position is changing, can we be certain that it has a nonzero velocity? Can we be certain that it has a nonzero acceleration?[14]

_____ 10. The noun clause in the passage is a subject complement.

Stonehenge perhaps also predicted eclipses of the moon, an impressive feat for people who did not use writing. Eclipses occur in an irregular and apparently random pattern that repeats itself only over a 56-year cycle. Even to have been aware that a repeated pattern exists required enormous dedication and attention to detail.[15]

How did you do? Are there topics you need to review?

Exercise 5 Apply It to Speaking

Reread the student essay in Exercise 4 about changing concepts regarding the composition of matter. Take notes about the various hypotheses advanced by different people in different eras. Then, with a partner, take turns summarizing the main ideas by answering the following questions. Use noun clauses in your discussion.

1 Tell your partner about the very earliest idea regarding the composition of matter proposed by the ancient Greek Democritus. What did he think?

2 Explain how the concept of matter changed around 1900. How did scientists imagine the smallest particles of matter?

3 Describe what happened to scientists' ideas between 1930 and 1950. What was the new hypothesis?

4 What is the most recent hypothesis about the composition of matter? Why do physicists think it is the best hypothesis yet?

Exercise 6 Apply It to Writing

Write two paragraphs about the student essay in Exercise 4. Be sure to use noun clauses in your discussion. See Appendix B for help.

1 In the first paragraph, use your notes from Exercise 5 to summarize what you have learned from the essay and your discussion about changing concepts regarding the composition of matter.

2 In the second paragraph, talk about your own reaction to the information presented in the essay. Do you feel that the changing hypotheses are persuasive and logical? What do you think will happen in the future? Do you believe that concepts about matter will continue to evolve?

Check Your Writing

Which of the following noun clauses did you use in your paragraphs? Did you use them correctly? Double-check your work.

- [ ] Noun clauses used as objects introduced by *that*
- [ ] Subjunctive noun clauses
- [ ] Noun clauses used as objects introduced by *wh-* words
- [ ] Noun clauses used as objects introduced by *if* or *whether*
- [ ] Noun clauses used as subjects
- [ ] Noun clauses used as complements
- [ ] Noun clauses used as appositives
- [ ] Noun clauses used for hedging
- [ ] Direct speech with the correct punctuation
- [ ] Reported speech to support your ideas

REFERENCES

Chapter 1

[1] Brookshear, J. G. (2012). *Computer Science: An Overview.* 11th ed. Upper Saddle River, NJ: Pearson. All material cited in this chapter is quoted from this text.

[2] page 8

[3] page 462

[4] page 9

[5] page 3

[6] page 156

[7] page 158

[8] page 438

[9] page 438

[10] page 10

[11] page 5

[12] page 5

[13] page 301

[14] page 198

[15] page 6

[16] pages 202 and 203

[17] page 2

[18] page 306

[19] page 472

[20] pages 8 and 9

[21] page 8

[22] pages 9 and 10

Chapter 2

[1] Brookshear, J. G. (2012). *Computer Science: An Overview.* 11th ed. Upper Saddle River, NJ: Pearson. All material cited in this chapter is quoted from this text.

[2] pages 8 and 9

[3] page 140

[4] page 111

[5] page 454

[6] page 454

[7] page 426

[8] page 337

Chapter 3

[1] Brookshear, J. G. (2012). *Computer Science: An Overview.* 11th ed. Upper Saddle River, NJ: Pearson. All material cited in this chapter is quoted from this text.

[2] pages 500 and 501

[3] page 113

[4] page 116

[5] page 140

[6] page 157

[7] page 158

[8] page 329

[9] page 500

[10] page 15

[11] page 16

[12] page 283

[13] page 306

[14] page 332

[15] page 465

[16] page 508

[17] page 414

[18] page 414

[19] page 14

[20] page 494

[21] pages 14 and 15

[22] page 329

[23] page 329

[24] page 500

[25] page 501

[26] page 500

[27] page 329

[28] page 329

[29] page 332

[30] page 465

[31] pages 415 and 416

[32] page 332

[33] page 465

[34] pages 14 and 15

[35] page 329

[36] page 508

[37] page 501

[38] page 414

[39] pages 497 and 498

PART 1 Putting It All Together

[1] Brookshear, J. G. (2012). *Computer Science: An Overview. 11th ed*. Upper Saddle River, NJ: Pearson. All material cited in this chapter is quoted from this text.

[2] page 10

[3] pages 9 and 10

[4] page 2

[5] page 77

[6] page 6

[7] page 175

[8] page 154

[9] pages 4 and 5

[10] page 10

[11] page 16

[12] page 17

Chapter 4

[1] Marshall, S. G., H. O. Jackson, and M. S. Stanley. (2012) *Individuality in Clothing Selection and Personal Appearance,* 7th ed. Upper Saddle River, NJ: Pearson. All material cited in this chapter is quoted from this text.

[2] pages 36 and 37

[3] page 26

[4] page 36

[5] page 26

[6] page 22

[7] page 7

[8] page 41

[9] page 29

[10] page 42

[11] page 110

[12] page 36

[13] page 41

[14] page 27

[15] page 31

[16] page 42

[17] page 110

[18] page 30

[19] page 38

[20] page 36

[21] page 47

[22] page 51

Chapter 5

[1] Marshall, S. G., H. O. Jackson, and M. S. Stanley. (2012) *Individuality in Clothing Selection and Personal Appearance,* 7th ed. Upper Saddle River, NJ: Pearson. All material cited in this chapter is quoted from this text.

[2] pages 42 and 43

[3] page 46

[4] pages 36 and 37

[5] page 36

[6] page 47

[7] page 37

[8] page 37

[9] page 107

[10] pages 42 and 43

[11] page 43

[12] page 43

[13] page 31

[14] page 37

[15] page 45

[16] page 28

[17] page 17
[18] page 47
[19] page 104
[20] page 51
[21] page 51
[22] page 47

Chapter 6

[1] Marshall, S. G., H. O. Jackson, and M. S. Stanley. (2012) *Individuality in Clothing Selection and Personal Appearance,* 7th ed. Upper Saddle River, NJ: Pearson. All material cited in this chapter is quoted from this text.
[2] page 39
[3] page 49
[4] page 51
[5] page 39
[6] page 41
[7] page 29
[8] page 39
[9] page 49
[10] page 28
[11] page 28
[12] page 45
[13] page 51
[14] pages 27 and 28

PART 2 Putting It All Together

[1] Marshall, S. G., H. O. Jackson, and M. S. Stanley. (2012) *Individuality in Clothing Selection and Personal Appearance,* 7th ed. Upper Saddle River, NJ: Pearson. All material cited in this chapter is quoted from this text.
[2] page 305
[3] page 306
[4] page 306
[5] page 320
[6] page 299
[7] page 305
[8] page 22

Chapter 7

[1] Kishlansky, M., P. Geary, and P. O'Brien. (2007). *Civilization in the West.* Vol. I, *To 1715.* 6th ed. Upper Saddle River, NJ: Pearson. All material cited in this chapter is quoted from this text.
[2] page 4
[3] page 32
[4] page 112
[5] page 56
[6] page 342
[7] page 256
[8] page 11

[9] page 12
[10] page 16
[11] page 19
[12] page 19
[13] page 31
[14] page 31
[15] page 72
[16] page 72
[17] pages 78 and 79

Chapter 8

[1] Kishlansky, M., P. Geary, and P. O'Brien. (2007). *Civilization in the West*. Vol. I, *To 1715*. 6th ed. Upper Saddle River, NJ: Pearson. All material cited in this chapter is quoted from this text.
[2] pages 50 and 51
[3] page 12
[4] page 12
[5] page 16
[6] page 16
[7] page 19
[8] page 73
[9] page 72
[10] page 72
[11] page 11
[12] page 11
[13] page 84
[14] page 232

Chapter 9

[1] Kishlansky, M., P. Geary, and P. O'Brien. (2007). *Civilization in the West*. Vol. I, *To 1715*. 6th ed. Upper Saddle River, NJ: Pearson. All material cited in this chapter is quoted from this text.
[2] page 121
[3] page 4
[4] page 473
[5] page 452
[6] page 72
[7] page 345
[8] page 40
[9] page 6
[10] page 356
[11] page 38
[12] page 49
[13] page 365
[14] page 12
[15] page 31
[16] page 356
[17] page 390

[18] page 73
[19] page 121
[20] page 452
[21] page 166
[22] page 6
[23] page 342
[24] page 12
[25] page 514
[26] page 571
[27] page 644
[28] page 921

PART 3 Putting It All Together

[1] Kishlansky, M., P. Geary, and P. O'Brien. (2007). *Civilization in the West*. Volumes I and II. Upper Saddle River, NJ: Pearson. All material cited in this chapter is quoted from this text.

[2] Volume II, page 708

[3] Volume I, page 102

[4] Volume I, page 330

[5] Volume I, page 49

Chapter 10

[1] Ember, C. R., M. Ember, and P. N. Peregrine. (2011). *Anthropology*. 13th ed. Upper Saddle River, NJ: Pearson. All material cited in this chapter is quoted from this text.

[2] page 272

[3] page 52

[4] pages 16 and 17

[5] pages 156

[6] page 165

[7] page 17

[8] page 222

[9] page 411

[10] page 298

[11] page 17

[12] page 353

[13] page 298

[14] pages 275 and 276

[15] pages 275 and 276

[16] page 279

[17] page 447

[18] page 373

[19] page 302

[20] page 241

[21] page 302

[22] page 284

[23] page 370

[24] page 369

Chapter 11

[1] Ember, C. R., M. Ember, and P. N. Peregrine. (2011). *Anthropology*. 13th ed. Upper Saddle River, NJ: Pearson. All material cited in this chapter is quoted from this text unless otherwise noted.

[2] page 229

[3] page 92

[4] page 357

[5] page 336

[6] page 298

[7] pages 22 and 23

[8] page 276

[9] page 240

[10] page 102

[11] page 259

[12] page 14

[13] page 470

[14] page 251

[15] pages 276 and 277

[16] page 283

[17] page 226

[18] page 227

[19] page 175

[20] page 149

[21] page 390

[22] page 446

[23] page 36

[24] page 252

[25] page 440

[26] page 72

[27] page 256

[28] page 314

[29] page 113

[30] page 201

[31] page 288

[32] page 102

[33] page 292

[34] page 222

[35] www.pewresearch/2008/02/06/where-men-and-women-differ-in-following-news/

Chapter 12

[1] Modified figure "Tiv Lineage Segments and Their Territories" and caption from Ember, C. R., M. Ember, and P. N. Peregrine. (2011). *Anthropology*. 13th ed. Upper Saddle River, NJ: Pearson, p. 426. Figure adapted from P. Bohannan (1954).

[2] Ember, C. R., M. Ember., and P. N. Peregrine. (2011). *Anthropology*. 13th ed. Upper Saddle River, NJ: Pearson. All material cited in this chapter is quoted from this text unless otherwise noted.

[3] page 426

[4] page 481

[5] page 411

[6] page 257

[7] page 487

[8] page 280

[9] page 11

[10] page 316

[11] page 42

[12] page 288

[13] page 453

[14] page 502

[15] page 248

[16] page 429

[17] page 273

[18] page 270

[19] page 281

[20] page 167

[21] page 183

[22] page 236

[23] pages 243 and 244

[24] page 434

[25] Table, "Worldwide Patterns in the Division of Labor by Gender," from page 351

PART 4 Putting It All Together

[1] Ember, C. R., M. Ember, and P. N. Peregrine. (2011). *Anthropology*. 13th ed. Upper Saddle River, NJ: Pearson. All material cited in this chapter is quoted from this text.

[2] pages 500 and 502

Chapter 13

[1] Hobson, A. (2010) *Physics: Concepts and Connections*. 5th ed. Upper Saddle River, NJ: Pearson. All material cited in this chapter is from this text unless otherwise noted.

[2] pages 4, 5, and 8

[3] page 79

[4] page 414

[5] page 10

[6] page 111

[7] page 11

[8] page 38

[9] page 31

[10] page 9

[11] page 11

[12] page 21

[13] page 20

[14] page 296

[15] page 414

[16] page 281

[17] page 249

[18] page 110

[19] page 110

[20] page 25

[21] page 125

[22] page 38

[23] page 4

[24] page 111

[25] pages 196

[26] page 90

[27] page 20

[28] page 31

[29] page 60

[30] page 157

[31] Figure, "The earliest Greek conception, around 500 B.C.E., of the layout of the universe," from page 9

Chapter 14

[1] Hobson, A. (2010) *Physics: Concepts and Connections*. 5th ed. Upper Saddle River, NJ: Pearson. All material cited in this chapter is from this text unless otherwise noted.

[2] pages 210 and 215

[3] page 201

[4] page 46

[5] page 217

[6] pages 216 and 217

[7] page 405

[8] pages 38 and 39

[9] page 102

[10] page 373

[11] page 48

[12] page 91

[13] page 290

[14] page 280

[15] page 22

[16] page 407

[17] page 124

[18] page 14

[19] page 307

[20] page 426

[21] page 111

[22] pages 21

[23] page 430

[24] pages 103 and 104

[25] page 108

[26] Figure, "Decline in the area covered by Arctic sea ice from 1978 through 2007," from page 214

[27] Figure, "Variations in Earth's surface temperature from 1860 through 2005," from page 217

[28] Figure, "World annual carbon emissions from fossil-fuel burning, 1950–2006, in gigatons of carbon," from page 218

[29] Figure, "Per Capita CO_2 Emissions," from page 219. Source: World Bank, online database, 2004.

Chapter 15

[1] Hobson, A. (2010) *Physics: Concepts and Connections*. 5th ed. Upper Saddle River, NJ: Pearson. All material cited in this chapter is from this text.

[2] pages 44 and 46

[3] page 34

[4] page 111

[5] page 20

[6] page 57

[7] page xi

[8] page xi

[9] page 3

[10] page 289

[11] page 3

[12] page 227

[13] page 299

[14] page 258

[15] page 71

[16] page 209

[17] page 207

PART 5 Putting It All Together

[1] Hobson, A. (2010) *Physics: Concepts and Connections*. 5th ed. Upper Saddle River, NJ: Pearson. All material cited in this chapter is from this text.

[2] pages 405 and 406

[3] page 414

[4] page 416

[5] page 9.

[6] page 60

[7] page 276

[8] page 425

[9] page 394

[10] page 408

[11] page 42

[12] page 235

[13] page 410

[14] page 68

[15] page 5

BIBLIOGRAPHY

PART 1
Brookshear, J. G. (2012). *Computer Science: An Overview.* 11th ed. Upper Saddle River, NJ: Pearson.

PART 2
Coulson, D. (1999). "Ancient art of the Sallara," *National Geographic* 195(8): 98–119.

Dodd, A. (2000, July 12). "Casual dressing is not so easy." *Daily News Record*, 6.

Huang, S., P. Teo, and S. A. Yeoh (2000). "Diaspora subjects and identity negotiations: Women in and from Asia." *Women's Studies International Forum* 23(4): 391–398.

Koretz, G. (2001, April 25). "A white-collar job squeeze." *Business Week*. http://www.businessweek.com.

Marshall, S. G., H. O. Jackson, and M. S. Stanley (2012) *Individuality in Clothing Selection and Personal Appearance,* 7th ed. Upper Saddle River, NJ: Pearson.

Reid, T. R. (2002). "The new Europe." *National Geographic* 201(1): 32–47.

Ryder, M. (2000). "The functional history of clothing." *The Textile Institute* 29(3): 42–61.

Smith, R. (2008a, June 4). "Tie association, a fashion victim, calls it quits as trends change." *Wall Street Journal*, A1.

Smith, S. (2008b, June 6). "Fashion tips for interns from the pros." *Women's Wear Daily*, 24.

PART 3
Kishlansky, M., P. Geary, and P. O'Brien. (2007). *Civilization in the West.* Volumes I and II. 6th ed. Upper Saddle River, NJ: Pearson.

PART 4
Adams, Robert McCormick. (1981). *Heartland of Cities: Surveys of Ancient Settlement and Land Use on the Central Floodplain of the Euphrates.* Chicago: University of Chicago Press.

Aptekar, Lewis. (1994). *Environmental Disasters in Global Perspective.* New York: G.K. Hall / Macmillan.

Balikci, Asen. (1970). *The Netsilik Eskimo.* Garden City, NY: Natural History Press.

Barry, Herbert III, Irvin L. Child, and Margaret K. Bacon. (1959). "Relation of child training to subsistence economy." *American Anthropologist* 61:51–63.

Bickerton, Derek. (1983, July). "Creole languages." *Scientific American* 116–22.

Bilby, Kenneth. (1996). "Ethnogenesis in the Guianas and Jamaica: Two Maroon cases." *In History, Power, and Identity: Ethnogenesis in the Americas,* edited by J. D. Hill, 119–41. Iowa City: University of Iowa Press.

Bohannan, Paul. (1954). "The migration and expansion of the Tiv." *Africa* 24:2–16.

Bourguignon, Erika. (2004). "Suffering and healing, subordination and power: Women and possession trance." *Ethos* 32:557–74.

Chagnon, Napoleon. (1983). *Yanomamö: The Fierce People.* 3rd ed. New York: Holt, Rinehart & Winston.

Darwin, Charles. (1970/1859). "The origin of species." *In Evolution of Man,* edited by L. B. Young. New York: Oxford University Press.

Dentan, Robert K. (1968). *The Semai: A Nonviolent People of Malaya.* New York: Holt, Rinehart & Winston.

De Waal, Frans. (2001). *The Ape and the Sushi Master: Cultural Reflections of a Primatologist*. New York: Basic Books.

Durham, William H. (1991). *Coevolution: Genes, Culture and Human Diversity*. Stanford, CA: Stanford University Press.

Durkheim, Emile. (1938/1895). *The Rules of Sociological Method*. 8th ed. Translated by Sarah A. Soloway and John H. Mueller. Edited by George E. Catlin. New York: Free Press.

Ember, Carol R., and Melvin Ember. (1993). "Issues in cross-cultural studies of interpersonal violence." *Violence and Victims* 8:217–33.

Ember, C. R., M. Ember, and P. N. Peregrine. (2011). *Anthropology*. 13th ed. Upper Saddle River, NJ: Pearson.

Ember, Melvin, and Carol R. Ember. (1992). "Cross-cultural studies of war and peace: Recent achievements and future possibilities." *In Studying War,* edited by S. P. Reyna and R. E. Downs. New York: Gordon and Breach.

Foster, Brian L. (1974). "Ethnicity and commerce." *American Ethnologist* 1:437–47.

Gould, Richard A. (1969). *Yiwara: Foragers of the Australian Desert*. New York: Scribner.

Hames, Raymond. (2009). "Yanomamö: Varying adaptations of foraging horticulturalists." *In MyAnthroLibrary,* edited by C. R. Ember, M. Ember, and P. N. Peregrine. MyAnthroLibrary.com. Pearson.

Hoebel, E. Adamson. (1968/1954). *The Law of Primitive Man*. New York: Atheneum.

Hoogbergen, Wim (1990). *The Boni Maroon Wars in Suriname*. Leiden: E.J. Brill.

Huang, H. T. (2002). "Hypolactasia and the Chinese diet." *Current Anthropology* 43:809–19.

Itkonen, T. I. (1951). "The Lapps of Finland." *Southwestern Journal of Anthropology* 7:32–68.

Kelly, Raymond C. (1985). T*he Nuer Conquest: The Structure and Development of an Expansionist System*. Ann Arbor: University of Michigan Press.

Lawless, Robert, Vinson H. Sutlive Jr., and Mario D. Zamora, eds. (1983). *Fieldwork: The Human Experience*. New York: Gordon and Breach.

Leacock, Eleanor, and Richard Lee. (1982). "Introduction." *In Politics and History in Band Societies*, edited by E. Leacock and R. Lee. Cambridge: Cambridge University Press.

Linton, Ralph. (1937). "One Hundred Per-Cent American." *American Mercury* 40:427–29.

Loustaunau, Martha O., and Elisa J. Sobo. (1997). *The Cultural Context of Health, Illness, and Medicine*. Westport, CT: Bergin & Garvey.

Malinowski, Bronislaw. (1939). "The group and the individual in functional analysis." *American Journal of Sociology* 44:938–64.

Malinowski, Bronislaw. (1954). "Magic, science, and religion." In B. Malinowski, *Magic, Science, and Religion and Other Essays*. Garden City, NY: Doubleday.

McCracken, Robert D. (1971). "Lactase deficiency: An example of dietary evolution." *Current Anthropology* 12:479–500.

Middleton, Russell. (1962). "Brother-sister and father-daughter marriage in ancient Egypt." *American Sociological Review* 27:603–11.

Mooney, Kathleen A. (1978). "The effects of rank and wealth on exchange among the coast Salish." *Ethnology* 17:391–406.

Motulsky, Arno. (1971). "Metabolic polymorphisms and the role of infectious diseases in human evolution." In *Human Populations, Genetic Variation, and Evolution*, edited by L. N. Morris. San Francisco: Chandler.

Peacock, James L. (1986). *The Anthropological Lens: Harsh Light, Soft Focus*. Cambridge: Cambridge University Press.

Pryor, Frederic L. (2005). *Economic Systems of Foraging, Agricultural, and Industrial Societies*. Cambridge: Cambridge University Press.

Pryor, Frederic L. (1977). *The Origins of the Economy: A Comparative Study of Distribution in Primitive and Peasant Economies*. New York: Academic Press.

Radcliffe-Brown, A. R. (1922). *The Andaman Islanders: A Study in Social Anthropology*. Cambridge: Cambridge University Press.

Roberts, John M. (1967). "Oaths, autonomic ordeals, and power." In *Cross-Cultural Approaches*, edited by C. S. Ford. New Haven, CT: HRAF Press.

Rubin, J. Z., F. J. Provenzano, and R.F. Haskett. (1974). "The eye of the beholder: Parents' views on the sex of newborns." *American Journal of Orthopsychiatry* 44:512–19.

Sahlins, Marshall D. (1961). "The segmentary lineage: An organization of predatory expansion." *American Anthropologist* 63:332–45.

Schlegel, Alice, and Rohn Eloul. (1988). "Marriage transactions: Labor, property, and status." *American Anthropologist* 90:291–309.

Service, Elman R. (1978). *Profiles in Ethnology.* 3rd ed. New York: Harper & Row.

Spencer, Robert F. (1968). "Spouse-exchange among the North Alaskan Eskimo." *In Marriage, Family and Residence,* edited by P. Bohannan and J. Middleton. Garden City, NY: Natural History Press.

Sussman, Robert W., and Peter H. Raven. (1978). "Pollination by lemurs and marsupials: An archaic coevolutionary system." *Science* 200 (May 19): 734–35.

Textor, Robert B., comp. (1967). *A Cross-Cultural Summary.* New Haven, CT: HRAF Press.

Trouillot, Michel-Rolph. (2001). "The anthropology of the state in the age of globalization: Close encounters of the deceptive kind." *Current Anthropology* 42:125–38.

Trudgill, Peter. (1983). *Sociolinguistics: An Introduction to Language and Society,* rev. ed. New York: Penguin.

Whitaker, Ian. (1955). *Social Relations in a Nomadic Lappish Community.* Oslo: Utgitt av Norsk Folksmuseum.

Whiting, John W. M. (1941). *Becoming a Kwoma.* New Haven, CT: Yale University Press.

Winkelman, Michael. (1986b). "Trance states: A theoretical model and cross-cultural analysis." *Ethos* 14:174–203.

PART 5

Hobson, A. (2010) *Physics: Concepts and Connections.* 5th ed. Upper Saddle River, NJ: Pearson.

APPENDIX A

VOCABULARY PRACTICE

Practice pronouncing the vocabulary words and then discuss their meanings. Pay particular attention to "word families," that is, words with more than one form (noun, verb, adjective, or adverb) and meaning.

Chapter 1

Self-Assessment

Here are some of the terms you will encounter in Chapter 1. How much do you know about each one? Score yourself from 1 to 4.

> 1: I don't know this term.
>
> 2: I have seen this term, but I am not sure of the meaning.
>
> 3: I understand this term, but I don't know how to use it in speaking and writing.
>
> 4: I know this term and can use it in my speaking and writing.

____ 1. algorithm	____ 6. contend
____ 2. application	____ 7. impact
____ 3. array	____ 8. miniaturization
____ 4. artificial intelligence	____ 9. program
____ 5. autonomous	____ 10. task

Exercise 1 Defining the Terms

Match each definition in the right column with the corresponding term in the left column.

____ 1. algorithm	a. to argue
____ 2. application	b. a field of computer science
____ 3. array	c. a set of instructions for a procedure or process
____ 4. artificial intelligence	d. the act of making something very small
____ 5. autonomous	e. an ordered set of numbers; a collection
____ 6. contend	f. a set of instructions for a computer
____ 7. impact	g. effect
____ 8. miniaturization	h. use
____ 9. program	i. a job or assignment
____ 10. task	j. independent

Exercise 2 Expanding Your Vocabulary

Use your dictionary to find the answers to the questions. Write them down on a separate sheet of paper.

1. Which four words can function as both nouns and verbs?
2. What adverb has the same root as *autonomous*?
3. Find the verb form in the same word family as *miniaturization*.
4. Find the noun forms in the same word family as *contend*.
5. Find the verb form and the adjective form in the same word family as *application*.

Exercise 3 Supplying the Missing Words

Complete the paragraph with the correct forms of the vocabulary words from this chapter. All of the words are used.

Engineers in the field of _____ have given themselves the _____ of creating completely _____ human-like machines, or robots. The job involves the development of a suitable _____ , writing a(n) _____ that computers can understand, and the _____ of computer parts so that they will fit into small spaces. There is a(n) _____ of reactions to these developments. Some people _____ that such robots will have a disastrous _____ on society. Others believe that the useful _____ of robots far outweigh the possible disadvantages.

Chapter 2

Self-Assessment

Here are some of the terms you will encounter in Chapter 2. How much do you know about each one? Score yourself from 1 to 4.

> 1: I don't know this term.
> 2: I have seen this term, but I am not sure of the meaning.
> 3: I understand this term, but I don't know how to use it in speaking and writing.
> 4: I know this term and can use it in my speaking and writing.

_____ 1. device   _____ 6. legitimize

_____ 2. embed   _____ 7. manipulation

_____ 3. equip   _____ 8. potential

_____ 4. evolve   _____ 9. stream

_____ 5. implement   _____ 10. virtual

Exercise 1 Defining the Words

Match each definition in the right column with the corresponding term in the left column.

____ 1. device   a. possibility

____ 2. embed   b. computer generated

____ 3. equip   c. to start a process

____ 4. evolve   d. to put something into something else

____ 5. implement   e. moving or turning something by using the hands

____ 6. legitimize   f. to play sound or video on a computer, directly from the Internet

____ 7. manipulation   g. to develop by gradually changing

____ 8. potential   h. to provide a person or place with the things that are needed for a particular activity or type of work

____ 9. stream

____ 10. virtual   i. to make something official that had not been before

     j. a machine or small object that does a special job

Exercise 2 Expanding Your Vocabulary

Use your dictionary to find the answers to the questions. Write them down on a separate sheet of paper.

1. Which words can function as both nouns and verbs?
2. What is the noun form of the verb *equip*?
3. What is the noun form of the verb *evolve*?
4. Which noun has the same adjective form?
5. What is the adjective form of the verb *legitimize*? The noun form? The adverb form?
6. What is the verb form of the noun *manipulation*?

Exercise 3 Supplying the Missing Words

Complete the paragraph with the correct forms of the vocabulary words from this chapter.
All of the words are used.

Is it legitimate to be developing machines to replace human beings? Researchers in the field of robotics are working to _____ plans to develop robots that are almost human. Engineers will _____ miniature computers in humanoid bodies and _____ the robots with _____ that have the _____ of taking over many human tasks such as the _____ of small machine parts. Engineers will probably _____ information over the Internet or other sources to the robots to tell them what to do. People say that robots will _____ into more and more intelligent machines and will eventually _____ their existence by helping mankind solve the problems of the world. Both robots and humans will use _____ situations to make decisions about how to deal with dangerous challenges.

Chapter 3

Self-Assessment

Here are some of the terms you will encounter in Chapter 3. How much do you know about each one? Score yourself from 1 to 4.

> 1: I don't know this term.
>
> 2: I have seen this term, but I am not sure of the meaning.
>
> 3: I understand this term, but I don't know how to use it in speaking and writing.
>
> 4: I know this term and can use it in my speaking and writing.

---- 1. appall   ---- 6. expediency

---- 2. catastrophic   ---- 7. maneuver

---- 3. credit   ---- 8. mimic

---- 4. dignity   ---- 9. onslaught

---- 5. ethics   ---- 10. uncharted

Exercise 1   Defining the Words

Match each definition in the right column with the corresponding term in the left column.

---- 1. appall   a. self-respect

---- 2. catastrophic   b. to shock someone by being very bad or immoral

---- 3. credit   c. to recognize for an achievement

---- 4. dignity   d. disastrous

---- 5. ethics   e. morals, principles

---- 6. expediency   f. convenience

---- 7. maneuver   g. unknown, unexplored

---- 8. mimic   h. to move or turn (something) skillfully, especially something large and heavy

---- 9. onslaught   i. to imitate

---- 10. uncharted   j. a very strong attack

Exercise 2   Expanding Your Vocabulary

Use your dictionary to find the answers to the questions. Write them down on a separate sheet of paper.

1. Which word has the same form as a noun, verb, and adjective?
2. Which three words have the same form as a noun and a verb?
3. Which word has a prefix meaning *not*? Is the word a noun, verb, adjective, or adverb?
4. What is the noun form of *catastrophic*? The adverb form?
5. How many different words and word forms can you find for the verb *expediency*?

Supplying the Missing Words

Complete the paragraph with the correct forms of the vocabulary words from this chapter. All of the words are used.

Nineteenth century people would probably be _____ by computer science today. There has been a(n) _____ of new technology unlike anything that has happened before. Computer engineers have even created robots that _____ human behavior. Robots can manipulate tiny devices and _____ large heavy machinery. When we see a robot that looks and behaves like a human, we tend to _____ it with human judgment, too. But we have to remember that robots do not understand _____ in the way humans do. They do not realize that human _____ is extremely important to us. If we trust computers to make decisions that affect people's lives, we will be entering _____ territory. The results could be _____ . We should not simply do the easiest thing just because it seems _____ .

Chapter 4

Self-Assessment

Here are some of the terms you will encounter in Chapter 4. How much do you know about each one? Score yourself from 1 to 4.

1: I don't know this term.
2: I have seen this term, but I am not sure of the meaning.
3: I understand this term, but I don't know how to use it in speaking and writing.
4: I know this term and can use it in my speaking and writing.

____ 1. adornment   ____ 6. indicator

____ 2. component   ____ 7. nature

____ 3. denote   ____ 8. practice

____ 4. diversity   ____ 9. status

____ 5. image   ____ 10. tight

Exercise 1 Defining the Words

Match each definition in the right column with the corresponding term in the left column.

_____	1. adornment	a. very close fitting
_____	2. component	b. one's level in society
_____	3. denote	c. a customary way of doing something
_____	4. diversity	d. a decoration of the body such as jewelry
_____	5. image	e. a part of something
_____	6. indicator	f. to mean or stand for something
_____	7. nature	g. the impression one gives to others
_____	8. practice	h. a variety
_____	9. status	i. a sign of something
_____	10. tight	j. the character or kind

Exercise 2 Expanding Your Vocabulary

Use your dictionary to find the answers to the questions. Write them down on a separate sheet of paper.

1. Which word has the same form as a noun and a verb?
2. Which word has the same form as a noun and an adjective?
3. How many different nouns, verbs, adjectives, and adverbs can you find that are related to *diversity*?
4. Find another noun form, the verb form, and the adjective form of *indicator*.
5. Which three words in the vocabulary list that have a noun form ending in *-tion*?

Exercise 3 Supplying the Missing Words

Complete the paragraph with the correct forms of the vocabulary words from this chapter. All of the words are used.

There is great _____ in what gives a person high _____ . One _____ of culture is clothing and _____ styles. Some groups have a(n) _____ of wearing gold jewelry to _____ a person's status. The more gold, the higher the status. Another _____ of social level might be the _____ of a person's clothing. For example, rock and roll musicians in the 1970s enhanced their _____ by wearing _____ leather pants and extremely long hair.

Chapter 5

Self-Assessment

Here are some of the terms you will encounter in Chapter 5. How much do you know about each one? Score yourself from 1 to 4.

> 1: I don't know this term.
>
> 2: I have seen this term, but I am not sure of the meaning.
>
> 3: I understand this term, but I don't know how to use it in speaking and writing.
>
> 4: I know this term and can use it in my speaking and writing.

____ 1. attire

____ 2. distinctive

____ 3. fan

____ 4. flamboyantly

____ 5. garment

____ 6. intricate

____ 7. masculine

____ 8. pattern

____ 9. trousers

____ 10. wrapped

Exercise 1 Defining the Words

Match each definition in the right column with the corresponding term in the left column.

____ 1. attire

____ 2. distinctive

____ 3. fan

____ 4. flamboyantly

____ 5. garment

____ 6. intricate

____ 7. masculine

____ 8. pattern

____ 9. trousers

____ 10. wrapped

a. characteristic

b. design

c. clothing

d. an admirer

e. in a showy, flashy, colorful way

f. a piece of clothing

g. long pants

h. elaborate, complicated

i. male

j. covered by cloth folded around it

Exercise 2 Expanding Your Vocabulary

Use your dictionary to find the answers to the questions. Write them down on a separate sheet of paper.

1. What part of speech is *distinctive*? Which other words are in the same word family as *distinctive*? Indicate the part of speech of each word.

2. What part of speech is *flamboyantly*? What are two other forms of *flamboyant*? Indicate the part of speech of each word.

3. Which three words in the list that have the same forms as nouns and verbs?

4. What part of speech is *intricate*? Find other words in the same word family and write their part of speech after them.

5. What part of speech is *masculinity*? Find other words in the same word family and write their part of speech after them.

Exercise 3 Supplying the Missing Words

Complete the paragraph with the correct forms of the vocabulary words from this chapter. One word is not used.

Different cultures have _____ fashions. Many Western cultures consider _____ to be clothing for men only, a sign of _____ . Other cultures, notably in the South Pacific, consider a(n) _____ skirt with colorful _____ to be suitable _____ for both men and women. Some African cultures wear brightly colored _____ and head wraps. Finally, many cultures favor _____ men's and women's clothing and _____ jewelry for weddings.

Chapter 6

Self-Assessment

Here are some of the terms you will encounter in Chapter 6. How much do you know about each one? Score yourself from 1 to 4.

> 1: I don't know this term.
>
> 2: I have seen this term, but I am not sure of the meaning.
>
> 3: I understand this term, but I don't know how to use it in speaking and writing.
>
> 4: I know this term and can use it in my speaking and writing.

____ 1. accessories

____ 2. apparel

____ 3. austere

____ 4. designate

____ 5. elaborate

____ 6. excess

____ 7. magnificent

____ 8. opulent

____ 9. striped

____ 10. sweeping

Exercise 1 Defining the Words

Match each definition in the right column with the corresponding term in the left column.

____ 1. accessories   a. shoes, bags, belts, and jewelry

____ 2. apparel   b. strict, plain

____ 3. austere   c. extra, too much

____ 4. designate   d. made from expensive materials

____ 5. elaborate   e. marvelous

____ 6. excess   f. clothing

____ 7. magnificent   g. a pattern of lines

____ 8. opulent   h. to demonstrate, show

____ 9. striped   i. intricate and rich looking

____ 10. sweeping   j. covering a large area, widespread

Exercise 2 Expanding Your Vocabulary

Use your dictionary to find the answers to the questions. Write them down on a separate sheet of paper.

1. What part of speech is *austere*? What is the adverb form? What are the noun forms?

2. What part of speech is *designate*? What are the noun forms?

3. Which two adjectives have the same ending (suffix) in the adjective form and the same suffix in the noun form?

4. Which two adjectives have endings that are derived from verb forms?

5. Which word has the same form for the noun and adjective?

Exercise 3 Supplying the Missing Words

Complete the paragraph with the correct forms of the vocabulary words from this chapter.
One word is not used.

Groups often distinguish themselves with their _____ and _____ . Some groups wear _____ clothing and _____ jewelry to show off their _____ wealth. Other people favor _____ clothing to demonstrate loyalty to their group. Some tribal groups have chosen black-and-white _____ skirts and head wraps, while others _____ brightly colored robes covered with _____ designs as their tribal costume.

Chapter 7

Self-Assessment

Here are some of the terms you will encounter in Chapter 7. How much do you know about each one? Score yourself from 1 to 4.

1: I don't know this term.

2: I have seen this term, but I am not sure of the meaning.

3: I understand this term, but I don't know how to use it in speaking and writing.

4: I know this term and can use it in my speaking and writing.

____ 1. blade

____ 2. contemporary

____ 3. decade

____ 4. descendant

____ 5. nomadic

____ 6. peasant

____ 7. remains

____ 8. sophistication

____ 9. trait

____ 10. weapon

Exercise 1 Defining the Words

Match each definition in the right column with the corresponding term in the left column.

_____ 1. blade   a. a dead body

_____ 2. contemporary   b. anything used to fight

_____ 3. decade   c. modern

_____ 4. descendant   d. traveling from place to place to find food

_____ 5. nomadic   e. a person who comes from a particular ancestor

_____ 6. peasant   f. ten years

_____ 7. remains   g. the edge, cutting part

_____ 8. sophistication   h. characteristic

_____ 9. trait   i. worldly education and experience

_____ 10. weapon   j. a farmer of low rank

Exercise 2 Expanding Your Vocabulary

Use your dictionary to find the answers to the questions. Write them down on a separate sheet of paper.

1. What part of speech is *nomadic*? What is the noun form of *nomadic*?

2. Which words have the same form as an adjective and as a noun?

3. What part of speech is *descendant*? Is there a variation in the spelling of this word?
   Does it have other forms?

4. What part of speech is *weapon*? Is there another noun form? What does it mean?
   What is the verb form of *weapon*?

Exercise 3 Supplying the Missing Words

Complete the paragraph with the correct forms of the vocabulary words from this chapter.
All of the words are used.

Several _____ ago, some hikers found the _____ of a five-thousand-year-old _____ hunter who was carrying several _____ when he died. One of his weapons was a knife with a copper _____ . _____ farmers who are _____ of this hunter live in the same alpine valleys where he hunted so long ago. These _____ still have physical _____ that can be traced back to the original nomad. They live very simply and do not have a lot of _____ , but they thrive on farming and hunting.

Chapter 8

Self-Assessment

Here are some of the terms you will encounter in Chapter 8. How much do you know about each one? Score yourself from 1 to 4.

1: I don't know this term.
2: I have seen this term, but I am not sure of the meaning.
3: I understand this term, but I don't know how to use it in speaking and writing.
4: I know this term and can use it in my speaking and writing.

____ 1. block

____ 2. counterpart

____ 3. defeat

____ 4. disgrace

____ 5. dowry

____ 6. endure

____ 7. fare

____ 8. glorify

____ 9. inherit

____ 10. prestigious

Exercise 1 Defining the Words

Match each definition in the right column with the corresponding term in the left column.

____ 1. block

____ 2. counterpart

____ 3. defeat

____ 4. disgrace

____ 5. dowry

____ 6. endure

____ 7. fare

____ 8. glorify

____ 9. inherit

____ 10. prestigious

a. to get along, cope, manage

b. to praise; to make something seem better than it really is

c. a person or thing with the same function as another person or thing

d. money or property brought into a marriage by the bride

e. a kind of stone used in buildings

f. to receive money, property, or physical characteristic from parents or ancestors

g. shame

h. to win a victory, beat

i. to undergo and tolerate a hardship

j. respected and admired by people

Exercise 2 Expanding Your Vocabulary

Use your dictionary to find the answers to the questions. Write them down on a separate sheet of paper.

1. Which words in the list have the same form as a noun and as a verb?
2. Which two words have the same adjective ending (suffix)?
3. Which two pairs of words have the same noun ending (suffix)?
4. Which word ends in *-ies* in the plural form?
5. What are the two forms and meanings of *block*?

Exercise 3 Supplying the Missing Words

Complete the paragraph with the correct forms of the vocabulary words from this chapter. Note the time frame of the passage. One word is not used.

In the Middle Ages (approximately 500 A.D. to 1400 A.D.), young noblewomen of marriageable age from _____ families were given large _____ when they married. They were also in line to _____ titles, property, and money when their parents died. At the time there were a number of young noblemen with no money who needed to marry well in order to succeed in society. These men _____ many hardships as they attempted to win a rich bride. They would challenge each other to combat with various weapons. Each one struggled to _____ his _____ to obtain the hand of the lady in marriage. One man out of many _____ well in these contests; the others faced _____ and dishonor. Throughout history these fights have been _____ and admired, but in truth, life for the penniless nobleman was a constant struggle.

Chapter 9

Self-Assessment

Here are some of the terms you will encounter in Chapter 9. How much do you know about each one? Score yourself from 1 to 4.

1: I don't know this term.
2: I have seen this term, but I am not sure of the meaning.
3: I understand this term, but I don't know how to use it in speaking and writing.
4: I know this term and can use it in my speaking and writing.

_____ 1. column

_____ 2. courtyard

_____ 3. dwelling

_____ 4. elegant

_____ 5. flow

_____ 6. luxurious

_____ 7. marble

_____ 8. mosaic

_____ 9. painting

_____ 10. wealth

Exercise 1 Defining the Words

Match each definition in the right column with the corresponding term in the left column.

_____ 1. column

_____ 2. courtyard

_____ 3. dwelling

_____ 4. elegant

_____ 5. flow

_____ 6. luxurious

_____ 7. marble

_____ 8. mosaic

_____ 9. painting

_____ 10. wealth

a. liquid or gas that moves in a continuous way

b. a picture or design made with paint, a liquid in which colored material is suspended

c. extravagantly comfortable

d. an open space surrounded by a building or buildings

e. high quality, tasteful and beautiful

f. a picture or design made of small colored pieces of glass or stone

g. money, possessions, and property

h. a kind of stone used in buildings

i. a residence or house; shelter

j. a long pillar of stone used to support a building

Exercise 2 Expanding Your Vocabulary

Use your dictionary to find the answers to the questions. Write them down on a separate sheet of paper.

1. Which word has the same forms as a noun, verb, and adjective?
2. What part of speech is *elegant*? Are there other forms? What are they?
3. What other forms can you find for the word *luxurious*?
4. Which two words are nouns formed from verbs? What were the original verbs?

Exercise 3 Supplying the Missing Words

Complete the paragraph with the correct forms of the vocabulary words from this chapter. All of the words are used.

_____ Roman citizens lived in _____ , _____ houses. These citizens built their _____ with blocks of _____ placed around a central area called a(n) _____ . In the center were a garden and a pool into which water from a fountain _____ . Around the courtyard were _____ of ancestors and colorful, decorative _____ of famous scenes. Tall marble _____ were located around the edges of the courtyard to support the roof of the house.

Chapter 10

Self-Assessment

Here are some of the terms you will encounter in Chapter 10. How much do you know about each one? Score yourself from 1 to 4.

> 1: I don't know this term.
>
> 2: I have seen this term, but I am not sure of the meaning.
>
> 3: I understand this term, but I don't know how to use it in speaking and writing.
>
> 4: I know this term and can use it in my speaking and writing.

____ 1. betrothed   ____ 6. game

____ 2. ceremony   ____ 7. immunity

____ 3. courtship   ____ 8. kin

____ 4. feast   ____ 9. survive

____ 5. forager   ____ 10. yield

Exercise 1   Defining the Words

Match each definition in the right column with the corresponding term in the left column.

____ 1. betrothed   a. a rich and delicious meal for many guests

____ 2. ceremony   b. all of a person's family

____ 3. courtship   c. to produce

____ 4. feast   d. resistance to disease

____ 5. forager   e. a person searching for food

____ 6. game   f. to remain alive or continue existing

____ 7. immunity   g. engaged to be married

____ 8. kin   h. a formal activity to celebrate a special occasion

____ 9. survive   i. animals hunted

____ 10. yield   j. a period of time when one person seeks to persuade another to marry

Exercise 2   Expanding Your Vocabulary

Use your dictionary to find the answers to the questions. Write them down on a separate sheet of paper.

1. Which two words have the same ending as nouns?
2. Which word ends in the same letters as the words in item 1, but is an adjective?
3. Which three words have the same form as a noun and as a verb?
4. Which two nouns end in -*ies* in plural form?
5. How many different word forms can you find that are related to *immunity*?

Exercise 3   Supplying the Missing Words

Complete the paragraph with the correct forms of the vocabulary words from this chapter.
One word is not used.

The process of getting married is similar in many cultures. It includes several steps beginning with a
period of _____ during which a young man tries to convince a young woman to marry him. During
this period, the family of the young woman often agrees to give her a dowry of money, possessions, or
perhaps property. If the young woman agrees to the marriage, we say that the couple is _____ or
engaged. After a suitable period, the marriage is finalized with a wedding _____ attended by the
bride's and groom's _____ . Following the wedding, there is usually a great _____ consisting
of all kinds of delicious foods from the harvest _____ and fish or _____ as well. In time the
young family produces a child that may or may not _____ the first year if the living conditions are
poor. If the child lives through childhood diseases, he or she will have lifetime _____ to them.

Chapter 11

Self-Assessment

Here are some of the terms you will encounter in Chapter 11. How much do you know about each
one? Score yourself from 1 to 4.

1: I don't know this term.
2: I have seen this term, but I am not sure of the meaning.
3: I understand this term, but I don't know how to use it in speaking and writing.
4: I know this term and can use it in my speaking and writing.

____ 1. aggression

____ 2. assertiveness

____ 3. behavior

____ 4. compliant

____ 5. constraint

____ 6. dating

____ 7. gender

____ 8. misinterpret

____ 9. sample

____ 10. strive

Exercise 1 Defining the Words

Match each definition in the right column with the corresponding term in the left column.

___ 1. aggression	a. to struggle
___ 2. assertiveness	b. a small amount of something that shows what the whole thing is like
___ 3. behavior	c. violence
___ 4. compliant	d. self-assured, forceful conduct
___ 5. constraint	e. limitation
___ 6. dating	f. going out socially
___ 7. gender	g. sex, male or female
___ 8. misinterpret	h. conduct, how a person acts
___ 9. sample	i. obedient, conforming
___ 10. strive	j. to understand incorrectly

Exercise 2 Expanding Your Vocabulary

Use your dictionary to find the answers to the questions. Write them down on a separate sheet of paper.

1. Which word has the same form as a noun, verb, and adjective?
2. Which word has a prefix meaning "not"?
3. Which word in the list is an adjective?
4. How many parts of speech can you find for the word *assertive*? Write the word and its part of speech.
5. How many forms can you find for the word *aggression*? Write each word and its part of speech.

Exercise 3 Supplying the Missing Words

Complete the paragraph with the correct forms of the vocabulary words from this chapter.
Two words are not used.

A person's _____ when he or she goes out socially on a(n) _____ differs from person to person. Some people think that a person's _____ determines whether he or she is _____ or timid. After years of _____ of the evidence, research using a(n) _____ of university students revealed certain regularities; there are both women and men who are _____ , cooperating and allowing the other person to choose what they will do on a date , and others who _____ to control every situation.

Chapter 12

Self-Assessment

Here are some of the terms you will encounter in Chapter 12. How much do you know about each one? Score yourself from 1 to 4.

> 1: I don't know this term.
>
> 2: I have seen this term, but I am not sure of the meaning.
>
> 3: I understand this term, but I don't know how to use it in speaking and writing.
>
> 4: I know this term and can use it in my speaking and writing.

____ 1. engage (in combat)

____ 2. exercise (leadership)

____ 3. hierarchical

____ 4. inclusive

____ 5. integrate

____ 6. labor

____ 7. lineage

____ 8. role

____ 9. segment

____ 10. tribe

Exercise 1 Defining the Words

Match each definition in the right column with the corresponding term in the left column.

____ 1. engage (in combat)   a. a person's usual function in society

____ 2. exercise (leadership)   b. physical work

____ 3. hierarchical   c. including everyone or everything

____ 4. inclusive   d. to mix, combine

____ 5. integrate   e. arranged according to a system of ranking people or things

____ 6. labor   f. people who trace their descent from a common ancestor

____ 7. lineage   g. a part or piece of something that is divided into equal parts

____ 8. role   h. a group of families and relatives with the same culture and language descended from an ancestor

____ 9. segment

____ 10. tribe   i. to take part in, be involved

                                    j. to perform, demonstrate

Exercise 2 Expanding Your Vocabulary

Use your dictionary to find the answers to the questions. Write them down on a separate sheet of paper.

1. Which word has the same form as a noun, verb, and adjective?
2. Which two words have the same form as nouns and verbs?
3. What form is the word *inclusive*? What other forms does it have?
4. What form is the word *hierarchical*? What other forms are there?
5. How many different meanings can you find for the verbs *engage* and *exercise*? What are they?

Exercise 3 Supplying the Missing Words

Complete the paragraph with the correct forms of the vocabulary words from this chapter.
One word is not used.

In many areas of the world, groups of people who descend from a single ancestor, in other words, who
have the same _____ , are called a(n) _____ . Within the tribe, parts or _____ of the
tribe who are closely related are known as families, and within a family, each person has a(n) _____ .
The men are usually responsible for the most physically demanding jobs, the _____ . These jobs are
all _____ and often involve many activities such as farming, building shelters, hunting, and fishing.
Men may even _____ in combat if the tribe goes to war. Women's roles include child care and food
collection and preparation. The members of a tribe are often arranged in a(n) _____ of status levels;
the highest status individuals _____ the leadership roles, while the remaining members fulfill other
necessary functions.

Chapter 13

Self-Assessment

Here are some of the terms you will encounter in Chapter 13. How much do you know about each
one? Score yourself from 1 to 4.

> 1: I don't know this term.
>
> 2: I have seen this term, but I am not sure of the meaning.
>
> 3: I understand this term, but I don't know how to use it in speaking and writing.
>
> 4: I know this term and can use it in my speaking and writing.

____ 1. axis

____ 2. fluctuate

____ 3. horizon

____ 4. hypothesize

____ 5. matter

____ 6. spherical

____ 7. spin

____ 8. stipulate

____ 9. symmetry

____ 10. transparent

Exercise 1 Defining the Words

Match each definition in the right column with the corresponding term in the left column.

____ 1. axis   a. the substance composing all physical objects

____ 2. fluctuate   b. to require something in an agreement

____ 3. horizon   c. round

____ 4. hypothesize   d. an imaginary line around which a planet turns

____ 5. matter   e. able to be seen through

____ 6. spherical   f. regularity, balanced proportions

____ 7. spin   g. to rotate very quickly

____ 8. stipulate   h. to become higher or lower in strength

____ 9. symmetry   i. to suggest a theory

____ 10. transparent   j. the line where the earth appears to meet the sky

Exercise 2 Expanding Your Vocabulary

Use your dictionary to find the answers to the questions. Write them down on a separate sheet of paper.

1. How many different meanings can you find for the word *matter*? Which is the most common meaning?
2. What form is the word *axis*? What is the plural form?
3. What forms does the word *spin* have? What is the past tense of *spin*?
4. How many forms does the word *hypothesize* have? What are they?
5. What word form is *spherical*? What other form does this word have?
6. Which two verbs in the list have the same ending in their noun forms?

Exercise 3 Supplying the Missing Words

Complete the paragraph with the correct forms of the vocabulary words from this chapter.
One word is not used.

The early Greeks held that the Earth was flat because when they looked out to sea, they could see a flat
_____ where the sea seemed to meet the sky. Pythagorean astronomy also _____ that the
most perfect, pure shape was a circle. For this reason, a sphere, being the most _____ shape, had
to be the shape of the universe. At first they _____ that the sun and and stars were attached to the
inside of a huge _____ sphere that moved around the Earth. However, that theory did not explain
why ships at sea disappear over the horizon little by little with the top of their masts disappearing last.
Eventually, scientists concluded that the Earth is not flat but _____ and turns or _____ on its
_____ . In fact, the Earth is just a tiny part of the millions of planets and stars in the universe. At the
same time, astronomers were noticing that the light from some stars varies in intensity or _____ in
brightness. This phenomenon led to the notion that some of the heavenly bodies were stars and some were
planets.

Chapter 14

Self-Assessment

Here are some of the terms you will encounter in Chapter 14. How much do you know about each one? Score yourself from 1 to 4.

> 1: I don't know this term.
>
> 2: I have seen this term, but I am not sure of the meaning.
>
> 3: I understand this term, but I don't know how to use it in speaking and writing.
>
> 4: I know this term and can use it in my speaking and writing.

_____ 1. analogous

_____ 2. CO_2

_____ 3. electromagnetic (EM)

_____ 4. emissions

_____ 5. fossil fuel

_____ 6. galaxy

_____ 7. photon

_____ 8. radiation

_____ 9. skeptical

_____ 10. vapor

Exercise 1 Defining the Words

Match each definition in the right column with the term in the left column.

_____ 1. analogous   a. a quantum of light

_____ 2. CO_2 b. a cluster of stars

_____ 3. electromagnetic (EM)   c. energy sent forth in rays or waves, such as light waves

_____ 4. emission   d. carbon dioxide

_____ 5. fossil fuel   e. the combined effects of electric and magnetic forces

_____ 6. galaxy   f. water in a gaseous state

_____ 7. photon   g. unbelieving

_____ 8. radiation   h. coal, oil, and natural gas

_____ 9. skeptical   i. substance that is discharged or released

_____ 10. vapor   j. similar

Exercise 2 Expanding Your Vocabulary

Use your dictionary to find the answers to the questions. Write them down on a separate sheet of paper.

1. What word form is the word _emissions_? What other form is there?
2. What form is the word _skeptical_? What other forms are there?
3. There are two noun forms of _skeptical_. What is the difference in their meanings?
4. What word form is _analogous_? What other forms are there?
5. Which word has a verb ending in _-ize_?

Exercise 3 Supplying the Missing Words

Complete the paragraph with the correct forms of the vocabulary words from this chapter. Two words are not used.

Have you ever owned a magnet? It's a small bar of iron that attracts other pieces of iron. If you have two, you will see that they pull together on one end and push apart on the other. Both electric and magnetic forces come from electric charge. Michael Faraday, a nineteenth-century English physicist, did experiments with _____ (EM) fields. What he discovered became extremely important in the production of energy by power plants where _____ are burned. These power plants still use EM energy to produce electricity, but an unfortunate result is air pollution containing _____ such as _____ and water _____ .

Later, in the early twentieth century, physicists studying rays and waves of _____ developed the quantum theory, the idea that the smallest unit of measurement should be called a quantum of energy. They named a quantum of light a(n) _____ . At about the same time, Albert Einstein came up with his theory of relativity. He was always _____ of quantum theory, which he thought was "spooky."

Chapter 15

Self-Assessment

Here are some of the terms you will encounter in Chapter 15. How much do you know about each one? Score yourself from 1 to 4.

1: I don't know this term.
2: I have seen this term, but I am not sure of the meaning.
3: I understand this term, but I don't know how to use it in speaking and writing.
4: I know this term and can use it in my speaking and writing.

_____ 1. analog   _____ 6. microscopic

_____ 2. digital   _____ 7. particle

_____ 3. disdainfully   _____ 8. tide

_____ 4. inert   _____ 9. trace

_____ 5. initial   _____ 10. vibrate

Exercise 1 Defining the Words

Match each definition in the right column with the corresponding term in the left column.

____ 1. analog	a. with contempt
____ 2. digital	b. having no power or ability to react
____ 3. disdainfully	c. an extremely tiny piece of something
____ 4. inert	d. representing data with numbers rather than a pointer
____ 5. initial	e. a very small amount of something
____ 6. microscopic	f. to shake
____ 7. particle	g. something you cannot see, but which is there
____ 8. tide	h. the way something is changing or developing, rising, and falling
____ 9. trace	i. first
____ 10. vibrate	j. representing data through physical properties such as a pointer or dial

Exercise 2 Expanding Your Vocabulary

Use your dictionary to find the answers to the questions. Write them down on a separate sheet of paper.

1. What is the verb form of *digital*?
2. What form of the word is *disdainfully*? What other forms are there?
3. What form of the word is *initial*? What other forms are there?
4. There is another noun form of *initial*. What does it mean?
5. Which three words have the same form as nouns and verbs?

Exercise 3 Supplying the Missing Words

Complete the paragraph with the correct forms of the vocabulary words from this chapter.
All of the words are used.

Research has shown that quantum effects change only in _____ (you can't see them) jumps from one energy level to the next in what is known as the Planck distance. This is analogous to a(n) _____ clock that jumps from one number to the next rather than a(n) _____ clock, whose hands move slowly and continuously from one number to the next. _____ , skeptical physicists greeted this idea _____ because they still believed that all matter was composed of small pieces or _____ called atoms that moved in a continuous manner. Then scientific opinion changed and the _____ turned in favor of quantum theory. There are still _____ of doubt, but most scientists now realize that far from being _____ particles that resemble tiny solar systems, quanta are made up of tiny loops or strings of energy that _____ in particular ways. This has become known as the string theory.

APPENDIX B

WRITING AND SPEAKING GUIDELINES

APPENDIX B-1
Basic Paragraph Structure and Development

CHART B-1	The Well-Developed Paragraph

A well-developed paragraph moves from a topic sentence that makes a general statement about the content of the paragraph to sentences that provide increasingly specific information. The numbers here represent levels of generality:

- **(1)** = most general
- **(2)** = background of the topic sentence
- **(3)** = specific examples of the preceding sentences

Paragraph 1

(1) Topic sentence = This sentence tells the reader what the paragraph will be about. It is the most general sentence in the paragraph.

(2) These sentences give background information about the topic sentence and provide a transition from the most general idea in the topic sentence to the specific example that will come next. Note that the level 2 sentences may provide different types of information about the topic sentence, depending on the nature and needs of the paragraph

(3) Each of these sentences describes a specific example of the preceding topic sentence and background.

(1) Money plays an important role in the economic and social affairs of a community. **(2)** Before coins were invented in the seventh century B.C., people exchanged something of value such as cattle or agricultural products to obtain other goods. **(2)** Later, commodities such as gold and silver and eventually paper, whose value was based on the commodities, were used as money. **(2)** Nowadays, money may play a purely economic role in that it is exchanged for goods and services, or its role may be more ceremonial. **(3)** The island of Yap, located in the Pacific Ocean south of Japan and east of Philippines, has a curious kind of disk-shaped ceremonial stone money, which can be up to 12 feet in diameter and weigh thousands of pounds. The stone disk looks like a millstone with a hole in center so that a pole or coconut rope can be used to carry it.

A well-developed paragraph should have at least three levels. Number the levels in your paragraphs to check your organization.

Notice that a well-organized paragraph, like Paragraph 1, contains connectors (*before, later, nowadays*) to indicate chronological order; reference pronouns (*it, its*), and repetition of key words (*commodities, money*) to help the reader follow the description.

Paragraph 2

(1) Topic sentence = This sentence tells the reader what the paragraph will be about. It is the most general sentence in the paragraph.	**(1) One of the advantages of caffeine is its psychological effects. (2)** Caffeine helps increase the speed of rapid information processing about 10 percent by improving alertness and concentration. **(3)** These findings were discovered by Smith et al (Euan,1992), who conducted a study in 1993 to examine the effects of coffee on daytime and nighttime performance and alertness.
(2) This sentence explains the topic sentence.	
(3) This sentence gives details about the preceding (level 2) sentence.	

The numbers again represent levels of generality:

> **(1)** = most general
> **(2)** = background of the topic sentence
> **(3)** = specific examples of the preceding sentences

However, this paragraph is slightly different from the preceding one in that level 2 gives an explanation of the topic sentence rather than providing background information.

APPENDIX B-2
Paraphrasing and Summarizing Written Content

Paraphrasing

To paraphrase an original text, restate the author's ideas and words in your own words. A paraphrase is approximately the same length as the original text.

Work with just one or two sentences at a time. Use a combination of the following methods, as appropriate:

1. Change as many of the words as you can by substituting synonyms. Remember that some words must stay the same because there is no good synonym to convey the same meaning.
2. Change the sentence from affirmative to negative or negative to affirmative.
3. Change the word order and structure; change active to passive or passive to active; change from one kind of clause to another.
4. Substitute different forms of names and/or use pronouns.
5. Combine sentences.
6. Finally, rewrite the author's ideas and words using your paraphrased sentences.

SAMPLE ORIGINAL PARAGRAPH:

     Money plays an important role in the economic and social affairs of a community. Before coins were invented in the seventh century B.C., people exchanged something of value such as cattle or agricultural products to obtain other goods. Later, commodities such as gold and silver and eventually paper, whose value was based on the commodities, were used as money. Nowadays, money may play a purely economic role in that it is exchanged for goods and services or its role may be more ceremonial. The island of Yap, located in the Pacific Ocean south of Japan and east of the Philippines, has a curious kind of disk-shaped stone money, which can be up to 12 feet in diameter and weigh thousands of pounds. The stone disk looks like a millstone with a hole in center so that a pole or coconut rope can be used to carry it.

CHART B-2-1 | How to Paraphrase

Example: Original first sentence:
Money plays an important role in the economic and social affairs of a community.

1. Begin the paraphrase by using synonyms.	Money has a significant function in society and the economy.

Example: Original second, third, and fourth sentences:
Before coins were invented in the seventh century B.C., people exchanged something of value such as cattle or agricultural products to obtain other goods. Later, commodities such as gold and silver and eventually paper, whose value was based on the commodities, were used as money. In some communities, money played a purely economic role in that it could exchanged for goods and services or its role was more ceremonial.

2. First paraphrase by using synonyms.	Before 700 B.C., people bartered for goods. After some time, gold and silver replaced the system of bartering. Gold and silver coins and then paper—assigned a comparable value—were employed as currency. In some places, currency served both economic and ceremonial functions.
3. Improve the paraphrase by changing active to passive or passive to active.	Before 700 B.C., goods were bartered. Around 700 B.C., currency was devised to take the place of bartering. First, people used gold and silver coins. Then people assigned paper money the same value as the precious metals and employed it as currency. In some places, currency served both economic and ceremonial functions.
4. Continue the paraphrase by combining sentences by changing two simple sentences into a complex sentence.	Although goods were bartered at first, around 700 B.C., currency was devised to take the place of bartering. After people had used gold and silver coins for some time, they assigned paper money the same value as the precious metals and employed it as currency. In some places, currency served both economic and ceremonial functions.

Example: Original fifth and sixth sentences:
The island of Yap, located in the Pacific Ocean south of Japan and east of the Philippines, has a curious kind of disk-shaped stone money, which can be up to 12 feet in diameter and weigh thousands of pounds. The stone disk looks like a millstone with a hole in center so that a pole or coconut rope can be used to carry it.

5. Use synonyms, change word order, and change singular nouns into plural.	Yap, a Pacific island east of the Philippines and south of Japan, has a strange variety of plate-shaped ceremonial money stones, which can be as large as 12 feet wide and have a weight of more than a thousand pounds. The stones resemble wheels with round openings through the middle so that ropes or poles can be employed to transport them.

6. Reverse the word order and structure of the sentences by changing active to passive. Move modifiers around. Expand an adjective phrase into an adjective clause. Change the original adjective clause into a simple sentence.	A strange variety of ceremonial money <u>made of stone in the shape of a plate or wheel as large as 12 feet wide with a weight of more than a thousand pounds</u> is used in Yap, a Pacific island, <u>which is east of the Philippines and south of Japan. The stones can be transported with poles or ropes through the circular openings in the middle of the wheels.</u>
Complete your paraphrase of the paragraph: Put all of your paraphrased sentences together. Finally, compare the original passage and your paraphrase to make sure that they have the same meaning. If not, make changes so that they do.	**Final paraphrase:** A significant function in society and the economy is fulfilled with money. Although goods were bartered at first, around 700 B.C., currency was devised to take the place of bartering. After people had used gold and silver coins for some time, they assigned paper money the same value as the precious metals and employed it as currency. In some places, currency served both economic and ceremonial functions. A strange variety of ceremonial money made of stone in the shape of a plate or wheel as large as 12 feet wide with a weight of more than a thousand pounds is used in Yap, a Pacific island, which is east of the Philippines and south of Japan. The stones can be transported with poles or ropes through the circular openings in the middle of the wheels.

Summarizing

A summary should be one-third to one-half the length of the original text.

CHART B-2-2	**Writing a Summary**
Choose the key ideas from the original paragraph.	**Original:** <u>Money plays an important role in the economic and social affairs of a community.</u> Before coins were invented in the seventh century B.C., people exchanged something of value such as cattle or agricultural products to obtain other goods. Later, commodities such as gold and silver and eventually paper, whose value was based on the commodities, were used as money. <u>Nowadays, money may play a purely economic role in that it is exchanged for goods and services, or its role may be more ceremonial. The island of Yap, located in the Pacific Ocean south of Japan and east of the Philippines, has a curious kind of disk-shaped ceremonial stone money, which can be up to 12 feet in diameter and weigh thousands of pounds.</u> The stone disk looks like a millstone with a hole in center so that a pole or coconut rope can be used to carry it.
Use some of the techniques for paraphrasing to summarize the key ideas.	**Paraphrased summary:** A significant function in society and the economy is fulfilled with money. In some places, currency served both economic and ceremonial functions. A strange variety of ceremonial money made of stone in the shape of a plate or wheel as large as 12 feet wide with a weight of more than a thousand pounds is used in Yap, a Pacific island, which is east of the Philippines and south of Japan.

APPENDIX B-3
Summarizing a Discussion

Summarizing a discussion is similar to summarizing a piece of writing. Begin by introducing the discussion topic. What do you remember about the discussion in general?

EXAMPLE:

"In a recent discussion about ____, we agreed that . . ."
  OR
"Recently, a group discussion revealed a disagreement over the topic of . . ."
  OR
"A second topic of discussion compared _____ and _____. One group explained that . . ."

- If you took notes during a discussion, look them over and see if you can group the comments that were centered around one or more particular ideas.

- List the ideas and the central focus of the ideas that you discussed (report what the members of the group said). It is not necessary to use names of the participants, especially if there was some disagreement.

- Add explanations of what was said if necessary.

- Interpret the main points made. What did they mean?

- To conclude, answer this question: What did you learn from the discussion?

EXAMPLE:

   Recently, a class discussion revealed a disagreement over the topic of government subsidies to the poor, also known as welfare. Two members of the group expressed the idea that the poor should be supported by the federal government because they are unable to earn a living for themselves. One of the students claimed that many citizens have been deprived of the education necessary to hold a job in today's world. The other student agreed and added that because these citizens have inadequate education, they are not be able to learn as adults and so will become criminals if the government does not support them. In contrast, three members of the group insisted that the opposite is true. They argued that there are dozens of facilities offering training in basic computer operator skills and that anyone can learn to type. They assured the group that businesses are eager to hire people who have gone through such training. This discussion reflects the basic differences of opinion regarding government aid to the poor in the country as a whole. It became clear to me that this disagreement will not be easy to resolve.

APPENDIX B-4
How to Give an Oral Presentation

CHART B-4-1	Planning Your Oral Presentation
What is your topic?	Money
Why are you giving the presentation? • Is your purpose to inform? • Is your purpose to persuade?	To inform
Who is your audience? • Experts in your field? Use specific technical language with experts. • A general audience (lay people)? Use simpler language and more definitions for a general audience.	Professors and other students
What is your main idea?	Money has caused enormous problems throughout history.

CHART B-4-2	Preparing Your Oral Presentation
The introduction will establish a relationship with the audience.	
Begin with an attention getter: • An interesting quotation related to your topic	"An old saying goes, 'Money is the root of all evil.'"
• A surprising fact or statistic	"One of the earliest forms of money was cattle."
• A rhetorical question	"Did you know that at one time, there was no such thing as money?"
• An anecdote	"Thousands of years ago, a wealthy man in Rome gave his son a large amount of gold. This gold . . . "
Identify the topic in a single topic sentence. Be specific.	"In this presentation I'm going to show / demonstrate . . . " "This presentation traces the history of money . . . " "From the beginning, money has indeed been the root of all evil."

Organize what you will say in one of three ways:

- Chronological order (what happened first, second, third)
- Cause and effect order (how and why something happens)
- Divided into parts (description of an object or a place)

Write a brief outline of your presentation to use as notes. You can also write your notes on separate cards. Plan not to write your presentation out in full sentences and read it aloud. That would be extremely boring!

- Cover only the main points and use key words to remind yourself of examples you will use.

- Give proof, facts.

- Use clear, interesting examples.

1. Early forms of exchange (Stone Age)
   - cattle; other animals; grains
   - problems with theft (quote from history book)

2. The invention of currency in 700 B.C.
   - metal coins (copper, bronze, silver, gold)
   - commodity money (shells)
   - paper money
   - problems with theft and counterfeit money (quote from Internet source)

3. Modern money and banking
   - electronic and Internet banking
   - problems with identity theft (Experts estimate that . . .)

Use clear transitions between points: *first, second, third, in addition, next, later, moreover, finally, in contrast, similarly, although.*

"First, early people bartered cattle and other agricultural products. Next, the country of Lydia began to use precious metals as money. Later, paper money was introduced."

Plan a conclusion that includes, as appropriate:

- A short summary

- A call to action

- A suggestion

- A prediction

"The history of money has been long and complicated . . . "

"It is important for us to . . . "

"Perhaps if we all work together . . . "

"Someday, money may no longer exist . . . "

CHART B-4-3	**Giving Your Presentation**

Practice, practice, practice. • Practice exactly as you hope to give the presentation. • Look at your audience, smile, and introduce yourself. • Begin with the attention getter. • Preview the main points. • Speak slowly and clearly in a conversational tone. • Be enthusiastic about your topic. • Be confident.	"Good afternoon. My name is Helen Schmidt. You may have heard the famous saying that money is the root of all evil. In fact, that has been shown to be true through research. Today I am going to trace the history and show how the development of money has been the cause of a great many problems throughout history."
Avoid these bad habits: • Apologizing or making excuses • Hesitations. • Using extra words	~~"This presentation is too long."~~ ~~"I didn't have time to add all the material I would have liked."~~ ~~"I'm not very good at public speaking, sorry."~~ ~~"Uhhh, ummm . . ."~~ ~~"You know, like . . ."~~
Give a cue that the speech is about to end.	"Let me end by saying, . . . " "I'd like to finish by emphasizing . . . " "So . . . / To sum up . . . / To summarize . . . "
End in a way that the audience will remember.	"We must be aware that while money is necessary for life, it can also cause unbelievable problems." "There is a story about a poor man who won more than a million dollars in the lottery. . . ."
Close.	"Thank you very much, any questions?"

APPENDIX C

ANSWER KEY FOR APPENDIX A

Chapter 1

Exercise 1 Defining the Words

1 c, 2 h, 3 e, 4 b, 5 j, 6 a, 7 g, 8 d, 9 f, 10 i

Exercise 2 Expanding Your Vocabulary

1. array, impact, program, task
2. autonomously
3. miniaturize
4. contention, contender
5. apply, applicable

Exercise 3 Supplying the Missing Words

Engineers in the field of <u>artificial intelligence</u> have given themselves the **task** of creating completely **autonomous** human-like machines, or robots. The job involves the development of a suitable **algorithm**, writing a **program** that computers can understand, and the **miniaturization** of computer parts so that they will fit into small spaces. There is an **array** of reactions to these developments. Some people **contend** that such robots will have a disastrous **impact** on society. Others believe that the useful **applications** of robots far outweigh the possible disadvantages.

Chapter 2

Exercise 1 Defining the Words

1 j, 2 d, 3 h, 4 g, 5 c, 6 i, 7 e, 8 a, 9 f, 10 b

Exercise 2 Expanding Your Vocabulary

1. implement, stream
2. equipment
3. evolution
4. potential
5. legitimate; legitimization; legitimately
6. manipulate

Exercise 3 Supplying the Missing Words

Is it legitimate to be developing machines to replace human beings? Researchers in the field of robotics are working to **implement** plans to develop robots that are almost human. Engineers will **embed** miniature computers in humanoid bodies and **equip** the robots with **devices** that have the **potential** of taking over many human tasks such as the **manipulation** of small machine parts. Engineers will probably **stream** information over the Internet or other sources to the robots to tell them what to do. People say that robots will **evolve** into more and more intelligent machines and will eventually **legitimize** their existence by helping mankind solve the problems of the world. Both robots and humans will use **virtual** situations to make decisions about how to deal with dangerous challenges.

Chapter 3

Exercise 1 Defining the Words
1 b, 2 d, 3 c, 4 a, 5 e, 6 f, 7 h, 8 i, 9. j, 10 g

Exercise 2 Expanding Your Vocabulary
1. mimic
2. credit, maneuver, mimic
3. uncharted; *an adjective*
4. catastrophe; catastrophically
5. expediency (*n.*); expedience (*n.*); expedient (*n.*); expedient (*adj.*); expediently (*adv.*)

Exercise 3 Supplying the Missing Words

Nineteenth century people would probably be **appalled** by computer science today. There has been an **onslaught** of new technology unlike anything that has happened before. Computer engineers have even created robots that **mimic** human behavior. Robots can manipulate tiny devices and **maneuver** large heavy machinery. When we see a robot that looks and behaves like a human, we tend to **credit** it with human judgment, too. But we have to remember that robots do not understand **ethics** in the way humans do. They do not realize that human **dignity** is extremely important to us. If we trust computers to make decisions that affect people's lives, we will be entering **uncharted** territory. The results could be **catastrophic**. We should not simply do the easiest thing just because it seems **expedient**.

Chapter 4

Exercise 1 Defining the Words

1 d, 2 e, 3 f, 4 h, 5 g, 6 i, 7 j, 8 c, 9 b, 10 a

Exercise 2 Expanding Your Vocabulary

1. practice
2. component
3. at least 6: diverseness (*n.*), diversification (*n.*), diversifier (*n.*) diversify (*v.*), diverse (*adj.*), diversely (*adv.*)
4. indication (*n.*), indicate (*v.*), indicative (*adj.*)
5. denotation, diversification, indication

Exercise 3 Supplying the Missing Words

There is great **diversity** in what gives a person high **status**. One **component** of culture is clothing and **adornment** styles. Some groups have a **practice** of wearing gold jewelry to **denote** a person's status. The more gold, the higher the status. Another **indicator** of social level might be the **nature** of a person's clothing. For example, rock and roll musicians in the 1970s enhanced their **image** by wearing **tight** leather pants and extremely long hair.

Chapter 5

Exercise 1 Defining the Words

1 c, 2 a, 3 d, 4 e, 5 f, 6 h, 7 i, 8 b, 9 g, 10 j

Exercise 2 Expanding Your Vocabulary

1. *adjective*; distinction (*n.*), distinguish (*v.*), distinct (*adj.*)
2. *adverb*; flamboyant (*adj.*), flamboyance (*n.*), flamboyancy (*n.*)
3. attire, fan, pattern
4. *adjective*; intricacy (*n.*), intricateness (*n.*), intricately (*adv.*)
5. *noun*; masculine (*adj.*), masculinize (*v.*), masculinist (*n.*/*adj.*)

Exercise 3 Supplying the Missing Words

Different cultures have **distinctive** fashions. Many Western cultures consider **trousers** to be clothing for men only, a sign of **masculinity**. Other cultures, notably in the South Pacific, consider a **wrapped** skirt with colorful **patterns** to be suitable **attire / garments** for both men and women. Some African cultures wear brightly colored **garments / attire** and head wraps. Finally, many cultures favor **flamboyant** men's and women's clothing and **intricate** jewelry for weddings.

Chapter 6

Exercise 1 Defining the Words

1 a, 2 f, 3 b, 4 h, 5 i, 6 c, 7 e, 8 d, 9 g, 10 j

Exercise 2 Expanding Your Vocabulary

1. *adjective*; austerely (*adv.*); austereness (*n.*), austerity (*n.*)
2. *verb*; designation, designator
3. opul**ent** (*adj.*), magnific**ent** (*adj.*); opul**ence** (*n.*), magnific**ence** (*n.*)
4. strip**ed**, sweep**ing**
5. excess

Exercise 3 Supplying the Missing Words

Groups often distinguish themselves with their **apparel / accessories** and **accessories / apparel.** Some groups wear **opulent / elaborate / magnificent** clothing and **opulent / elaborate / magnificent** jewelry to show off their **excess** wealth. Other people favor **austere** clothing to demonstrate loyalty to their group. Some tribal groups have chosen black-and-white **striped** skirts and head wraps, while others **designate** brightly colored robes covered with **magnificent / elaborate / opulent** designs as their tribal costume.

Chapter 7

Exercise 1 Defining the Words

1 g, 2 c, 3 f, 4 e, 5 d, 6 j, 7 a, 8 i, 9 h, 10 b

Exercise 2 Expanding Your Vocabulary

1. *adjective*; nomad
2. contemporary, descendant
3. *noun; yes*: descendent; *yes*: descend (*v.*); descendent (*adj.*)
4. *noun; yes*: weaponry; weapons *in general*; weapon *or* weaponize

Exercise 3 Supplying the Missing Words

Several **decades** ago, some hikers found the **remains** of a five-thousand-year-old **nomadic** hunter who was carrying several **weapons** when he died. One of his weapons was a knife with a copper **blade**. **Contemporary** farmers who are **descendants** of this hunter live in the same alpine valleys where he hunted so long ago. These **peasants** still have physical **traits** that can be traced back to the original nomad. They live very simply and do not have a lot of **sophistication**, but they thrive on farming and hunting.

Chapter 8

Exercise 1 **Defining the Words**

1 e, 2 c, 3 h, 4 g, 5 d, 6 i, 7 a, 8 b, 9 f, 10 j

Exercise 2 **Expanding Your Vocabulary**

1. block, defeat, disgrace, fare
2. glorious, prestigious
3. endurance, inheritance and glory, dowry
4. dowry: dowries
5. block (*n.*) = *a kind of stone used in buildings;* block (*v.*) = *to obstruct*

Exercise 3 **Supplying the Missing Words**

In the Middle Ages (approximately 500 A.D. to 1400 A.D.), young noblewomen of marriageable age from <u>prestigious</u> families were given large <u>dowries</u> when they married. They were also in line to <u>inherit</u> titles, property, and money when their parents died. At the time there were a number of young noblemen with no money who needed to marry well in order to succeed in society. These men <u>endured</u> many hardships as they attempted to win a rich bride. They would challenge each other to combat with various weapons. Each one struggled to <u>defeat</u> his <u>counterparts</u> to obtain the hand of the lady in marriage. One man out of many <u>fared</u> well in these contests; the others faced <u>disgrace</u> and dishonor. Throughout history these fights have been <u>glorified</u> and admired, but in truth, life for the penniless nobleman was a constant struggle.

Chapter 9

Exercise 1 **Defining the Words**

1 j, 2 d, 3 i, 4 e, 5 a, 6 c, 7 h, 8 f, 9 b, 10 g

Exercise 2 **Expanding Your Vocabulary**

1. marble
2. *adjective*; *yes*; elegance (*n.*), elegantly (*adv.*)
3. luxury (*n., adj.*), luxuriant (*adj.*), luxuriance (*n.*), luxuriantly (*adv.*)
4. Dwelling *and* painting *are nouns formed from the verbs* dwell *and* paint.

Exercise 3 **Supplying the Missing Words**

<u>Wealthy</u> Roman citizens lived in <u>elegant</u>, <u>luxurious</u> houses. These citizens built their <u>dwellings</u> with blocks of <u>marble</u> placed around a central area called a <u>courtyard</u>. In the center were a garden and a pool into which water from a fountain <u>flowed</u>. Around the courtyard were <u>paintings</u> of ancestors and colorful, decorative <u>mosaics</u> of famous scenes. Tall marble <u>columns</u> were located around the edges of the courtyard to support the roof of the house.

Chapter 10

Exercise 1 Defining the Words
1 g, 2 h, 3 j, 4 a, 5 e, 6 i, 7 d, 8 b, 9 f, 10 c

Exercise 2 Expanding Your Vocabulary
1. ceremony *and* immunity. *Both end in* -y.
2. ceremonial (*adj.*)
3. feast, game, yield
4. ceremonies, immunities
5. immune (*adj.*), immunize (*v.*), immunization (*n.*), immunizer (*n.*)

Exercise 3 Supplying the Missing Words

The process of getting married is similar in many cultures. It includes several steps beginning with a period of **courtship** during which a young man tries to convince a young woman to marry him. During this period, the family of the young woman often agrees to give her a dowry of money, possessions, or perhaps property. If the young woman agrees to the marriage, we say that the couple is **betrothed** or engaged. After a suitable period, the marriage is finalized with a wedding **ceremony** attended by the bride's and groom's **kin**. Following the wedding, there is usually a great **feast** consisting of all kinds of delicious foods from the harvest **yield** and fish or **game** as well. In time the young family produces a child that may or may not **survive** the first year if the living conditions are poor. If the child lives through childhood diseases, he or she will have lifetime **immunity** to them.

Chapter 11

Exercise 1 Defining the Words
1 c, 2 d, 3 h, 4 i, 5 e, 6 f, 7 g, 8 j, 9 b, 10 a

Exercise 2 Expanding Your Vocabulary
1. sample
2. misinterpret; *"mis" means* not.
3. compliant
4. 4; assertive (*adj.*), assertiveness (*n.*), assert (*v.*), assertively (*adv.*)
5. 4; aggression (*n.*), aggressor (*n.*); aggressive (*adj.*), aggressively (*adv.*)

Exercise 3 Supplying the Missing Words

A person's **behavior** when he or she goes out socially on a **date** differs from person to person. Some people think that a person's **gender** determines whether he or she is **assertive** or timid. After years of **misinterpretation** of the evidence, research using a **sample** of university students revealed certain regularities; there are both women and men who are **compliant**, cooperating and allowing the other person to choose what they will do on the date, and others who **strive** to control every situation.

Chapter 12

Exercise 1 Defining the Words

1 i, 2 j, 3 e, 4 c, 5 d, 6 b, 7 f, 8 a, 9 g, 10 h

Exercise 2 Expanding Your Vocabulary

1. labor
2. exercise, segment
3. *adjective*; inclusiveness (*n.*), inclusively (*adv.*)
4. *adjective*; hierarchy (*n.*), hierarchies (*n. pl.*), hierarchically (*adv.*)
5. engage = *at least 5 (to pay for, to get and keep, to start fighting against, to move something, to promise to marry)*; exercise = *at least 4 (to do physical activity, to use, to cause an animal to do physical activity, to practice a particular skill)*

Exercise 3 Supplying the Missing Words

In many areas of the world, groups of people who descend from a single ancestor, in other words, who have the same <u>lineage</u>, are called a <u>tribe</u>. Within the tribe, parts or <u>segments</u> of the tribe who are closely related are known as families, and within a family, each person has a <u>role</u>. The men are usually responsible for the most physically demanding jobs, the <u>labor</u>. These jobs are all <u>inclusive</u> and often involve many activities such as farming, building shelters, hunting, and fishing. Men may even <u>engage</u> in combat if the tribe goes to war. Women's roles include child care and food collection and preparation. The members of a tribe are often arranged in a <u>hierarchy</u> of status levels; the highest status individuals <u>exercise</u> the leadership roles, while the remaining members fulfill other necessary functions.

Chapter 13

Exercise 1 Defining the Words

1 d, 2 h, 3 j, 4 i, 5 a, 6 c, 7 g, 8 b, 9 f, 10 e

Exercise 2 Expanding Your Vocabulary

1. *18 for the noun form, 2 for the verb form;* "the matter" *meaning* trouble *or* problem *as in "What's the matter?"*
2. *noun*; axes
3. *noun and verb*; spun
4. *4*; hypothesize (*v.*), hypothesis (*n.*), hypothetical (*adj.*), hypothetically (*adv.*)
5. *adjective*; sphere (*n.*)
6. fluctuate *and* stipulate (fluctuation *and* stipulation)

Exercise 3 Supplying the Missing Words

The early Greeks held that the Earth was flat because when they looked out to sea, they could see a flat <u>horizon</u> where the sea seemed to meet the sky. Pythagorean astronomy also <u>stipulated</u> that the most perfect, pure shape was a circle. For this reason, a sphere, being the most <u>symmetrical</u> shape had to be the shape of the universe. At first they <u>hypothesized</u> that the sun and stars were attached to the inside of a huge <u>transparent</u> sphere that moved around the Earth. However, that theory did not explain why ships at sea disappear over the horizon little by little with the top of their masts disappearing last. Eventually, scientists concluded that the Earth is not flat but <u>spherical</u> and turns or <u>spins</u> on its <u>axis</u>. In fact, the Earth is just a tiny part of the millions of planets and stars in the universe. At the same time, astronomers were noticing that the light from some stars varies in intensity or <u>fluctuates</u> in brightness. This phenomenon led to the notion that some of the heavenly bodies were stars and some were planets.

Chapter 14

Exercise 1 Defining the Words

1 j, 2 d, 3 e, 4 i, 5 h, 6 b, 7 a, 8 c, 9 g, 10 f

Exercise 2 Expanding Your Vocabulary

1. *noun*; emit (*v.*)
2. *adjective*; skeptic (*n.*), skepticism (*n.*)
3. *A* skeptic *is a person;* skepticism *is the act of being skeptical.*
4. *adjective*; analogy (*n.*) analogousness (*n.*), analogously (*adv.*)
5. vaporize

Exercise 3 Supplying the Missing Words

Have you ever owned a magnet? It's a small bar of iron that attracts other pieces of iron. If you have two, you will see that they pull together on one end and push apart on the other. Both electric and magnetic forces come from electric charge. Michael Faraday, a nineteenth-century English physicist, did experiments with <u>electromagnetic</u> (EM) fields. What he discovered became extremely important in the production of energy by power plants where <u>fossil fuels</u> are burned. These power plants still use EM energy to produce electricity, but an unfortunate result is air pollution containing <u>emissions</u> such as CO_2 and water <u>vapor</u>.

Later, in the early twentieth century, physicists studying rays and waves of <u>radiation</u> developed the quantum theory, the idea that the smallest unit of measurement should be called a quantum of energy. They named a quantum of light a <u>photon</u>. At about the same time, Albert Einstein came up with his theory of relativity. He was always <u>skeptical</u> of quantum theory, which he thought was "spooky."

Chapter 15

Exercise 1 Defining the Words

1 j, 2 d, 3 a, 4 b, 5 i, 6 g, 7 c, 8 h, 9 e, 10 f

Exercise 2 Expanding Your Vocabulary

1. digitize
2. *adverb;* disdain (*n.*), disdainful (*adj.*)
3. *adjective;* initially (*adv.*), initialness (*n.*)
4. *the first letter of a word*
5. initial, tide, trace

Exercise 3 Supplying the Missing Words

Research has shown that quantum effects change only in <u>microscopic</u> (you can't see them) jumps from one energy level to the next in what is known as the Planck distance. This is analogous to a <u>digital</u> clock that jumps from one number to the next rather than an <u>analog</u> clock, whose hands move continuously from one number to the next. <u>Initially</u>, skeptical physicists greeted this idea <u>disdainfully</u> because they still believed that all matter was composed of small pieces or <u>particles</u> called atoms that moved in a continuous manner. Then scientific opinion changed and the <u>tide</u> turned in favor of quantum theory. There are still <u>traces</u> of doubt, but most scientists now realize that far from being <u>inert</u> particles that resemble tiny solar systems, quanta are made up of tiny loops or strings of energy that <u>vibrate</u> in particular ways. This has become known as the string theory.

APPENDIX D

ANSWER KEY FOR "WHAT DID YOU LEARN?"

PART 1 Putting It All Together
WHAT DID YOU LEARN?

A. Answers may vary. Here are some possible answers.

_I_ 1. History tells us that the abacus had its roots in ancient China and *was* used in the early Greek and
Roman civilizations.

_I_ 2. For control of an algorithm's execution, the machine ~~is~~ relies on the human operator.

_C_ 3. As desktop computers were being accepted and used in homes, the miniaturization of
computing machines continued.[3]

_C_ 4. The algorithm followed by the loom could changed to produce different woven designs.

_I_ 5. John Atanasoff from Iowa State University and Clifford Berry, his assistant, *have* ~~has~~ finally received
credit for creating the first electronic digital computer.

_C_ 6. Once an algorithm for performing a task has been found, the performance of the task no longer
requires an understanding of the principles on which the algorithm is based.[4]

_I_ 7. Pascal *had* ~~has~~ already designed a computing machine by the time that Babbage created his
Difference Engine.

_I_ 8. In the field of artificial intelligence, autonomous machines *are* ~~were~~ being built that can operate
without human intervention.

OR

In the field of artificial intelligence, autonomous machines were being built that *could* ~~can~~ operate
without human intervention.

_C_ 9. Thomas Edison is credited with inventing the incandescent lamp, but other researchers were
developing similar lamps and in a sense Edison was lucky to be the one to obtain the patent.[5]

_I_ 10. Computer scientists want to develop their knowledge about artificial intelligence—knowledge
that *allows / will allow* ~~allowed~~ them to create new intelligent machines.

B. Answers may vary. Here are some possible answers.

1. The paragraph is in the past time frame. The simple past is used to express a past fact. Then the past perfect and a perfect modal are used to speculate about that past fact.

2. The paragraph is in a present time frame to express facts. *Might be installed* is used to express a possibility in the present or future.

C. Answers may vary. Here are some possible answers.

1. The passive is used because the paragraph describes a process.

2. We can interpret the choice of passive in two ways. The passive verbs *was built, was embedded, could be modified,* and *was designed* were used because the agents in these sentences are understood, so it is not necessary to mention them. The use of passive also improves the flow of the sentences in the paragraph. In the first sentence, the focus is on "these machines" at the end of the sentence. The second sentence begins with "Pascal's machine." The use of "machine" first in the second sentence makes it easier to read the sentence. In other words, it improves the flow. Similarly, the third sentence ends with "machine itself" and the next sentence uses a synonym, "Babbage's Difference Engine," to begin. This is another case of improving the flow by using passive verbs.

D. Answers may vary. Here are some possible answers.

1. The verb *sees* describes a fact, so it is not a hedge. A hedge is expressed with a modal auxiliary.

2. The sentence is a hedge because by using the modal auxiliary *may argue,* the writer avoids expressing certainty about the statement that the study of human-machine interfaces is an entire field in its own right.

PART 2 Putting It All Together
WHAT DID YOU LEARN?

A. Noun Functions

1. *Possessions*: s; *indicators*: sc; *position*: op

2. *Experts*: s; *concept*: do; *body image*: oc

3. *expression*: do; *white-collar worker*: oc

4. *1960s*: op; *women*: s; *hair*: do

5. *clothing*: s; *athleisure*: a; *development*: do; *apparel*: op

6. *choices*: s; *people*: io; *information*: do

7. *1980s*: op; *products*: s; *business*: sc

B. Elements of Noun Phrases

1. *some*: det; *magnificent*: adj; *creative*: adj; *stitchery*: hn

2. *the*: det; *increasingly*: adv; *global*: adj; *designer*: nm; *influence*: hn

3. *body-conforming*: nm; *jeans*: hn; *worn*: part; *by*: prep; *men*: hn

4. *rich and powerful*: adj; *English*: adj; *businessmen*: hn

5. *highly*: adv; *appropriate*: adj; *work and play*: nm; *garments*: hn; *for*: prep; *women*: hn

6. *flamboyantly*: adv; *dressed*: adj or part; *rock-and-roll*: nm; *stars*: hn

7. *the*: det; *standard*: adj; *businessmen's*: nm; *white*: adj; *dress*: nm; *shirt*: hn

8 *dark*: adj; *kimonos*: hn; *in*: prep; *a*: det; *solid*: adj; *color*: hn; *for*: prep; *women*: hn

C. Order of Elements in a Noun Phrase

1. lowly manual tasks

2. many regional peasant costumes

3. the bright red-orange silk garment of Afghanistan

4. somber-colored, body-concealing dresses

5. a vertically striped woven skirt with a heavily embroidered border
   OR
   a heavily embroidered skirt with a vertically striped woven border
   OR
   a heavily woven skirt with a vertically striped embroidered border

6. clean, uncluttered, body-conforming lines

7. the working dress of the fisherman's wife

8. stitched-skin clothing preserved in permafrost

PART 3 Putting It All Together
WHAT DID YOU LEARN?

A. Answers may vary. Here are some possible answers.

  _I_ 1. The five-thousand-year-old man who found **was** was named Ötzi.

  _C_ 2. Several hikers, many of whom were German, found Ötzi.

  _I_ 3. Scientists were mystified by Ötzi's death, the reason for ~~that~~ **which** they were unable to discover.

  _C_ 4. The earliest human, named Lucy by the scientists who found her, lived in Ethiopia.

  _C_ 5. The Neanderthals, whose disappearance has never been explained, looked much like modern humans.

  _I_ 6. The Olympic Games were the most prestigious athletic events ~~holding~~ **held** in Greece.

  _C_ 7. Some of the athletes racing in the games had prepared for many years.

  _I_ 8. One Greek athlete, ~~was~~ Theogenes, competed for more than twenty years.

  _C_ 9. Women did not compete in the male-dominated Greek Olympics.

  _I_ 10. It was the ancient Greeks ~~what~~ **who** focused the most attention on athletes.

B. 1. *C*

2. *C*

3. *C*

4. *C*

5. *I* It describes the noun *woman*, not the noun *discipline*.

6. *C*

7. *C*

8. *I* It emphasizes the Roman women.

9. *I* It describes Bulla the Lucky.

PART 4 Putting It All Together

WHAT DID YOU LEARN?

A. Answers may vary. Here are some possible answers.

C   1. The bride's family may provide the dowry; meanwhile, the groom's family may plan a special gift for the couple.

I   2. Many newly married couples may live with the groom's family at first even ^*though* they would prefer their own apartments.

C   3. Women in some cultures are expected to marry; nonetheless, some decide not to marry at all.

I   4. Although matchmakers are used in some cultures, ~~but~~ in other cultures they are not.

     OR

     ~~Although~~ ^*M* matchmakers are used in some cultures, but in other cultures they are not.

I   5. Marriage provides happiness and security to a couple ~~unless~~ ^*if* the relationship is a good one.

I   6. In the past, if a hunter had been successful, his family ~~will have~~ ^*would have had* enough to eat.

C   7. Given that a hunting and fishing community is dependent upon the supply of meat and fish, the people there know that they need to care for the environment.

I   8. The Dinka and the Nuer were neighbors, but the Nuer had the advantage, ~~moved~~ ^*moving* into Dinka territory with little difficulty.

I   9. When ~~facing~~ ^*faced* with invasion, the Dinka were unable to defend themselves.

     OR

     When facing ~~with~~ invasion, the Dinka were unable to defend themselves.

C   10. Having taken over Dinka land, the Nuer military force dissolved.

C   11. Research results being important, anthropologists study lineage systems carefully.

C   12. Albeit needing immediate results, the anthropologist took the time to double-check the data.

<u>_I_</u> 13. The anthropologist was extra careful, thereby ~~discovered~~ *discovering* a few errors in the results.

<u>_I_</u> 14. The results showed some errors in the data despite ~~of~~ the researcher's efforts.

<u>_C_</u> 15. Without further research, the results cannot be verified.

B. 1. *I* The adverb clause beginning with *although* expresses concession, an unexpected result.

2. *I* The adverb phrase beginning with *if* expresses condition.

3. *C*

4. *C*

5. *C*

6. *I* To correct this sentence, change the comma after *anthropologists* to a semicolon.

7. *C*

8. *C*

9. *C*

10. *I* The adverb clause expresses time.

PART 5 Putting It All Together
WHAT DID YOU LEARN?

A. Answers may vary. Here are some possible answers.

<u>_C_</u> 1. The ancient Greeks were certain that the stars were placed in an invisible sphere surrounding Earth.

<u>_I_</u> 2. Ancient Greeks supported the theory ~~what~~ *that* Earth was at the center of the universe.

<u>_C_</u> 3. One false idea is that theories are absolutely certain.

<u>_I_</u> 4. ~~If~~ *Whether* Earth or the sun is at the center of the universe was debated among philosophers for centuries.

<u>_I_</u> 5. Aristarchus, a Greek astronomer, was the first to claim ~~whether~~ *that* the sun was the center of the universe and Earth and other planets moved around the sun.

<u>_C_</u> 6. Pythagoras believed that the most perfect ideas were mathematical because they could be stated so precisely yet abstractly.[5]

<u>_C_</u> 7. It is surprising that Artistarchus's theory was ignored for so long.

<u>_I_</u> 8. It is always possible ~~if~~ *that* new evidence will contradict an accepted theory.

<u>_C_</u> 9. The notion that Earth circled the sun seemed impossible to ancient Greeks.

<u>_C_</u> 10. A big difficulty for the sun-centered astronomy proposed by Copernicus around 1550 was the problem of how Earth could keep moving with nothing to push it.[6]

B. 1. *C*

2. *I* The noun clause is the direct object.

3. *C*

4. *I* The noun clause in the first sentence functions as a direct object.

The noun clause in the *second* sentence functions as the object of a preposition.

5. *C*

6. *I* The noun clause is direct speech.

7. *C*

8. *C*

9. *C*

10. *I* The noun clause in the passage is an adjective complement following the adjective *aware*.

GLOSSARY OF GRAMMAR AND WRITING TERMS

Each term is introduced in the chapter indicated in parentheses at the end of the definition.

Abstract noun – a noun that represents an idea, something one cannot touch rather than something one can touch. An abstract noun is usually a noncount noun. (5)
- **Knowledge** is a concept that includes **information** and **wisdom**.

Active verb – a verb that expresses an action that the subject of a sentence does to an object (1)
- Charles Babbage **invented** a machine.

Adjective – a word that describes a noun (1)
- Smartphones are **essential** to **young** people today.

Adjective clause – a dependent clause that can follow any noun in a sentence and describe it (7)
- Students **who study** are successful.

Adjective complement – a phrase or noun clause that follows an adjective and gives more information about it. (14)
- The students are uncertain **of the results.**
- The students are sure **that they are well prepared for the examinations.**

Adverb – a word that describes a verb, an adjective, or another adverb (1)
- People **quickly** adopted the new phones.
- The new phones are **extremely** small.
- They are **really** beautifully designed.

Adverb clause – a combination of words including a subject and a verb introduced by a subordinating conjunction such as *because, since, before, after,* and *although* (10)
- **Although the aborigines work extremely hard**, they are content with their lives.

Agent – the word(s) used to describe the doer in a passive sentence. The agent is often preceded by the word *by.* (2)
- The Difference Engine was invented by **Charles Babbage**.

Appositive – a noun following another noun that means the same thing (4)
- The most popular course, **Psychology 101**, is always full.

Article – the word *a, an,* or, *the* (5)
- **The** large international enrollment is due to **a** good economy.

Auxiliary verb – a verb used with a main verb and sometimes other auxiliary verbs in a verb phrase to express tense or aspect, how something is to be viewed with respect to time (1)
- Computers **have been** changing for the last twenty years.

Base form – the form of the verb that is found in the dictionary (13)
- **go, run, write, be**

Cleft sentence – a sentence that is used to focus on one element of a sentence. The emphasized element can be a noun, phrase, or clause. (9)
- It was **Rome** that was the center of the empire.
- It is in **New York** that you can find the Metropolitan Museum of Art.
- It is **because people are catching the measles** that doctors are recommending the vaccine.

Common noun – a word for a person, place, or thing (4)
- The **textbook** for this **class** can be purchased in the **bookstore**.

Complex sentence – a sentence composed of an independent clause and a dependent clause (7)
- Before students register for classes, they are supposed to see their advisors.

Compound modifier – a usually hyphenated combination of adverbs, adjectives, prepositional phrases, and nouns used to describe a head noun (5)
- The department is in a **ten-story** building. Several **well-known** professors have their offices there.

Compound sentence – two simple sentences joined with a coordinating conjunction (7)
- Ross Hall has six floors, but Carver Hall only has two floors.

Compound-complex sentence – a combination of a compound and a complex sentence (7)
- Ross Hall has six floors, but Carver Hall only has two floors, although they were built at about the same time.

Conjunction (also called a **connector**) – a word used to connect words, phrases, or clauses (7)
- Students **and** professors use the university library.

Conjunctive adverb – a word such as *because, before, after, although,* and *whereas* used to join an adverb clause (dependent clause) to an independent clause (10)
- Aborigines hunt every day **because** they need fresh meat.

Connector (also called a **coordinating conjunction, subordinating conjunction, conjunctive adverb,** and **transition)** – a word used to connect words and sentences (10)
- The aborigines work extremely hard; **however**, they are content with their lives. **As a result,** they have few mental problems.

Coordinating conjunction – a word such as *and, but, or, nor, for,* and *yet* used to connect nouns, verbs, adjectives, and adverbs as well as independent clauses to form a compound sentence (10)
- The women **and** children work to gather **and** cook plants, **but** they rarely hunt.

Count noun – a noun that can be counted and has a plural form (4)
- Three **professors** teach the team teaching class.

Demonstrative adjective – the adjective *this, that, these,* or *those* used with a noun to indicate which noun one is referring to (5)
- It's important to buy **this** access code rather than **that** one.

Dependent clause (also called a **subordinate clause**) – a clause introduced by a subordinating conjunction such as *who, what, before, after,* and *because.* This clause cannot stand alone as a sentence. It needs to be used with an independent clause to form a complete sentence. (7)
- Taxes have been raised **because the city needs money.**

Determiner – a word such as an article, quantifier, possessive adjective, possessive noun, or demonstrative adjective that begins a noun phrase (5)
- **Every** student must purchase **his** or **her** textbooks early in **the** semester.
- **These** textbooks are required.

Direct object – a noun, pronoun, gerund, or infinitive that receives the action of a transitive verb (4)
- Professor Williams assigned a **project**. We didn't expect **it**, but we enjoyed **writing** it.

Direct quotation (also called **direct speech**) – the exact words a person says, usually written surrounded by quotation marks (15)
- Einstein remarked, **"I thought of that while I was riding my bicycle."**

Gerund – a verb ending in *-ing* that is used as a noun (4)
- **Seeing** is **believing**.

Head noun – the most important noun in a noun phrase. It is usually the last word in the phrase. (5)
- The large international **enrollment** is due to a good **economy**.

Hedge – a way of speaking or writing that avoids taking a position or giving a direct answer (**to hedge** is the verb form) (3)
- **It appears that** people are not being vaccinated.
- This **could be** the result of fear.

Hyphenated – a word written with the punctuation mark known as a hyphen (-) (5)
- It is important to have a **well-thought-out** plan.

Independent clause (also called a **main clause**) – a clause that could stand alone as a simple sentence (7)
- **Taxes have been raised** because the city needs money.

Indirect object – a noun or pronoun that receives the direct object (use *to)* or its benefit (use *for).* The indirect object sometimes precedes the direct object. (4)
- Several students wrote papers for the **professor**. They sent the papers to **him**.
- The students sent the **professor** the paper.

Infinitive – the basic dictionary form of the verb usually preceded by the word *to* (2)
- Most people want **to improve** their health.

Intransitive verb – a verb that cannot be followed by an object (2)
- Some students **listen** carefully.

Linking verb – a verb that is used between the subject of a sentence and a noun with the same meaning as the subject, or between the subject of a sentence and an adjective describing the subject (1)
- Computers **are** electronic devices.
- Computers **seem** difficult to use at first.

Main verb – the verb that expresses the lexical meaning of a verb phrase. It is usually the last word in a verb phrase (1)
- Computers have been **changing** dramatically since 1990.

Manner – an adverb or adverb clause that tells how something happens or is done (10)
- The students worked **rapidly** to complete their task.
- They did **as they were told**.

Modal – an auxiliary verb that expresses the speaker's attitude about something (3)
- Everyone **can** save the environment.
- Old computers **should** be recycled.

Noncount noun (also called a **mass noun**)– a noun that cannot be counted (4)
- We need several pieces of **information**. An answer will require a great deal of **research**.

Nonrestrictive adjective clause – an adjective clause that does not identify the noun it follows but adds information about it. These clauses are set off with commas. (7)
- New York City, **which is my favorite city to visit**, is an exciting tourist destination.

Noun modifier – a noun that is used with a head noun to describe it (5)
- Several students have become **business** executives.

Noun phrase – a group of words often including an article, perhaps an adverb, one or more adjectives, sometimes a noun modifier, and the head noun (5)
- **The extremely large international enrollment** is due to a **good business environment**.

Object (also called a **direct object**) – a noun or pronoun that is the receiver of the action of an active verb (1)
- Designers invent new **devices**.
- Engineers build **them**.

Object complement – a noun or adjective that follows a direct object and describes it (4)
- We elected Obama **president**. The voters called the president **intelligent**.

Object of the preposition – the noun that follows a preposition in a prepositional phrase (4)
- Most of the **students** study from **morning** until **night**.

Participial phrase – the combination of a participle and the prepositional phrase or noun that follows it. A participle is derived from a verb, so it can be followed by an object, which can be a noun phrase or pronoun. (6)
- The classes **chosen by the students** are already full.
- The student **choosing her classes** is my roommate.

Participle – The forms of the participle are the present participle = verb + *-ing* and the past participle = verb + usually *-ed* or *-en*. Participles are used as part of the verb or as adjectives. (5)
- The students are **choosing** classes this week. The students have **chosen** their classes.
- The student **choosing** her classes is my roommate.
- The classes **chosen** by the students are already full.

Passive voice – a sentence in which the subject of the verb is acted upon and the verb is a form of *be* + past participle (1)
- The smartphone **was created** by Steve Jobs.
- Smartphones **are used** all over the world.

Possessive adjective – a word such as *his, her, my, our,* or *their* that indicates ownership of a noun (5)
- Students may use **their** access codes until the end of the semester.

Possessive noun – a common noun or proper noun form ending with *'s or s'* that indicates ownership of another noun (5)
- Professor **Allen's** access code was free.
- The **students'** access codes were quite expensive to purchase.

Postmodifier – the word or group of words that follow a head noun and describe it. Prepositional phrases and participial phrases are the most common postmodifiers. (6)
- The students **sitting in the classroom** are waiting to hear whether the professor **from Harvard** will arrive.

Premodifier – the word or group of words that can precede the head noun in a noun phrase, including, for example, quantifiers, articles, adverbs, adjectives, and noun modifiers (5)
- **A few extremely intelligent graduate** students graduated with honors.

Preposition – a word that precedes a noun and shows the relationship of the noun to other words in a sentence. Examples include *in, on, at, about, with, of, to, for, from, around, above,* and *until.* (4)
- Classes usually begin **in** the morning and end late **at** night.

Prepositional phrase – a phrase containing a preposition and its object, which is a noun or pronoun (2)
- Computers will be very different **in the future**.

Pronoun – a word that takes the place of a noun (4)
- **She** is one of the international students. Most of **them** live in the dormitories where **they** can have roommates who speak English.

Proper noun – a word for a particular person, place, or thing; a person's name, the name of a city, the name of a building. A proper noun is always capitalized. (4)
- **Dr. Roberts** is the professor who teaches this class.
- The professor was born in **Boston, Massachusetts**.
- The class is in **Ross Hall** at **Iowa State University**.

Quantifier – a word used at the beginning of a noun phrase that expresses how much or how many (5)
- **Some** graduate students enroll in a **few** undergraduate courses.

Relative pronoun – a subordinating conjunction used to introduce an adjective clause (*who, whom, which, that*) (7)
- Bill Gates, **who** founded Microsoft, lives in Seattle, Washington.

Reported speech (also called **indirect speech**) – a report of what a person says, thinks, or believes (15)
- Einstein remarked that he had thought of that while he had been riding his bicycle.

Restrictive adjective clause – an adjective clause that is essential to identify the noun it describes. These clauses have no commas. (7)
- The man **who is wearing the gray suit** is my professor.
- The city **in which I was born** is in the Northeast.

Semimodal auxiliary verbs – a group of auxiliary verbs not considered modals that express the speaker's attitude about something (3)
- People **need to** become aware of the environment.
- Something **had better** be done.

Simple sentence – a sentence composed of one independent clause (7)
- Ötzi lived five thousand years ago.

Subject – a noun or pronoun in a sentence that is the doer of an action or that is being described (1)
- **Steve Jobs** created many devices. **He** lived in California. **He** was a multi-talented genius.

Subject complement – a noun or adjective that means the same as or describes the subject of a sentence. Subject complements follow linking verbs. (4)
- Most graduate students are **women**.
- Many business students are **overworked**.

Subordinating conjunction – one of a number of words used to connect dependent clauses to independent clauses (*who, that, which, before, after, what,* and *how* are some examples) (7)
- Few people understand **how** a computer operates.

Time frame conventions – the way English-speaking writers organize the verb tense usage in their paragraphs when they write or speak formally so as to make it easier for the reader or listener to understand. For example, paragraphs discussing past time usually include mostly past tense verbs, and paragraphs about the present usually contain mostly present tenses. (1)
- Digital computers **were developed** during the 1960s. Most of these computers **were created** by universities and small companies. Before the 1960s, people like Charles Babbage **had built** analog machines that they **called** computing machines. At the same time as Babbage **was working** on his machines, other engineers **were developing** their own versions. (past time frame)

Transitions – words and phrases such as *soon, besides, as a result, in contrast, for example, in the meantime,* and compared to that are used to connect sentences and paragraphs to make ideas flow smoothly (10)
- The men repaired their tools. **In the meantime**, the women cooked the meal.

Transitive verb – a verb that is followed by an object (2)
- People **buy** phones every year.

Verb – a word that expresses an action or state of being (1)
- Computers **began** as simple adding machines.
- Computers **are** not easy to use.

Verb phrase – a combination of verbs including a main verb and an auxiliary verb and perhaps an adverb (1)
- Simple computing machines **have been** in existence since the nineteenth century.
- Computers **will always be** useful devices.

Verb tense – the time expressed by a verb or verb phrase (1)
- A computer program **begins** with a particular symbol.
- Smartphones **began** to replace laptops eight to ten years ago.

CREDITS

Photo Credits

Page 2 Nmedia/Fotolia; **p. 4** (left) Photos 12/Alamy, (right) GL Archive/Alamy; **p. 5** Science & Society Picture Library/Getty Images; **p. 11** Xuejun li/Fotolia; **p. 13** Juulijs/Fotolia; **p. 22** miro kovacevic/Fotolia; **p. 26** Petr Malyshev/Shutterstock; **p. 27** photorebelle/Fotolia; **p. 31** Petair/Fotolia; **p. 34** 145/Maciej Frolow/Ocean/Corbis; **p. 39** Reddogs/Shutterstock; **p. 41** Rebel/Fotolia; **p. 49** Paul Fleet/Fotolia; **p. 50** (left) YOSHIKAZU TSUNO/ AFP/Getty Images, (right) Stocktrek Images, Inc./Alamy; **p. 53** Pete Saloutos/Shutterstock; **p. 56** Brian Senic/ Shutterstock; **p. 60** Portrait of the Empress Dowager Cixi (1835-1908) (oil on canvas) (see also 209281 for detail), Chinese School, (19th century) / Summer Palace, Beijing, China / Bridgeman Images; **p. 62** (left) Amoret Tanner/Alamy, (right) Lisa F. Young/Fotolia; **p. 74** Henry Westheim Photography/Alamy; **p. 82** North Wind Picture Archives/Alamy; **p. 84** (left) sharplaninac/Fotolia, (middle left) michaeljung/Fotolia, (middle right) Elnur/Fotolia,(right) vadymvdrobot/Fotolia; **p. 86** Gunter Marx/EV/Alamy; **p. 94** Ambrophoto/Fotolia; **p. 98** Flashon Studio/Shutterstock; **p. 99** (top) WavebreakMediaMicro/Fotolia, (bottom) Andrey Kiselev/Fotolia; **p. 101** wong yu liang/Fotolia; **p. 102** siloto/Fotolia; **p. 104** MARKA/Alamy; **p. 117** Bastos/Fotolia; **p. 118** The Print Collector/Alamy; **p. 126** North Wind Picture Archives/Alamy; **p. 135** The LIFE Picture Collection/Getty Images; **p. 139** National Geographic Image Collection/Alamy; **p. 142** JOE CICAK/E+/Getty Images; **p. 144** Blend Images/ Alamy; **p. 146** Penny Tweedie/Alamy; **p. 159** Freesurf/Fotolia; **p. 161** antoni halim/Shutterstock; **p. 162** Peter Bernik/Shutterstock; **p. 163** Jasmin Awad/Shutterstock; **p. 180** Mark Pearson/Alamy; **p. 195** Agencja Fotograficzna Caro/Alamy; **p. 202** agsandrew/Shutterstock; **p. 204** B Christopher/Alamy; **p. 205** Mike Norton/Shutterstock; **p. 218** Nickolay Khoroshkov/Shutterstock; **p. 230** Bettmann/Corbis; **p. 241** agsandrew/Shutterstock; **p. 244** (left) Aleksandr Bedrin/Fotolia, (right) fotoliaxrender/Fotolia.

Text Credits

PART 1
Chapters 1-3, PIAT 1

87 excerpts from *Computer Science: An Overview*, 11th Edition, by J. Glenn Brookshear, Chapters 0, 3, 4, 5, 6, 7, 9, 11 Addison-Wesley Pearson Education Inc., 2012, ISBN 10: 0-13-256903-5, ISBN 13: 978-0-13-256903-3, Pearson Education; BROOKSHEAR, J. GLENN, *COMPUTER SCIENCE: AN OVERVIEW*, 11th Ed., (c) 2012. Reprinted and electronically reproduced by permission of Pearson Education, Inc., Upper Saddle River, New Jersey.

PART 2
Chapters 4-6, PIAT 2

Ch4(02-07), Ch5(02-07), Ch6(01-09), PIAT(01-03): 56 excerpts from *Individuality in Clothing Selection and Personal Appearance*, 7th Edition, by Suzanne G. Marshall, Hazel O. Jackson, and M. Sue Stanley, Prentice Hall, 2012, ISBN-13: 978-0-13-613626-2, ISBN-10: 0-13-613626-5, Pearson Education, 3, 7, 17, 22, 26-28, 31, 36-39, 41-43, 45-47, 49; Ch4(02-07), Ch5(02-07), Ch6(01-09), PIAT(01-03): MARSHALL, SUZANNE; JACKSON, HAZEL; STANLEY, SUE, *INDIVIDUALITY IN CLOTHING SELECTION AND PERSONAL APPEARANCE*, 7th Ed., (c) 2012. Reprinted and electronically reproduced by permission of Pearson Education, Inc., Upper Saddle River, New Jersey.

PART 3
Chapter 7

Civilization in the West: Seventh Edition, by Mark Kishlansky - Harvard University; Patrick Geary - University of California, Los Angeles; Patricia O'Brien - University of California, Los Angeles, Chapter 1, Pearson, 2008, Combined Volume ISBN-10 0-205-55684-1; **26: Mark Kishlansky, Patrick Geary, Patricia O'Brien, "It is often argued that a Neanderthal, properly groomed and dressed, could today be lost in the crowd of an European city." (22 words),** *Civilization in the West:* **Seventh Edition, by Mark Kishlansky - Harvard University; Patrick Geary - University of California, Los Angeles; Patricia O'Brien - University of California, Los Angeles, Chapter 1, Pearson, 2008, Combined Volume ISBN-10 0-205-55684-1, Pearson Education**

Chapter 8

"With the Dutch already well established in Java, France, Great Britain, and the United States each established a center of power in southeast Asia and sought a balance of strength there to complement their global efforts to keep any one of them from getting ahead of the others." (43 words), *Civilization in the West: Volume II: Since 1555,* **Sixth Edition, by Mark Kishlansky - Harvard University; Patrick Geary - University of California, Los Angeles; Patricia O'Brien - University of California, Los Angeles, Chapter 25, Pearson, 2007, eText ISBN-10 0-321-34145-7 ISBN-13 978-0-321-34145-7 p. 789, Pearson Education**; 18: *Civilization in the West: Volume II: Since 1555,* Sixth Edition, by Mark Kishlansky - Harvard University; Patrick Geary - University of California, Los Angeles; Patricia O'Brien - University of California, Los Angeles, Chapter 25, Pearson, 2007, eText ISBN-10 0-321-34145-7 ISBN-13 978-0-321-34145-7 p. 789

Chapters 7-9

4, 5, 17-21,23-25/ 1, 2, 11, 13-15, 18/2-5,9-18: KISHLANSKY, MARK; GEARY, PATRICK; O'BRIEN, PATRICIA, *CIVILIZATION IN THE WEST, VOLUME I (To 1715),* 6th Ed., (c) 2006. Reprinted and electronically reproduced by permission of Pearson Education, Inc., Upper Saddle River, NJ.; **4, 5, 17-21,23-25/ 1, 2, 11, 13-15, 18/2-5,9-18: Mark Kishlansky, Patricia O'Brien, Patrick Geary, 132 excerpts from** *Civilization in the West: Volume I: To 1715,* **Sixth Edition,** *Civilization in the West: Volume I: To 1715,* **Sixth Edition, by Mark Kishlansky - Harvard University; Patrick Geary - University of California, Los Angeles; Patricia O'Brien - University of California, Los Angeles, Chapters 1, 2, 3, 4, 9, 11, 12, 16, Pearson, 2007, eText ISBN-10 0-321-34144-9, ISBN-13 978-0-321-34144-0, Pearson Education**

Chapter 9, PIAT 3

9-11, 13, 14: KISHLANSKY, MARK; GEARY, PATRICK; O'BRIEN, PATRICIA, *CIVILIZATION IN THE WEST, VOLUME II (SINCE 1555),* 6th Ed., (c) 2006. Reprinted and electronically reproduced by permission of Pearson Education, Inc., Upper Saddle River, NJ; **9-11, 13, 14: Mark Kishlansky, Patrick Geary, Patricia O'Brien, 13 excerpts from** *Civilization in the West: Volume II: Since 1555,* **Sixth Edition,** *Civilization in the West: Volume II: Since 1555,* **Sixth Edition, by Mark Kishlansky - Harvard University; Patrick Geary - University of California, Los Angeles; Patricia O'Brien - University of California, Los Angeles, Chapter 25, Pearson, 2007, eText ISBN-10 0-321-34145-7 ISBN-13 978-0-321-34145-7, Pearson Education**

PART 4
Chapter 10

28 excerpts from *Anthropology,* Thirteenth Edition, Carol R. Ember, Melvin Ember, Peter N. Peregrine, *Anthropology,* Thirteenth Edition Author(s): Carol R. Ember; Melvin Ember; Peter N. Peregrine Publisher: Pearson, © 2011, ISBN-13: 978-0-205-73882-3, eText: ISBN-10 0-205-73883-4, ISBN-13 978-0-205-73883-0, Print: ISBN-10 0-205-73882-6, ISBN-13 978-0-205-73882-3, Pearson Education, 2011; EMBER, CAROL R.; EMBER, MELVIN; PEREGRINE, PETER N., *ANTHROPOLOGY,* 13th Ed., (c) 2011. Reprinted and electronically reproduced by permission of Pearson Education Inc., Upper Saddle River, New Jersey.

Chapter 11

Gender Profile of News Audiences "Online papers Modestly Boost Newspaper Readership," Pew Research Center for the People & the Press, July 30, 2006. Reprinted with permission.; **34: Gender Profile of News Audiences, Article Feb 6, 2008, "Where Men and Women Differ in Following the News" www.pewresearch/2008/02/06/where-men-and-women-differ-in-following-news/, Pew Research Center for the People & the Press**

Chapter 12

EMBER, CAROL R.; EMBER, MELVIN; PEREGRINE, PETER N., *ANTHROPOLOGY*, 13th Ed., (c) 2011. Reprinted and electronically reproduced by permission of Pearson Education Inc., Upper Saddle River, New Jersey; **2: Tiv lineage segments and their territories, Carol R. Ember, Melvin Ember, Peter Peregrine, *Anthropology*, Thirteenth Edition Author(s): Carol R. Ember; Melvin Ember; Peter N. Peregrine Publisher: Pearson, Copyright year: © 2011, ISBN-13: 978-0-205-73882-3, eText: ISBN-10 0-205-73883-4, ISBN-13 978-0-205-73883-0, Print: ISBN-10 0-205-73882-6, ISBN-13 978-0-205-73882-3, Pearson Education**; 30: EMBER, CAROL R.; EMBER, MELVIN; PEREGRINE, PETER N., *ANTHROPOLOGY*, 13th Ed., (c) 2011. Reprinted and electronically reproduced by permission of Pearson Education Inc., Upper Saddle River, New Jersey.; **30: Table 20-1 Worldwide Patterns in the Division of Labor by Gender, Carol R Ember, Melvin Ember, Peter Peregrine, *Anthropology*, Thirteenth Edition Author(s): Carol R. Ember; Melvin Ember; Peter N. Peregrine Publisher: Pearson, Copyright year: © 2011, ISBN-13: 978-0-205-73882-3, eText: ISBN-10 0-205-73883-4, ISBN-13 978-0-205-73883-0, Print: ISBN-10 0-205-73882-6, ISBN-13 978-0-205-73882-3, page 351, Pearson Education**

Chapters 11-12, PIAT 4

\02-30 (11), 02-24 (12), 1 (PIAT): 119 excerpts from *Anthropology*, 13e, Carol R. Ember, Melvin Ember, Peter N. Peregrine, *Anthropology*, Thirteenth Edition Author(s): Carol R. Ember; Melvin Ember; Peter N. Peregrine Publisher: Pearson, Copyright year: © 2011, ISBN-13: 978-0-205-73882-3, eText: ISBN-10 0-205-73883-4, ISBN-13 978-0-205-73883-0, Print: ISBN-10 0-205-73882-6, ISBN-13 978-0-205-73882-3, Pearson Education, 2011; 02-30 (11), 02-24 (12), 1 (PIAT): EMBER, CAROL R.; EMBER, MELVIN; PEREGRINE, PETER N., *ANTHROPOLOGY*, 13th Ed., (c) 2011. Reprinted and electronically reproduced by permission of Pearson Education Inc., Upper Saddle River, New Jersey.

PART 5
Chapters 13-15, PIAT 5

114 excerpts from *Physics: Concepts & Connections*, 5th Edition, by Art Hobson, Pearson, ISBN_978-0-321-66113-5, Pearson Education; HOBSON, ART, *PHYSICS: CONCEPTS AND CONNECTIONS*, 5th Ed., (c) 2010. Reprinted and electronically reproduced by permission of Pearson Education, Inc., New Jersey.

SUBJECT INDEX